Advance Praise for
Saṃsāra, Nirvāṇa, and Buddha Nature

"*Saṃsāra, Nirvāṇa, and Buddha Nature* is the third volume in the series of books coauthored by Venerable Thubten Chodron and His Holiness the Dalai Lama. This has proven to be a remarkable partnership, producing lucid, accessible articulations of Buddhadharma and demonstrating the relevance of philosophy to practice. The present volume ably advances the project begun in the first two volumes and expands its scope enormously. His Holiness and Ven. Thubten Chodron together set out a comprehensive vision of the nature of saṃsāra and nirvāṇa, of the Buddhist understanding of the nature of mind, and of the path to liberation grounded in the realization of our buddha nature. The philosophical analysis is precise and comprehensive. The application to personal practice is insightful, direct, and easy to apply. This is a wonderful example of how Buddhist philosophy and Buddhist practice can be integrated."

—Jay L. Garfield, Doris Silbert Professor in the Humanities, Smith College and Harvard Divinity School

"This third volume in the Wisdom Publications series *The Library of Wisdom and Compassion* presents an in-depth examination of the idea of 'buddha nature' and explores and illustrates how the mind itself serves as the basis for both our suffering and our liberation. Helpful reflections throughout the text guide our journey. These are truly textbooks tailored for our times."

—Jan Willis, author of *Dreaming Me: Black, Baptist, and Buddhist—One Woman's Spiritual Journey*

"This third volume of the marvelous *Library of Wisdom and Compassion* series provides an exploration of saṃsāra—the painful cycle of unenlightened existence—as well as its causes and how to attain freedom from it. [illegible] a beautiful elucidation of the nature of the mind [illegible] that every living being has [illegible]

[illegible] material in th[illegible]

sincerely wish to understand the Buddhist path and begin following it."

—Venerable Sangye Khadro, author of *How to Meditate*

THE LIBRARY OF WISDOM AND COMPASSION

The Library of Wisdom and Compassion is a special multivolume series in which His Holiness the Dalai Lama shares the Buddha's teachings on the complete path to full awakening that he himself has practiced his entire life. The topics are arranged especially for people not born in Buddhist cultures and are peppered with the Dalai Lama's unique outlook. Assisted by his long-term disciple, the American nun Thubten Chodron, the Dalai Lama sets the context for practicing the Buddha's teachings in modern times and then unveils the path of wisdom and compassion that leads to a meaningful life, a sense of personal fulfillment, and full awakening. This series is an important bridge from introductory to profound topics for those seeking an in-depth explanation from a contemporary perspective.

Volumes:

1. *Approaching the Buddhist Path*
2. *The Foundation of Buddhist Practice*
3. *Saṃsāra, Nirvāṇa, and Buddha Nature*

More volumes to come!

LIBRARY OF WISDOM AND COMPASSION · VOLUME 3

Saṃsāra, Nirvāṇa, and Buddha Nature

Bhikṣu Tenzin Gyatso,
the Fourteenth Dalai Lama

and

Bhikṣuṇī Thubten Chodron

Wisdom

Wisdom Publications
199 Elm Street
Somerville, MA 02144 USA
wisdompubs.org

Library of Congress Cataloging-in-Publication Data
Names: Bstan-dzin-rgya-mtsho, Dalai Lama XIV, 1935– author. | Thubten Chodron, 1950– author.
Title: Samsara, Nirvana, and Buddha Nature / Bhiksu Tenzin Gyatso, the Fourteenth Dalai Lama and Bhiksuni Thubten Chodron.
Description: Somerville, MA: Wisdom Publications, 2018. | Series: The library of wisdom and compassion; volume 3 | Includes bibliographical references and index. |
Identifiers: LCCN 2018010703 (print) | LCCN 2018028973 (ebook) | ISBN 9781614295556 (ebook) | ISBN 9781614295365 (hardcover: alk. paper)
Subjects: LCSH: Buddhism—Psychology. | Life—Religious aspects—Buddhism. | Happiness—Religious aspects—Buddhism. | Nirvana. | Buddhism—Doctrines.
Classification: LCC BQ4570.P76 (ebook) | LCC BQ4570.P76 B78 2018 (print) | DDC 294.3/420423—dc23
LC record available at https://lccn.loc.gov/2018010703

ISBN 9781614295365 ebook ISBN 9781614295556

22 21 20 19 18 5 4 3 2 1

Cover and interior design by Gopa & Ted2, Inc. Set in Diacritical Garamond Pro 11/14.6.
Photo credits: pp. vi, 276, Olivier Adam; p. xii, Jamyang Zangpo; p. xx, Traci Thrasher; p. 4, © Religious Images/Universal Images Group/Getty Images; p. 38, © kingxhuang / stock.adobe.com; p. 142, © Stocksnapper/stock.adobe.com; p. 192, Stephen Ching; pp. 216, 230, Thubten Jigme; p. 252, Libby Kamrowski; p. 290, Dmitry Rukhlenko; p. 318, Mike Novak. All photos reprinted with permission.

Wisdom Publications' books are printed on acid-free paper and meet the guidelines for permanence and durability of the Production Guidelines for Book Longevity of the Council on Library Resources.

♲ This book was produced with environmental mindfulness.
For more information, please visit wisdompubs.org/wisdom-environment.

Printed in the United States of America.

PUBLISHER'S ACKNOWLEDGMENT

The publisher gratefully acknowledges the generous help of the Hershey Family Foundation in sponsoring the production of this book.

Contents

Preface by Bhikṣuṇī Thubten Chodron xiii

Abbreviations xxi

Introduction by His Holiness the Dalai Lama 1

1. The Self, the Four Truths, and Their Sixteen Attributes 5
   - Three Questions about the Self 5
   - The Four Truths 10
   - The Coarse and Subtle Four Truths 18
   - The Sixteen Attributes of the Four Truths of Āryas 19

2. Revolving in Cyclic Existence: The Truth of Duḥkha 39
   - Knowing Duḥkha for What It Is 39
   - Realms of Existence 41
   - Three Types of Duḥkha 47
   - Feelings, Afflictions, and Duḥkha 50
   - Six Disadvantages of Cyclic Existence 51
   - Eight Unsatisfactory Conditions 53
   - Examining True Duḥkha via Ten Points 54
   - Our Human Value 57

3. True Origins of Duḥkha 63
   - The Six Root Afflictions 64

More Types of Defilements 87
Afflictions 88
Underlying Tendencies 88
Auxiliary Afflictions 92
Fetters 97
Pollutants 98
Hindrances 99

4. Afflictions, Their Arising, and Their Antidotes 101
Eighty-Four Thousand Afflictions 101
The Order in Which Afflictions Arise 104
Factors Causing Afflictions to Arise 106
Feelings That Accompany Afflictions 109
The Ethical Dimension of Afflictions 110
Counterforces to the Afflictions 112
Afflictions, Our Real Enemy 119

5. Afflictions and Karma, Their Seeds and Latencies 123
Acquired and Innate Afflictions 124
Coarse and Subtle Afflictions 126
Seeds, Latencies, and Having-Ceased 126
Latencies and Ideas in Other Religions and in Psychology 135
Virtue, Nonvirtue, Merit, and Roots of Virtue 137

6. Karma, the Universe, and Evolution 141
The Origin of the Universe 141
Mind and the External World 144
The Laws of Nature and the Law of Karma and Its Effects 148
Karma and Our Present Environment 150
Karma, Instinctual Behavior, and Our Bodies 152

7. Revolving in Cyclic Existence: The Twelve Links of Dependent Origination 155
Dependent Arising 156
How Cyclic Existence Occurs 158
1. Ignorance (*avidyā*) 159
2. Formative Action (*saṃskāra karman*) 165
3. Consciousness (*vijñāna*) 168
4. Name and Form (*nāma-rūpa*) 170
5. Six Sources (*ṣaḍāyatana*) 172
6. Contact (*sparśa*) 176
7. Feeling (*vedanā*) 176
8. Craving (*tṛṣṇā*) 179
9. Clinging (*upādāna*) 182
10. Renewed Existence (*bhava*) 185
11. Birth (*jāti*) 188
12. Aging or Death (*jarāmaraṇa*) 190

8. Dependent Origination: Cycling in Saṃsāra 193
How the Twelve Links Produce a Life 193
An Example 197
Flexibility 200
Pāli Tradition: How We Cycle 200
An Example from a Pāli Sūtra 202
Who Revolves in Cyclic Existence? 204
The Ultimate Nature of the Twelve Links 211

9. The Determination to Be Free 217
The Benefits of Meditating on the Twelve Links 217
Invigorating a Dry Dharma Practice 219
Can a Leper Find Happiness? 222
Compassion for Ourselves and Others 225
The Demarcation of Generating the Determination to Be Free 227

10. Seeking Genuine Peace 231
The "Ye Dharmā" Dhāraṇī 232
Forward and Reverse Orders of the Afflictive and Purified Sides of the Twelve Links 234
Transcendental Dependent Origination (Pāli Tradition) 238
Karma in Saṃsāra and Beyond 249

11. Freedom from Cyclic Existence 253
Stages Leading to Liberation and Full Awakening 254
The Two Obscurations 259
Nirvāṇa 262
Pāli Tradition: Nirvāṇa 266
Bodhi 274

12. The Mind and Its Potential 277
The Mind's Potential 277
Is Liberation Possible? 279
Excellent Qualities Can Be Cultivated Limitlessly 281
Afflictive Mental States and the Nature of the Mind 283
The Equality of Saṃsāra and Nirvāṇa 284
Levels of Mind 286

13. Buddha Nature 291
The Mind's Potential according to the Pāli Tradition 291
Ārya Disposition according to the Vaibhāṣikas and Sautrāntikas 292
Buddha Nature according to the Cittamātra School 293
Buddha Nature according to the Madhyamaka School 296
Buddha Nature according to Tantra 301
Nine Similes for Tathāgatagarbha 302
Three Aspects of the Tathāgatagarbha 310
Three Aspects of Buddha Disposition 314
A Puzzle 315

14. Going Deeper into Buddha Nature 319
The Three Turnings of the Dharma Wheel and Buddha Nature 319
A Link between Sūtra and Tantra 322
Nothing Is to Be Removed 325
The Capacity Giving Rise to the Three Kāyas 327
A Buddha's Nature Dharmakāya 328
Pristine Wisdom Abiding in the Afflictions 330
Causal Clear Light Mind 332
What Continues to Awakening? 332
Dzogchen and Mahāmudrā 334
Are We Already Buddhas? 337
Awareness of Our Buddha Nature Eliminates Hindrances 341

Notes 343
Glossary 353
Further Reading 367
Index 371
About the Authors 409

Preface

THE FIRST VOLUME of *The Library of Wisdom and Compassion*, *Approaching the Buddhist Path*, explored the Buddhist view of life, mind, and emotions. It provided historical background, introduced us to a systematic approach to the spiritual path, and discussed how Buddhist ideas could pertain to contemporary issues. The second volume, *The Foundation of Buddhist Practice*, discussed gaining nondeceptive knowledge, rebirth, spiritual mentors, and how to structure a meditation session. From there we considered the essence of a meaningful life and karma—the ethical dimension of our actions. If we use our lives wisely and make good ethical decisions, our deaths will be free from regret and fear. Having fortunate rebirths in the future, we will have conducive circumstances to continue our spiritual practice.

A fortunate rebirth is definitely desirable, but it is still within cyclic existence (*saṃsāra*), bound by ignorance, afflictions, and polluted karma. The unsatisfactory circumstances (*duḥkha*) of saṃsāra are immense and, knowing that, we seek to free ourselves from it. To do so, we must know its causes and whether those causes can be ceased. When convinced the causes can be stopped, we learn the path to eradicate them. Knowledge of guideposts along the way is helpful, as is continuously keeping our goal—the genuine peace and freedom of nirvāṇa for all living beings—in mind. Self-confidence and joyous effort are good friends on our journey to buddhahood.

While ostensibly this volume is about saṃsāra and nirvāṇa, it is actually about our minds—our minds that are sometimes tumultuous and at other times peaceful. Although our minds are always with us and are the basis of designation of the person, I, our minds remain a mystery to us. How can it be both the basis for the extreme duḥkha of saṃsāra and the incredible bliss and fulfillment of nirvāṇa?

Knowledge of the two types of buddha nature answers this question. One is the naturally abiding buddha nature—the emptiness of inherent existence of our minds—which has always been and will always be the ultimate nature of our minds. The second is the transforming buddha nature—the mind whose continuity goes on to awakening but at present is not yet freed from defilement. This mind serves as the basis for the emptiness that is the naturally abiding buddha nature. These two types of buddha nature are already present within us. The afflictions are not embedded in our minds; our minds are obscured by defilements but are not the nature of defilement. These obscuring factors can be forever eliminated by applying suitable antidotes.

This buddha nature is an indelible part of us. Each sentient being has it, so no matter how low we or others may fall as a result of our afflictions, afflictions and suffering are not our nature. We are worthwhile beings who deserve happiness. Our buddha nature can never be lost and we do not need to prove ourselves to anyone. The unpurified mind is saṃsāra; the purified mind is the basis of nirvāṇa. All that is needed is our confidence and sincere effort to follow the path, purify our buddha nature, and cultivate awakened qualities. These are the topics of the present volume.

How This Book Came About

The prefaces of volumes 1 and 2—*Approaching the Buddhist Path* and *The Foundation of Buddhist Practice*—contain longer explanations of the origin of the Library of Wisdom and Compassion. To give a brief account, it began with my requesting His Holiness in 1995 to write a short text on the stages of the path (*lamrim*) that lamas could use when teaching serious students new to Buddhism. Much to my surprise, His Holiness responded by saying that a larger book needed to be compiled first. Because the existing lamrim texts are excellent, there was no need to repeat them. This book needed to be different: It must contain material from the philosophical treatises so that readers will gain a deeper and more detailed explanation of the important points. It must contain material from the Pāli Buddhist tradition so that Tibetan Buddhists will have a more expanded view of the Buddha's teachings that will lessen sectarianism and help students to appreciate the Buddha's remarkable skill and versatility in instructing people with diverse interests, aptitudes, and dispositions.

Using material from His Holiness's teachings in Asia and the West, I began writing. I also compiled questions from his non-Tibetan disciples to ask during the series of interviews that occurred over the years. These questions dealt with topics that the authors of lamrim texts either assumed readers already knew or didn't discuss because they weren't pertinent at that time or in that culture. The book was also designed to clarify misunderstandings that arise when the meaning from another faith is superimposed onto Buddhism—for example, when people mistakenly understood karma and its effects to be a system of reward and punishment, as in theistic religions.

His Holiness often invited two, three, or four geshes to join the interviews, and engaged them in intriguing discussions about the topics I raised. The section on karmic seeds and having-ceaseds in chapter 5 of this volume came from such an interview. I asked about the similarities and differences between karmic seeds and having-ceaseds and a lengthy energetic discussion, punctuated with much laughter, followed. The discussion and debate continued after the session with His Holiness as I asked the geshes more questions over tea. At the end, we concluded that there were many more questions and points of debate to explore.

While writing, it sometimes seemed that I was "translating from English into English." The philosophical texts are lengthy, filled with debates, and often have sentences that are one page long. We had to extract the important points and express them in easy-to-understand English, including background material when necessary and examples to help the reader understand. As the manuscript increased in length, we realized that instead of being a book it would become a series.

In oral teachings, His Holiness weaves various topics together in a way that we listeners may not have considered before, opening up new meanings and perspectives. He also goes from simple to complex topics and back again in a matter of minutes, making one talk pertinent for both beginners and advanced practitioners. He doesn't expect us to understand everything at the first explanation and knows that our understanding will grow slowly as new layers of meaning are revealed to our minds as a result of our purification, collection of merit, study, and reflection. For this reason, the volumes in this series are meant to be read again and again, so that each time you will discover new gems. The books may also be read individually if you are interested in a particular topic, or be used as a resource when you need to look up specific points.

Overview of Saṃsāra, Nirvāṇa, and Buddha Nature

This book will lead us through a fascinating journey regarding our present situation and the possibility of attaining unsurpassed awakening where all duḥkha and its causes have been forever ceased and all excellent qualities have been developed limitlessly. Underlying both our saṃsāra and nirvāṇa is the fundamental innate clear light mind that by nature is empty of inherent existence. When obscured by defilements, it is buddha nature; when purified of defilements, it is the truth body (*dharmakāya*) of a buddha.

The book begins with an examination of the self: Is there a self? Does it have a beginning and an end? This leads into a discussion of the four truths—*duḥkha* (unsatisfactory circumstances), its origin, its cessation, and the path to that cessation—in both its coarse and subtle forms. We then delve into each truth, examining its four attributes, which reveals misunderstandings we may have about them and how to remedy those misconceptions.

With a clearer understanding of the four truths, in chapter 2 we look closely at true duḥkha—the realms of saṃsāric existence and our experiences in them. This exposes the many repugnant faults of saṃsāra and gives us a lens through which to see our present situation as it is. Chapter 3 identifies the chief causes of duḥkha—the six root afflictions. Investigating more closely, we find many other defilements obscuring our mindstreams. These bring psychological disturbances and have physical ramifications. This chapter provides a mirror for us to identify disturbing emotions and afflictive views that may otherwise go unnoticed.

In chapters 4 and 5 we examine the origins of duḥkha more thoroughly: the factors causing the arising of afflictions, feelings accompanying various afflictions, and temporary antidotes to subdue afflictions. We also learn about seeds of afflictions that provide continuity between one instance of an affliction and the next, latencies of afflictions that obscure the mind even after the afflictions have been eradicated, and karmic seeds and having-ceaseds that connect an action with its result. Chapter 6 deals with the way karma affects the evolution of the universe and our bodies.

The twelve links of dependent origination—which describe how rebirth in saṃsāra occurs and how the chain of events leading to it can be cut—is an important teaching in both the Pāli and Sanskrit traditions. With it comes the question, "Who revolves in cyclic existence and who is liberated?" which leads us to investigate the nature of the person. Chapters 7 and 8 explore the afflictive side of dependent origination and encourage us to renounce duḥkha and aspire for liberation, as explained in chapter 9. Chapters 10 and 11 describe the purified side of dependent origination, focusing especially on nirvāṇa, the ultimate true cessation. True path will be explained extensively in volume 4.

In order to aspire to liberation, we must know that liberation is possible. Elaborated on in chapter 12, this depends on understanding both the conventional and ultimate natures of our minds. If defilements were embedded in the nature of the mind, liberation would be impossible. Similarly, if the mind existed inherently, it could never change, and trying to attain liberation and awakening would be fruitless. But thankfully none of these is the case. Since ignorance is a faulty mind, it can be removed by correct wisdom.

Chapters 13 and 14 come from some of the most vibrant interviews with His Holiness, where he traced the explanation of true cessation from the first turning of the Dharma wheel to its more elaborate form in the second turning. He also traced the explanation of true path—the mind that realizes emptiness—from the Sūtra to the Tantra perspective, as hinted at in the third turning of the Dharma wheel. Listening to this was confusing and enlightening at the same time; there is a lot of profound meaning in these chapters that opens the way to gaining conviction that awakening is indeed possible.

Please Note

Although this series is coauthored, the vast majority of the material is His Holiness's instruction. I researched and wrote the parts pertaining to the

Pāli tradition, wrote some other passages, and composed the reflections. For ease of reading, most honorifics have been omitted, but that does not diminish the great respect we have for these most excellent sages and practitioners. Foreign terms are given in parentheses at their first usage. Unless otherwise noted with "P" or "T," indicating Pāli or Tibetan, respectively, italicized terms are Sanskrit. When two italicized terms are listed, the first is Sanskrit, the second Pāli. For consistency, Sanskrit spelling is used for Sanskrit and Pāli terms used in common language (nirvāṇa, Dharma, arhat, and so forth), except in citations from Pāli scriptures. *Śrāvaka* encompasses solitary realizers, unless there is reason to specifically speak of them. To maintain the flow of a passage, it is not always possible to gloss all new terms on their first use; a glossary is provided for you at the end of the book. "Sūtra" often refers to Sūtrayāna and "Tantra" to Tantrayāna. When these two words are not capitalized, they refer to two types of discourses: sūtras and tantras. Unless otherwise noted, the personal pronoun "I" refers to His Holiness.

Appreciation

I bow to Śākyamuni Buddha and all the buddhas, bodhisattvas, and arhats who embody the Dharma and with compassion teach it to us unawakened beings. I also bow to all the realized lineage masters of all Buddhist traditions through whose kindness the Dharma still exists in our world.

Since this series will appear in consecutive volumes, I will express my appreciation of those involved in each particular volume. This volume, the third in *The Library of Wisdom and Compassion*, is due to the talents and efforts of His Holiness's translators—Geshe Lhakdor, Geshe Dorji Damdul, and Mr. Tenzin Tsepak. I am grateful to Geshe Dorji Damdul, Geshe Dadul Namgyal, and Ven. Sangye Khadro for checking the manuscript, and to Samdhong Rinpoche, Geshe Sonam Rinchen, and Geshe Thubten Palsang for clarifying important points. I also thank Bhikkhu Bodhi for his clear teachings on the Pāli tradition and for generously answering my many questions. The staff at the Private Office of His Holiness facilitated the interviews, and Sravasti Abbey and Dharma Friendship Foundation kindly supported me while I worked on this series. Mary Petrusewicz skillfully edited this book, and Traci Thrasher was a tremendous help in gathering the photographs. I thank everyone at Wisdom Publications who contributed to the successful production of this series. All errors are my own.

Bhikṣuṇī Thubten Chodron
Sravasti Abbey

Abbreviations

Translations used in this volume, unless noted otherwise, are as cited here. Some terminology has been modified for consistency with the present work.

ADK *Treasury of Knowledge* (*Abhidharmakośa*) by Vasubandhu.

ADS *Compendium of Knowledge* (*Abhidharmasamuccaya*).

AN Aṅguttara Nikāya. Translated by Bhikkhu Bodhi in *The Numerical Discourses of the Buddha* (Boston: Wisdom Publications, 2012).

BCA *Engaging in the Bodhisattvas' Deeds* (*Bodhicaryāvatāra*) by Śāntideva.

CMA *Abhidhammattha Saṅgaha* by Anuruddha. In *A Comprehensive Manual of Abhidhamma*, edited by Bhikkhu Bodhi (Seattle: BPS Pariyatti Editions, 2000).

CŚ *The Four Hundred* (*Catuḥśataka*) by Āryadeva. Translated by Ruth Sonam in *Āryadeva's Four Hundred Stanzas on the Middle Way* (Ithaca, NY: Snow Lion Publications, 2008).

DN Dīgha Nikāya. Translated by Maurice Walshe in *The Long Discourses of the Buddha* (Boston: Wisdom Publications, 1995).

DS *Praise to the Sphere of Reality* (*Dharmadhātu-stava*) by Nāgārjuna.

EPL *Elucidating the Path to Liberation: A Study of the Commentary on the Abhidharmakosa* by the First Dalai Lama. Translated by David Patt (PhD dissertation, University of Wisconsin–Madison, 1993).

LC *The Great Treatise on the Stages of the Path* (T. *Lam rim chen mo*) by Tsongkhapa, 3 vols. Translated by Joshua Cutler et al. (Ithaca, NY: Snow Lion Publications, 2000–2004).

LS *Praise to the Supramundane* (*Lokātītastava*) by Nāgārjuna.

MMK *Treatise on the Middle Way* (*Mūlamadhyamakakārikā*) by Nāgārjuna.

MN Majjhima Nikāya. Translated by Bhikkhu Ñāṇamoli and Bhikkhu Bodhi in *The Middle-Length Discourses of the Buddha* (Boston: Wisdom Publications, 2005).

OR *Ocean of Reasoning* by rJe Tsong Khapa. Translated by Geshe Ngawang Samten and Jay L. Garfield (New York: Oxford University Press, 2006).

P Pāli.

PV *Commentary on the "Compendium of Reliable Cognition"* (*Pramāṇavārttika*) by Dharmakīrti. Hereafter *Commentary on Reliable Cognition.*

RA *Precious Garland* (*Ratnāvalī*) by Nāgārjuna. Translated by John Dunne and Sara McClintock in *The Precious Garland: An Epistle to a King* (Boston: Wisdom Publications, 1997).

RGV *Sublime Continuum* (*Ratnagotravibhāga, Uttaratantra*) by Maitreya.

SN Saṃyutta Nikāya. Translated by Bhikkhu Bodhi in *The Connected Discourses of the Buddha* (Boston: Wisdom Publications, 2000).

T Tibetan.

Vism *Path of Purification* (*Visuddhimagga*) by Buddhaghoṣa. Translated by Bhikkhu Ñāṇamoli in *The Path of Purification* (Kandy: Buddhist Publication Society, 1991).

Introduction

How to Study the Teachings

As with all activities, our attitude and motivation for learning and practicing the Buddhadharma affect the value of our action. Keeping six factors in mind will enable you to have a beneficial motivation. First, see yourself as a sick person who wants to recover. Our illness is cyclic existence and the duḥkha—unsatisfactory circumstances—that permeate it. Duḥkha includes being subject to birth, aging, sickness, and death under the influence of afflictions and karma, as well as not getting what we want, being separated from what we love, and encountering problems we don't want. Seeing ourselves as ill, we will approach the teachings with sincerity and receptivity.

Second, regard the teacher as a kind doctor who correctly diagnoses our illness and prescribes the medicine to cure it. Our saṃsāra is rooted in mental afflictions, the chief of which is ignorance that misapprehends the ultimate nature of phenomena. Although we want happiness, our minds are continually overwhelmed by attachment, anger, and confusion that cause us misery here and now and create the karma for future duḥkha.

Third, see teachings as medicine to cure our illness. The Buddha prescribes the medicine of the three higher trainings in ethical conduct, concentration, and wisdom, and the medicine of bodhicitta and the six perfections—generosity, ethical conduct, fortitude, joyous effort, meditative stability, and wisdom. Fourth, understand that practicing the teachings is the method to heal.

When we are ill, we naturally respect the doctor, trust the medicine, and want to take it, even if it doesn't taste so good. If we second-guess the doctor or complain about the medicine, we won't take it. Similarly, if we don't respect the Buddha and the Dharma, we won't practice. Likewise, if we have a prescription but don't fill it, or fill it but don't take the medicine, we won't recover. We must make an effort to learn and practice the Dharma and not simply collect statues, texts, and prayer beads. Curing the illness is a collaborative process between doctor and patient; we must both do our parts. The *King of Concentration Sūtra* says (LC 1:60–61):

> Some people are ill, their bodies tormented;
> for many years there is not even temporary relief.
> Afflicted with illness for a very long time,
> they seek a doctor, in search of a cure.
>
> Searching again and again,
> they at last find a physician with skill and knowledge.
> Treating the patients with compassion,
> the doctor gives medicine, saying, "Here, take this."
>
> This medicine is plentiful, good, and valuable.
> It will cure the illness, but the patients do not take it.
> This is not a shortcoming of the doctor, nor the fault of
>   the medicine.
> It is just the negligence of those who are ill.
>
> I have explained this very good teaching.
> Yet if you, having heard it, do not practice correctly,
> then just like a sick person holding a bag of medicine,
> your illness cannot be cured.

Taking the medicine entails looking beyond the words we hear and trying to understand their deeper meaning. When that is clear in our minds, we must then consistently put it into practice. Then, and only then, will our disease of duḥkha and afflictions be cured. When taking ordinary medicine, we must follow the instructions properly and take the whole cycle. If we take the medicine for a few days and then stop, we won't get well. Similarly, if we don't like the taste of the medicine and so mix in all sorts of better-tasting things, we won't recover. Our commitment to practicing the teachings as we are able to is a crucial element in our awakening.

Fifth, regard the buddhas as excellent, wise, and compassionate beings, and sixth, pray that the teachings will exist for a very long time so that many sentient beings can benefit from them.

Then cultivate an altruistic motivation, thinking, "I want to be free from the duḥkha of saṃsāra and will seek the Buddha's medicine that, when practiced properly, will lead me to good health. But I am not the only sick person; countless sentient beings also wander in saṃsāra and suffer from the afflictions. May I become a skillful and compassionate doctor like the Buddha, so that I can help all other sentient beings to be free from the duḥkha of saṃsāra."

1 | The Self, the Four Truths, and Their Sixteen Attributes

THE FOUR TRUTHS of the āryas are four facts that āryas—beings who directly see the ultimate nature of all persons and phenomena—know as true. These four truths establish the fundamental framework of the Buddhadharma, so a good understanding of them is essential. In this chapter we will look at the four truths in general, and in subsequent chapters will examine each one in detail.

The four truths describe the unawakened and awakened experiences of this merely designated self, so to begin with I would like to share some reflections on the self—the person who is reborn in cyclic existence, practices the path, and attains awakening.

Three Questions about the Self

I enjoy interfaith gatherings and appreciate the genuine in-depth dialogue and cooperation that result from them. At one such gathering in Amritsar, India, each participant was asked three questions: Is there a self? Is there a beginning to the self? Is there an end to the self? Here are my thoughts.

Is There a Self?

Most non-Buddhists assert an independent self—an *ātman* or soul—that takes rebirth. What leads them to say this? Although we know that our adult bodies did not exist at the time of our births, when we say, "At the time I was born . . ." we feel there was a self that was born and that this same self exists today. We also say, "Today my mind is calm," indicating that our mind is different today than yesterday when it was disturbed. But we feel the I is the same as yesterday. When we see a flower, we think, "I see," and it feels that there is a real person who sees it.

In all these cases, although we know that the body and mind change, we still have the sense of an enduring I that is the owner of the body and mind. This is the basis for believing there is a permanent, unitary, independent self that goes to heaven or hell or is reborn in another body after death. From this comes the conclusion that there must be an unchanging, independent I that is present throughout our lives and remains the same although the mental and physical aggregates change. This I is the agent of all actions such as walking and thinking.

While both Buddhists and non-Buddhists accept the existence of the self, our ideas of what the self is differ radically: most non-Buddhists accept the existence of a permanent, unchanging soul or independent self, while Buddhists refute it. Although no Buddhist philosophical school asserts a permanent, unitary, independent self, these schools have various ideas of what the self is: the mental consciousness, the continuum of consciousness, the collection of aggregates, or the mere I that is merely designated. The Prāsaṅgika Madhyamaka, which is generally accepted as the most refined system of tenets, says the self is merely designated in dependence on the body and mind. Because the self is merely imputed, we can say, "I am young or old" and "I think and feel." If the person were a completely different entity from the body and mind, it would not change when either the body or mind changes.

Is There a Beginning to the Self?

Those who believe in an external creator assert an autonomous intelligence that does not depend on causes and conditions. This being, they say, created the world and the sentient beings in it. For many people the notion that God created life fosters the feeling of being close to God and willingness to follow God's advice to be kind and refrain from harming others. Their belief in a creator spurs them to live ethically and to help others.

Some faiths such as Jainism and Sāṃkhya do not assert a creator, but I do not know if they believe the ātman has a beginning.

A repeated theme in Buddhism is dependent arising, one aspect of which is that functioning things arise due to causes and conditions. When explaining the twelve links of dependent origination, the Buddha said,

"Because of this, that exists. Because this has arisen, that arises." *Because of this, that exists* points out that things come into existence due to causes and conditions; they do not appear without a cause. If something has no causes, what makes it arise? If things do not depend on causes and conditions, why does a seed grow into a plant in the spring but not in the winter? If our lunch came into being without a cause, it would arise without groceries, pots, or cooks! Therefore everything—the body, the mind, and the external universe—depends on causes and conditions.

Because this has arisen, that arises illustrates that causes, like their results, are impermanent. If causes did not change, they would continue to exist even after producing their results. However, for a result to arise, its cause must cease; for an apple tree to grow, the apple seed must cease. It is not possible for a permanent creator or prior intelligence to create the universe and beings in it without itself changing. Each person, thing, and event arises due to its own causes, which in turn have come about in dependence on their causes. There is no discernable beginning.

Furthermore, things are produced by their own unique causes, not by discordant causes—things that do not have the capability to produce them. It is not the case that anything can produce anything. A daisy grows from daisy seeds, not from metal. Our bodies and minds each have their own unique causes.

Causes depend on conditions to produce their results. If conditions were unnecessary, a sprout could grow in the dead of winter or in parched soil; it would not depend on warmth and moisture to grow. Multiple causes and conditions are necessary to bring a result.

Each cause not only produces its own results but also arose due to the causes that produced it. The sprout is the cause of the tree that grows from it as well as the result of the seed from which it grew. If an external creator were the cause of the universe, he or she would also have to be the result of a previous cause. He would be a caused phenomenon and could not exist independent of causes.

If Buddhists do not accept a self, who takes rebirth? Although the Buddha refutes a self that exists independent of all other factors, he accepts a conventional self that is dependent on causes, conditions, and parts. This self is designated in dependence on the body and mind, so the question of whether the self has a beginning depends on if the body and mind have beginnings. The body is material in nature. Scientists currently say that all matter can be traced back to the Big Bang. How did the Big Bang occur? There must have been some material substances, energy, or potential for matter that existed before the Big Bang, and conditions must have been such that it exploded. Here, too, we see that things must have causes that are affected by other conditions and therefore change and give rise to something new.

Our minds change moment by moment; the mind is impermanent and arises due to causes that have the ability to produce each moment of mind. The first moment of mind in this life has a cause, because without a cause it could not exist. The cause of our minds was not our parents' minds, because both of our parents have their own individual continuity of consciousness, as do we. The substantial cause (*upādānakāraṇa*) of our minds—the cause that turns into the mind—cannot be our bodies or the sperm and egg of our parents, because the mind and body have different natures: the mind is formless and has the nature of clarity and cognizance, while the body has physical and material characteristics. The only thing we can point to as the cause of the first moment of mind in this life is the previous moment of that mind in the previous life. This continuity can be traced back infinitely, with one moment of mind producing the next moment of mind; there is no beginning.

REFLECTION

Consider:

1. Everything that is produced arises from causes; nothing can arise causelessly.
2. Causes are impermanent; they must cease in order for their result to arise.
3. There is concordance between a cause and its result. A specific result can only arise from the causes and conditions that are capable of producing it.
4. Apply this understanding to the existence of the physical universe and of your mind.

Is There an End to the Self?

Within Buddhism there are two positions regarding this question. Some Vaibhāṣikas say that when an arhat (someone who has attained liberation from saṃsāra) passes away (attains nirvāṇa without remainder of the polluted aggregates), the continuum of the person ceases to exist, like the flame of a lamp going out due to lack of fuel. Because the polluted aggregates are produced by afflictions and karma, when arhats pass away there is no continuity of their aggregates, since their causes—afflictions and polluted karma—have been ceased. Because the aggregates are necessary for the existence of a person, they say that the person no longer exists.

There are difficulties with this assertion: when the person is alive, there is no nirvāṇa without remainder of the polluted aggregates, and when this nirvāṇa has been attained, there is no person who attained it. In that case, how could we say, "This person attained this nirvāṇa?"

Furthermore, there is nothing that can eradicate the mindstream—the continuity of mind. The wisdom realizing selflessness eradicates afflictive obscurations, but it cannot destroy the clear and cognizant nature of the mind. For this reason Mādhyamikas and most Cittamātrins assert that after a person attains parinirvāṇa—the nirvāṇa after death—the continuum of the purified aggregates exists. These purified aggregates are the basis of designation of that arhat; thus the person does not cease to exist when he or she attains parinirvāṇa. Motivated by compassion, bodhisattvas who have overcome afflictive obscurations continue to take rebirth in cyclic existence. The continuity of buddhas' mindstreams also remain forever.

From the viewpoint of Tantrayāna, after an arhat passes away the subtlest mind-wind continues to exist and a person is posited in dependence on this. That self is called an *arhat*. Someone who has attained full awakening obtains the four bodies (here "body" means collection) of a buddha. Since the mind's ultimate nature is emptiness, the emptiness of the awakened mind becomes the nature truth body—the final true cessation of a buddha and the emptiness of that buddha's mind. The subtlest mind becomes the wisdom truth body—the omniscient mind of a buddha. The subtlest wind becomes the form bodies of a buddha—the enjoyment body and the emanation bodies. An *ārya* buddha—a person who is a buddha—exists by being merely designated in dependence on these four bodies.

The Four Truths

In classical India, many spiritual traditions spoke about the unawakened state of saṃsāra and the awakened state of nirvāṇa, each tradition having its own description of duḥkha, its origins, cessation, and the path leading to cessation. Saṃsāra means to be reborn with karmically conditioned aggregates. Specifically, it is our five aggregates, subject to clinging (*upādāna*) and appropriated due to afflictions and karma.[1]

Liberation is freedom from the bondage of rebirth with polluted aggregates, impelled by afflictions and karma. *Polluted* means under the influence of ignorance. Liberation comes about by ceasing the ignorance and karma that cause cyclic existence. The mind renouncing duḥkha and intent on liberation is a precious mind that needs to be cultivated with care. Renunciation does not mean relinquishing happiness; it is the aspiration for liberation, the determination to seek a higher and more enduring happiness than saṃsāra can offer.

The first teaching the compassionate Buddha gave was the four truths: true duḥkha, true origins, true cessations, and true paths. These four truths cover our present state, one that is replete with unsatisfactory conditions (*duḥkha*) and their origins, and presents an alternative: nirvāṇa (true cessations) and the path leading to that. The Buddha did not create the four truths; he simply described the truth about saṃsāra and its origins as well as the truth that a path exists to cease those and bring about nirvāṇa.

We may wonder why these truths are sometimes called the *four noble truths*. After all, what is noble about suffering? *Noble* indicates (1) they were directly realized and taught by noble ones—āryas, those who have realized the ultimate nature directly, and (2) knowing these truths ennobles us by enabling us to become āryas. They are called *truths* because it is true that duḥkha and its origins are to be abandoned and it is true that cessations and paths are to be adopted. These four are true according to the perception of the āryas, and they are true in the sense that they form a nondeceptive explanation that will lead us beyond suffering.

The Buddha spoke of the four truths in many sūtras. In the first turning of the Dharma wheel, the Buddha presented the four truths by means of three cycles: first he identified the *nature* of each truth, then he spoke of *how to engage* with each one, and finally he described the *result* of realizing each truth.

The Nature of Each Truth

In terms of their nature, *true sufferings* (*duḥkha*) are the polluted aggregates that are principally caused by afflictions and polluted karma. More broadly, true duḥkha consists of polluted bodies, minds, environments, and the things we use and enjoy. In *Compendium of Knowledge* Asaṅga says, "If one asks what is true duḥkha, it is to be understood both in terms of the sentient beings who are born as well as the habitats in which they are born." The body and mind are internal true duḥkha because they are in the continuum of a person; the environment and the things around us are external true duḥkha, which are not part of a person's continuum. All true origins are also true duḥkha, although not all true duḥkha is true origins. All afflictions are unsatisfactory, but our bodies and our habitats, which are unsatisfactory, are not causes of saṃsāra.

What propels this process of uncontrollably and repeatedly taking the psychophysical aggregates of a being of one of the three realms? It is the *true origins* of duḥkha—afflictions and polluted karma (actions). The chief affliction that is the root of saṃsāra is the ignorance grasping inherent existence—a mental factor that apprehends phenomena as existing in the opposite way than they actually exist. Whereas all phenomena exist dependently, ignorance apprehends them as existing independently. The Tibetan term for ignorance—*ma rig pa*—means not knowing. Even its name implies something undesirable that disturbs the mind and interferes with happiness and fulfillment. Since the cause of cyclic existence is inauspicious, its effect—our bodies, habitats, and experiences in cyclic existence—will not bring stable joy.

Ignorance narrows the mind, obscuring it from seeing the multifarious factors involved in existence. From ignorance stems various distorted conceptualizations that foster the arising of all other afflictions—especially the "three poisons" of confusion, attachment, and animosity. Afflictions in turn create karma that propels saṃsāric rebirth. In the context of the four truths, the Buddha identified craving as the principal example of the origin of duḥkha to highlight its prominent role.

True cessations are the exhaustion of true duḥkha and true origins. From the Prāsaṅgika viewpoint, they are the emptiness of an ārya's mind, specifically the purified aspect of the ultimate nature of a mind that has abandoned some portion of obscurations through the force of a true path.

True paths are āryas' realizations informed by the wisdom directly realizing selflessness. With the exception of ethical restraints that are imperceptible forms, true paths are consciousnesses. Pāli sūtras emphasize the eightfold path, which is subsumed into the three higher trainings, as the true path. Of the eight, right view—the wisdom realizing selflessness—is what actually cuts the root of cyclic existence.

The four truths comprise two pairs, each pair having a cause-and-effect relation. True origins cause true duḥkha, and true paths bring about true cessations. Technically speaking, true cessation—nirvāṇa—is not an effect, because it is unconditioned and permanent.[2] However, attaining nirvāṇa is due to a cause, which is the true path. The Buddha goes into more depth about the nature of each truth in the *Establishment of Mindfulness Sutta* (DN 22:18–21):

> And what, monastics, is the ārya truth of duḥkha? Birth is duḥkha, aging is duḥkha, death is duḥkha, sorrow, lamentation, pain, dejection, and despair are duḥkha. Encountering the undesired is duḥkha, being separated from the desired is duḥkha, not getting what one wants is duḥkha. In short, the five aggregates subject to clinging are duḥkha . . .
>
> And what, monastics, is the ārya truth of the origin of duḥkha? It is that craving that gives rise to rebirth, bound up with delight and attachment, seeking fresh delight now here, now there: that is to say, sensual craving, craving for existence, and craving for nonexistence.
>
> And what, monastics, is the ārya truth of the cessation of duḥkha? It is the remainderless fading away and ceasing, the giving up, abandoning, letting go, and detachment from it [craving].
>
> And what, monastics, is the ārya truth of the way leading to the cessation of duḥkha? It is just this ārya eightfold path—namely, right view, right intention, right speech, right action, right livelihood, right effort, right mindfulness, right concentration.

To look more closely at the Buddha's description of *true duḥkha*: We are already aware of the suffering involved in birth, sickness, aging, and death. *Sorrow* is our response to misfortune and disagreeable situations. When sorrow intensifies so that it becomes unbearable, we cry out or weep. This is *lamentation*. *Pain* refers to physical pain of whatever sort; *dejection* is mental pain, unhappiness, and depression. Due to pain or dejection, suffering becomes overwhelming and we *despair*, giving up hope because we see no recourse to solve our difficulties.

Encountering the undesired is meeting with what is disagreeable. However much we try to avoid difficulties, they keep coming in one form or another. We encounter relationship and financial problems as well as prejudice, injustice, and climate change.

Being separated from the desired occurs when we have what we like and then are separated from it. Once we have friends, relatives, a job and income, a good reputation, and so forth, we do not want to lose them. Although we cling to these, it is impossible to hold on to them forever because they are transient by their very nature. The greater our attachment, the more painful our eventual separation from them will be. For this reason the Buddha said that worldly things are unsatisfactory and lack the ability to bring lasting happiness.

Not getting what we want is the situation of having unfulfilled wishes and needs. We seek good health, financial security, and stable relationships; we wish to stay young forever and have an excellent reputation. However much we want these, we cannot achieve them to a degree that fulfills us, and fall prey to frustration, moodiness, and despondency. This experience is common to the rich and the poor, the popular and the lonely, the healthy and the ill.

The above circumstances are fairly easy to discern in our lives. In them we find three types of duḥkha. There are (1) evident pain—the *duḥkha of pain*—and (2) the unsatisfactory situation of not being able to hold on to the pleasant—the *duḥkha of change*. (3) The basis upon which these arise is the body and mind—the five aggregates subject to clinging. Because we have these five aggregates, all the other unsatisfactory situations arise. This is the *pervasive duḥkha of conditionality*, which is intrinsic to the five aggregates that are clung to with ignorance.

The five aggregates are momentary processes, bound together in relationships of mutual conditionality. We believe ourselves to be independent persons, existing above and beyond the body and mind or existing within the body and mind and having control over them. This idea of being an independent self is delusion. Until now we have never examined how we grasp the self and simply assume there is a self in control of the aggregates.

When we look deeply into the nature of the five aggregates, we see that they are simply momentarily changing processes that are in a constant flux. They arise and pass away without interruption, giving rise to the next moment in the same continuum. What we consider to be the person consists of only momentary material and mental aggregates.

Our bodies and minds are transient by nature. There is no further cause or external condition for their changing and passing away other than their having arisen. The Buddha said, "Whatever has the nature of arising, all of it has the nature of ceasing." This is subtle impermanence, and to realize it clearly through direct experience requires great mindfulness and concentration. This realization is very valuable because, when coupled with the understanding that our aggregates will never be something secure that we can take comfort in, it leads us to seek the *origin of duḥkha* and to investigate if it can be eradicated and, if so, how.

Repeatedly taking the five aggregates occurs due to ignorance, craving, and karma. Not only are our present aggregates the product of past ignorance, craving, and karma, but they also become the basis in this life for the arising of more ignorance, craving, and karma, which lead to taking another set of five aggregates subject to clinging in the future, which are under the control of ignorance, craving, and karma.

In pointing to craving as the prime example of the origin of duḥkha in the above passage, the Buddha was not disregarding the role of ignorance, other afflictions, and karma. Ignorance obscures the mind from knowing things as they are, and within that unclarity, craving is an active force that creates duḥkha. It does this in several ways: First, craving arises toward whatever is pleasurable. It seeks out objects, cognitive faculties, consciousnesses, contacts, feelings, intentions, thoughts, and images that are agreeable. In short, craving makes us into addicts who perpetually seek more and better physical and mental pleasures. Causing us to cling to the objects that appear to give us pleasures, craving breeds dissatisfaction and a sense of lacking. Thinking that gratifying all our desires will bring us happiness, we find ourselves immersed in cheating, lying, backbiting, and other harmful behaviors. In sum, craving lies behind much of the karma that projects rebirth in cyclic existence.

In addition to motivating many of the destructive actions we engage in during our lives, craving arises forcefully at the time of death, ripening the karmic seeds that project the next rebirth. As death approaches, craving seeks to preserve our sense of being an independent person; we do not want to separate from the body and mind of this life that are the basis for fabricating an independent self. However, during the death process, the body's ability to act as the support for consciousness ebbs, and craving gives rise to clinging, which propels the mind to seek rebirth in another body. According to the karmic seeds fertilized by craving and clinging, the mind connects to another body at the moment of rebirth. For human rebirths, this is the moment of conception. When consciousness joins the fertilized egg, all five aggregates of the next rebirth come into existence together. The fertilized egg is the body; and along with consciousness come feeling, discrimination, and miscellaneous factors, thus forming the basis of the person of the new life.

The *true cessation of duḥkha* is the relinquishment of the afflictive obscurations, especially craving. In our daily lives, we may experience facsimiles of cessation—for example, the peace and relief we feel when we let go of having our way or of insisting on being right and having the last word in an argument. While the final true cessation is nirvāṇa, āryas attain several partial cessations while on the path each time they abandon a certain portion of afflictions and their seeds.

The Pāli tradition speaks of four types of cessation; not all of these are nirvāṇa:

(1) *Cessation by factor substitution* (P. *tat anga nirodha*) occurs after we have cultivated the antidote to a particular affliction and temporarily eliminated it. When angry, we meditate on fortitude, and when filled with sensual craving, we contemplate the unattractiveness of the body. By substituting a virtuous state of mind for a nonvirtuous one, there is a cessation by factor substitution.

(2) *Cessation through suppression* (P. *vikambana nirodha*) is the result of attaining the meditative absorptions. Strong samādhi temporarily overcomes the manifest forms of the five hindrances and other defilements

(P. *saṃkleśa, saṃkilesa*), bringing the peace and bliss of concentration. Since the defilements are not active during meditative absorption, it seems that they have been eradicated. However, they have only been suppressed and their seeds remain in the mindstream.

(3) *Cessation through eradication* (P. *samucheda nirodha*) is the cessation attained through penetrative wisdom that cuts off the defilements so that they can never arise again. This cessation is attained beginning at the stage of stream-enterer (path of seeing), progresses through the stages of once-returner and nonreturner (path of meditation), and culminates in arhatship (path of no more learning).

(4) The *ultimate cessation of defilement* (P. *achanta nirodha*) as explained in the Pāli tradition is the reality that is the ultimate absence of all defilements. Cutting off defilements completely depends on a reality that is completely free from defilements, a reality that is ever-existing, unconditioned, and unborn. It is the existence of this unborn state—the reality of nirvāṇa—that makes the eradication of all defilements possible.[3] This nirvāṇa is the object of penetrating wisdom. When wisdom sees the truth of nirvāṇa and actualizes true cessation, defilements are eradicated.

REFLECTION

1. Remember a time when you applied an antidote to an affliction such as greed or the wish for revenge, and that affliction temporarily subsided.
2. Consider that it is possible for afflictions to subside for a longer period of time due to the force of having strong concentration that makes the mind extremely tranquil and peaceful.
3. Consider that it is possible to perceive reality directly and, by this, eradicate some level of defilement.
4. Consider that it is possible to deepen and stabilize that perception of reality so that all afflictive obscurations are eradicated such that they can never return.
5. Make a strong determination to do this.

True cessation is attained not by wishing or praying for it but by means of training the mind. The principal *true path* that trains the mind is the right view—the wisdom realizing selflessness. We must put energy into understanding the four truths, first intellectually, then experientially, and finally with penetrative wisdom. When a person on the śrāvaka path penetrates the four truths with direct realization, she becomes a stream-enterer and has entered the stream leading to nirvāṇa. She becomes an ārya who will proceed to nirvāṇa and never again be an ordinary being. When those following the bodhisattva path gain this realization, they become ārya bodhisattvas and will irreversibly proceed to full awakening.

How to Engage with Each Truth

How do we engage with or practice the four truths? True duḥkha is to be fully known or understood, true origins is to be abandoned, true cessations is to be actualized, and true paths is to be cultivated. Maitreya's *Sublime Continuum* (*Ratnagotravibhāga*, *Uttaratantra*) says (RGV 4.57):

> In the case of disease, we need to diagnose it, remove its causes,
> attain the happy state [of health], and rely on suitable medicine.
> Similarly, we need to recognize our duḥkha, remove its causes,
> actualize its cessation, and rely on the suitable path.

The Result of Each Truth

In terms of the resultant understanding of the four truths, true duḥkha is to be fully understood, but there is no duḥkha to understand; true origins are to be abandoned, but there are no origins to abandon; true cessation is to be actualized, but there is no cessation to actualize; and true paths are to be cultivated, but there are no paths to cultivate.

This may be understood in two ways. The first is common to all Buddhist schools: once we have completely understood duḥkha, there is no more duḥkha to understand; once we have totally overcome its origins, there are no more causes of suffering to overcome; once we have perfectly actualized cessation, our liberation is complete and there are no more cessations to actualize; and once we have fully cultivated the path, there is nothing more to cultivate.

According to the uncommon Madhyamaka approach, the Buddha is referring to the ultimate nature of the four truths, their emptiness. His thought is that it is possible for us to overcome true duḥkha and its origins and to actualize true cessations and true paths because their very nature is empty of inherent existence. Since they are primordially empty and have never existed inherently, duḥkha and its origins can be eliminated, and true cessations and true paths can be actualized. Their ultimate nature, emptiness, is also called *natural nirvāṇa*, and this allows for us to attain the three other types of nirvāṇa: nirvāṇa without remainder, nirvāṇa with remainder, and nonabiding nirvāṇa.[4]

According to the Madhyamaka approach, true duḥkha is to be fully understood on the conventional level, but on the ultimate level there is no true duḥkha. That is, true duḥkha exists on the conventional level by being merely designated by concept and term, but on the ultimate level there has never been inherently existent true duḥkha; true duḥkha is naturally empty of inherent existence. It is similar for the other three of the four truths: they exist conventionally, but ultimately cannot be found by ultimate analysis.

The Coarse and Subtle Four Truths

According to the Prāsaṅgikas' unique presentation, the four truths have both a coarse and a subtle form. Vasubandhu's *Treasury of Knowledge* (*Abhidharmakośa*) and Asaṅga's *Compendium of Knowledge* (*Abhidharmasamuccaya*) described the coarse four truths: True duḥkha is all unsatisfactory circumstances arising from grasping a self-sufficient substantially existent person. True origins are grasping a self-sufficient substantially existent person and the afflictions and polluted karma arising from this grasping. True cessations are the abandonment of the duḥkha and origins that arise from grasping a self-sufficient substantially existent person. True path is the wisdom that sees the absence of a self-sufficient substantially existent person. This is the view held by the lower philosophical tenet systems.

The subtle four truths are described by the Prāsaṅgikas: True duḥkha is the unsatisfactory circumstances that are rooted in grasping inherent existence and karma. True origins are grasping inherent existence of persons and phenomena and the afflictions and polluted karma that arise from this grasping. True cessations are the complete eradication of these, and true path is the wisdom realizing the emptiness of inherent existence. As true origin, grasping inherent existence is much subtler and more tenacious than grasping a self-sufficient substantially existent person. It is also more difficult to identify when meditating on selflessness.

Ordinary beings can directly realize coarse selflessness—the lack of a self-sufficient substantially existent person. But this realization alone cannot remove the root of cyclic existence, the ignorance grasping inherent existence. At best, it can temporarily abandon coarse self-grasping and the afflictions that depend on it. Therefore the wisdom realizing the lack of a self-sufficient substantially existent person is not an actual true path capable of cutting the root of cyclic existence, and the cessation of this grasping is not an actual true cessation. Here we see the far-reaching implications of the Prāsaṅgikas' way of positing the object of negation and the importance of identifying it correctly in order to cultivate the wisdom that sees it as nonexistent.

The Sixteen Attributes of the Four Truths of Āryas

The sixteen attributes of the four truths are found in the *Treasury of Knowledge*, Asaṅga's *Śrāvaka Grounds* (*Śrāvakabhūmi*), and Dharmakīrti's *Commentary on Reliable Cognition*. They are taught to protect sentient beings from duḥkha by helping them to develop wisdom and insight (*vipaśyanā*). Each truth has four attributes, which counteract four distorted conceptions about each truth. In addition to eliminating these sixteen misconceptions, which are obstacles to attaining liberation, the sixteen attributes establish the existence of liberation and the method to attain it. Each attribute is a quality of that truth and reveals a specific function of that truth.

If you have doubts regarding the possibility of eradicating duḥkha forever and if you wonder if nirvāṇa exists and if it is possible to attain it, contemplation on the sixteen attributes of the four truths will be very helpful. As we reflect on them, we may discover that we hold some of the misconceptions that are refuted. Making effort to understand the sixteen attributes will help us to dispel these, clearing the way for wisdom to arise.

Unless otherwise noted, the sixteen attributes are presented according to the common view acceptable to all Buddhist tenet systems. The unique

Prāsaṅgika meaning is also presented when it differs from this.[5] Please note that while each truth is often stated in the singular (e.g., true origin), it has many components, so sometimes it is expressed in the plural (true origins).

Four Attributes of True Duḥkha

True duḥkha (*duḥkha-satya*) is the polluted aggregates principally caused by afflictions and karma. They include internal true duḥkha, such as our polluted bodies and minds, and external true duḥkha, such as our habitats and the things in it.

The four attributes of true duḥkha—impermanent, duḥkha (unsatisfactory), empty, and selfless—counteract four distorted conceptions (*ayoniśo manaskāra*) or conceptualizations (*vikalpa viparyāsa*)—believing impermanent things to be permanent, things that are by nature unsatisfactory to be pleasurable, the unattractive to be attractive, and what lacks a self to have one.[6] The Buddha said in *Distortions of the Mind* (AN 4.49):

> Perceiving permanence in the impermanent,
> perceiving pleasure in what is duḥkha,
> perceiving a self in what is not-self,
> and perceiving beauty in what is foul,
> beings resort to wrong views,
> their minds deranged, their perception twisted.
>
> Such people are bound by the yoke of Māra[7]
> and do not reach security from bondage.
> Beings continue in saṃsāra,
> going repeatedly from birth to death.
>
> But when the buddhas arise in the world
> and send forth a brilliant light,
> they reveal this teaching that leads
> to the stilling of duḥkha.
>
> Hearing it, wise people regain their sanity.
> They see the impermanent as impermanent,

and what is duḥkha as duḥkha.
They see what is not-self as not-self,
and the unattractive as unattractive.
By acquiring the right view,
they overcome all duḥkha.

The four attributes of true duḥkha counteract the four distorted conceptions.[8] Understanding the first two attributes prepares us to realize the last two, which are the main antidotes that bring true cessations. While our physical and mental aggregates are pinpointed as an example of true duḥkha because they are the basis of designation of the self, the explanation pertains to everything conditioned by afflictions and karma.

1. The physical and mental aggregates are *impermanent* (*anitya*) because they undergo continuous, momentary arising and disintegrating.

Overwhelmed by ignorance, we apprehend transient things—such as our bodies, relationships, and possessions—as unchanging, stable, and enduring, and expect them to remain the same and always be there. We do not feel that we are going to die—at least not any time soon. Believing that we are the same person we were yesterday, we expect our lives to be constant and predictable. We are surprised by a car accident or a sudden change in our conditions at work. As a result of holding what is impermanent to be permanent, we don't prepare for death or future lives by avoiding harmful actions and engaging in constructive ones. Telling ourselves we will practice Dharma later when we have more time, we waste our precious human lives.

Coarse impermanence is perceptible by our senses: the sun sets, a building is constructed and later decays, babies become adults and then die. All of these coarse changes happen due to subtle impermanence—changes occurring in each moment. These subtle changes are built into the nature of conditioned things; no other external factor is necessary to make things arise and cease in each moment.

Arising is something new coming into existence, abiding is the continuation of something similar, and ceasing is the disintegration of what was. These three occur simultaneously in each moment. From the moment something arises, it is changing and ceasing. There is no way to halt this process or take a time-out. Because everything changes in each moment, there is no stability or security to be found in saṃsāra. Understanding this gives us a more realistic view of life. This, in turn, helps us to release attachment to saṃsāric enjoyments and birth in saṃsāra in general, and frees our mind to seek a more reliable happiness that comes from Dharma practice.

2. The aggregates are *unsatisfactory by nature* (*duḥkhatā*) because they are under the control of afflictions and karma.

Believing that what is unsatisfactory by nature—food, possessions, reputation, friends, relatives, our bodies, and so forth—is actual pleasure and happiness, we jump into the world of transitory pleasures expecting lasting joy. Viewing our bodies to be a source of great pleasure, we expend great effort to secure and experience sensual delights. In doing so we consume more than our fair share of the Earth's resources and spend a lot of time chasing illusions. In actuality, our bodies have constant aches and pains and are seldom comfortable for long. If we saw them more realistically, we would keep them healthy in order to use them to practice the Dharma, but we would not expect true happiness from them.

Contemplating that the objects, people, and activities we see as enjoyable are actually unsatisfactory in nature because they are under the influence of afflictions and karma remedies the distorted belief that they are a source of secure happiness. What we commonly call pleasure is actually a state where one discomfort has decreased and a newer discomfort is just beginning. For example, when we've been standing a long time, sitting brings a feeling of relief and pleasure. But slowly, the discomfort of sitting increases, and after a while we want to stand up and walk around.

Our aggregates are subject to the three types of duḥkha mentioned above—the duḥkha of pain, which is physical and mental pain; the duḥkha of change, in which pleasurable circumstances do not last; and the pervasive duḥkha of conditioning, a body and mind conditioned by afflictions and karma. This last one is the source of the first two. Afflictions and karma condition our experiences, and without choice, our bodies fall ill, age, and die. Our minds are overwhelmed by disturbing emotions such as despair and rage. Understanding that whatever is under the power of afflictions and karma cannot be a source of lasting joy, we release unrealistic expectations and distance ourselves from the useless pursuit of clinging to saṃsāric pleasures. Instead we direct our energy toward actualizing true cessations.

The attributes of impermanence and duḥkha are linked. Āryadeva says (CŚ 50):

> The impermanent is definitely harmed.
> What is harmed is not pleasurable.
> Therefore all that is impermanent
> is said to be duḥkha.

Gyaltsab explains:

> Whatever is impermanent, such as the body, which is a maturation of polluted past karma and afflictions, is definitely damaged by factors causing disintegration and therefore produces aversion. Anything affected by causes of harm, whose character is to produce aversion, is not pleasurable. Therefore all that is impermanent and polluted is said to be duḥkha, just as anything that falls into a salt pit become salty.

Impermanent and polluted things, such as our bodies, are under the influence of afflictions and karma that cause them to disintegrate. An aged or dead body is considered undesirable and unclean, just as beautiful flowers are ugly when they decay and rot. Anything that disintegrates under the influence of afflictions and karma and produces aversion and distaste in us is by nature duḥkha. It lacks a findable essence; it is empty. Seeing this leads to disenchantment with saṃsāra and inspires us to turn our attention to liberation.

3. The aggregates are *empty* (*śūnya*) because they lack a permanent, unitary, and independent self.

The third distorted conception holds what is foul—specifically our bodies—as beautiful. Our own and others' bodies are filled with ugly substances—blood, bones, muscles, organs, tissue, excrement, and so on. Because of ignorance, we preen our own bodies and see others' bodies as desirable and lust after them. Needless to say, our infatuation with the body is misplaced and leads to disappointment and misery.

There are two aspects to seeing the aggregates as unattractive. The first focuses on the body and sees that its organs, fluids, and so forth are foul. No one finds the inside of the body gorgeous, and we clean away everything that the body excretes. The second understands that since the aggregates are impermanent and are unsatisfactory by nature, the body is unattractive and our afflictive thoughts are undesirable. As such, our saṃsāric aggregates are not worth craving and clinging to, for they lack the capacity to bring us enduring well-being. This inspires us to turn our attention to creating the causes for liberation.

The aggregates being empty refutes the permanent, unitary, independent self or ātman as conceived by the non-Buddhists. *Permanent* here means the self is eternal and does not change from one life to the next. *Unitary* means not made of parts, and *independent* in this context means not depending on causes and conditions. Such a self or soul has a nature that is entirely different from that of the aggregates: it is forever unchanged, monolithic, all-pervasive, and completely separate from conditioned phenomena. The aggregates, in contrast, change, consist of parts, and are influenced by causes and conditions. The aggregates cannot possibly be such a self. The attribute of empty also refutes the existence of an independent creator who is unchanging, monolithic, and not affected by causes and conditions.

How does the third attribute—empty—counteract the notion of the body as attractive? Our mistaken belief that the foul body is attractive and pure involves holding the person and the aggregates to be separate when in fact they are the same nature. During the Buddha's time, people adhered strongly to the caste system and the brahmins prided themselves on being pure because they were born from Brahmā's mouth, while those of lower castes were born from lower parts of Brahmā's body and thus were considered impure. Brahmins maintained strict rules of cleanliness to the extent that they did not touch the bodies of lower-caste people, eat with them, or use the same utensils. The Buddha opposed the caste system and the notion of a "pure self" that was its basis. By teaching that there is no pure, eternal, monolithic self that is separate from the aggregates, he pointed out that all saṃsāric bodies—no matter what caste people belonged to—were unattractive and impure.

Although Prāsaṅgikas agree with the above, their unique viewpoint of the third attribute is expressed in the following syllogism: The aggregates are *empty* because of arising dependently. This expresses the emptiness of inherent existence of phenomena. If the subject were the person, it would express the emptiness of the person. The reason—dependent arising—proves the emptiness of both the person and the aggregates because in both cases inherent existence is being negated. The reason in this syllogism could also be "because of depending on causes and conditions" or "because they depend on parts."

4. The aggregates are *selfless* (*nairātmya*) because they lack a self-sufficient substantially existent person.

If a self-sufficient substantially existent person existed, it would be the same nature as the aggregates. When we say "I" or "my body and mind," we have the impression that there is a self who is the owner and controller of the body and mind. This I instructs the mind to think and the body to move. Whereas we usually identify a person by seeing his body, hearing her voice, or thinking of her mind, a self-sufficient substantially existent person could be identified without cognizing any of the aggregates. The fourth attribute negates the existence of such a self.

According to Prāsaṅgikas' unique view, a self-sufficient substantially existent self is a coarse object of negation, one that can be refuted by a conventional reliable cognizer. They assert that the fourth distorted conception is grasping all phenomena whatsoever as inherently existent, meaning they have their own intrinsic essence and exist under their own power, independent of all other factors. For Prāsaṅgikas emptiness and selflessness come to the same point.

The ignorance that grasps inherent existence is a big troublemaker. Based on it, we incorrectly consider ourselves to be self-enclosed entities, become attached to our individual well-being, and see everything in relationship to ourselves. Grasping inherent existence stimulates distorted conceptualization, which projects attractiveness and ugliness on people and things that don't have them. As a result, we become indignant when criticized and arrogant when praised. This leads to manipulative behavior, personal anguish, societal discord, and vicious wars. It is important to understand this by examining our own experiences.

Because all phenomena are baseless—they lack an inherent nature—it is possible for the wisdom realizing the emptiness of inherent existence to overcome and dispel self-grasping ignorance, which holds phenomena to exist inherently. Seeing with wisdom that all persons and phenomena are selfless—that they lack inherent existence—is the path freeing us from saṃsāra.

In conclusion, based on not knowing the four attributes of true duḥkha, the four distorted conceptions arise in our minds one after the other. They give rise to afflictions, which instigate disturbing mental, verbal, and physical actions, which in turn leave karmic seeds on our mindstreams. Some of these karmic seeds ripen at the time of death and cause our next rebirth; others ripen in our future lives, affecting our environments, habits, and the experiences we undergo. This is the meaning of being under the control of afflictions and polluted actions, and it clearly illustrates that we are not free to experience the joy and fulfillment we seek. We must understand the four distorted conceptions well in order to overcome them, just as in ordinary warfare one has to learn about one's enemies in order to defeat them.

The four attributes of true duḥkha build on one another. Our bodies and minds change moment by moment. This is their nature; once they arise, no further cause is needed to make them change. Knowing this contradicts the belief that they are static and unchanging.

Impermanent things are produced by causes and conditions; our aggregates are controlled by their causes—afflictions and karma—which are ultimately rooted in ignorance. Anything caused by or rooted in ignorance is unsatisfactory; this is the pervasive duḥkha of conditioning. Once we understand this, no matter how beautiful, pleasurable, and enticing things may appear, we know they are not worthy of our clinging to them.

The first two attributes center on the aggregates being dependent on causes and conditions. They lead to understanding the last two attributes that deny the existence of any kind of independent self or person. We aren't free from these aggregates, so how could there be a permanent, unitary, independent self that is a different entity from the aggregates? We cannot prevent our bodies and minds from aging and dying, so how could there be a self-sufficient substantially existent person that controls the aggregates?

Whether we initially approach the four attributes from the viewpoint of reasoning or meditation, we must later combine the knowledge gained from both to attain a yogic direct reliable cognizer that realizes impermanence, duḥkha, emptiness, and selflessness. This mind is a mental consciousness that is a union of serenity and insight that directly realizes these four attributes.

Reflecting on the four attributes of true duḥkha makes us yearn to be free from our polluted aggregates and to attain nirvāṇa, a state of true freedom. The practice of the four establishments of mindfulness is one way to realize the four attributes of true duḥkha and to overcome the four distorted conceptions. Mindfulness of the body overcomes holding it as attractive; mindfulness of feelings overcomes seeing the aggregates as pleasurable and desirable; mindfulness of the mind counteracts grasping a permanent, unitary, independent self; and mindfulness of phenomena leads us to understand selflessness. The realization of subtle emptiness and subtle selflessness frees us from the bonds of cyclic existence.

DISTORTED CONCEPTIONS OF TRUE DUḤKHA		ATTRIBUTES OF TRUE DUḤKHA *The polluted aggregates are*
1.	Believing impermanent things to be permanent	Impermanent, because they undergo continuous, momentary arising and disintegrating
2.	Believing unsatisfactory things to be pleasurable	Duḥkhatā, because they are under the control of afflictions and karma
3.	Believing the unattractive to be attractive	Empty, because they lack a permanent, unitary, and independent self
4.	Believing what lacks a self to have a self	Selfless, because they lack a self-sufficient substantially existent self

REFLECTION

1. Remember a situation in which you had strong animosity toward someone. Observe how you believed that person to be fixed and unchanging. It seems as if all he has ever been or done is condensed as that horrible person who harmed you.

2. Ask yourself if this is true. Is the person frozen in time like this? Or does he change depending on causes and conditions? Is there an independent person who always has been and always will be the image you currently have of him?

3. Seeing that the person is neither permanent nor independent, allow your anger to dissipate. Enjoy the feeling of being free from hurt and anger.

Four Attributes of True Origins

True origins (*samudaya-satya*)—afflictions and karma—are the principal causes of true duḥkha. Actions come from afflictions, especially craving and ignorance, the root of all afflictions. Buddhist tenet systems have various ideas of what ignorance is and how it relates to the view of a personal identity. These will be explained later.

A prominent example of afflictions is craving (*tṛṣṇā*), a strong liking for an object and unwillingness to let it go. Looking closely at our life experiences, we see that much of our suffering is due to craving—holding on to something or someone outside of ourselves as the source of happiness, security, and success. Craving creates feelings of dissatisfaction and inadequacy, so that no matter what we accomplish or possess, or who loves and appreciates us, we still feel discontent, pervaded by the longing for more and better.

The four attributes of true origins are cause, origin, strong producers, and conditions.

1. Craving and karma are the *causes* (*hetu*) of duḥkha because they are the chief causes of duḥkha.

Our suffering is not haphazard but has causes—craving and karma. Under the control of ignorance, we crave to experience pleasant feelings and crave to not experience painful ones. This leads us to act, creating karma. Craving also spurs different karmas to ripen into their results, especially during the dying process. This attribute refutes the idea that duḥkha is random or causeless, as asserted by the Materialists (Cārvāka), a philosophical school in ancient India. By rejecting the law of karma and its effects, many

Materialists denied ethical responsibility and lived hedonistic lifestyles, indulging in sense pleasures with little thought of the long-term effects of their actions on themselves or others.

2. Craving and karma are *origins* (*samudaya*) of duḥkha because they repeatedly produce all of the diverse forms of duḥkha.

Afflictions and karma create not just a portion of our mental and physical misery but all of it in the past, present, and future. Understanding this dispels the idea that duḥkha comes from only one cause, such as an external deity or a primal cosmic matter. If duḥkha rested on only one cause, cooperative conditions would be unnecessary, in which case either that cause would never produce a result or it would never stop producing a result. If a sprout depended only on a seed and nothing else, the seed would continually grow because the change of seasons would not affect it at all; or it would not grow at all because the presence of warm weather, water, and fertilizer would not affect it. Duḥkha depends on the coming together of many changeable factors. It is not predestined or fated.

Seeing the diverse forms of duḥkha that sentient beings repeatedly experience under the control of afflictions and karma can be shocking at first. However, since they are conditioned phenomena, when conditions change or cease, duḥkha will similarly change or cease.

3. Craving and karma are *strong producers* (*prabhava*) because they act forcefully to produce strong duḥkha.

We tend to think that our problems come from causes outside of ourselves—an external creator or another person. When some people experience illness or accidents, they attribute it to God, who willed that event. On a more mundane level, we blame our unhappiness on other people or external circumstances. This way of thinking locks us into a victim mentality where we believe we are unable to change our experiences because they are caused by someone outside of ourselves. Understanding the third attribute dispels the notion that duḥkha arises from discordant causes—for example, the motivation of an external creator.

Afflictions and karma bring intense duḥkha in both lower and higher realms, and they forcefully keep us bound in saṃsāra. When we understand that afflictions and karma are the actual origins of our problems, we accept responsibility for our actions and our lives. We become empowered, knowing that we have the ability to change our situation and create the causes for the happiness we want. Having correctly identified the origins of our misery, we learn, reflect on, and meditate on the Dharma to counteract afflictions and purify karma. Understanding this stimulates us to dispel these origins of duḥkha.

4. Craving and karma are *conditions* (*pratyaya*) because they also act as the cooperative conditions that give rise to duḥkha.

Craving and karma are not only the primary causes of duḥkha but also the cooperative conditions that enable karma to ripen. When craving manifests in our minds, it acts like fertilizer enabling karmic seeds to ripen. Understanding that duḥkha depends on causes and conditions dispels the notion that it is fixed and unalterable and counteracts the idea that duḥkha is fundamentally permanent but temporarily fleeting—that is, thinking our unsatisfactory state cannot be overcome even though there are temporary times of reprieve. When the causes and conditions are eliminated, the resultant unsatisfactory and suffering experiences will also cease. Knowing this brings resilience to our Dharma practice.

Contemplating these four attributes strengthens our determination to abandon true origins.

DISTORTED CONCEPTIONS OF TRUE ORIGINS		ATTRIBUTES OF TRUE ORIGINS *Afflictions (especially craving) and karma are*
1.	Believing that duḥkha is random or causeless (Cārvāka)	Causes of duḥkha, because they are the chief causes of duḥkha
2.	Believing that duḥkha comes from only one cause	Origins, because they repeatedly produce all the diverse forms of duḥkha
3.	Believing that duḥkha arises from discordant causes, such as an external creator (Vaiśeṣika)	Strong producers, because they act forcefully to produce strong duḥkha
4.	Believing that duḥkha is fundamentally permanent but temporarily fleeting (Nirgrantha)	Conditions, because they act as cooperative conditions that give rise to duḥkha

REFLECTION

1. Examine the role of craving in your life. What do you crave? Do these things actually satisfy you when you get them?
2. Does craving come from outside yourself? Is it from a creator, another person, the object you crave? How is craving related to ignorance?
3. What do you do under the influence of craving? What are the results of these actions?
4. Make a strong determination to overcome ignorance and craving by practicing the path.

Four Attributes of True Cessations

True cessations (*nirodha-satya*) include the cessations of various levels of afflictions that are actualized as we progress through the paths to arhatship and full awakening. Prāsaṅgikas add to this that a true cessation is the purified ultimate nature of the mind that has removed that level of afflictions.

An arhat's true cessation of all afflictions and karma causing saṃsāric rebirth is taken as the example. This true cessation in the continuum of an arhat is the cessation of innate (*sahaja*) afflictions that have existed since beginningless time and acquired (*parikalpita*) afflictions that were learned from incorrect philosophies.

Prāsaṅgikas assert that the true cessations of the coarse four truths are not actual true cessations because eliminating the ignorance grasping a self-sufficient substantially existent person does not eradicate true duḥkha and its origins, although it will temporarily stop the manifest coarse afflictions explained in the two *Knowledges*. They also assert that a buddha's true cessation is also the cessation of the cognitive obscurations that prevent full awakening.

The four attributes of true cessation address concerns that you may have. If you believe that afflictions exist inherently in sentient beings, so that a state of final peace is impossible, reflect on the first attribute. If you wonder if heaven is better than nirvāṇa, contemplate the second attribute. If you think that nirvāṇa isn't total freedom, reflect on the third attribute. And if you wonder if it's possible for nirvāṇa to deteriorate, contemplate the fourth attribute.

The four attributes of true cessation are cessation, peace, magnificence, and definite emergence (freedom).

1. Nirvāṇa is the *cessation* of duḥkha (*nirodha*) because it is a state in which the origins of duḥkha have been abandoned, and it thus ensures that duḥkha will no longer arise.

Thinking that afflictions are an inherent part of sentient beings, some people believe that trying to eliminate them is futile. They do not try to remedy their situation and consequently continue to be reborn in cyclic existence. Understanding that attaining true cessations is possible by eliminating afflictions and karma dispels the misconception that liberation does not exist, immediately freeing us from a defeatist, and often cynical, attitude.

2. Nirvāṇa is *peace* (*śānta*) because it is a separation in which afflictions have been eliminated.

Unable to correctly identify the qualities of liberation, some people mistake other polluted states, such as meditative absorptions in the form and formless realms, as liberation. Although these meditative absorptions are much more tranquil than our human existence, they have only suppressed manifest afflictions and have not eliminated subtle afflictions and their seeds from the root. Not understanding that nirvāṇa is ultimate peace, people do not try to attain it and are satisfied with a temporary, superior saṃsāric state. This attribute counteracts the belief that states polluted by ignorance are nirvāṇa. People who are convinced of the harm of afflictions and karma know that their cessation is a state of peace and joy that will not vanish.

3. Nirvāṇa is *magnificence* (*praṇīta*) because it is the superior source of benefit and bliss.

Because nirvāṇa is completely nondeceptive and no other state of liberation supersedes it, it is supreme and magnificent. Nirvāṇa is total freedom from all three types of duḥkha. Knowing this prevents mistaking certain states of temporary or partial cessation as nirvāṇa. It also prevents thinking that there is some state superior to the cessation of duḥkha and its origins. Someone who mistakes a saṃsāric state as liberation will follow a detour that does not lead to their destination. For example, someone who enjoys the tranquility of suppressing the conceptual mind in blank-minded meditation does himself a disservice, because nirvāṇa will elude him.

4. Nirvāṇa is *freedom* or *definite emergence* (*niḥsaraṇa*) because it is total, irreversible release from saṃsāra.

Nirvāṇa is a definite abandonment because it is an irrevocable release from saṃsāra's duḥkha. This counters the mistaken notion that nirvāṇa can degenerate. Because nirvāṇa is the elimination of all afflictions and karma causing saṃsāric rebirth, there no longer exists any cause for such rebirth or for the suffering it entails.

Contemplating these four attributes encourages us not to stop partway but to continue practicing until we actualize full nirvāṇa.

DISTORTED CONCEPTIONS OF TRUE CESSATIONS		ATTRIBUTES OF TRUE CESSATIONS *Nirvāṇa—an arhat's true cessation of all afflictions and karma that cause saṃsāric rebirth through the force of antidotes—is*
1.	Believing that liberation does not exist	Cessation of duḥkha, because it is a state in which the origins of duḥkha have been abandoned
2.	Believing that other polluted states (such as meditative absorptions in the form and formless realms) are liberation	Peace, because it is a separation in which afflictions have been eliminated
3.	Believing that a state of temporary or partial cessation is nirvāṇa/liberation	Magnificence, because it is the superior source of benefit and bliss
4.	Believing that nirvāṇa can degenerate, that it is reversible	Freedom, because it is total, irreversible release from saṃsāra

REFLECTION

1. To get a small taste of what nirvāṇa could be like, imagine that an affliction such as anger is totally absent from your mind. No matter what someone says or does, no matter what happens, you will never get angry again.
2. Nirvāṇa is the complete absence of all afflictions forever. Aspire to attain it.

Four Attributes of True Paths

The true path (*mārgasatya*) *is the wisdom realizing the sixteen attributes of the four truths, especially true cessation.* Existing in the mindstreams of āryas of all three vehicles, true paths eradicate ignorance and other afflictions. When afflictions cease, polluted karma is no longer created and that which has already been created cannot ripen into a saṃsāric rebirth; liberation is attained.

The Pāli tradition says that the āryas' eightfold path constitutes true paths, while Prāsaṅgikas say it is an ārya's realization informed by the wisdom directly realizing the emptiness of inherent existence. The wisdom realizing emptiness is the principal true path because it views phenomena's mode of existence opposite to the way ignorance does. While ignorance grasps inherent existence, the wisdom directly realizing emptiness realizes the absence of inherent existence. In this way, it is able to completely counteract ignorance and all afflictions rooted in it.

As above, these four attributes assuage doubts that we may have about the true path. If you fear that there is no path to peace, reflect on the first attribute. If you think that the wisdom realizing emptiness cannot counteract the afflictions, reflect on the second attribute. If you wonder if the wisdom realizing emptiness will actually eliminate all afflictions, ponder the third attribute. If you wonder if meditating with the wisdom realizing emptiness will bring nirvāṇa and not some other state, reflect on the fourth attribute.

The four attributes of true paths are path, suitable, accomplishment, and deliverance. These are explained according to the Prāsaṅgika viewpoint.[9]

1. The wisdom directly realizing selflessness is the *path* (*mārga*) because it is the unmistaken path to liberation.

This wisdom leads to liberation. Knowing this counters the misconception that there is no path to liberation from saṃsāra. People who believe no path exists will not venture to cultivate it and will remain endlessly trapped in cyclic existence.

2. The wisdom directly realizing selflessness is *suitable* (*nyāya*) because it acts as the direct counterforce to the afflictions.

The wisdom realizing selflessness is the suitable path leading to nirvāṇa because it is the powerful antidote that directly counteracts self-grasping ignorance and eliminates duḥkha. Understanding this eliminates the misconception that this wisdom is not a path to liberation. Having confidence that it is the correct path to nirvāṇa, we will be eager to cultivate the wisdom that knows the nature of bondage in and release from saṃsāra just as they are. This wisdom also knows the faults of the afflictions and the meaning of selflessness.

3. The wisdom directly realizing selflessness is *accomplishment* (*pratipatti*) because it unmistakenly realizes the nature of the mind.

Unlike worldly paths that cannot accomplish our ultimate goals, the precious wisdom directly realizing emptiness leads to unmistaken spiritual attainments because it is an exalted wisdom that directly realizes the final mode of existence of the mind, its emptiness of inherent existence. In this way, it accomplishes the eradication of afflictions and attainment of liberation.

Understanding this counteracts the misconception that worldly paths eliminate duḥkha. Worldly paths are of many types, such as meditative absorptions that are mistaken for liberation. Blissful as they may be, they do not secure a true state of liberation. Some people practice the worldly path of extreme asceticism, mistakenly believing that harsh treatment of the body will eliminate craving for pleasure. This method does not bring the desired result, as the Buddha attested to by practicing—and then relinquishing—torturous asceticism for six years.

4. The wisdom directly realizing selflessness is the *way of deliverance* (*nairyāṇika*) because it overcomes afflictions and duḥkha from their root and brings irreversible liberation.

Inherent existence and noninherent existence are contradictory. By realizing the lack of inherent existence, the ignorance that grasps inherent existence can be conclusively removed. This wisdom is able to overpower ignorance because it knows things as they are, whereas ignorance relies on faulty fabrications. Because it definitely abandons all duḥkha and obscurations, this wisdom does not stop partway, but definitively delivers us from cyclic existence. This attribute counteracts the misconception that afflictions can regenerate and cannot be removed completely. It also counteracts the mistaken notion that while some paths may partially cease duḥkha, no path can cease it completely.

Contemplating these four attributes encourages us to meditate on true paths in order to destroy duḥkha and its origins and to actualize nirvāṇa.

DISTORTED CONCEPTIONS OF TRUE PATHS		ATTRIBUTES OF TRUE PATHS *The wisdom directly realizing selflessness is*
1.	Believing that there is no path to liberation	Path, because it is an unmistaken path to liberation
2.	Believing that this wisdom is not a path to liberation	Suitable, because it acts as the direct counterforce to the afflictions
3.	Believing that worldly paths (e.g., meditative absorptions) can eliminate duḥkha and are liberation	Accomplishment, because it unmistakenly realizes the nature of the mind
4.	Believing that afflictions and duḥkha cannot be removed completely, or that once removed, they can reappear	Way of deliverance, because it overcomes afflictions and duḥkha from their root and brings irreversible liberation

REFLECTION

1. Contemplate that true duḥkha—everything produced by afflictions and polluted karma—lacks any inherent essence.

2. Contemplate that all duḥkha as well as the origins of duḥkha depend on causes. Because they are dependent and do not exist under their own power, true duḥkha and true origins lack independent essence.

3. Contemplate the four attributes of true cessation. Abide in the certainty that nirvāṇa—a lasting state of peace and joy—can be attained, and let your mind be imbued with the optimism that brings.

4. Contemplate that true paths are also conditioned phenomena that depend on other factors. They too do not exist from their own side and thus are empty of inherent existence.

In conclusion, according to the Prāsaṅgika perspective, the entire complex of all sufferings and unsatisfactory circumstances of cyclic existence is rooted in self-grasping ignorance. This grasping at objective existence underpins our emotional reactions, such as craving, anger, jealousy, arrogance, guilt, and so forth. Cultivating the view of emptiness undermines this grasping and overcomes the four distorted conceptions. So there is a direct connection between the understanding of emptiness and our day-to-day engagement with the world.

While I have not realized emptiness directly, I can assure you that as a result of cultivating and deepening an understanding of emptiness and familiarizing myself with this understanding over time, I can see a progressive reduction of the influence of the afflictions that usually dominate our ordinary minds. There is a real impact and transformative power in this practice. If you make sincere effort to study, contemplate, and meditate on emptiness, the four distorted conceptions will no longer be able to nourish afflictions in your mind. When your afflictions have been eliminated, engaging in polluted actions ceases, and without these, rebirth due to afflictions and karma comes to an end.

2 | Revolving in Cyclic Existence: The Truth of Duḥkha

THE FOUR TRUTHS directly apply to our lives: they lay out the framework for understanding our situation and our potential. Having a general understanding of them, we will now go into more depth regarding each truth, beginning with the truth of duḥkha, the unsatisfactory circumstances in which we are bound. These include the three realms of saṃsāric existence into which we are born, the disadvantages of being born there, and the value of our human lives to reverse this situation.

Knowing Duḥkha for What It Is

The Buddha said that true duḥkha is to be known, true origins are to be eliminated, true cessations are to be actualized, and true paths are to be cultivated. In specifying that true duḥkha is to be known, the Buddha was giving us an important message: unless we identify the unsatisfactory circumstances that afflict us, we will never attempt to free ourselves from them. If we don't know we are ill or deny the fact that we are, we will not go to the doctor or take the prescribed medicine. Meanwhile, an insidious disease will fester inside us.

In spiritual practice, the first step is to identify true duḥkha, the unsatisfactory situation in which we live. Once we know this, we will search out its causes, eliminate them by cultivating true paths, and actualize true cessations, the state of lasting peace and happiness that we want. When reflecting on the various types of duḥkha, keep in mind that the purpose is to generate the determination to be free from saṃsāra and attain liberation.

Seeing others' duḥkha, with compassion we will want to help them attain liberation as well. Otherwise there is no purpose to reflecting on suffering.

Having properly identified our duḥkha, it is essential to cultivate the proper attitude toward it. Many of us, when confronted with pain or injustice, respond with anger or self-pity. We try to blame someone else for our misery. Meditating on true duḥkha involves taking responsibility for our situation and our problems and dealing with them wisely.

We may think that we're already aware of our misery, so there's no need to contemplate it. Although we may be aware of our gross duḥkha, we probably are not aware of duḥkha's subtler levels. Until we recognize these, we won't seek to be free from them.

Initial-level practitioners identify the obviously painful suffering of unfortunate migrations and its causes—destructive actions. They wish to attain a good rebirth (the cessation of that suffering), and observe karma and its effects as the path to accomplish this. Nevertheless, these people do not yet understand the full meaning of duḥkha, nor can they actualize the full cessation of all duḥkha.

We may know the various divisions of duḥkha into three, six, and eight types and have intellectual knowledge of them, but real understanding comes from observing our own experiences—our bodies and minds, our lives and deaths. It involves facing the disparity between the belief that we are in control of our lives and the reality of what actually is.

When reflecting on duḥkha, keep in mind that understanding duḥkha and its origins is just the beginning. The Buddha also taught the last two truths, directing us to the state of genuine peace and showing us the method to attain it. With those, we will have a complete picture. As Buddhaghoṣa said (Vism 16.97):

> The truth of duḥkha should be regarded as a burden, the truth of origin as the taking up of the burden, the truth of cessation as the putting down of the burden, the truth of the path as the means to put down the burden. The truth of duḥkha is like a disease, the truth of origin is like the cause of the disease, the truth of cessation is like the cure of the disease, and the truth of the path is like the medicine.

Realms of Existence

As beings in cyclic existence, we are reborn in different realms (*dhātu*) of existence. A realm is primarily the five aggregates projected by our karma, although it also includes the environment. All of these are considered true duḥkha. One way of expressing the realms of saṃsāra is the schema of the three realms (*tridhātu* or *trailokya*). Beings in the *desire realm* are completely immersed in objects that are attractive to the six senses. They are obsessed with fulfilling their desires by possessing these objects. This is the realm in which we presently live. The *form realm* comprises beings who have attained the four levels of single-pointed concentration or meditative stabilization (*dhyāna, jhāna*). The *formless realm* consists of beings in even deeper states of meditative absorption (*samāpatti*),[10] such that they do not have bodies. While these realms are manifestations of our karma, they are not merely projections of mind or metaphors for states we experience as human beings. When we are born in a realm, it appears as real to us as our present human life and environment appear to us now.

Sentient beings in saṃsāra can be subdivided into six classes (*ṣaḍgati*). From the highest to the lowest, they are devas (gods or celestial beings in the desire, form, and formless realms), asuras (anti-gods), human beings, hungry ghosts, animals, and hell beings. Sometimes the devas and asuras are considered as one, in which case there are five classes.

The three realms can be expanded into thirty-three classes of beings or planes of existence, which are listed from the highest to the lowest.[11]

(1) Formless Realm (*Ārūpyadhātu*)

33. Peak of Saṃsāra (Neither-discrimination-nor-nondiscrimination, *Naivasaṃjñānā-saṃjñāyatana* or *Bhavāgra*)
32. Nothingness (*Ākiñcanyāyatana*)
31. Infinite Consciousness (*Vijñānānantyāyatana*)
30. Infinite Space (*Ākāśānantyāyatana*)

Ordinary beings are born in these four realms due to invariable karma—that is, in the immediately preceding life, they attained the corresponding level of meditative absorption. Lacking a coarse body, these beings have only the four mental aggregates. They remain in deep states of meditative absorption for eons, experiencing no coarse suffering at all. These four meditative absorptions are distinguished based on the mental factor of discrimination that accompanies them, which becomes increasingly subtle, culminating in the peak of saṃsāra. These states are so subtle and blissful that some meditators confuse them with liberation. However, when the karma for these rebirths is exhausted, those beings take rebirth in the desire realm again, usually as hell beings, hungry ghosts, or animals.

(2) Form Realm (*Rūpadhātu*)

Fourth Dhyāna (*Caturthadhyāna*)

29. Highest Pure Abode (*Akaniṣṭha*)
28. Clear-Sighted (*Sudarśana*)
27. Beautiful (*Sudṛśa*)
26. Untroubled (*Atapa*)
25. Not Great (Free from Afflictions, *Avṛha*)[12]
24. Unconscious Beings without Discrimination (*Asaṃjñasattva*). Ordinary beings who have attained the fourth dhyāna and cultivate meditative absorption without discrimination are born here, where the beings are nonpercipient and have no mental activity except at the moments of birth and death.[13]
23. Great Fruit (*Bṛhatphala*)
22. Increasing Merit (*Puṇyaprasava*) [14]
21. Cloudless (*Anabhraka*)

Ordinary beings are born in these three dhyānas by the invariable karma of having previously attained that state of concentration.

Third Dhyāna (*Tṛtīyadhyāna*)

20. Devas of Refulgent Glory (*Śubhakṛtsna*)[15]
19. Devas of Measureless Glory (*Apramāṇaśubha*)
18. Devas of Limited Glory (*Parīttaśubha*)

Ordinary beings are born in the third dhyāna by the invariable karma of having previously attained that state of concentration.

Second Dhyāna (*Dvitīyadhyāna*)

17. Devas of Total Radiance (*Ābhāsvara*)
16. Devas of Limitless Radiance (*Apramāṇābha*)
15. Devas of Limited Radiance (*Parīttābha*)

These beings are born in the second dhyāna by the invariable karma of having previously attained that state of concentration.

First Dhyāna (*Prathamadhyāna*)

14. Great Brahmā (*Mahābrahmā*). Great Brahmā, who mistakenly considers himself the creator of the universe, dwells here.
13. Ministers of Brahmā (In Front of Brahmā, *Brahmapurohita*)
12. Retinue of Brahmā (Brahmā Type, *Brahmakāyika*)

These beings are born in the first dhyāna by the invariable karma of having previously attained that state of concentration.

The four dhyānas of the form realm differ in terms of the mental factors that accompany them.[16] The four formless absorptions differ in terms of their object. The depth of concentration increases as one ascends these eight meditative absorptions.

Only āryas who are not yet free from saṃsāra are born in the five pure abodes in the fourth dhyāna, although after nonreturners become arhats they dwell there until attaining final nirvāṇa. The cause for rebirth there is the cultivation of alternating concentrations. This is a practice done by āryas, which involves first entering an unpolluted fourth dhyāna, then a polluted dhyāna, followed by another unpolluted dhyāna. This is extremely difficult to do, and the number of times a yogi can go back and forth between unpolluted and polluted dhyānas determines which pure abode he or she will be born in. Āryas who have attained liberation do these meditations to distance themselves from afflictions even more and to experience bliss in this life.

Śrāvakas who are nonreturners take rebirth in the five pure abodes to experience the specific bliss of the pure abodes. Ārya solitary realizers are not born there because they pray in their last life to be born where there is no buddha. Ārya bodhisattvas are born in the pure abodes to benefit the śrāvaka arhats there by encouraging them to enter the bodhisattva path after they arise from their blissful meditation in nirvāṇa.

The five pure abodes are saṃsāric realms. These differ from both *nirmāṇakāya* (emanation body) pure lands—such as Amitābha Buddha's pure land Sukhāvatī and Akṣobhya Buddha's pure land Abhirati—and enjoyment body (*saṃbhogakāya*) pure lands, which are not saṃsāric realms. Several places have the name Akaniṣṭha. The Akaniṣṭha that is one of the five pure abodes is a saṃsāric abode, whereas the Densely Arrayed Akaniṣṭha is not: there a buddha's enjoyment body teaches ārya bodhisattvas.

According to the Pāli tradition, only arhats and nonreturners dwell in the five pure abodes. Those who become nonreturners in other realms are reborn in these pure abodes, where they attain arhatship. New arhats remain here until the end of their natural lifespans and then attain parinirvāṇa.

According to the *Treasury of Knowledge*, the beings in the form realm lack the sense of smell and taste.[17] While they have some sensual desire for sights and sounds, it is weak—beings with strong desire are born in the desire realm. They do not sleep or eat, nor do they have sexual desire, because they do not have sexual organs in that realm. Their bodies are subtle forms made of the four elements. Their basic state of consciousness is samādhi, although they do emerge from it and interact with one another.

The form and formless realms are collectively known as the higher realms owing to the refined states of mind of the beings born in them. Beings are born in these realms by attaining various degrees of meditative absorption—for example, when they were human meditators. All of these meditative absorptions can be attained by human beings as well, in which case it is said that the person is in the desire realm because of being a human being, but has a form-realm sphere of consciousness (*vacaracitta*) because of the level of concentration they have attained.

(3) Desire Realm (*Kāmadhātu*)

Desire-Realm Devas (*Kāmadhātudeva*)

11. Controllers of Others' Emanations Devas (*Paranirmitavaśavartin*) enjoy sense pleasures others create for them. Māra, the personification of delusion and desire, dwells here.
10. Devas Delighting in Emanations (*Nirmāṇarati*) enjoy the sense pleasures they created themselves.

9. Joyful Devas (*Tuṣita*) experience pure delight. According to the Pāli tradition, Maitreya (Metteya), the bodhisattva who will become the next wheel-turning buddha, dwells here, as do other bodhisattvas in the life prior to their becoming buddhas. The Sanskrit tradition says that Maitreya lives in the pure land Tuṣita, which is on the outskirts of the deva realm with the same name.
8. Suyāma Devas (*Suyāma*) live in the air and are free from all problems.
7. The Thirty-Three Devas (*Trāyastriṃśa*) is so-called because thirty-three young people were born there as a result of their meritorious actions. The leader of this group of youths became the deva Śakra, who presides over this realm and is a devotee of the Buddha. Many devas dwelling here live in mansions in the air.[18] During one rains retreat, the Buddha went here to teach his mother, who had been reborn in this realm.
6. Devas of the Four Great Kings (*Cāturmahārājika*). The four great kings, who are Dharma protectors, rule this land. Their images are often near the door of Mahāyāna temples. The causes for rebirth here are ethical conduct and generosity.

Other Desire-Realm Beings

5. *Anti-gods* (asuras). Asaṅga includes the asuras in the deva realm and says that they experience great sense pleasure, even though they suffer from jealousy and constant battles with higher devas. The *Smṛtyupasthāna Sūtra* puts them with the hungry ghosts and animals.[19]
4. *Human beings* (*manuṣya*) have the necessary balance of happiness and suffering that is conducive for Dharma practice. The primary cause for rebirth here is ethical conduct.
3. *Animals* (*tiryañc*) suffer from hunger and thirst, being enslaved by human beings, and being eaten by others.
2. *Hungry ghosts* (*preta*) suffer from constant hunger and thirst that is never satisfied.[20]
1. *Hell beings* (*nāraka*) experience great physical pain due to heat, cold, and torture.

Unethical actions and wrong views are the primary cause for rebirth as a hungry ghost, animal, or hell being. Stinginess is especially affiliated with rebirth as a hungry ghost, while violent activities are associated with rebirth in the hells.

Rebirth in any of the six realms is not eternal. When the karma causing that rebirth is exhausted, the being is born in another realm. None of the realms are rewards or punishments. They are all simply results of our actions, our karma.

According to the Pāli tradition, *nāgas* (snake-like beings who live in or near water), *gandharvas* (celestial musicians), and *yakṣas* (tree spirits of varying degrees of ethical purity, who resemble goblins, trolls, and fairies) live in the Realm of the Four Great Kings. The *Treasury of Knowledge* says some yakṣas are in the deva realm and some are in the hungry ghost realm. Gandharvas are included with the devas because they are the musicians of the devas. *Garuḍas* (large birds), *kiṃnaras* (beings who are half human and half horse), and nāgas are included among animals. *Piśāca* (a class of demons), *unmada* (crazy makers), *apasmāra* (forgetful makers), and *mātṛka* (a type of wicked demon) are included with hungry ghosts.

These realms are actual realms of rebirth. We can get an idea of life in them by comparing them to some experiences that occur in the human realm. The Indian sage Kamalaśīla says:

> Humans also experience the sufferings of hell beings and so forth. Those who are afflicted here by having their limbs cut off, being impaled, hanged, and so forth by thieves and the like, suffer like hell beings. Those who are poor and deprived and are pained by hunger and thirst suffer like hungry ghosts. Those in servitude and so forth, whose bodies are controlled by others and who are oppressed, suffer from being struck, bound, and so forth, like animals.[21]

The magnificent pleasures of the deva realms can be understood by comparing them to some of the greatest pleasures we human beings experience. However, these are simply analogies; they are not the actual experience. The actual bliss of the deva realms is beyond our imagination, as is the misery of the unfortunate realms.

Seeing the various realms as psychological states can be helpful for recognizing mental characteristics we may have. For example, the mental state of a hungry ghost is similar to that of a person who goes here and there looking for someone to love them, but is perpetually dissatisfied with every relationship. The mental state of a hell being resembles the mind of someone overwhelmed by fear, animosity, and violence. These human mental states could motivate actions that cause rebirth in those realms, but the actual realms are not simply psychological states of human beings.

In the *Treasury of Knowledge*, Vasubandhu states that the world with its realms and its sentient beings is created by karma and he describes the location of some realms in relation to our human realm. Although his account is contradicted by modern knowledge, that does not disprove the general existence of these realms. We know the animal realm exists. People with the paranormal power of the divine eye can see some of the other realms.

Three Types of Duḥkha

When *duḥkha* is translated as suffering, people easily have the wrong idea that it refers only to pain. But unsatisfactory experiences are more than that. In a previous chapter, I briefly outlined the three types of duḥkha and now would like to explain them in more depth.

(1) The *duḥkha of pain* is the manifest physical and mental pain that all beings recognize as suffering. It includes suffering from heat, cold, hunger, thirst, stress, anxiety, depression, loneliness, and so forth.

(2) The *duḥkha of change* is subtler and more difficult to identify; it includes what worldly beings usually call happiness. Why is the happiness we experience when eating a good meal, hearing the music we like, or experiencing other sensual pleasures unsatisfactory? If they were truly pleasurable, the more we did them, the happier we would be. However, that is not the case. If we keep eating, we feel ill. Jogging after a long day sitting at work initially feels wonderful, but after a while we are tired and want to sit down. When we are lonely, seeing a friend initially alleviates the feeling of isolation and makes us happy. But if we stay with that person hour after hour, we get tired, bored, and want to be alone. When we don't have a high-status job, we want one. After we are promoted, we are initially happy but later resent having to work longer hours. Āryadeva comments (CŚ 37):

Pleasure, when it increases,
is seen to change into pain.
Pain, when it increases,
does not likewise change into pleasure.

Examining the experiences we call happiness, we see that they are not true happiness. They feel good for a short while and then turn into overt discomfort or even pain. For this reason they are unsatisfactory in nature, and the Buddha with compassion directs us toward a more satisfying joy—the peace of liberation and awakening.

(3) The *pervasive duḥkha of conditioning* is even subtler and more difficult to identify. It refers to our five psychophysical aggregates—our bodies, feelings, discriminations, miscellaneous factors, and consciousnesses—that are unsatisfactory because they are produced by afflictions and karma. The result of our previous saṃsāric rebirths, our aggregates are the basis for our present duḥkha when our destructive karma ripens as the physical and mental pain we experience in this life.

Although our bodies and minds may not experience pain at this very moment, with the slightest change in circumstances, they easily will. They have the potential to experience horrible pain. Also, our five aggregates propel us to create the causes for more duḥkha in the future. By reacting to the pain and pleasure of this life with afflictions such as attachment, anger, and confusion, we again create more karmic causes to take another saṃsāric rebirth where we will again experience all three types of duḥkha. Dharmakīrti says (PV):

> Because they are the basis of faults [i.e., duḥkha] and also because they are under the power of [polluted] causes, they are duḥkha.

At present, we are under the illusion that happiness can be attained with this body. We cling to the hope that scientists will discover and root out the causes for depression, unhappiness, disease, substance abuse, aging, and death. While scientific endeavors have remedied much suffering, they cannot stop the basic causes of suffering because our body itself is unsatisfactory by nature. No matter how much a cook tries to slow the disintegration of rotten vegetables or covers them with delicious sauce, making a tasty dish out of them is impossible. Similarly, once we have taken a body and mind under the control of afflictions and karma, we are set up to experience duḥkha. For this reason our aggregates are considered unsatisfactory by nature. Āryadeva tell us (CŚ 32–33):

> The body, however long one spends,
> will not in itself become pleasurable.
> To say its nature can be overruled
> by other factors is improper.
>
> The high have mental suffering;
> for the common it comes from the body.
> Day by day, both kinds of duḥkha
> overwhelm people in the world.

When contemplating the three types of duḥkha and the disadvantages of cyclic existence, reflect that you have experienced these since beginningless time. These meditations on duḥkha are not idle speculation; being repeatedly subjected to the miseries of cyclic existence is serious. In the *Tears Sutta*, the Buddha gave a series of vivid examples illustrating the length of time afflictions and karma have bound us in saṃsāra (SN 15.3).

> The stream of tears that you have shed as you roamed and wandered through this long course [of saṃsāra], weeping and wailing because of being united with the disagreeable and separated from the agreeable—this alone is more than the water in the four great oceans. For a long time, monastics, you have experienced the death of a mother . . . father . . . brother . . . sister . . . son . . . daughter . . . the loss of relatives . . . the loss of wealth . . . loss through illness. As you have experienced this, weeping and wailing because of being united with the disagreeable and separated from the agreeable, the stream of tears that you have shed is more than the water in the four great oceans. For what reasons? Because, monastics, this saṃsāra is without discoverable beginning. A first point is not discerned of beings roaming

> and migrating hindered by ignorance and fettered by craving. For such a long time, monastics, you have experienced suffering, anguish, and disaster, and swelled the cemetery. It is enough to experience revulsion toward all formations, enough to become dispassionate toward them, enough to be liberated from them.

While such a message may initially be unpleasant to hear, the Buddha says it with compassion so that we can act now while we have the opportunity to remedy the situation and free ourselves from such misery.

Feelings, Afflictions, and Duḥkha

Each of the three types of duḥkha is associated with a specific feeling: the duḥkha of pain with painful feelings; the duḥkha of change with pleasant feelings, because when we initially engage in certain activities or have particular possessions we feel happy; and the pervasive duḥkha of conditioning with neutral feelings, because all beings in cyclic existence experience this duḥkha even when they are not actively feeling pain or pleasure. We will explore this more in the practice of the four establishments of mindfulness in a future volume.

These feelings in turn prompt afflictions. Anger easily arises toward painful physical and mental feelings. Attachment manifests when pleasurable feelings are experienced; we crave these feelings, do not want them to cease, and cling to the objects that seem to cause them. Ignorance increases when neutral feelings are present because we hold the aggregates as permanent when in fact they are momentary.

Under the influence of these afflictions, we create karma. While attachment may fuel actions that lead to rebirth in any of the six classes of beings, anger makes us miserable in this life and creates the causes for unfortunate rebirths. Ignorance keeps us bound in cyclic existence, unable to help ourselves, let alone others.

Recognizing pleasant feelings as duḥkha enables us to release craving and clinging to them, and as a result, attachment subsides. Accepting that by nature our bodies are unsatisfactory makes it easier to avoid anger or anxiety with respect to painful feelings. Seeing that neutral feelings are transient in nature diminishes ignorance. In this way, although the three feelings may arise, we stop responding to them with attachment, anger, and ignorance, thus reducing the karma created by afflictions.

REFLECTION

1. Think of a situation in which you felt happy. Observe how attachment arises for the pleasant feeling as well as for the people, objects, or situations that seem to cause it.
2. Observe the actions you do motivated by attachment. How do they cause problems in this life? How do they create karma for suffering in future lives? Think of the kinds of rebirth those actions could propel.
3. Contemplate that pleasant feelings are unsatisfactory in nature because they do not last and degenerate into pain if we keep doing the action over time. After contemplating the disadvantages of the duḥkha of change, observe your attachment subside. As your mind becomes more balanced, enjoy that peace.
4. While this peace is not the tranquility of nirvāṇa, it does give us the knowledge that relinquishing attachment at any level makes the mind more peaceful.

Six Disadvantages of Cyclic Existence

Not only is saṃsāra unsatisfactory in nature, it is also bereft of advantages. Nāgārjuna's *Letter to a Friend* (*Suhṛi-lekha*) speaks of six disadvantages of saṃsāra:

(1) There is no security or certainty. We may work hard for a certain goal, but unexpected hindrances block our attaining it. We may live in a pleasant environment and suddenly be forced to leave. Our situation can change dramatically in a short period of time. Our relatives and friends change from one life to the next; saṃsāra lacks consistency and predictability.

(2) We are never satisfied with what we are, do, or have. We always want more and better of whatever we find desirable. No matter what we have

accomplished or how much we excel, we never feel good enough about ourselves.

(3) We die repeatedly, each time leaving behind everything and everyone we know. Everything we worked so hard for during our life cannot come with us to the next life. Death naturally follows birth, and when we die nothing from this life except our karmic seeds and mental habits accompany us.

(4) We are reborn in cyclic existence repeatedly with all the problems and struggles that exist in each life. Our saṃsāra is beginningless, and unless we exert effort to attain liberation, it will be endless.

(5) We repeatedly change status from superior to inferior and vice versa. In one life we may change social position, health, financial status, relationships, and so on. From one life to the next we may go from the deva realm to a hell realm to birth as a human or an animal.

(6) We experience suffering alone; others cannot experience it for us no matter how much they love us. We are born alone and die alone. Our feelings are felt by ourselves alone. While we may be inseparable from certain people during our lives, at death separation is guaranteed.

The Buddha did not point these disadvantages out so that we would become depressed. Rather, with compassion, he asked us to look closely at our experiences in cyclic existence and see them for what they are. Knowing that we have the potential to be free from them, he then described their causes, the path to counteract them, and the state of liberation.

REFLECTION

1. Contemplate each of the six disadvantages of cyclic existence, making examples of them from your life.

2. Contemplate that they originate in ignorance and that it is possible to eliminate ignorance through cultivating the wisdom realizing the emptiness of inherent existence.

3. Knowing you have the potential to attain nirvāṇa, generate a strong determination to be free from saṃsāra and attain liberation or full awakening.

4. Use this firm and clear aspiration to inspire your Dharma practice and clarify your priorities in life.

5. Observe that the eight worldly concerns become uninteresting when your sights are focused on higher aims such as the true freedom of nirvāṇa or full awakening.

Eight Unsatisfactory Conditions

In describing true duḥkha in his first teaching, the Buddha said (SN 56.11):

> Now this, monastics, is the ārya truth of duḥkha: (1) birth is duḥkha, (2) aging is duḥkha, (3) illness is duḥkha, (4) death is duḥkha, (5) union with what is displeasing is duḥkha, (6) separation from what is pleasing is duḥkha, (7) to not get what one wants is duḥkha, in brief (8) the five aggregates subject to clinging are duḥkha.

It is not difficult to make examples of these eight in our lives, for they describe much of what we experience on a daily basis. For many people, being able to acknowledge the presence of these unsatisfactory conditions in their lives is a relief. They no longer feel "something is wrong with me," but know that all ordinary beings have these experiences. They see these events as part of life, not as punishments or personal failures.

At the beginning of our lives we are born. Coming out of the womb into a new environment is physically painful for the child as well as the mother. At the end of our lives we die, experiencing suffering mentally if not physically. Between these two are aging and illness, which are also undesirable experiences. On top of these, problems, which we don't want, come uninvited. We exert great effort to have conditions that bring happiness, but our efforts are not always successful. Even when we do find good circumstances they change and we have to separate from what we like, or we are disappointed because they don't bring the enduring happiness we expected. Clearly this situation is unsatisfactory. Our human potential must involve more than experiencing just this.

Our five aggregates subject to clinging are in the nature of duḥkha. They are a container in which past karma ripens, and the body in particular is the basis for aging, sickness, and death. Clinging to our present aggregates, our mind generates more afflictions, which create more karma, which causes future rebirths as well as pain and dissatisfaction during those lives. For example, being angry at our present problems, we may steal, lie, or criticize others, creating the karma to have more misery in the future. Clinging to worldly success in this life habituates us with this mental state, setting the stage for it to increase in future lives. In short, the aggregates are the basis in which the three, six, and eight types of duḥkha run rampant. Contemplating this deeply leads to the arising of a clear and powerful intention to renounce the bondage of saṃsāra and seek freedom.

Examining True Duḥkha via Ten Points

In the *Śrāvakabhūmi*, Asaṅga speaks of the four attributes of true duḥkha by way of ten points. Points 1–5 pertain to impermanence, points 6–8 to duḥkha, point 9 to emptiness, and point 10 to selflessness.[22]

1. To understand the *impermanence of change*—that is, coarse impermanence—we examine changes that are easy to observe: our bodies are born and die; our health, appearance, and physiques may change suddenly as a result of injury or illness. Everything in our environment—trees, buildings, cities—and all the objects we use—food, transportation, buildings, medicine, and clothing—likewise are consumed or destroyed. The fleeting character of our happy, suffering, and neutral feelings and the swiftness by which our thoughts change from one moment to the next are also examples of coarse change. The objects we see, hear, smell, taste, touch, and think about all change, as do the cognitive faculties that enable us to apprehend them. Meditating on this in depth leads us to understand that all conditioned things are unstable and unreliable and therefore cannot bring us true satisfaction.

2. Reflecting on the *impermanence of perishability* leads to an inferential cognizer that knows subtle impermanence. Here we contemplate that the coarse change we see could not occur without imperceptibly subtle moment-to-moment change. Nothing can stop functioning things from changing. They need no cause other than their arising to bring their disintegration; perishing is in their very nature. We may think that a volcano erupts suddenly, when in fact the pressure inside it has been building imperceptibly for a long time. We see the sun rise and set, but it goes across the sky moment-by-moment. As Candrakīrti says:

> Just as consciousness is momentary, all [other] conditioned things have the same momentary nature as the mind, because nothing obstructs the perishing of all conditioned things as soon as they appear and because the impermanence [of things] depends only upon [their] arising.[23]

The impermanence of perishability also points to the multiplicity of situations in which we sentient beings find ourselves and to the diversity of our physical beauty, intelligence, wealth, fame, lifespans, contentment, and so forth. The vastness of these alternatives are conditioned by the countless and complex virtuous and nonvirtuous karma we create, not by chance and not by the will of an external creator. By meditating on this, we develop the conviction that conditioned factors in one lifetime—specifically our physical, verbal, and mental actions—bring about our experiences in future lives.

3. To understand the *impermanence of separation*, we reflect on the changeability of our personal situation and the separation from desirable circumstances that we experience without choice. We are healthy and then fall ill, we have freedom and then fall under the control of others, we have a happy family life but then circumstances change and it evaporates.

4. To reflect on the *impermanence of the dharmatā* or nature of things, we consider that while we may not be experiencing the impermanence of change or the impermanence of separation in this moment, we will in the future. There is no way to continue whatever good circumstances we presently have, for change is the nature of everything in saṃsāra.

5. The *impermanence of the present* is the perishability and separation that we presently undergo. Contemplating this reinforces the above contemplations, for we see that perishability and separation are occurring in this very instant.

These reflections on impermanence bring home the fact that every facet of our being and every aspect of our lives and our world is transitory and unstable. This leads to a sense of unease regarding life in cyclic existence. Contemplating the next three points—the three forms of duḥkha—will increase our discomfort with remaining in saṃsāra.

6. The *duḥkha of pain* is called "the aspect of being undesirable" because painful physical and mental experiences are unwanted. Still, they keep coming, counter to our wish for happiness.

7. The *duḥkha of change* is called "the aspect of fetters and bondage" because even when our bodies and minds experience pleasure, that pleasure leads to the fetter of craving, which in turn gives rise to the bondage of birth, aging, sickness, death, sorrow, lamentation, pain, grief, and despair.

8. *The pervasive duḥkha of conditioning* is called "the factor of our welfare not being secure" because even though we may experience a neutral feeling now, our aggregates are under the control of afflictions and karma. They possess the potential to experience the first two types of duḥkha with the slightest change of circumstances.

Understanding impermanence leads to understanding duḥkha. Birth in cyclic existence is unsatisfactory because it is permeated with unwanted change: aging, sickness, death, meeting with the disagreeable, separating from the desirable, and not getting what we want. Contemplating duḥkha on the basis of understanding subtle impermanence jars our complacency. A deep sense of vulnerability arises because happiness and suffering are entirely at the whim of afflictions and karma. In our ignorant state, we have so little control over these.

9. The *aspect of unobservability* refers to not being able to observe or discern a real self that exists separate from the aggregates. Here we contemplate that there is no self over and above all the instances of each of the aggregates. For example, when we say "I see," there is merely a visual object, the eye faculty, and an immediately preceding consciousness. Together they cause a visual consciousness that perceives the object. I and mine are mere names, mere figures of speech; the aggregates are not possessed by a real self. Nor can a person be found among the aggregates. There is no observable self that creates karma and experiences its results. There is no findable self that circles in saṃsāra or attains liberation. These conditioned aggregates are completely empty of a self.

10. The *aspect of a lack of independence* refers to the aggregates not being under the control of a self. The aggregates are dependent arisings that lack self-determination; they lack a controlling self.

The understandings of impermanence, duḥkha, emptiness, and selflessness evolve in that order. Subtle impermanence means the aggregates arise due to causes and conditions: specifically afflictions and karma. Those causes and conditions bring about the three types of duḥkha, which give rise to craving and thus renewed cyclic existence. Understanding the pervasive duḥkha of conditioning in particular leads us to examine the relationship between the aggregates and self, and therefore to understand emptiness and selflessness. As Dharmakīrti points out (PV 2:254cd):

> For this very reason, the [Buddha] taught duḥkha through impermanence, and selflessness through duḥkha.

Why does true duḥkha receive so much attention? It would be so much more pleasant to think of light, love, and bliss. However, encouraging us to contemplate duḥkha is the best way for the Buddha to rouse us from our complacency so that we will take advantage of our amazing opportunity to practice the Dharma. Just as a person won't seek freedom if he is unaware that he is imprisoned or if he thinks prison is a comfortable environment, we will not seek liberation from cyclic existence without a clear awareness of what it is and why it is unsatisfactory. Deeply meditating on the above topics will energize us to turn away from the prison of saṃsāra and pursue the path to nirvāṇa.

REFLECTION

1. Reflect on Asaṅga's ten points, one by one, making examples of each in your life.
2. Focus on the conclusion that everything in cyclic existence is transient, unsatisfactory in nature, empty, and selfless.
3. Aspire to attain liberation.

Our Human Value

Reflecting on the above descriptions of true duḥkha by applying them to our own lives and by observing the experiences of others is crucial for making this teaching come alive. By doing that, a sincere aspiration to be free from saṃsāra and attain liberation or awakening will arise in our minds.

Those aspirations are the fuel for our Dharma practice. As our understanding of duḥkha gradually increases, so will our faith in the Three Jewels as qualified guides.

Slowly we awaken to the fact that money, social status, popularity, power, praise, and appreciation—while useful in this life—do not bring lasting happiness and instead bring more worries and difficulties. We begin to see that chasing them is like riding a roller-coaster or merry-go-round—it may temporarily seem thrilling, but at the end we are back where we started. Enduring peace still eludes us, and deep inside we still lack a stable sense of self-worth. No matter how much luxury surrounds us, how exciting our jobs are, how famous we are, or how many people love us, we still are not beyond aging, sickness, and death.

In response to this predicament, in their confusion some people self-medicate with any number of addictions—drugs, alcohol, work, sex, digital games, TV, gambling, shopping, and so on—but those only serve as short-term distractions that bring more suffering. Other people think life is meaningless and consider ending their lives. This is very foolish, for we all have great potential—the potential to become fully awakened buddhas, the potential to experience reliable joy and fulfillment.

When we analyze how suffering and happiness arise in our minds, we see that they come about from our actions, which are motivated by our disturbing emotions and distorted views. Without even considering past lives, we can see that the more subdued our minds are, the more peaceful and happy we are. Even if our external environment is tumultuous, with inner mental peace we can transform external difficulties into the path to awakening by practicing mind-training teachings. But when our minds are upset, agitated, or obscured, we are miserable even when the external environment is fantastic. This clearly shows that happiness and suffering are related to our mental attitudes. Therefore training our minds is worthwhile.

By reflecting on duḥkha in this way, we become less infatuated with saṃsāra and turn our natural aspiration for well-being to nirvāṇa. Gyelsay Togme Zangpo's poem *The Thirty-Seven Practices of Bodhisattvas* (9) sums it up:

> Like dew on the tip of a blade of grass,
> pleasures of the three worlds last only a while and then vanish.

Aspire to the never-changing supreme state of liberation—
this is the practice of bodhisattvas.

In describing his own spiritual journey before attaining awakening, the Buddha said (MN 26.13):

> Before my awakening, while I was still only an unawakened bodhisatta, I too, being myself subject to birth, sought what was also subject to birth. Being myself subject to aging, sickness, death, sorrow, and defilement, I sought what was also subject to aging, sickness, death, sorrow, and defilement. Then I considered, thus: "Why, being myself subject to birth, do I seek what is also subject to birth? Why, being myself subject to aging, sickness, death, sorrow, and defilement, do I seek what is also subject to aging, sickness, death, sorrow, and defilement? Suppose . . . I seek the unborn supreme security from bondage, nibbāna. Suppose . . . I seek the unaging, unailing, deathless, sorrowless, and undefiled supreme security from bondage, nibbāna."

While subject to the unsatisfactory circumstances of saṃsāra, we ignorant beings take refuge in people and things that are also subject to the vagaries of saṃsāra. What if we were to turn to the Three Jewels for refuge and seek nirvāṇa instead? Practitioners with this aspiration are not distracted by the appeal of saṃsāra's pleasures, riches, power, and fame, and they easily stay focused on their spiritual aims. This leads to mental peace in this life as well as to liberation. Bodhisattvas expand on this aspiration for freedom to include all sentient beings and generate bodhicitta, the aspiration for full awakening.

Lessening our attachment to saṃsāric pleasures does not mean having aversion toward our bodies, relationships, good food, praise, reputation, and other sense objects. These things, in and of themselves, are neither virtuous nor nonvirtuous; it is our craving for them that is the source of difficulties. The purpose of seeing the things of saṃsāra as unsatisfactory is to eliminate our craving for and clinging to them, because these emotions keep us bound in saṃsāra. To live in society, money and possessions are necessary. We can use them without attachment and share them with others to create merit. We human beings are social creatures and our lives depend on the kindness of others. We can appreciate the people in our lives and be compassionate toward them without being attached to them.

Relinquishing attachment to our bodies doesn't mean we ignore our health and neglect to go to the doctor and dentist. Our bodies are the physical support of our precious human lives that we use to practice the Dharma, so we must care for the body and keep it healthy. Caring for our bodies in a practical way is very different from indulging in sensual pleasures with attachment.

With all of this talk about duḥkha, we may mistakenly believe that Dharma practitioners must relinquish all of the usual activities that bring them happiness and instead practice extreme asceticism and self-denial. We may fear that there is no happiness to be experienced until we reach nirvāṇa. This is not the case at all. In fact, it is important to have a happy mind while practicing the Dharma. As we go deeper into practice, we realize that there are many types and levels of happiness and pleasure. Having food, shelter, clothing, medicine, and friends bring us some well-being—enough that we can practice the Dharma without being in dire suffering, which would make practice difficult. As we practice more, we discover the internal peace arising from living ethically and the pleasant, relaxed feeling that comes from improving our concentration. As we lessen our attachment and open our hearts to others, the joy derived from connecting with others on a heart level and acting with kindness toward them brings us a sense of fulfillment that is greatly superior to any sense pleasure that money and possessions can afford.

Although most people in the world have intimate emotional and sexual relationships, some people choose not to have them. This is a valid lifestyle choice, whether people are Buddhist or not, whether they are monastics or lay practitioners. They are not avoiding intimacy; they prefer to use their life energy doing other things that are more important to them. In short, giving up our addiction to pleasure derived from external objects and people opens the door to experience other types of happiness.

Some people wonder if it's possible to become attached to the Dharma and crave liberation. Attachment is based on projecting or exaggerating qualities and then clinging to an object. In general it is not possible to exaggerate the excellent qualities of the Three Jewels, liberation, and full awakening. Furthermore, appreciation of the Dharma's excellent qualities and the aspiration to attain liberation are very different from being attached to them with obsessive longing or possessiveness.

If someone perchance builds an ego-identity, thinking, "*I* am a Buddhist and *my* religion is the best," he has not understood Buddhism very well. His attitude is not one of attachment to Buddhism; rather his mind is afflicted with self-grasping and arrogance.

3 | True Origins of Duḥkha

WE LIVE AMIDST true duḥkha day in and day out. It is our close companion, never letting us be peaceful in our own hearts or with others. Since we do not like duḥkha and want to be free from it, we must seek out its causes, examine whether they can be eliminated, and if so, learn the path to do so. The Buddha identified afflictions and karma as the true origins of duḥkha. Karma arises from afflictions, the chief of which is ignorance. In this chapter we will examine the defilements that are the origins of duḥkha. These mental factors keep us bound in cyclic existence and prevent our attainment of nirvāṇa and awakening.

Buddhist psychology is profound and reveals parts of our minds that we may have been oblivious to. Virtuous and variable mental factors were described in chapter 3 of the previous volume, *The Foundation of Buddhist Practice*. The following afflictive mental factors are explained in the context of factors that produce duḥkha and interfere with attaining liberation and full awakening.

It's important to approach the topic of afflictions with the correct attitude. Avoid using the various lists of defilements to criticize yourself, thinking, "I have so much anger. I'm also so jealous. What a bad person I am!" Remember that gaining knowledge about mental defilements gives us the power to free ourselves from them and arrive at a state of true peace. We have the potential to do this. Chapters 12–14 will discuss the possibility to attain liberation and our buddha nature that makes that possible.

Describing afflictions is similar to identifying the thieves in our house who have been masquerading as our friends while all the time stealing our happiness. When we know their characteristics, we can catch them, evict them, and lock the door behind them so they can never return. But unlike living thieves who can regroup later, once evicted, afflictions vanish completely.

Like all other phenomena, mental defilements are empty of inherent existence. They are transient like bubbles that quickly burst; they have no essence like the trunk of a plantain tree. Rather than think of anger, or any other affliction, as a solid emotion that is always lurking under the surface of your mind, ready to explode, spewing its vitriol, recognize that it exists by being merely designated: in dependence on some moments of mind that share some common characteristics, we designate "anger." That's all anger is. It's not a monster that is an inherent part of us; it is not who we are. We need to view our afflictions from two perspectives: on the one hand they are the source of our misery; on the other they lack essence and can be completely eradicated from our mindstreams. There are many ways of classifying mental defilements; we will begin with the six root afflictions, the most prominent group in the Sanskrit tradition.

The Six Root Afflictions

Studying the laboratory that is our own mind, we notice that we can have radically different emotions at different times. We can be loving one moment and irritated the next. Some emotions arise more easily or are more habitual than others: our anger surges in a moment; fortitude is difficult to cultivate. Some emotions bring peace, others disturb our mental tranquility. The later are called *afflictions*. Asaṅga identifies these in his *Compendium of Knowledge* (LC 1:298):

> An affliction is defined as a phenomenon that, when it arises, is disturbing in character and that, through arising, disturbs the mindstream.

Afflictions are distinct mental factors that, when they arise in our minds, cause our minds to be unpeaceful and unsubdued. Afflictions may be emotions, attitudes, or views, and they usually arise without our choice. The three principal afflictions are ignorance, anger, and attachment. Although compassion may disturb our minds, it isn't an affliction. Genuine compassion—as opposed to pity, or personal distress when seeing others suffer—is deliberately cultivated for a good purpose and is supported by reasoning. Unable to ignore sentient beings' duḥkha, compassion wishes them to be free of it. Our minds may be temporarily disturbed because our apathy has been challenged, but this type of mental disturbance spurs us to be more tolerant and kind; it makes our minds strong and determined to aid others and brings benefit to ourselves and others.

Afflictions, on the other hand, arise without good reasons and lack foundation in reality. Because we are habituated with afflictions, they arise easily when we encounter certain conditions. They disturb the tranquility of the mind and have the long-term effect of increasing our problems and unhappiness. Unlike virtuous mental states such as integrity and compassion, afflictions lack mental clarity, and we often find ourselves justifying their presence: "I have a right to be angry because he criticized me unfairly." But think about it: Why must we be angry when someone criticizes us? Is anger the only possible response to this situation? Does anger increase our ability to communicate well or destroy it? Questioning ourselves in this way clears away confusion and enables us to see the faulty "logic" behind the afflictions and thus to dispel them.

Afflictions give rise to actions that are considered destructive in all cultures—such as killing, stealing, and lying. These actions perpetuate the cycle of misery. Because they bring our ruin, we need to be aware of their nature, causes, functions, and disadvantages. If a country has an enemy that is destroying its well-being, it tries to learn everything it can about that enemy in order to combat it and prevent it from devastating the country. Similarly, we need to know everything we can about the enemy—the afflictions that destroy our own and others' happiness. But simply learning about the afflictions is not sufficient; we must also combat them by hearing, thinking, and meditating on their counterforces as described in the Buddha's teachings. Doing this is the crux of Dharma practice.

The Buddha listed eighty-four thousand afflictions, the most prominent of which are the root afflictions (*mūlakleśa*) and auxiliary afflictions (*upakleśa*). In the *Treasury of Knowledge*, Vasubandhu spoke of six root afflictions, the last one being afflictive views, which in turn is subdivided into five. In the *Compendium of Knowledge*, his older brother Asaṅga listed ten root afflictions—the first five that Vasubandhu listed plus the five afflictive views. Although the two lists come to the same point, there are some differences in how a few of the afflictions are described because the *Treasury of Knowledge* was written from the Vaibhāṣika viewpoint while the *Compendium of Knowledge* is from the Cittamātra viewpoint. In general we will follow the latter, except when the Prāsaṅgika presentation differs. This occurs mainly in the descriptions of ignorance and the view of a personal identity. The six root afflictions are attachment (*rāga*), anger (*pratigha*), arrogance (*māna*), ignorance (*avidyā*), deluded doubt (*vicikitsā*), and afflictive views (*kliṣṭadṛṣṭi*).

Attachment

Attachment is a mental factor that, based on distorted attention that exaggerates the attractiveness of a polluted object (an object under the influence of ignorance), wishes for and takes a strong interest in it. The object could be a material object, a person or a place, or it could be praise or an idea. Attachment functions to produce discontent and to perpetuate the cycle of existence. Looking at our own experiences, we can see how true this is.

This is a general description of attachment; there are many degrees and variations of attachment. Some instances of attachment that arise in daily life are greed that wants more than our fair share, attachment to our ideas that leads to stubborn insistence on being right, attachment to reputation, praise, pleasing sensory experiences, and so on. We also become attached to people, which leads to having unrealistic expectations of them or of our relationships with them. This in turn leads to disappointment and friction in those relationships, and feelings of bitterness or betrayal when the relationships don't continue as expected.

Covetousness is a coarse form of attachment. As one of the ten nonvirtues, covetousness easily leads to actions that directly harm others, such as stealing or unwise sexual relationships. Other afflictions derived from attachment are miserliness that doesn't want to share our possessions, haughtiness that is attached to our good fortune, and restlessness that distracts the mind to desirable objects during meditation.

Attachment and aspiration are distinct mental factors with different functions. Although both are attracted to their object, attachment is based on distorted attention that exaggerates its attractiveness or projects good qualities that are not there. Seeing the object inaccurately, attachment clings to it and does not want to be separated from it. We become attached to people, money and possessions, love and approval, good food and other pleasurable sensory experiences, and so on, and are certain that the good qualities we see inhere in that person or thing. If our perception were accurate, everyone should see the person or thing as attractive as we do and desire it as much as we do. Clearly that is not the case.

Aspiration focuses on its intended object and takes a strong interest in it, but it is not necessarily based on exaggerating or projecting the object's good qualities. The aspirations seeking a good rebirth, liberation, and full awakening are based on realistically seeing beneficial qualities that are present. In his Abhidharma text, the Tibetan scholar Chim Jampelyang (ca. 1245–1325) clarified that the aspirations for a fortunate rebirth, liberation, or awakening are virtuous; they are not attachment.

Furthermore, Vasubandhu said that objects giving rise to afflictions are polluted. Since buddhahood and the Three Jewels are unpolluted, they cannot induce afflictions in others' minds. If someone thinks, "When I'm a buddha, everyone will respect me," he suffers from attachment to reputation, not attachment to buddhahood.

Craving is a form of attachment and is usually seen as nonvirtuous. However, "craving" can refer to other forms of attachment that may be temporarily useful. For example, in the case of someone who is miserly and doesn't want to part with his possessions, the craving to be wealthy in a future life can motivate him to counteract his stinginess and become generous in this life. Even though this craving seeks happiness in saṃsāra, it is a step up from craving the happiness of only this life and thus is considered virtuous. For someone who lives an ethically corrupt life, desire to be reborn as a deva can induce him to relinquish harmful behaviors and keep precepts. Craving for the bliss of samādhi in the form and formless realms can inspire someone to cultivate concentration in order to be reborn in those realms. These types of attachment are useful in those specific situations. However, for someone intent on liberation, those same cravings are hindrances because they are enamored with saṃsāric pleasures.

Ānanda says that based on the craving for liberation—our highest spiritual aspiration, which is certainly virtuous—the unwanted forms of craving can be eliminated (AN 4.159, AN 2.145). The postcanonical Pāli text *Nettippakaraṇa* speaks of virtuous and nonvirtuous forms of craving and confirms that virtuous craving leads to the end of craving. For example, one monastic learns that another has become an arhat, and with the desire to attain arhatship too, she practices diligently and becomes an arhat, one who has abandoned craving. Similarly, a monastic motivated by arrogance thinks, "I am as capable as that person who attained arhatship." This propels him to make effort and he becomes an arhat, someone who has abandoned arrogance. This is similar to the idea of taking attachment on the path in Tantrayāna. Here attachment is employed to make manifest the subtlest mind and use it to realize emptiness and destroy all obscurations, including attachment.

How do we reconcile these examples with a statement of Nāgārjuna, the great second-century Indian sage who spread the Madhyamaka (Middle Way) view (RA 20ab)?

> Attachment, anger, confusion,
> and the karma that arises from them are nonvirtuous.

"Attachment" here refers to selfish desire for material possessions, praise, good reputation, and pleasant sensory experiences. Such attachment often leads to nonvirtuous actions, while aspiration for the happiness of future lives can lead to virtuous actions. Anger and hatred, however, can never be the motivating factors for virtue; they always lead to nonvirtue. Here confusion refers not to the self-grasping ignorance that is the root of saṃsāra, but to the ignorance that does not understand karma and its effects. While self-grasping ignorance can also precede virtuous actions, the ignorance that has a skewed view of ethical conduct will lead to mental, verbal, and physical nonvirtuous paths of action.

Similarly, there are different ways to be "attached" to a beautiful statue of the Buddha. One person wants a beautiful statue to inspire his daily meditation practice. Another person wants the same statue to show off to his friends or to sell for a profit. These different motivations will bring different results in the present life and in future lives.

In short, "attachment" may have diverse meanings in different contexts. This is illustrated by the four types of clinging mentioned in the teaching

Parting from the Four Clingings that Mañjuśrī gave to the great Sakya lama Sachen Kunga Nyingpo:

> If you cling to this life, you are not a true spiritual practitioner.
> If you cling to saṃsāra, you do not have renunciation.
> If you cling to your own self-interest, you have no bodhicitta.
> If there is grasping, you do not have the view.

The first line indicates clinging to the happiness of this life, which is invariably an obstacle for Dharma practice. The presence or absence of this type of attachment is the demarcation between an action that is Dharma and one that is not. The second, clinging to cyclic existence, prevents us from embarking on the path to liberation, although it could lead to happiness within saṃsāra, as exemplified by the person who is attached to the bliss of samādhi and is born in the form or formless realms.

Clinging to our self-interest prevents us from entering the bodhisattva path, although it could support the attainment of arhatship—for example, by a person who clings to be free of saṃsāra and seeks his own liberation alone. The most deeply ingrained attachment is grasping inherent existence, which prevents the attainment of both liberation and full awakening.

The Tibetan term *chags pa* may also be translated as "attachment" and is sometimes used to indicate strong affection and care. In this sense, buddhas are "attached" to sentient beings, indicating that because of their strong compassion, they will never abandon sentient beings and will continuously work to lead them to temporal and ultimate happiness. This feeling of closeness and care that buddhas have for sentient beings is very different from attachment in the minds of sentient beings.

Anger

Anger is a mental factor that, referring to one of three objects, agitates the mind by being unable to bear or through wanting to harm the object or person. The three objects can be expanded to nine: (1–3) he harmed me in the past, he is harming me now, he will harm me in the future; (4–6) she harmed my dear friend or relative, is harming them, will harm them; (7–9) he helped my enemies, is helping them now, will help them in the future. Here *enemy* includes people we don't like or disagree with as well as those who harm us or interfere with our happiness. Anger functions to disturb our minds. As the basis for harming ourselves and others, it involves us in destructive actions and increases suffering in the world.

Anger is based on distorted attention that exaggerates or projects defects onto people and things. Our minds create many reasons to validate our anger and give us a false sense of power in situations where we feel afraid or hurt. Anger has many forms, and several other afflictions are derived from it, including irritation, annoyance, frustration, hatred, rebelliousness, belligerence, resentment, vengeance, spite, cruelty, violence, and jealousy.

Behind each episode of anger are many stories—conceptualizations proliferated by our minds—in which we impute motivations to people that they do not have, interpret actions from our own standpoint, and favor our own concerns while ignoring or demeaning the concerns of others. Although we may try to justify, rationalize, or deny our anger, the truth is that we are unhappy when our minds are overcome by anger. Sometimes we vent our anger to friends, hoping that they will take our side. (If they didn't, how could they be our friends?) Other times we speak or act in ways that harm others. Here we can see the relationship of attachment and anger: the more distorted attention has exaggerated someone's good qualities, increasing the strength of our attachment, the more distorted attention exaggerates that person's bad qualities when he or she doesn't meet our expectations. We become discontent, and this mental unhappiness inflames our anger, resulting in aggressive behavior that breaks the trust of the people we care about the most. Anger is a mental state, it is not the behavior. While some of us may not think of ourselves as angry because we don't throw things or scream at others, inside our anger rages. In these cases, ignoring the other person or refusing to have anything to do with them may be considered harmful behavior. We should not be fooled into thinking that passive behavior like withdrawing from a situation and refusing to communicate indicates a lack of anger.

Anger may also be a reaction to fear. When fearful we usually feel powerless, whereas anger gives us a false sense of power by sending adrenaline coursing through our body. Although anger may sometimes seem to make us courageous, our behavior when angry seldom remedies the problem and usually makes it worse.

Arrogance

Arrogance is a mental factor that, based on the view of a personal identity that misapprehends how the I or mine exists, strongly grasps an inflated image of ourselves. It functions to prevent us from learning and increasing our virtue and causes us to disrespect or denigrate others. Vasubandhu mentions seven types of arrogance:

1. Arrogance thinking, "I am superior" in relation to someone who is "inferior." In this and the next two forms of arrogance, we compare ourselves with others in terms of wealth, looks, knowledge, social standing, athletic ability, fame, and other factors.
2. Arrogance thinking, "I am superior" in relation to someone who is our equal.
3. Arrogance thinking, "I am superior" in relation to someone who is better than us.
4. Arrogance that regards our aggregates and thinks, "I." This is also called the *conceit of I am* (*asmimāna*). Based on self-grasping, we believe ourselves to be inherently existent and very important.
5. Arrogance that thinks we have good qualities that we don't have.
6. Arrogance thinking we are just a little bit inferior to someone who is really wonderful. We may think, "In this group of esteemed people, I am the least qualified," implying that although we are less than those who are experts, we are definitely better than the majority of other people. It also claims status by being associated with someone who is better than us: "I am the disciple of a truly great spiritual master."
7. Arrogance thinking our faults are virtues; for example, an ethically degenerate person thinks he is upstanding and righteous.

In the *Precious Garland* Nāgārjuna (RA 407–12) delineates seven types of arrogance in a slightly different way, although the meaning is generally the same as above. The one exception is the arrogance of inferiority. Here Nāgārjuna describes it as the arrogance of disparaging ourselves and thinking that we are useless and incapable. The Pāli tradition agrees with Nāgārjuna's gloss.

(1) Concerning these, the [first] is called *arrogance*;
it is where one thinks of oneself
as even inferior to the inferior, equal to the equal,
or greater than or equal to the inferior.

(2) It is *presumptive arrogance* for one to presume
that one is equal to someone who is better.

(3) If one presumes oneself to be
even better than one's betters,
this is *arrogance beyond arrogance*;
thinking oneself to be even loftier than the lofty.
It is excessively bad,
like developing sores on top of one's boils.

(4) The five empty aggregates
are called the *[aggregates] subject to clinging.*
When one apprehends them as I,
this is called the *conceit of thinking "I am."*

(5) To presume that one has attained a result
that one has not attained is to have *conceited arrogance.*

(6) The wise know that boasting
about one's negative deeds is *erroneous arrogance.*

(7) Deriding oneself, thinking,
"I cannot manage,"
is the *arrogance of inferiority.*
Such are the seven forms of arrogance, in brief.

Arrogance blocks us from gaining new qualities; when we believe we are already top-notch, we are not receptive to learning. Instead we remain complacent, or even smug, without endeavoring to cultivate virtuous qualities. Arrogance due to our Dharma knowledge or accomplishments does not plague beginners; at that time we are aware of how little we know and how much we need to learn and practice. But after we have studied and practiced for a while, arrogance can easily set in and arrest our spiritual growth.

It is important to discriminate between arrogance and self-confidence. Arrogance is often a cover for insecurity, whereas self-confidence acknowledges our abilities without inflating them. Self-confident people have no need to boast of their achievements. Self-confidence, an essential factor on the spiritual path, should be nurtured. Having the thought "As I progressively practice the path, I'll be able to accomplish all the bodhisattva activities" is a helpful and necessary attitude; it is not arrogance. Awareness of our potential boosts our enthusiasm to engage in Dharma study and practice. Similarly, rejoicing at our virtue with a sense of satisfaction, thinking, "I feel good because I kept my precepts in a challenging situation," is not arrogance, it's a way of reinforcing our virtue.

Ignorance

Ignorance is an afflictive state of unknowing brought about by the mind's lack of clarity regarding the nature of things such as the four truths, Three Jewels, and karma and its effects. It functions as the basis and root of all other afflictions and the afflictive actions and rebirths they produce. This is a general definition of ignorance accepted by all Buddhist tenet systems. However, each system has its own unique definition as well. Furthermore, the meaning of ignorance differs according to the context; some of these meanings are explained below. Unless otherwise noted, they accord with the Prāsaṅgikas' view, which may or may not be shared by other systems. As we delve into the correct view of emptiness later in the series, the meanings of ignorance in the various schools will be clarified. Ignorance (*avidyā*) is often, but not always, synonymous with confusion (*moha*).[24]

1. *Ignorance that is a mental factor* is ignorance as defined above.

2. *Ignorance of selflessness*, in the meaning common to all Buddhist tenet schools, does not understand the selflessness of persons.

3. *Ignorance of the ultimate truth* does not know the mode of existence of all persons and phenomena. This meaning is accepted by the Cittamātra and Madhyamaka schools. When this ignorance gives rise to afflictions that produce karma, which in turn projects rebirths in saṃsāra, it is ignorance that is the first link of dependent origination (see #6).

4. *Ignorance of karma and its effects* underlies all destructive actions,

especially those that lead to unfortunate rebirths. It is not simply not knowing about karma and its effects, but either strong disbelief in it or temporary disregard for it. This ignorance cannot discern virtuous from nonvirtuous actions, does not accept that happiness comes from virtuous actions and unhappiness from nonvirtuous actions, or does not fully believe this. For example, under the influence of this ignorance we don't see the faults of engaging in business deals that deprive others of what is rightly theirs. We may generally believe in karma and its effects, but when given the opportunity for personal gain, we justify lying to obtain what we like (see #5).

5. *Ignorance that is one of the three poisons* of ignorance, attachment, and animosity is one of the three basic factors spurring the creation of destructive karma. This is ignorance of karma and its effects. Often translated as "confusion," it accompanies all nonvirtuous mental states and is a cause of unfortunate rebirths.

6. *Ignorance that is the first link of dependent origination* starts a new set of twelve links that leads to rebirth in saṃsāra. Tenet systems have different assertions about this ignorance. According to the Prāsaṅgikas, it grasps our own I and mine as inherently existent, which is based on grasping our aggregates as inherently existent.

7. *Self-grasping ignorance* grasps persons and phenomena as inherently existent. It first grasps the aggregates as inherently existent, and on that basis grasps the person to be inherently existent. Self-grasping ignorance is synonymous with ignorance grasping inherent existence, ignorance grasping true existence, ignorance grasping things to exist from their own side, and so on. Sometimes when used loosely, "self-grasping ignorance" may refer to grasping a self-sufficient substantially existent person.

8. *Ignorance of the four distorted conceptions* grasps the impermanent as permanent, that which is duḥkha by nature as pleasurable, the unattractive as beautiful, and that which lacks a self as having one. This description is accepted by all tenet systems.

9. In the Pāli tradition ignorance is explained as not knowing the four truths—the aggregates, their origin, cessation, and the way to that cessation (SN 22.135)—past and future lives, and dependent origination. In specific contexts, it is described as not knowing the impermanent nature of the aggregates (SN 22.126); not understanding the gratification, danger, and

escape with respect to the five aggregates (SN 22.129); and so forth.[25] In all these cases, true knowledge—the mind that understands these clearly, as they are—is the opposite.

Vasubandhu states that ignorance (see #1) accompanies all afflictions.[26] Prāsaṅgikas assert that self-grasping ignorance provokes coarse afflictions but does not accompany them because the two have different functions. Self-grasping ignorance grasps its object as inherently existent, while attachment craves an object seen as attractive and desirable. Self-grasping ignorance arises first and attachment follows. Because they perform different functions and do not occur at the same time, Prāsaṅgikas say self-grasping ignorance and attachment do not share the same primary mind and do not accompany each other.

However, they say that self-grasping ignorance can accompany subtle afflictions because subtle attachment and anger have an element of grasping phenomena as inherently existent. Subtle attachment grasps its object as inherently desirable and craves to possess it. Subtle anger grasps its object as inherently undesirable and craves to be separated from it. These subtle afflictions are obstacles to attaining nirvāṇa, but do not necessarily hinder having a good rebirth. The lower schools do not consider subtle afflictions to prevent liberation because they assert inherent existence.

According to Prāsaṅgikas, ignorance (see #3, 7) grasps persons and phenomena as inherently existent. Grasping the self as self-sufficient and substantially existent is also a form of ignorance, but is not the ignorance that is the root of saṃsāra. The ignorance grasping inherent existence arises first, followed by the ignorance grasping the self as self-sufficient substantially existent. The former does not accompany the latter, because they grasp their object differently and do not occur simultaneously: the former grasps the self to be inherently existent, the latter grasps the self to be self-sufficient substantially existent. Similarly, in cases when grasping a self-sufficient substantially existent person causes anger to arise, it does not accompany anger due to the different ways these mental factors grasp their object.

Technically speaking, self-grasping ignorance and self-grasping are not the same. *Self-grasping ignorance* refers to the mental factor of ignorance that grasps inherent existence, while *self-grasping* refers to the entire mental state—the primary consciousness and its accompanying mental factors that include self-grasping ignorance. In other words, when ignorance grasping inherent existence accompanies a mental state, all aspects of that mental state grasp inherent existence.

However, sometimes *self-grasping* and *self-grasping ignorance* are used interchangeably. In this case, the speaker's purpose is not to distinguish the mental factor from the entire mental state, but to identify inherent existence and how we grasp objects and people to exist in this way.

As you can see, the topic of ignorance is complex and we need a lot of wisdom to understand it!

Deluded Doubt

Deluded doubt is a mental factor that is indecisive and wavers toward an incorrect conclusion concerning important spiritual topics such as the ultimate nature of phenomena, the four truths, Three Jewels, and karma and its effects. Keeping us in a constant state of uncertainty about what we believe, which path to follow, and what to practice, deluded doubt immobilizes and prevents us from going forward spiritually. Doubting ourselves, the path, and the result, we spin in circles and spend days, months, and years stuck in indecision. Deluded doubt is compared to trying to sew with a two-pointed needle: we accomplish nothing. It has only an acquired, not an innate, form.

Deluded doubt differs from doubt inclined toward the correct conclusion or doubt wavering in the middle. It differs from curiosity, which propels us to ask questions and learn more until we come to a sound conclusion.

REFLECTION

1. Review each of the five afflictions above, one by one. Think of at least three instances when each affliction has arisen in your mind.
2. What were the bare facts of the situation that sparked it? What did distorted attention add on to these bare facts, for example, by imputing qualities onto the object or person?
3. What effect did that affliction have on your mind? How did it influence your deeds and words?
4. Which Dharma points or teachings would help you to subdue that affliction?

Afflictive Views

The above five root afflictions are non-views, whereas the sixth, afflictive views, includes five erroneous views. These five erroneous views are forms of corrupt intelligence that either grasp the I to exist inherently or, based on that, develop further mistaken conceptions. They act as the basis for all problems caused by afflictions and all other mistaken outlooks and create turmoil in our lives. Wisdom is their antidote.

Saying these views are "corrupt intelligence" (T. *shes rab nyon mong chan*) means they are incorrect speculations or conclusions reached by incorrect analysis. They are unreliable minds that lack a realistic foundation. They are called intelligence (*prajñā*) because they distinguish their object and know its qualities; they are corrupt (*kleśa*) because they misapprehend their object. Although afflictive views are numerous, these five are prominent: view of a personal identity (*satkāyadṛṣṭi*), view of extremes (*antagrāhadṛṣṭi*), view holding erroneous views as supreme (*dṛṣṭi-parāmarśa*), view of bad rules and practices (*śīlavrata-parāmarśa*[27]), and wrong views (*mithyādṛṣṭi*).

View of a personal identity

According to all Buddhist schools except the Prāsaṅgikas, the view of a personal identity is a corrupt intelligence that, referring to the mental and physical aggregates, grasps them to be either a self-sufficient substantially existent I or mine. According to the Prāsaṅgikas, it is a corrupt intelligence that, observing the nominally existent I or mine, grasps it to exist inherently. Of the two self-graspings—of persons and of phenomena—view of a personal identity is included in self-grasping of persons. However, self-grasping of persons includes grasping all persons as inherently existent, whereas the view of a personal identity grasps our own I and mine as inherently existent.

The aggregates are collections of many moments or many parts; they are transitory, perishing in each moment. Translated literally, the Tibetan term for *satkāyadṛṣṭi*—*'jig tshogs la lta ba*—is "view of the transitory collection" or "view of the perishing aggregates." Specifying that they are transitory or perishing shows they are not permanent; saying "aggregates" indicates they are plural, not unitary. The term itself eliminates the possibility of a permanent, unitary person based on the aggregates.

Whereas the I is imputed in dependence on the collection of aggregates, view of a personal identity holds it to exist as an independent entity. All Buddhist schools refute the belief in a permanent soul or self that is asserted by non-Buddhists. According to the lower Buddhist schools, view of a personal identity observes the aggregates and mistakenly believes them to be a self-sufficient substantially existent I and mine—a person that controls the aggregates and a person that owns the aggregates. Here the observed object (*ālambana,* T. *dmigs pa*) is the aggregates, and the apprehended object (*muṣṭibandhaviṣaya,* T. *'dzin stangs kyi yul*) and conceived object (T. *zhen yul*) are a self-sufficient substantially existent person. The view of a personal identity is mistaken with respect to its apprehended and conceived objects because it believes the aggregates to be a self-sufficient substantially existent person, although they are not.

According to the view unique to the Prāsaṅgikas, view of a personal identity observes the mere I and mine—the I and mine that exist by being merely designated in dependence on the aggregates—and erroneously grasps them to be inherently existent. Here the observed object is the mere I and mine, and the apprehended and conceived objects are an inherently existent I and mine. This view is erroneous with respect to its apprehended and conceived objects because it mistakenly grasps the mere I and mine to exist inherently, as an independent entity unrelated to any other factors. To Prāsaṅgikas, grasping a self-sufficient substantially existent I and mine is a coarse grasping. It is not an actual view of a personal identity, but is only imputed as such. The subtle view of a personal identity that grasps the I and mine to be inherently existent is the actual view of a personal identity. This has ramifications for the meditation on selflessness, because realizing the selflessness that is the absence of only a self-sufficient substantially existent I and mine will not free us from saṃsāra.

Prāsaṅgikas assert that the view of a personal identity is a form of the ignorance that is the root of cyclic existence; it is an innate affliction that is present in all sentient beings, including babies and animals, as an instinctive sense of an inherently existent I and mine. Its artificial form is expounded and justified by incorrect philosophies.

The view of a personal identity has two facets, one grasping *I* as inherently existent (*ahaṃkāra,* T. *ngar 'dzin pa*) and the other grasping *mine* as inherently existent (*mamakāra,* T. *nga yir 'dzin pa*). *I* refers to the person, while *mine* refers to what makes things mine. Based on grasping *I*, grasping at *mine* or *my* arises. The *I* and *mine* are one nature but different isolates; they cannot be separated but are nominally distinct.

Our aggregates are examples of *mine*—conventionally the five aggregates are said to be mine; they belong to the I. However, grasping them to be inherently existent is self-grasping of phenomena. The view of a personal identity grasps the mere I to be inherently existent and views the aggregates as being under the control of this person who makes things mine.

Once we designate something as mine—be it our bodies, minds, material objects, ideas, or relationships—we relate to it in a very different way. If a new car on the showroom floor is dented, we aren't disturbed, but once we see this car as mine, we become incensed when a small scratch appears on it. *My* body being attractive or unhealthy invokes strong feelings of delight or worry; *my* ideas being accepted is a source of great pride.

Holding the strong notion of an inherently existent I, we cherish our selves more than anything else. Everything that gives us pleasure is seen as good; we cling to it and want more. All that interferes with our happiness or harms us is considered bad; we become hostile toward it and seek to destroy or avoid it. To obtain and protect our objects of attachment and to defend them against any harm, we engage in many destructive actions that harm others and plant seeds of destructive karma on our mindstreams that will ripen as future painful experiences.

Because the view of a personal identity is an erroneous consciousness that misapprehends the I, it can be eradicated through realizing the wisdom that knows how the I actually exists. Identifying the disadvantages of the view of a personal identity motivates us to cultivate this liberating wisdom.

Both the Pāli and Sanskrit traditions speak of twenty false views of a real self that stem from the view of a personal identity. *The Shorter Series of Questions and Answers* (*Cūḷavedalla Sutta*, MN 44) records a lay follower questioning Bhikkhunī Dhammadinnā about how the view of a personal identity comes to be. She responds:

> An untaught ordinary person who has no regard for āryas and is unskilled and undisciplined in their Dhamma . . . regards (1) the body as the self, or (2) the self as possessing the body, or (3) the

> body as [contained] in the self, or (4) the self as [contained] in the body. He regards feelings as the self, or the self as possessing feelings, or feelings as [contained] in the self, or self as [contained] in feelings. He regards discrimination as the self, or the self as possessing discrimination, or discrimination as [contained] in the self, or self as [contained] in discrimination. He regards miscellaneous factors as the self, or the self as possessing miscellaneous factors, or miscellaneous factors as [contained] in the self, or the self as [contained] in miscellaneous factors. He regards consciousness as the self, or the self as possessing consciousness, or consciousness as [contained] in the self, or the self as [contained] in consciousness.

Pāli commentaries explain these four positions for each aggregate using the example of the relationship between the self and the body:

1. Regarding the body as self is like regarding the flame of an oil lamp as identical to the color of that flame.

2. Regarding the self as possessing the body is like regarding a tree as possessing its shadow.

3. Regarding the body as being in the self or being part of the self or dependent on the self is like regarding the scent as being in the flower. In the Sanskrit tradition, the analogy is a bag (I) with many items (aggregates) in it.

4. Regarding the self as being in the body or part of the body or dependent on the body is like regarding a jewel in a box. In the Sanskrit tradition, the analogy is the self being like a lion in a forest.

Regarding the first three, we may think, "The flame is not identical to its color, a tree does not really possess a shadow, and the scent is not in the flower, but a jewel can be in a box. Since this last analogy is true, perhaps the self is in the body." To understand the analogy, we must ask ourselves if the relationship between the self and the body is like the relationship between a jewel and the box it is in. A jewel is a distinct phenomenon from the box and can be removed from the box and looked at alone without seeing the box. However, removing the self as an entity totally distinct from the body and looking at it in its own right, divorced from the body, is not possible because the self is dependent on the body. It is designated in dependence on the aggregates. Similarly, the lion is a distinct entity from the forest, whereas the I depends on the aggregates.

These twenty false views are not the view of a personal identity itself: the observed objects of the first and third are one of the aggregates and the observed objects of the second and fourth are the I. These false views are not innate grasping because, according to Prāsaṅgikas, view of a personal identity does not innately grasp the I as either inherently one with or entirely separate from the aggregates. Because the twenty false views present only these two possibilities and neither of them is how the view of a personal identity innately grasps the I, they are acquired false views. However, if the I inherently existed it would have to be one of four positions. Thus to refute the view of a personal identity, we must also refute these twenty.

View of extremes

The view of extremes is a corrupt intelligence that, referring to the I and mine apprehended by the view of a personal identity, regards them in either an absolutist or nihilistic manner. Based on grasping the I as inherently existent, view of the extremes holds either (1) an absolutist perspective that the I exists as an eternal, immutable soul or self that continues in future lives, or (2) a nihilistic outlook that the I becomes totally nonexistent after death, there being no continuum of the mere I in future lives. View of the extremes prevents us from finding the middle way view, free from the two extremes of absolutism and nihilism. It also causes us to neglect creating the virtuous causes for higher rebirth and liberation.

The absolutist view is also called the view of existence, eternalism,[28] superimposition, or permanence because it projects a false mode of existence on the person. The nihilistic view is called the view of nonexistence, annihilation, or deprecation because it denies the continuity of the self that actually exists. In doing so, it negates future rebirth as well as the possibility of liberation and awakening. The Buddha spoke of this view, saying its holders think (SN 24.4), "I may not be, it may not be for me, I shall not be, it will not be for me."

By identifying the view of extremes as erroneous, the Buddha clarified that although there is no inherently existent person, a conventionally existent person—the mere I—that is reborn and can attain liberation exists.

View holding erroneous views as supreme

The view holding wrong views as supreme is a corrupt intelligence that regards view of a personal identity, view of extremes, or wrong views as correct and supreme views, there being no higher views. It also views our own five aggregates as supreme, thinking there is no better body, feelings, and so forth. We ordinary beings easily become attached to our views, and the view holding wrong views as supreme functions to increase our attachment to erroneous views so that we arrogantly tout our wrong views as right ones. Holding erroneous views as supreme strongly holds to wrong views and serves as the basis for generating wrong views in this and future lives. It makes our minds very narrow and decreases our intelligence. While wrong views can be abandoned comparatively easily, when we hold them as supreme, they become deeply entrenched in our minds and thus more difficult to overcome.

The four distorted conceptions regarding true duḥkha correspond with the first three afflictive views: Viewing that which lacks a self as having one is view of a personal identity. Viewing the impermanent as permanent is the eternalistic extreme view. Viewing the foul body as clean and viewing what is in nature unsatisfactory as pleasurable are the view holding erroneous views as supreme.

View of rules and practices

The view holding bad rules and practices as supreme is a corrupt intelligence that believes purification of mental defilements is possible by ascetic practice and inferior ethical codes that are inspired by erroneous views. It causes us to engage in useless actions that make us exhausted but bring no spiritual benefit.

View of rules and practices thinks that what are not causes for higher rebirth and liberation are causes for them and what is not the path to liberation is the path. Under its influence people engage in nonvirtue, believing it to be virtue, and follow a path they believe will lead to liberation that leads instead to unfortunate rebirths. Examples of this erroneous view include thinking that killing in the name of one's religion will bring rebirth in a heavenly realm and that animal sacrifice pleases the gods and brings good fortune. Other instances are believing that the perfect performance of a ritual alone, without any mental transformation, is the path to liberation; that negativities can be purified by bathing in or drinking holy water; and that attachment is abandoned by extreme asceticism, such as fasting for days on end, walking through fire, or lying on a bed of nails. Although these people aspire for liberation, their aspiration remains unfulfilled.

Wrong views

Wrong views are a corrupt intelligence that denies the existence of something necessary to attain awakening that exists. This includes the denial of causes, saying that constructive and destructive actions don't exist; denial of effects, believing that the results of constructive and destructive actions don't exist; denial of functionality, believing that past and future lives are nonexistent; and denial of phenomena, asserting liberation, awakening, or the Three Jewels are nonexistent. These views are so damaging because when people hold them, they easily deny ethical responsibility for their actions and justify engaging in many destructive actions. Wrong views function to harm us because they serve as a basis for engaging in nonvirtue, cause us not to engage in virtue, and sever our roots of virtue. Adhering to wrong views cuts our opportunity to attain awakening.

In the *Supreme Net Sutta* (*Brahmajāla Sutta*) the Buddha spoke of sixty-two examples of wrong views advanced by various groups (DN 1.3.45–57):[29]

> The Eternalists proclaim the eternity of the self and the world . . . those who are partly Eternalists and partly Non-Eternalists proclaim the partial eternity and the partial non-eternity of the self and the world . . . the Finitists and Infinitists proclaim the finitude or infinitude of the world . . . the Eel-wriggles resort to evasive statements . . . the Chance Originationists proclaim the chance origin of the self and the world . . . those who speculate about the past, having fixed views about the past . . . those who claim a doctrine of conscious postmortem survival . . . those who proclaim a doctrine of unconscious postmortem survival . . . those who proclaim a doctrine of neither-conscious-nor-unconscious postmortem survival . . . Nihilists proclaim the annihilation, destruction, and

> nonexistence of beings . . . (and) there are proclaimers [of a self that realizes] nibbāna here and now . . . speculators about the future . . . speculators about the past, the future, or both . . .

As we can see, just as in modern times, at the Buddha's time too there were a plethora of views, each claiming to be the one correct truth.

The Buddha pinpointed three types of nihilistic views as views shunned by the wise because they do not bring liberation (MN 60, MN 76).

1. *Nihilistic view denying the continuation of the person after death* is often the result of a materialist outlook on life. In a modern context, it is thinking the mind is an emergent property of the brain, and since the brain ceases to function at death, so do the mind and the person. Since no one will experience the consequences of our actions in a future rebirth, as long as we avoid the authorities in this life, we won't experience any adverse repercussions from our nonvirtuous actions and therefore can do as we please.

2. *Nihilistic view denying the existence of constructive and destructive actions* negates ethical distinctions among actions. Killing and torturing others is not destructive, so no unpleasant results of engaging in such actions will follow. Generosity and kindness are not constructive, so there is no use engaging in them.

3. *Nihilistic view denying* causation holds that there are no causes or conditions for either the defilement or purification of sentient beings—sentient beings are defiled and purified by either chance or fate, and there is nothing we can do to prevent suffering or attain liberation. Some people may believe in the randomness of happiness and pain because they cannot see the link between causes created in one life bringing effects in another life. Alternatively, they are fatalistic and believe that everything is controlled by destiny or by the will of the creator.

The Buddha did not say these views are wrong because they contradicted his ideas but because they are based on misunderstanding, limited knowledge, or distorted thinking and will lead those who hold them to create the causes for their own future suffering.

Wrong views may be spoken of in two ways. In general, they include all five afflictive views. More precisely, they differ from other views because of their object: they negate the existence of past and future lives, the Three

Jewels, and the law of karma and its effects. Denying cause and effect is a serious wrong view, one that cuts the root of virtue.

Wrong views in the context of the ten paths of nonvirtue and in the context of the root afflictions differ slightly. The latter is more pervasive in that it includes not only negating what does exist—such as the Three Jewels and so forth—but also holding what does not exist—such as a creator god, or a metaphysical primal substance or universal mind—as the ultimate source of the world and the beings in it.

Wrong views cut the root of virtue gradually, not all at once. The roots of virtue decrease while the wrong views grow stronger. For example, although Sally practices generosity, her career does not advance. Meanwhile, she sees people who lie get promoted. The wrong view arises in her mind that it's useless to create virtue. Slowly this idea grows stronger, so that even if her teacher tries to explain that her hindrances are due to destructive karma from the past and her present constructive actions will bring agreeable results in the future, she doesn't listen. She completely dismisses the law of karma and its effects. Such an entrenched wrong view severs the root of virtue in her mind, destroying the seeds of virtue.

It is easy to glaze over wrong views in our own minds, believing them to be correct. Observing our views, assumptions, and beliefs and questioning their veracity helps us to become aware of wrong views we haven't yet recognized. People who were raised in another religion may find that deep in their minds they still hold beliefs they were taught as children—beliefs in a creator, a soul, reward and punishment for ethical and unethical behavior, and so on. These may distort our understanding of Buddhist concepts that sound similar, and they hinder our understanding the teachings correctly. Examining them closely and using reason to decide what we believe is important to resolve the confusion wrong views cause.

Wrong views are based on ignorance and arise due to incorrect logic. They are especially difficult to abandon because the mistaken reasons and beliefs that are their basis must be dismantled. Due to strong attachment, some people are reluctant to reexamine their cherished beliefs and are thus resistant to hearing reasons that refute the assumptions at their basis. But when we are open and someone points out to us the absurd consequences that result from our wrong views, we begin to reevaluate our beliefs. Once we doubt an incorrect view, we can use reasoning to generate a correct assumption and then an inferential understanding. As we do so, our minds become clearer and more peaceful.

Wrong views easily support unethical conduct. People who dismiss the law of karma and its effects and hold that there is no connection between our actions and our experiences may wave away any sense of responsibility for their actions. They believe that they can do anything they wish—including extortion, rape, and brutality—because their actions will not adversely affect themselves, the only possible consequence being arrest by the police, which they try to avoid.

Wrong views prevent people from attaining realizations of the path, liberation, and awakening. Someone with strong belief in an external creator will find the doctrine of emptiness uninteresting and make no attempt to learn or understand it. Someone who believes that sentient beings are inherently selfish does not think training our minds in compassion is worthwhile and considers the cultivation of bodhicitta a useless pursuit.

All Buddhist tenet systems agree that these five views are afflictive in that they disturb the mind; view of a personal identity and view of the extremes are ethically neutral, but the remaining three are nonvirtuous. The tenet systems also agree that all five afflictive views are rooted in ignorance and have an element of not knowing the object. Prāsaṅgikas take it a step further and say that all afflictive views are forms of ignorance.

According to the *Treasury of Knowledge*, wrong views are a kind of corrupt intelligence. According to the *Compendium of Knowledge*, they are called *corrupt intelligence* but are not actually intelligence because intelligence must necessarily be virtuous and afflictive views are nonvirtuous. However, both texts agree that the mental factor of wrong views and the mental factor of ignorance do not have a common locus. According to the *Compendium of Knowledge*, the path of action of wrong views (the tenth nonvirtue) is the mental factor of wrong views and is not ignorance. Asaṅga says this because wrong views are corrupt intelligence, and ignorance, being obscuration and unknowing, is not.

REFLECTION

1. Make examples from your own experience of times each of the five afflictive views have manifested in your mind.
2. Are these views easier or more difficult to notice than the first five afflictions?
3. What effect do afflictive views have on your Dharma practice?
4. What will help you to subdue them?

More Types of Defilements

To broaden our perspective on true origins, we will now look at other ways the sūtras and Abhidharma texts of both the Pāli and Sanskrit traditions describe the afflictive mental factors that propel saṃsāra.

There are many classification systems, each one looking at the defilements from a slightly different perspective that emphasizes particular points. The auxiliary afflictions emphasize the relationship of secondary afflictions and root afflictions. Abandonment or reduction in the ten fetters delineate attainment of the stages of stream-enterer (*srotāpanna*), once-returner (*sakṛdāgāmin*), nonreturner (*anāgāmi*), and arhat. The pollutants are discussed in the context of their being the basic mental contaminants that keep sentient beings revolving in cyclic existence because they are so well-entrenched in the mind.

Sometimes the description of a defilement varies from one text or tradition to another. This gives us more information about that defilement and its functions, making it easier for us to identify it when it arises in our minds.

What follows are not simply lists of defilements but mirrors to our minds that help us to identify the various attitudes, emotions, and views that disturb our minds. These defilements cause us to experience unhappiness here and now and instigate the creation of destructive karma that brings unpleasant results in future lives. As you read the descriptions of the various defilements, pause after each one and make an example of it in your own experience. This will bring these lists alive for you and reveal them as an excellent tool for identifying factors that hinder your happiness and the fulfillment of your spiritual aims.

Afflictions

In the Pāli sūtras the afflictions (P. *kilesa*) are mentioned often but are not itemized. Their enumeration is found in the *Vibhaṅga* and explained in the *Dhammasaṅgaṇi*, both canonical Abhidhamma texts. The *Path of Purification* also discusses them, saying they are called *afflictions* because they themselves are afflicted and because they afflict their associated mental states (Vism 22.49). They are ten in number:

(1–3) Greed (attachment, P. *lobha*), animosity (hatred, P. *dosa*), and confusion (P. *moha*) are called *roots* (P. *mūla*) because their presence determines the ethical quality of a mental state as well as the verbal and physical actions it motivates. Their opposites—liberality, loving-kindness, and wisdom—are the three roots of virtue. (4) Arrogance (P. *māna*) is one of the higher fetters, abandoned only at arhatship. On the basis of any of the five aggregates, which are impermanent, duḥkha, and not self, arrogance thinks, "I am superior, equal, or inferior." (5) Afflictive views (P. *diṭṭhi*) are numerous but can be condensed into eternalism and nihilism. (6–8) Deluded doubt (P. *vicikicchā*), restlessness (P. *uddhacca*), and lethargy (P. *thina*) are three of the five hindrances (P. *nīvaraṇa*), which will be explained later. (9–10) Lack of integrity (P. *ahirika*) and lack of consideration for others (P. *anottappa*) are instrumental in creating destructive karma. Lack of integrity is directed inward. Under its influence, we do not respect our principles and precepts and thus do not abandon nonvirtuous thoughts and behavior.[30] Lack of consideration for others is directed outward and does not abandon nonvirtuous thoughts and behavior even though they adversely affect others and their faith. Some of the above correspond to root afflictions in the Sanskrit tradition, whereas others are considered auxiliary afflictions.

Underlying Tendencies

The six root afflictions in the Sanskrit tradition are called underlying tendencies (*anuśaya, anusaya*) in the Pāli sūtras (MN 18.8) and Abhidharma.[31]

They are the same six, except attachment has been separated into two, making seven: attachment to sensuality (*kamaragā*), anger (P. *paṭigha*), views, deluded doubt, arrogance, existence (*bhavarāga*), and ignorance (P. *avijjā*). Vasubandhu lists the underlying tendencies in the same way.

Here *attachment to sensuality* is the attachment of the desire realm that hungers after sensory objects of the desire realm—sights, sounds, and so forth. *Attachment to existence* is attachment to birth in the form and formless realms; it is possessed by beings in all three realms who cling to the bliss of concentration. A human may abandon attachment for sensual objects in the desire realm but have strong attachment for meditative states in the form or formless realms. Beings born in the form realm are attached to existence in that realm or to existence in the formless realm and will strive to actualize that level of meditative absorption. Beings born in the formless realm are attached to existence there, although not to existence in the desire or form realms. Because they still hanker for saṃsāric existence, they lack the aspiration for liberation and cannot attain nirvāṇa unless they relinquish that attachment.

Although the main afflictive mental factors are listed as both underlying tendencies and root afflictions, they are seen differently in the Pāli Abhidhamma than in the *Compendium of Knowledge*. In the Pāli tradition, *anusaya* literally means "to lie down or to sleep along with." Firmly established in the mind, underlying tendencies "sleep alongside" the mental continuum, acting as the causes for manifest afflictions. They are latent dispositions present even in newborn infants that enable manifest afflictions to arise when the appropriate causes and conditions are present.

Although seven underlying tendencies are listed, all defilements have a dormant form that is also called an underlying tendency. These may be stronger or weaker depending on the person's actions and thoughts. When a certain view or emotion repeatedly arises in our minds—and especially when we act on it—its underlying tendency increases in strength. Saying someone has a hot temper means that his underlying tendency for anger is strong.

When afflictions arise and we counteract them by applying the antidotes, their underlying tendencies weaken. Training our minds in correct ways of thinking increases the strength of the antidotal mental factors, transforming someone who has a hot temper into someone who is kind and patient. Underlying tendencies begin to be eradicated from our mindstreams when we attain the supramundane path and become stream-enterers. This corresponds to the path of seeing in the Sanskrit tradition.

Vaibhāṣikas consider the underlying tendencies and the afflictions to be the same, whereas Sautrāntikas say that latent attachment is an underlying tendency and manifest attachment is a full entanglement. This difference in interpretation arose as the Abhidharmikas tried to explain how an affliction could be manifest now, disappear in fifteen minutes, and manifest again tomorrow. Without a permanent self, what connects the previous instance of an affliction to a later one? Sautrāntikas say that the underlying tendencies are latent forces, like seeds that produce manifest afflictions when the right conditions are present. Since the afflictions, like consciousnesses, are impermanent, the underlying tendency of anger connects one instance of anger to another instance of anger the next day.

Vaibhāṣikas do not agree, saying that if these dormant potentials were always alongside the consciousness, there could never be a virtuous mental state, because virtuous mental states and dormant potentials are incompatible. Thus they say the underlying tendencies and the afflictions are the same.

Another Abhidharma school (Yaśomitra says it is the Vātsīputrīya) asserts that the underlying tendencies are abstract composites (*viprayukta-saṃskāra*)—impermanent things that are neither form nor consciousness. Here the underlying tendencies are neutral—neither virtuous nor non-virtuous—and could abide alongside any mental state.[32] This is similar to Tibetan thought on this topic: afflictions are mental factors. When a manifest affliction fades, a seed of that affliction remains. The seed is a neutral abstract composite. When the correct conditions come together, the seed turns into the manifest affliction, in this way connecting one instance of an affliction with a later instance. The same mechanism works for virtuous mental factors.

The Buddha noted three underlying tendencies as being particularly dangerous (MN 148.28):

> When one is touched by a pleasant feeling, if one delights in it, welcomes it, and remains holding to it, the underlying tendency to attachment lies within one. When one is touched by a painful feeling, if one sorrows, grieves, laments, weeps, beating one's

> breast, and becomes distraught, the underlying tendency to anger lies within one. When one is touched by a neutral feeling, if one does not understand as it actually is the origination, disappearance, gratification, danger, and escape[33] in regard to that feeling, the underlying tendency to ignorance lies within one. Monastics, that one shall here and now make an end to duḥkha without abandoning the underlying tendency to attachment for pleasant feeling, without abolishing the underlying tendency to anger for painful feeling, without extirpating the underlying tendency to ignorance in regard to neutral feeling, without abandoning the ignorance [that is the root of saṃsāra] and arousing true knowledge—this is impossible.

Observing our lives, we clearly see that attachment immediately arises in response to pleasant feelings—for example, eating some tasty food; aversion arises in response to an unpleasant feeling, such as having a stomachache; ignorance arises in response to a neutral feeling. What is needed is wisdom, insight, and true knowledge to free our minds from these underlying tendencies.

However, these three underlying tendencies must not be abandoned in regard to all pleasant, unpleasant, and neutral feelings (MN 44.25–28). In fact, the joy (*prīti*) and bliss (*sukkha*) experienced in the first dhyāna overpower the underlying tendency to sensual attachment. The unpleasant feeling from thinking about duḥkha overcomes the underlying tendency to anger by inspiring us to become a nonreturner. The neutral feeling in the fourth dhyāna leads to equanimity and employing that dhyāna to realize the four truths leads to arhatship.

Even before attaining insight and wisdom, we can temporarily lessen the underlying tendencies. When a pleasant feeling arises, be mindful of it but do not delight in it. Instead of clinging to and wanting more of that experience, simply let it be. In that way the underlying tendency to sensual attachment isn't activated. Similarly, practice observing unpleasant feelings, and by recalling their transience, don't arouse anger. Restraining our senses is also helpful because by decreasing contact with sensual objects, we experience fewer pleasant and unpleasant feelings and thus fewer instances of sensual attachment and anger.

Auxiliary Afflictions

In the Sanskrit tradition, the *Compendium of Knowledge* presents twenty auxiliary afflictions (*upakleśa*) that disturb the mind. They are called *auxiliary* because they are close to or related to the root afflictions and are classified according to the root afflictions with which they are associated.[34]

Afflictions derived from anger

1. Wrath (belligerence, *krodha*) is a mental factor that, due to an increase of anger, is a thoroughly malicious state of mind wishing to cause immediate harm.

2. Resentment (grudge holding, vengeance, *upanāha*) is a mental factor that firmly holds on to the fact that in the past we were harmed by a particular person and wishes to retaliate.

3. Spite (*pradāsa*) is a mental factor that is preceded by wrath or resentment, is an outcome of malice, and motivates us to speak harsh words in response to unpleasant words said by others.

4. Jealousy (*īrṣyā*) is a mental factor that, out of attachment to respect and material gain, is unable to bear the good qualities, possessions, opportunities, or virtue of others.

5. Cruelty (*vihiṃsā*) is a mental factor that, with a malicious intention that lacks any compassion or kindness, desires to harm, belittle, or disregard others. It is usually directed toward those we consider inferior to ourselves.

Afflictions derived from attachment

6. Miserliness (*mātsarya*) is a mental factor that, out of attachment to respect and material gain, firmly holds on to our possessions with no wish to give them away.

7. Haughtiness (*mada*) is a mental factor that, being attentive to the good fortune we possess, produces a false sense of confidence or security that leads to complacency.

8. Restlessness (agitation, excitement, *auddhatya*) is a mental factor that, through the force of attachment, does not allow the mind to rest solely on a virtuous object but scatters it here and there to many other objects.

Afflictions derived from ignorance

9. Concealment (*mrakṣa*) is a mental factor that wishes to hide our faults whenever another person with a benevolent intention free of attachment, confusion, hatred, or fear talks about such faults.

10. Lethargy (dullness, *styāna*) is a mental factor that, having caused the mind to become dull and thereby insensitive, does not comprehend its object clearly.

11. Laziness (*kausīdya*) is a mental factor that, having firmly grasped an object offering temporary happiness, either does not wish to do anything constructive or, although wishing to, is weak-minded. Laziness leads to excessive sleep, involvement with meaningless activities, and discouragement.

12. Lack of faith (lack of confidence or trust, *āśraddhya*) is a mental factor that, causing us to have no belief in or respect for that which is worthy of confidence—such as karma and its results and the Three Jewels—is the complete opposite of faith. It acts as the basis for laziness and disrespect.

13. Forgetfulness (*muṣitasmṛtitā*) is a mental factor that, having caused the apprehension of a virtuous object to be lost, induces memory of and distraction to an object of affliction.

14. Non-introspective awareness (non-clear comprehension, *asaṃprajanya*) is a mental factor that, being an afflictive intelligence, has made no, or only a rough, analysis and is not fully alert to the conduct of our body, speech, and mind, and thus causes us to become carelessly indifferent.

Afflictions derived from both attachment and ignorance

15. Pretension (*māyā*) is a mental factor that, being overtly attached to respect or material gain, fabricates a particularly excellent quality about ourselves and wishes to make it known to others with the thought to deceive them.

16. Deceit (dishonesty, *śāṭhya*) is a mental factor that, being overtly attached to respect or material gain, wishes to deceive others by hiding our faults or preventing others from knowing our faults.

Afflictions derived from ignorance, anger, and attachment

17. Lack of integrity (*āhrīkya*) is a mental factor that does not avoid destructive actions for reasons of personal conscience or for the sake of our

Dharma practice. It is a supportive condition for all afflictions and the basis for not protecting our precepts.

18. Inconsideration for others (*anapatrāpya*) is a mental factor that, without taking others or their spiritual traditions into account, does not restrain from destructive behavior. It causes others to lose faith in us.

19. Heedlessness (negligence, *pramāda*) is a mental factor that, when we are affected by laziness, wishes to act in an unrestrained manner without cultivating virtue or guarding the mind from objects or people that spark afflictions.

20. Distraction (*vikṣepa*) is a mental factor that, arising from any of the three poisons, is unable to direct the mind toward a constructive object and disperses it to a variety of other objects.

The Pāli tradition lists sixteen auxiliary afflictions (P. *upakkilesa*) that are offshoots of the three root afflictions (MN 7.3). Many of these overlap with the twenty in the Sanskrit tradition.

1. Covetousness and greed (P. *abhijjhāvisamalobha*) are aspects of craving. One commentary says covetousness is desire for and attachment to our own belongings, and greed is desire for and attachment to the belongings of others. Another commentary states that covetousness is attachment to an object that is suitable and has been obtained (e.g., coveting a new shirt that you need and obtain legally), while greed is attachment to an object that is unsuitable and has not been obtained (e.g., greedily desiring illegal drugs).

2. Malice (P. *vyāpāda*, *byāpāda*) is aversion that arises in nine cases when thinking, "He harmed me, is harming me, will harm me. He harmed, is harming, will harm those who are dear to me. He helped, is helping, will help my enemies."

3. Wrath (P. *kodha*) is hatefulness and opposition that seeks to harm someone.

4. Resentment (P. *upanāha*) is accumulated anger and hostility. At first there is anger toward a person or situation. This anger persists and turns into resentment, which is continued animosity toward someone. Weighing us down emotionally and obscuring our mind spiritually, resentment grows when we insist on being right, make ourselves into a victim, or refuse to forgive.

5. Contempt (P. *makkha*) is ingratitude that denigrates those who have

been kind to us. A spiritual mentor may help her student for many years, training and teaching him. But when the student becomes well-known and respected, he disregards his teacher and thinks, "She did nothing for me."

6. Insolence (P. *paḷāsa*) is a sense of competitiveness that puts the other person down. We arrogantly consider ourselves to be above others who are more qualified.

7. Jealousy (P. *issā*) is resentment of the gain, honor, respect, esteem, veneration, and reverence shown to others.

8. Miserliness (P. *macchariya*) is stinginess and avarice. We cling to what we have and are unwilling to share our possessions, dwelling, food, reputation, praise, and so forth with others. We don't want the people who praise us to meet others because they may praise them. We don't want others to learn the Dharma because they may become as well respected as we are.

9. Pretension (P. *māyā*) craftily hides our faults and misdeeds. We do a nonvirtuous action and, not wanting others to know about it, pretend to be innocent.

10. Deceit (P. *sāṭheyya*) fraudulently claims excellent qualities, achievements, or status that are not so.[35] We pretend to be a loyal and dear friend who will never let others down.

11. Obstinacy (P. *thambha*) is rigidity and inflexibility. Such stubbornness often arises when, being insecure, we seek to control a situation or insist that we are right.

12. Competition (P. *sārambha*) seeks to rival and outshine others. We see someone dressed nicely and want to get better clothes to show off; we hear someone is learned and want to demonstrate our knowledge in order to receive more praise and a better reputation. Although such competition is defiled, it is possible to "compete" in a positive way. We see someone who is generous, and with a giving heart we wish to match or surpass her gift; we meet someone who is learned in the Dharma, and with a sincere desire to learn ourselves, we aspire to learn the Dharma as well as she has.

13. Arrogance (P. *māna*) is being puffed up on account of our social class, education, possessions, and so forth. There are three types of arrogance: thinking (1) I am better than others, (2) I am just as good as they are, and (3) I am worse than them. In the Pāli tradition, arrogance is listed both as an underlying tendency and an auxiliary affliction.[36]

14. Conceit (P. *atimāna*) is extreme elevation of the mind. Haughty and

dismissive of others, we are so wrapped up in our own greatness that others seem insignificant in comparison.

15. Haughtiness (P. *mada*). According to one commentary, it is similar to arrogance and conceit in that it concerns social class, clan, and so forth. The sūtras describe haughtiness as vanity in relationship to youth, health, and life. Young people are infatuated with their youth and think they will never get old, the healthy believe they will not become ill, and those who are alive think they will not die.

16. Heedlessness (P. *pamāda*) is the opposite of conscientiousness and allows the mind to roam among objects of sensual pleasure. Letting the mind be overwhelmed with afflictions without making any effort to restrain the mind, it leads to self-indulgent actions and ethical downfalls.

Of the sixteen auxiliary afflictions in the Pāli tradition, eight (wrath, resentment, jealousy, miserliness, deceit, pretention, haughtiness, and heedlessness) are auxiliary afflictions and one (arrogance) is a root affliction in the *Compendium of Knowledge*. Two (covetousness and malice) are two of the ten nonvirtues.

REFLECTION

1. Some people have difficulty identifying emotions because when they were children their parents did not name emotions or discuss them very much.
2. Some ways to learn to identify your emotions are to become aware of (a) sensations in your body, (b) the flow or "texture" of your breath, and (c) the "tone" or mood in your mind.
3. Using the above techniques, try to identify instances of each of the auxiliary afflictions in your life.
4. Examine the triggers that make the auxiliary afflictions arise. Examine the short- and long-term results of manifest auxiliary afflictions in your life.
5. Develop a strong determination to counteract the auxiliary afflictions by cultivating mental states that see the object in the opposite way.

Fetters

The ten fetters (*saṃyojana*) are spoken about extensively in the Pāli tradition and in the *Treasury of Knowledge*. They are called *fetters* because they keep us bound to cyclic existence and impede the attainment of liberation. The first five are *lower fetters* because they bind us to rebirth in the desire realm. The last five are *higher fetters* that prevent a nonreturner from becoming an arhat.

(1) View of a personal identity grasps a true self with respect to the aggregates—for example, thinking one of the aggregates is the self, the self is separate from the aggregates, the self is vast and the aggregates exist within it, or the self exists within the aggregates.

(2) Deluded doubt is a vacillating mind that equivocates about issues important for liberation, such as doubting that the Buddha is awakened, that the Dharma is the ultimate truth and the path out of saṃsāra, and that the Ārya Saṅgha has realized the Dharma.

(3) View of rules and practices clings to mistaken codes of ethics and mistaken practices as virtuous and as the path to awakening—for example, holding extreme ascetic practices of self-mortification, such as fasting for weeks or sitting in fire to be virtuous, or holding perfectly performed brahminic rituals to be the path.

(4) Sensual desire (*kāmacchanda*) is attachment to objects in the desire realm.

(5) Malice is the wish to harm another living being.

(6–7) Desire for existence in the form realm (*rūparāga*) and desire for existence in the formless realm (P. *arūparāga*) are attached to their respective realms and wish to continue to abide there. These correspond to the pollutant of craving for continued existence.

(8) Arrogance is the subtle, fundamental arrogance, the conceit of "I am" (*asmimāna*). This differs from view of a personal identity, which is a conceptual view holding a permanent, true self. After this view is eliminated, the thoughts "I am this" or "I am that" no longer arise, but the thought "I am" is still present. Even though a nonreturner knows this to be mistaken and does not hold on to the idea "I am," the thought "I am" still arises spontaneously.

(9) Restlessness is present in any mind that is not liberated. This

hindrance may still arise in nonreturners if they are not mindful and diligent, but they are able to overcome it quickly.

(10) Ignorance is the primordial ignorance that is the root of saṃsāra. It is blindness of the true nature, an obscuration that prevents us from seeing how things actually exist. Unlike the Prāsaṅgika, according to the Pāli tradition ignorance does not apprehend the opposite of how things exist.

The *Compendium of Knowledge* lists the fetters differently: attachment, anger, arrogance, ignorance, deluded doubt, afflictive views (view of a personal identity, view of extremes, and wrong views), holding wrong views as supreme, which includes the view of rules and practices, jealousy, and miserliness.

REFLECTION

1. Choose one of the fetters that is obvious in your experience. Be aware of it in its latent, manifest, and motivating forms.
2. While eliminating its latent form requires insight into selflessness, what ideas do you have to inhibit it manifesting, or once it has manifested, from motivating your deeds and speech?

Pollutants

Pollutants (*āsrava, āsava*) perpetuate saṃsāra. Most Pāli sūtras mention three pollutants, although a late addition to the *Mahāparinibbāna Sutta* and the Pāli Abhidhamma literature speak of four.

(1) The *pollutant of sensuality* (P. *kāmāsava*) is a deeply rooted tendency for sensual desire that causes us to get tangled up with sensual objects. It corresponds to the fetter of sensual desire.

(2) The *pollutant of existence* (P. *bhavāsava*) is a deep, fundamental craving to exist in some form. This pollutant is particularly insidious because it propels the mind to take rebirth repeatedly in cyclic existence. It encapsulates the fetters of desire for existence in the form and formless realms.

(3) The *pollutant of ignorance* (P. *avijjāsava*) is a lack of knowing and

understanding. Always present in saṃsāric beings, it sometimes surges and becomes very intense, inhibiting the mind from seeing reality clearly. The fetter of ignorance and the underlying tendency of ignorance are included in this pollutant.

(4) The *pollutant of views* (P. *diṭṭhāsava*) includes the fetters of view of a personal identity and view of rules and practices, and the underlying tendency to views. This pollutant is not included in the enumeration of pollutants in the early sūtras.

Pollutants are deeply rooted, primordial defilements that have kept us bound in saṃsāra without respite. Existing deep in the mind, they flow into conscious experience when provoked by contact with certain objects. For example, contact with pleasant sensory objects stimulates the pollutant of sensuality.

Āsrava was a word used by brahmins and ascetics before the Buddha. The Buddha gave the term a new meaning and delineated the first three pollutants. These are also forms of craving, each focused on its own object and functioning in its own way to keep us trapped in saṃsāra.

The *Treasury of Knowledge* lists three pollutants: (1) The *pollutant of desire or attachment* includes the afflictions and full entanglements of the desire realm, except for ignorance. These are nonvirtuous. (2) The *pollutant of existence* is directed inward and is interested in birth in the form or formless realm. It is ethically neutral and includes the underlying tendencies and afflictions of the form and formless realms, except for ignorance. (3) The *pollutant of ignorance* is the ignorance of the desire, form, and formless realms. It is listed as a separate pollutant to emphasize that it is the root of saṃsāra and that when it is eliminated, the other pollutants also cease. These are called *pollutants* because they establish us in cyclic existence; they are called *outflows* because they flow out of the mind through the six sense sources.[37]

Hindrances

Another group of obscurations explained in both the Pāli and Sanskrit traditions are the five hindrances: (1) sensual desire, (2) malice, (3) lethargy and sleepiness, (4) restlessness and regret, and (5) deluded doubt. They are called *hindrances* because they impede attaining the form- and formless-realm absorptions. These five are nonvirtuous and are found only in desire-realm beings. The five hindrances have been briefly discussed above in other classifications of defilements and will be explained in more depth when the method to gain serenity is presented.

In the above classifications of defilements, some defilements are found in multiple categories, others are present only once. Various forms of attachment, anger, and ignorance appear repeatedly, sometimes given different names or slightly different definitions. However, they still point to three strong tendencies of our minds that it behooves us to pay attention to.

When studying the defilements and observing how they function in our minds and the influence they have on our lives, it is important to remember that they are not embedded in the nature of our minds. Just as clouds in the sky obscure the clear nature of the sky but are not part of it, defilements obscure the clear light nature of the mind but are not embedded in that pure nature. Like the clouds, defilements can be removed. But unlike clouds, which can always reappear, when defilements are thoroughly cleansed from the mind, they can never return and the pure sky-like nature of the mind radiates forever unobscured.

4 | Afflictions, Their Arising, and Their Antidotes

As we've seen, when we delve into the categories and definitions of defilements according to various Buddhist traditions and tenet schools, the discussion becomes lengthy and complex. On the other hand, when we focus on the questions "What motivates me to act in ways that harm myself and others? What keeps me and others bound in cyclic existence?" the answer is succinct—afflictions rooted in ignorance. In this chapter we will learn more about how the afflictions operate.

Eighty-Four Thousand Afflictions

We may wonder why certain disturbing emotions—such as fear, anxiety, frustration, insecurity, and depression—are not mentioned in the classifications of defilements, although they disturb our minds and interfere with Dharma practice. It could be that because of the structure of contemporary society and world events, these afflictions have become more pronounced. However, they did not go unnoticed by the Buddha, who spoke of eighty-four thousand afflictions. The groups in the previous chapter contain the most prominent afflictions that keep us revolving in cyclic existence. These other afflictions are among the eighty-four thousand and are subtypes of the prominent ones.

For example, fear, insecurity, and anxiety are related to attachment. Based on distorted conceptions that see what is impermanent as permanent and what is unsatisfactory in nature as happiness, we become attached to certain people or things. Fear arises over the possibility of being separated from the people, situations, and things we are attached to. Anxiety and insecurity manifest when we consider unknown future events, such as possibly losing our job, our marriage dissolving, or receiving an unwanted medical diagnosis. Although these events have not happened yet and may never happen, distorted conceptions and afflictions run rampant in our minds, making us miserable.

Another type of anxiety is related to doubt, but unlike the doubt that is a root affliction, this doubt does not contemplate issues important to spiritual practice. Rather, we agonize over making decisions, wishing we could follow all the options simultaneously before choosing the best one. Plagued by doubt, we avoid making a decision and spin with anxiety. This, too, is related to attachment: our world has become narrowly focused on our own happiness and what benefits ourselves and the people we cherish. Our problem is that we don't know what will bring us the most happiness.

Depression that is not based on chemical activity in the brain or traumatic brain injury seems to be related to attachment. We want events to happen in ways that accord with our expectations and dreams, and we become despondent when they do not. That can lead to anger at ourselves and self-recrimination, both of which can contribute to depression.

Emotions such as depression, rage, and anxiety that manifests as hypervigilance may have multiple contributing factors—physical, sexual, or emotional abuse; combat trauma; poverty; prejudice and oppression; and irregularities in brain chemistry or traumatic brain injury, to name a few—so healing may require a multipronged approach. Within this, the Buddhist approach of analyzing the thoughts, mental habits, and so forth that lie behind disturbing emotions can be very helpful. If we attribute our problems only to external factors, healing can be difficult because we cannot undo past experiences. They happened and are over. Our present problems stem from unbeneficial ways of interpreting and responding to past events and present memories of them. By understanding the mistaken way in which disturbing emotions function and learning more realistic and beneficial ways of regarding situations, we can subdue these disturbing emotions and prevent the damaging behavior they can provoke.

When hearing our emotions analyzed in the above manner, we may feel piqued, thinking that the seriousness of our emotions is not being respected. As individuals we are very attached to what we term *my* emotions. Based on adhering to them as *mine*, we consider our emotions to be extremely serious, so much so that we feel hurt if others aren't as concerned with them as we are. While our emotions are important, it may not be for the reason we think. These emotions motivate our physical, verbal, and mental actions that not only affect us spiritually but also influence others around us. Our actions also influence our future lives. For these reasons, learning how to manage them effectively is important.

Some people are attached to predictability, even though saṃsāra is unpredictable in that previously created karma is continuously ripening. They wish to control other people and situations and become frustrated when they cannot. However, we cannot make others do what we think is best, nor can we control the aging of our bodies or make the body immune to illness or injury. Our wish to control and the belief that we should be able to is associated with the view of a personal identity, especially the form that grasps at a self-sufficient substantially existent person. Tsongkhapa uses the analogy of a master and servant to illustrate this grasping: the self is like a master who controls and gives orders, and the body and mind, like servants, should obey. However, such a self-sufficient substantially existent person does not exist, so thinking that we should be able to control everything around us is definitely unrealistic.

When we look from a global perspective, it is evident that all these defilements are in one way or another dependent on the obscuring and misleading force of ignorance and view of a personal identity. These are the root of saṃsāra. Seeing their disadvantages, we become determined to cultivate the wisdom that will eradicate them. Knowing that all ordinary beings suffer from them, our hearts open in compassion for ourselves and others.

REFLECTION

1. When afflictions that are not specifically named in the previous chapter arise in your mind, name them and observe how they function. See which of the root afflictions they are most closely related to.
2. Identify the distorted conceptions that lie behind that emotion.
3. Observe the other afflictions that arise either before or after it.
4. Question whether these afflictive emotions serve to promote your own

and others' well-being. Think of which Dharma teachings you could contemplate that would help counteract these afflictive emotions.

The Order in Which Afflictions Arise

The way the order in which afflictions arise is presented depends on whether ignorance and view of a personal identity are regarded as separate. Seeing them as different mental factors, the two *Knowledges* say that ignorance is mental obscuration that cannot see things clearly. On the basis of ignorance, view of a personal identity mistakenly believes the aggregates to be a self-sufficient substantially existent person. All other afflictions follow from this. This is analogous to not being able to see clearly in a dark room (ignorance) and mistaking a rope to be a snake (view of a personal identity). Attachment, anger, and other afflictions swiftly follow. Vasubandhu lays out their sequential development in the *Treasury of Knowledge*: ignorance, doubt, wrong views, view of a personal identity, view of extremes, view of rules and practices, view holding wrong views as supreme, arrogance, attachment, hatred.

> Initially from *ignorance* regarding the meaning of the [four] truths, *doubt* arises, wondering whether there is or is not duḥkha.
>
> From that, by relying on an inferior spiritual friend, one engages in erroneous teachings and learning, which produce the *wrong view* that duḥkha does not exist.
>
> From that arises the *view of a personal identity* that grasps the aggregates as I and mine.
>
> From that arises the *view of extremes* that grasps the permanence or annihilation of the aggregates [that is, that the I exists as an eternal, immutable soul or that it ceases to exist after death].
>
> From that arises the *view of rules and practices* that grasps the belief that there is purification from holding those extreme [views].
>
> From that arises the *view holding wrong views as supreme*,

> because what was believed to provide purification [is held as a supreme view].
>
> From that arise *arrogance* and *attachment* for one's own views and *hatred* that despises the views of others.

Sages such as Dharmakīrti and Candrakīrti and their followers, who assert that view of a personal identity is ignorance, present another sequence as outlined by Dharmakīrti in his *Commentary on Reliable Cognition* (LC 1:300).

> Once there is a self, there is an idea of an other.
> Discriminating self and other, attachment and animosity arise.
> All of the faults come about
> in association with these.

Tsongkhapa expands on this (LC 1:300):

> When the *view of a personal identity* [which is *ignorance*] apprehends the self, discrimination arises between self and other.
>
> Once you have made that distinction, you become *attached* to what is associated with yourself and *hostile* toward that which pertains to others.
>
> As you observe the self, your mind becomes inflated [with *arrogance*].
>
> You develop a belief that this very self is either eternal or subject to annihilation [*view of extremes*].
>
> You come to believe in the supremacy of a view of the self and the like [*view holding wrong views as supreme*], and you also come to believe in the supremacy of the detrimental practices associated with such views [*view of rules and practices*]. Similarly, you develop the *wrong view* that denies the existence of things such as the Teacher [Buddha], who taught selflessness and that which he taught—karma and its effects, the truths of the āryas, the Three Jewels, and so forth; or else you become *doubtful* as to whether such things exist or are real.

It is interesting to note that the Vaibhāṣika version of Vasubandhu places doubt and the various afflictive views before the disturbing emotions of attachment, anger, and arrogance, whereas in Dharmakīrti's version the disturbing emotions arise before the afflictive views and doubt.

Factors Causing Afflictions to Arise

Some people assert that afflictions are an inherent part of human nature and, as such, are hardwired in our nervous system or genes. Although we may be able to modify their effects, we can never be free of them. From a Buddhist viewpoint, this is a narrow view of human potential that offers little hope for the improvement of humanity. As described in volumes 1 and 2 of the Library of Wisdom and Compassion, the Buddhist view is that although coarse levels of consciousness and the brain are interdependent, they are not the same nature. Thus the subtlest minds are not bound by the physical limitations of our bodies and brains. In addition, as conscious phenomena, afflictions can be eliminated from the mindstream by applying their counterforces. They are not our inherent nature and liberation from afflictions is possible, as demonstrated by many highly realized practitioners throughout history.

The arising of afflictions in ordinary beings is to some extent related to our bodies. When we are physically weak or deprived of physical necessities, we are more susceptible to anger. We are more inclined toward attachment, especially sexual desire, when we are healthy and our bodies are comfortable. When we get angry, when we are hungry, or when we are depressed as a result of chemical imbalance in the brain, two factors are at work: one is our present physical situation, the other is the seed of afflictions in our mindstreams. Some people believe that scientists may one day be able to stop all disturbing emotions through medicines that regulate body chemistry and techniques that alter genetic makeup. However, as long as the seeds of afflictions are still present, afflictions will arise when suitable conditions come together. Afflictions can only be fully overcome through spiritual practice.

What are the principal factors that cause manifest afflictions to arise in our minds? Six conditions or a combination of them play a role.

(1) The *seeds of afflictions* are a prominent cause. Because they remain on our mindstreams and go from one life to the next, we are not free from

afflictions. An external or internal factor can stimulate these seeds to give rise to manifest afflictions.

(2) *Contact with certain objects* can stimulate afflictions to erupt. Attachment arises when good food or an attractive person is in front of us; anger springs up when we are around people who disagree with our ideas or challenge our opinions.

(3) *Detrimental influences* such as bad friends have a strong influence on our way of thinking and behaving. Adults recognize the strong influence of peer pressure on children, but they seldom take stock of the extent to which their own emotions and behavior are affected by the wish to be part of a group and the desire not to be seen as strange or different from others. Seeking the approval or praise of people we care about or respect can make us compromise our ethical values if we are not mindful. If a close friend is upset with someone, we tend to get angry at that person as well. If a family member is strongly attached to a particular political view, our attachment—or anger—toward it will easily arise.

(4) *Verbal stimuli*—news, books, TV, Internet, radio, magazines, films, social media, and so forth—impact our thoughts and emotions. In recent years the media has become a prominent conditioning force in our lives as we are exposed to hundreds, if not thousands, of advertisements each day. The daily news influences our thoughts and can easily provoke strong emotions. With the constant display of sexual images and violent pictures that we are exposed to from childhood, it is no wonder that attachment and hostility flare up so easily and frequently that we stop noticing them.

(5) *Habitual ways of thinking and habitual emotions* self-replicate in the future. The more familiar we are with certain afflictions and wrong views, the more we see them as true and reinforce them. Someone accustomed to concealing his or her faults and misdeeds will continue this mindset, making it more difficult to change. Resentment and belligerence arise easily in someone who is familiar with anger and has never applied counterforces to it. For this reason, it's advisable to learn and apply antidotes to our habitual afflictions and behaviors, because they are the most troublesome.

(6) *Distorted attention* (*ayoniśo manaskāra*) or distorted conceptions misinterpret events, superimpose attractive and unattractive qualities onto people and objects, and project motivations and meanings on other people's words and activities. This establishes the perfect setting for afflictions that

haven't arisen to arise and for those that have arisen to increase. However, when we train our minds to observe sense objects with mindfulness and wisdom, afflictions that haven't arisen do not arise, and the ones that have arisen subside.

For example, based on seeing a car as inherently existent, we see its marvelous qualities as existing in the car itself. In fact, distorted attention has exaggerated the car's good qualities and ignored its faults, making the car appear 100 percent desirable in our eyes. Our attachment for it explodes and we *must* buy it. By pausing to do some analysis, we will begin to see that distorted attention is fabricating the car's qualities and desirability and our life will be fine without buying that car.

The surroundings in which we live may contain many of the objects, detrimental social influences, and verbal stimuli that trigger our afflictions. For this reason, the great masters advise avoiding environments that trigger our afflictions. This is done not because those objects or people are bad, but because our afflictions are as yet uncontrolled. Living in an environment where distractions and commotion are minimal enables us to focus on developing counterforces to afflictions. Once these are strong, our external surroundings will not affect us as much.

REFLECTION

1. What kind of media are you exposed to throughout your day—Internet, TV, news, movies, smartphone, computer, advertising, billboards, magazines, and so forth.
2. How does each of these influence your thoughts and the decisions you make? Do they have a deleterious effect? For example, how do the sex and violence in movies influence your mind? Do you compare your body with the pictures in magazines and other media and feel that you're not attractive? Does watching people fighting in movies rev up your adrenaline and provoke hostility in your mind?
3. What would a healthy relationship with the media look like in your life? What do you need to do to bring that about?

Feelings That Accompany Afflictions

Previously we discussed one way in which feelings and afflictions are related: polluted feelings easily provoke afflictions to arise; when we are unhappy, anger and malice may soon follow. Here feelings are causes for afflictions. For this reason, we are advised to maintain a happy mind. In the second way, they are simultaneous—that is, feelings accompany afflictive mental states. Attachment in the desire realm is accompanied by pleasant feeling; anger and animosity are accompanied by unpleasant feeling. This may be one reason why we are less willing to apply the antidotes to attachment. Any of the three feelings—pleasant, unpleasant, or neutral—may accompany ignorance.

Mental happiness or unhappiness may accompany wrong views. If someone believes nonvirtuous actions have no result, he is happy; but if he thinks virtuous actions bring no result, he is unhappy. Mental unhappiness accompanies doubt; being indecisive is unpleasant. A happy feeling accompanies arrogance and the other four afflictive views. However, if the mind of a person in the desire realm is unclear, all ten root afflictions are accompanied by a neutral feeling.

The Pāli Abhidhamma says that all consciousnesses rooted in anger are accompanied by mental unhappiness. That means that whenever our minds are unhappy, anger is present even at a subtle level, and this mental state is nonvirtuous.

To the contrary, virtuous mental states are accompanied by either a happy feeling or equanimity. Consciously steering our thoughts so that they are constructive brings not only happiness or equanimity but also creates virtuous karma. When we act with genuine generosity or ethical restraint, our mind is happy here and now and we create the cause for happiness in the future. Of course when training in these practices we may not be continually happy because afflictions sometimes interfere, but as we continue to practice, afflictions will wane and virtue and joy will increase.

Of the auxiliary afflictions and variable mental factors that become nonvirtuous, regret, jealousy, belligerence, harmfulness, resentment, and spite are accompanied by mental unhappiness. Miserliness, being an aspect of attachment, is accompanied by a pleasant feeling. Either mental happiness or unhappiness may accompany deceit, pretension, concealment, and sleep because when those four mental factors do not accomplish the purpose that is their object, the mind becomes unhappy.

Haughtiness is usually accompanied by happiness, although above the third dhyāna (P. *jhāna*), neutral feeling is present. Lack of integrity, inconsideration for others, lethargy, and restlessness may be accompanied by any of the five feelings—physical and mental happiness, physical and mental unhappiness, and neutral feeling. Neutral feeling may accompany any of the afflictions.

There is no physical or mental unhappiness in the form and formless realms, and their afflictions are ethically neutral because they are weak. Of the dhyānas, the first three are accompanied by the feeling of bliss (a type of happy feeling) and the fourth by a neutral feeling. Formless realm absorptions are accompanied by only neutral feeling.

REFLECTION

1. Practice identifying the various virtuous and nonvirtuous mental factors as they arise in your mind.
2. Observe the feeling that accompanies each one.
3. How does the feeling of happiness that arises with attachment to sensual objects differ from the happiness that accompanies generosity or genuine affection?

The Ethical Dimension of Afflictions

Not all afflictions are nonvirtuous; by themselves, ignorance, view of a personal identity, and view of extremes are neutral. They are not nonvirtuous because by themselves they lack the capacity to produce pain. In addition, these three do not always give rise to nonvirtuous mental states.[38]

The *Treasury of Knowledge* speaks of mixed and unmixed ignorance. *Mixed ignorance* assists and accompanies the other five root afflictions and shares five similarities with them: they depend on the same cognitive faculty, have the same object, are generated in the same aspect, occur at the same time, and have the same entity.[39] Ignorance shares the same primary consciousness with all of the root and auxiliary afflictions. An example is the ignorance that shares a primary consciousness with attachment. This ignorance, as well as the primary consciousness and other mental factors accompanying it, become nonvirtuous by the power of attachment being nonvirtuous.

Unmixed ignorance doesn't share five similarities with any of the nonvirtuous afflictions and is ethically neutral. Examples of unmixed ignorance are the ignorance accompanying the view of a personal identity and the view of extremes, and the ignorance mistaking a pen for a stick.

The ignorance that is the first of the twelve links of dependent origination is unmixed ignorance. When it gives rise to anger, greed, or any other nonvirtuous mental factors, this new mental state is no longer the first link. This new mental state is accompanied by ignorance and is nonvirtuous due to the power of the other affliction that accompanies it. It leads to a nonvirtuous formative action that is the actual second link.

All afflictions of the desire realm are nonvirtuous, except unmixed ignorance, view of a personal identity, and view of extremes, which are neutral. All afflictions of the upper realms—the form and formless realms—are neutral. A degree of intensity is needed for an affliction to be nonvirtuous. Since the afflictions of beings in the upper realms are refined, they lack the intensity required to create nonvirtuous karma that ripens into painful experiences.

To apply this to the Prāsaṅgika view, the first-link ignorance that precedes a virtuous formative karma such as generosity is unmixed ignorance that grasps the agent, object, and action as inherently existent. It is ethically neutral. This ignorance gives rise to a virtuous mental state, such as compassion, that motivates the constructive karma of generosity, which is the second link. During the time of giving the gift, grasping inherent existence may continue, or we may simply apprehend ourselves, the offering, and the recipient without grasping them as either inherently existent or non-inherently existent. In the former case, the mental state grasping inherent existence is neutral and is a different mental state than the one that is generous, which is virtuous. Although the two mental states are closely related in time, they do not occur simultaneously.

Counterforces to the Afflictions

Whether we follow a religion or not, we can see that afflictions interfere with our personal happiness as well as the well-being of society in general. Most harmful events among individuals, groups, or nations are rooted in ignorance and motivated by hatred, greed, arrogance, jealousy, and so forth. These afflictions are the causes of killing, robbery, sexual abuse, political and financial scandals, prejudice, injustice, and inequality. Problems in society—including in our institutional structures—are rooted in people's afflictive mental states. Although this is the case, when we face personal or societal problems, we seldom look in our minds for the source of the problem. It is time that we do.

The law of the land punishes people engaged in harmful actions in an effort to stop such behavior. Although punishment may make someone so uncomfortable or fearful that they temporarily stop a certain behavior, it does not bring about lasting change. That comes only from changing our mental attitude. Unless the deeper source of harmful activities is eliminated, they will continue in one form or another. We need to identify the source of problems—which lies in the unsubdued mind—and employ preventative and remedial measures to tame our minds. This involves learning about the faults of afflictions and techniques to counteract them, applying these to our own minds, and sharing them with others. This can be done without using Buddhist vocabulary or religious concepts; it is common sense.

The first step in counteracting the afflictions is to notice when they manifest in our minds. While we may believe that we know ourselves well, our thoughts and emotions often go unnoticed. One factor contributing to this is the lack of mindfulness and introspective awareness—we neglect to focus our minds on what is beneficial and to monitor our minds' activities with wisdom. Sometimes we are distracted by sense objects and do not pay attention to our inner thoughts and emotions. Some people grew up in families where emotions and thoughts were not labeled or discussed, so they did not learn the vocabulary necessary to discuss the workings of their minds.

Here are some tips to help you identify thoughts and afflictions. First check in with your body; our physical sensations often tell us a lot about what is happening in our minds. When our hearts are racing, our faces flush, and our stomachs tight, chances are anger—which is often based on fear—is present. When our palms are sweaty and our breaths short, we are usually agitated or nervous.

Also check in with the mood in your mind. When thoughts about desirable objects are swirling in your mind, attachment is manifest. When you can't stand that someone else is better than you in a certain activity, that is jealousy. When you don't feel like doing anything but lounge around, that is the laziness of procrastination. When you put yourself down, that is the laziness of discouragement.

Also observe your behavior patterns; they can tell you if an affliction has arisen in your mind. If you find yourself going to the refrigerator repeatedly even though you aren't hungry, what affliction is present in your mind? If you continually check social media, what affliction is propelling this action? What are you really seeking when you engage in that behavior?

The next step is to differentiate constructive and neutral thoughts from afflictions. Some virtuous states of mind have "near enemies"—afflictions that are similar to them. Love and attachment are easily confused: both want another person to be happy. Love freely extends goodwill broadly to many people whereas attachment focuses on a small group of people and has expectations and strings attached. Righteous anger can be confused with compassion because they both seek to eliminate injustice and others' suffering. However, compassion seeks the best outcome for all those concerned in a conflict whereas righteous anger wants to harm those whom we see as perpetrating harm.

Sometimes we must tease apart different facets of a mental state to identify an affliction. For example, a friend deliberately runs a red light when there are no extenuating circumstances. Some people become angry at the driver—the agent who did the action. Other people disagree with the action—heedlessly endangering others. The first is anger, the second is not. The more we can separate the person from his action, the more we can avoid anger at the person. This change in attitude enables us to have a reasonable discussion with him about the possible effects of running a red light.

Then reflect on the disadvantages of whatever affliction is plaguing you. That will give you determination to apply its counterforce.

When working to subdue our afflictions, it is best to choose the one that causes the biggest problems for us. Beginners in meditation often recognize that they have attachment to food, but that may not be the affliction that is most problematic for them. Anger may be a bigger problem because it interferes with our relationships at work and at home and fuels destructive behavior. Possessiveness regarding other people, lusting for sexual pleasure, or greed for money or social status may cause more difficulties in our lives and prompt more destructive karma than attachment to food. On the other hand, if you are overweight and in poor health and your doctor advises you to eat more healthily, attachment to food may be the affliction to work with first. If you work on the most problematic affliction at the outset of your practice, you'll see the positive effects Dharma practice has on your life.

One of the connotations of the word *dharma* is to hold back or to prevent. In the case of the Buddhadharma, if we properly practice, it holds us back from saṃsāric duḥkha by subduing or destroying afflictions. The Dharma does this by providing the antidotes to these harmful mental factors. Everything taught in this book is meant to be a counterforce to the afflictions, their seeds, and latencies.

There are two types of counterforces. One is the all-encompassing counterforce that counteracts all afflictions. The other consists of counterforces that are specific to each affliction. The wisdom realizing emptiness is the all-encompassing counterforce that eradicates all afflictions. It directly opposes the ignorance grasping inherent existence, which is the root of afflictions. While ignorance grasps all phenomena, including the I, to exist inherently, the wisdom directly realizing emptiness apprehends the emptiness of inherent existence of all persons and phenomena. Because ignorance and wisdom are diametrically opposed in the way they apprehend phenomena and because ignorance is an erroneous consciousness, wisdom can overcome ignorance. When ignorance is uprooted, all the afflictions that depend on it also cease.

Other counterforces do not have the ability to eliminate ignorance but are applied to individual afflictions. Since cultivating the wisdom realizing emptiness requires much time, we must learn and apply these more limited antidotes in the meantime to prevent our afflictions from getting out of hand. Some antidotes to cultivate:

- To counteract attachment, craving, clinging, and greed, reflect on the impermanence of whatever person or object you are attached to. Contemplating the unattractive aspects of the person or object also works well.

- When you crave for existence in saṃsāra, contemplate the disadvantages of saṃsāra. This powerful antidote will redirect our aspiration to liberation.
- To pacify anger and vengeance, cultivate fortitude.
- To remedy hatred, hostility, resentment, and so forth, meditate on loving-kindness.
- To counteract conceit, contemplate the detailed divisions of phenomena, such as the eighteen elements, the twelve sources, and the twelve links of dependent origination. Seeing the enormity of what there is to understand, self-importance is deflated. In addition, by examining all the components of the self, attachment to a real self will diminish.
- To counteract arrogance, reflect on the kindness of others. Seeing that our abilities, talents, and knowledge are due to the kindness of others deflates puffed-up pride.
- To reverse jealousy, rejoice at others' happiness, good qualities, good opportunities, and merit.
- To remedy anxiety and deluded doubt, observe the breath. Focus your attention on the gentle flow of your breath without allowing the mind to spin with fabricated, self-centered stories.
- When you are confused and cannot discern virtue from nonvirtue or what to practice from what to abandon on the path, study the sūtras and scriptures. They will provide excellent guidance.
- To lessen disturbing emotions in general, remember that they are not you; they are not who you are and are not embedded in the nature of your mind.

At the initial stages of practice, lessening our afflictions is difficult. They seem to arise out of nowhere because we are so habituated to them. Our counterforces are weak, and time and continuous effort are needed to strengthen the antidotes and to develop positive qualities. Being patient with ourselves and going ahead with a determined, optimistic attitude are important to train our minds in new mental habits.

The above counterforces are temporarily effective for the specific affliction they counteract. To gain proficiency in them we must practice them regularly, especially when we are not in the heat of an affliction. Having a regular daily meditation practice, where you can imagine applying these techniques to situations you may encounter or have already encountered, is very effective in this regard.

The antidotes must be applied skillfully so that we don't go too far in the other direction. For example, the antidote to lust is reflecting on the foulness of the body. However, if done unskillfully, this could lead to hating our bodies or disparaging the person whose body we are attracted to. Similarly, if cultivated unskillfully, loving-kindness could lead to attachment.

While using these antidotes to temporarily reduce the force of coarse afflictions, we should also reflect on emptiness to cultivate the wisdom that will eliminate all afflictions forever. By combining single-pointed concentration with a correct understanding of emptiness, our wisdom will eventually become strong enough to uproot the afflictions and obscurations from the mind so that they never return.

REFLECTION

1. Which affliction is the strongest and most frequent in your mind?
2. Contemplate its disadvantages in this life and for your spiritual path.
3. What is the temporary antidote to that affliction? Remember situations when that affliction was strong and contemplate its antidote. See if the force of the affliction subsides even a little. When it does, rejoice.

I came across an interesting passage written by the Kadampa master Togme Zangpo that called the view of a personal identity "the spear of the buddhas." This is unusual because afflictions are typically said to lack any redeeming qualities. Here Togme Zangpo described a skillful way of using the view of a personal identity as a weapon to destroy the duḥkha caused by the view of a personal identity. Initially as beginners with strong self-grasping, we think, "*I* want to be free from saṃsāra." Although this aspiration is afflicted by the view of a personal identity, it motivates us to learn, think, and meditate on emptiness, which will eventually destroy the view of a personal identity. Here we see that for some people at a certain point in their practice, grasping at a truly existent self could spur them to practice.

A similar idea is found in a Pāli sūtra. Explaining the Dharma to a bhikṣuṇī, Ānanda said (AN 4.159):

> It has been said, "Bhikkhunī, this body has come into being through craving, yet based on craving, craving can be abandoned." With reference to what was this said? In this case, a monastic hears it said, "They say that a monastic named so-and-so, by the destruction of the pollutants, in this very life enters and dwells in the unpolluted liberation of mind, liberation by wisdom, having realized it for himself by direct knowledge." He thinks, "Oh, when shall I too realize the unpolluted liberation of mind, liberation by wisdom?" Sometime later, based on that craving, he abandons craving. It is on account of this that it was said, "This body has come into being through craving, yet based on craving, craving can be abandoned."

Characterized by this body, which is in the nature of duḥkha, saṃsāra comes about through craving, yet when a monastic hears that another monastic has attained liberation, he craves to attain this too. Motivated by this new craving, he practices well and attains nirvāṇa, the destruction of all craving. In the passage following this, Ānanda says the same regarding arrogance. Here a monastic hears that another monastic has attained nirvāṇa and his pride is wounded because the other monastic attained it first. Arrogance arises in him, and not wanting to be outshone, he is energized to prove that he can attain nirvāṇa as well. This motivation of arrogance instigates him to practice in such a way that all his arrogance is eradicated forever. Some teachers use a similar technique to energize lazy students on the debate ground. These are skillful ways to use afflictions to destroy afflictions.

When we first learn the Dharma, living without attachment seems impossible. We fear relinquishing attachment will turn us into uncaring, self-absorbed individuals. Thankfully, this is not the case. Some examples of how liberated beings respond to real human situations will give us a glimpse of what living with a transformed mind will be like.

Śāriputra, the Buddha's foremost disciple in wisdom, commented to some monastic friends that he wondered if there were anything in the world whose change or loss would cause him sorrow, lamentation, pain, or despair. Examining himself, he did not see anything that would destabilize his emotional balance. Ānanda, the Buddha's attendant, then asked him, "What would happen if our Teacher, the Buddha, were to undergo change and pass away? Wouldn't that cause you pain?" Śāriputra responded with all sincerity (SN 21.2):

> Friend, even if the Teacher himself were to undergo change and alteration, still sorrow, lamentation, pain, displeasure, and despair would not arise in me. However, it would occur to me, "The Teacher, so influential, so powerful and mighty, has passed away. If the Blessed One had lived for a long time, that would have been for the welfare and happiness of the multitude, out of compassion for the world, for the good, welfare, and happiness of devas and humans."

Stunned with admiration, Ānanda responded that Śāriputra's emotional balance and compassion even at the time of losing the most important person in his life were due to the depth of his Dharma practice:

> It must be because I-making, mine-making, and the underlying tendency to arrogance have been thoroughly uprooted in the Venerable Sāriputta for a long time that even if the Teacher himself were to undergo change and alteration, still sorrow, lamentation, pain, displeasure, and despair would not arise in him.

Śāriputra's equanimity in the face of his own personal loss was not due to repressing his emotions. The attainment of arhatship did not make him a cold person. He was certainly concerned and deeply moved by the prospect of the Buddha's passing, but it was not out of self-interest, for he had forsaken all grasping to I and mine as well as relinquished the deeply rooted conceit thinking, "*I* exist." He was moved because he saw the benefit of the Buddha's presence in the world and the loss of his passing for all beings who need the Dharma. His sorrow was for others, not himself.

Interestingly, when Śāriputra heard that the Buddha would soon attain parinirvāṇa, he told the Tathāgata that he could not bear to witness the event and chose to attain parinirvāṇa himself before the Buddha.

Afflictions, Our Real Enemy

When we face difficulties in life, we tend to attribute their causes to external factors: a friend's behavior, our employer's speech, governmental policies, and so forth. The Buddha questioned our assumption that the chief cause of our problems lies outside of ourselves; he pointed us back to our own minds, asking us to examine our thoughts and emotions to see how they create both internal unhappiness as well as disharmony in our relationships and in society. The disadvantages of distorted conceptions and disturbing emotions extend beyond this lifetime, adversely influencing all our lives. Śāntideva likened afflictions to vicious enemies whom, in our confusion, we treat as friends (BCA 4.28–30, 32–34).

> Enemies such as craving and hatred
> are without arms, legs, and so on.
> They are neither courageous nor wise.
> How is it that they have enslaved me?
>
> Dwelling in my mind, they ruin me;
> at their pleasure, they cause me harm.
> And yet I patiently endure them and do not get angry
> at my tolerance with this shameful and improper situation.
>
> If all devas and humans were my enemies,
> even they would be unable to bring me to the fire of Avīci Hell.
> When encountered, it consumes even the ashes of Mount Meru.
> Afflictions, the mighty enemies, instantly throw me there.
>
> All other enemies are incapable
> of remaining for such a length of time
> as can my afflictions, the enduring enemy
> that has neither beginning nor end [if left unopposed].

While in cyclic existence, how can I be joyful and unafraid
if, in my heart, I readily prepare a place
for this incessant enemy of long duration,
the sole cause for the increase of all that harms me?

And how shall I ever have happiness
if, in a net of attachment within my mind,
there dwell the guardians of the prison of cyclic existence,
these afflictions that are my butchers and tormentors in hell?

The afflictions don't have arms and legs; they cannot assault our bodies. Yet the harm they inflict on us is far worse than any external assailant or murderer. The worst thing other sentient beings can do is to take our lives, which indeed is horrible. But they cannot propel us into an unfortunate rebirth the way the afflictions can by motivating us to act nonvirtuously and to create the karma that propels us into rebirths of intense suffering.

Furthermore, harmful sentient beings will eventually die, while the afflictions have resided in our minds beginninglessly and will not depart of their own accord. They may even grow stronger. Seen this way, our patient acceptance of afflictions sabotages our own happiness. We will never have happiness as long as this enemy dwells cozily in our minds, constantly inflicting pain on us. We should be totally fed up with this situation and fight back. Śāntideva continues (BCA 4.39, 44, 46–48):

If even scars inflicted by meaningless enemies
are worn upon the body like ornaments,
then why is suffering a cause of harm to me
while impeccably striving to fulfill the great purpose?

It would be better for me to be burned,
to have my head cut off and be killed,
rather than ever bowing down
to those ever-present disturbing conceptions.

Deluded afflictions! When overcome by the eye of wisdom
and dispelled from my mind, where will you go?

Where will you dwell to be able to injure me again later?
Weak-minded, I have been reduced to making no effort.

If these afflictions do not exist within the objects, the cognitive faculties, between the two or elsewhere,
then where do they exist and how do they harm the world?
They are like an illusion—thus I should dispel the fear within my heart and strive resolutely for wisdom.
For no real reason, why should I suffer so much in hell?

Therefore, having thought about this well,
I should try to put these precepts into practice just as they have been explained.
If the doctor's instructions are ignored,
how will a patient in need of a cure be healed by the medicine?

Proud of their combat, warriors wear their battle scars like medals. While combating this most insidious enemy, our afflictions, we must not shirk from any harm that may come about. We will never bow down to this enemy or accept defeat. For the benefit of all sentient beings, we will generate the wisdom realizing emptiness that will obliterate the afflictions such that they can never return.

Afflictions do not exist in external objects or in our cognitive faculties. Inherently existent afflictions are impossible to find; they are like illusions that lack a real essence and can be overcome. Therefore we must put the Buddha's teachings into practice, for they are the medicine that will heal all the injuries of cyclic existence.

REFLECTION

1. Read and contemplate the above verses from *Engaging in the Bodhisattvas' Deeds* one by one, speaking to yourself just as Śāntideva speaks to himself.
2. Remember the afflictions are not who you are; they are not in the very nature of your mind and can be eliminated.

3. Cultivate antipathy toward the afflictions and generate strong determination to become familiar with the antidotes to them through having a daily Dharma practice.

Compassion acts like preventative medicine for many of our afflictions. The greater our compassion, the more peace we will experience. My personal experience is that meditating on the suffering of sentient beings and generating compassion for them helps me to develop inner strength. When inner strength and self-confidence increase, fear and doubt diminish. That makes us naturally more open to others. Others then reciprocate by being friendly, and this nourishes better communication and more positive interactions with them.

To the contrary, if we are full of partiality, fear, hatred, and doubt, the door to our heart is closed, and everyone we encounter appears suspicious to us. The sad thing is that we then believe that others are just as suspicious of us as we are of them. That creates distance between us, and this spiral fosters loneliness and frustration.

All of us, but especially the younger generation, has the responsibility to make sure that the world is a peaceful place for everyone. This can become reality if we all make an effort to cultivate compassion. Our educational system should focus not only on training the intellect but also on training the heart. Let's help future generations learn to be good citizens of the planet by modeling compassion and tolerance ourselves.

5 Afflictions and Karma, Their Seeds and Latencies

TRUE ORIGINS of duḥkha are those phenomena that give rise to cyclic existence and are in the nature of duḥkha. True origins consist of afflictions—which are rooted in ignorance—and polluted karma—actions created under the influence of ignorance that produce the three types of duḥkha. Of afflictions and karma, afflictions are chief because they give rise to karma and also act as conditions for karma to ripen. Without the presence of afflictions, polluted karma cannot be created, and even if seeds of previously created karma remain in our mindstreams, they cannot ripen into duḥkha without the presence of afflictions.

In the context of the twelve links of dependent origination that describe how we cycle in saṃsāra, karma refers to volitional actions done under the force of afflictions that bring rebirth in cyclic existence. This is a more specific meaning of karma than used in volume 2, where we spoke of many kinds of actions, not all of which propel rebirth. To attain liberation—the stoppage of uncontrolled rebirth in saṃsāra—we need to eliminate the afflictive obscurations that cause it. These are ignorance, all the other afflictions that it produces, and the seeds of these afflictions.[40]

In this chapter we will investigate different types of afflictions and karma: acquired and innate afflictions, coarse and subtle afflictions, underlying and manifest afflictions, seeds and latencies of afflictions, seeds of karma, and having-ceased. Knowing these expands our understanding of the workings of our minds, the evolution of saṃsāra, and the path to liberation.

Acquired and Innate Afflictions

Afflictions are of two kinds: innate and acquired. *Innate afflictions* have been with our mindstreams since beginningless time. We did not learn them from anyone and they continue from one rebirth to the next. Innate afflictions are present in babies, animals, insects, and beings born in other saṃsāric realms. At no time in our wandering in saṃsāra have we been free from them.

Acquired afflictions are those learned in this lifetime through adopting the flawed reasoning of mistaken philosophies and ideologies. For example, we may study a philosophy that asserts a permanent soul or an inherently existent creator and come to believe the arguments presented for their existence. Innate and acquired self-grasping ignorance do not differ in terms of how they grasp the object—both grasp it as inherently existent. They differ in that innate self-grasping ignorance is deeply ingrained and arises frequently and spontaneously. Acquired self-grasping is learned in this life through reflecting on fallacious reasonings. Although innate self-grasping ignorance is the root of cyclic existence, the acquired version is especially insidious because it is based on thinking about how things exist in an incorrect manner and reaching erroneous conclusions. It may cause someone to cling to wrong views and be unreceptive to teachings on emptiness.

Strong clinging to identities of this life—our nationality, religion, ethnicity, race, class, educational level, gender, sexual orientation, and so forth—is an acquired affliction. We learned these identities in this lifetime and were taught to be attached to them. We then think, "I am a this-and-that and you should treat me in such-and-such a way." While the specific identity is acquired, the mind that clings to "I am" is innate.

Acquired afflictions cannot come about without their innate forms. Acquired afflictions abound and cause horrible suffering. For example, innate anger exists in our mindstreams. If someone teaches us false reasons why a particular racial or ethnic group is inferior or violent, we may believe these and have strong prejudice and anger regarding anyone in that group. Holding the belief, "This land is mine because a religious scripture said so" is acquired attachment. Thinking, "Killing the enemies of my people is justified by this political theory or religious belief" is acquired hostility. "My racial or ethnic group is morally superior" is an example of acquired arrogance. Thinking, "The mind is the brain" is an acquired wrong view.

Although these particular manifestations of afflictions were not present in us at birth, they still can be extremely dangerous and harmful. When people are taught by friends, family, or society to adhere to acquired afflictions, wars, oppression, and environmental destruction easily follow.

Sages and tenet schools have differing views regarding when afflictions are abandoned on the path. According to the *Treasury of Knowledge*, all five afflictive views and deluded doubt are abandoned on the path of seeing, while the other four root afflictions—attachment, anger, ignorance, and arrogance—are abandoned on the path of meditation as well.

According to the *Ornament of Clear Realizations* (*Abhisamayālaṃkāra*) and the Prāsaṅgika school, deluded doubt, wrong views, holding wrong views as supreme, and view of rules and practices are abandoned on the path of seeing, whereas the acquired forms of view of a personal identity and view of extremes are abandoned on the path of seeing and their innate forms are abandoned on the path of meditation. The acquired forms of all other afflictions are abandoned on the path of seeing and their innate forms are abandoned on the path of meditation. All afflictions have been eradicated at the time of becoming an arhat or an eighth-ground bodhisattva. Since direct realization of emptiness is needed to eliminate acquired afflictions, we should not underestimate their power to cause harm in this life and to create the causes to experience unfortunate rebirths.

The Pāli tradition does not have an explicit division into acquired and innate afflictions. However, some afflictions are said to be easier to eradicate than others: some are abandoned by seeing while others are abandoned later by meditation.[41] The former are overcome by stream-enterers, the latter by nonreturners and arhats. Since stream-enterers' realization of the unconditioned—nirvāṇa—is not as strong as that of nonreturners and arhats, the fetters they abandon through this first seeing of nirvāṇa—view of a personal identity, deluded doubt, and view of rules and practices—are not as ingrained as the rest of the fetters that are abandoned by meditation on the higher paths.

REFLECTION

1. What is the difference between innate and acquired afflictions?
2. Make examples in your life of acquired afflictions—certain biases, prejudices, fears, resentments, or jealousies—that you learned from faulty philosophies or from listening to others who have those ideas.
3. Consider the many reasons why those beliefs are false. Try to view those people or places from a different perspective so that your mind can be clearer and free from anxiety, bias, and incorrect conceptions.

Coarse and Subtle Afflictions

Coarse and subtle afflictions are spoken of primarily in the Prāsaṅgika school because its definitions of ignorance and the object of negation when meditating on selflessness are unique. Lower Buddhist schools say that the ignorance that is the root of saṃsāra grasps a self-sufficient substantially existent person, whereas Prāsaṅgikas assert it grasps inherent existence. For them, grasping a self-sufficient substantially existent person is a coarse affliction, as are the anger, attachment, and other afflictions based on it, whereas the ignorance grasping inherent existence as well as the afflictions based on it are subtle afflictions. Because the lower schools accept the inherent existence of persons and phenomena, they do not negate the afflictions based on it.

Most of the afflictions ordinary beings experience on a daily basis are coarse ones. There is nothing subtle about a person who is exploding with anger or one overwhelmed by greed. It is possible to notice the subtle afflictions only after realizing the lack of a self-sufficient substantially existent person.

Seeds, Latencies, and Having-Ceased

In contemplating the Buddha's teachings, ancient Indian sages discussed many topics. One concerned continuity: How does a karmic action created in one life bring a result in another life? How can a mental factor such as anger or compassion be present in our mindstreams one day, fade away, and then manifest again the next day? This is where latencies, seeds, and having-ceased come in.

In his autocommentary to the *Supplement*, Candrakīrti says "that which pollutes the mindstream and also leaves imprints and causes the continuation of something" is called a *latency*. Other English synonyms for *latency* are predisposition, habitual tendency, imprint, and propensity. Of the three types of impermanent phenomena—forms, minds, and abstract composites—seeds and latencies are abstract composites.

In *Illumination of the Thought*, Tsongkhapa said:

> Of the two latencies—one that is a seed and the other that is non-seed—cognitive obscurations are the latter.

We can speak of latencies (*vāsanā*) in two forms: latencies in the form of seeds (*bīja*) and latencies in the form of potencies (*samartha*); the latter are called *non-seed latencies*. When the word *latency* is used in general, it refers to both seed and non-seed latencies. A seed is necessarily a latency, but a latency is not necessarily a seed; it could be a non-seed latency.

For the sake of ease, in English, we'll call non-seed latencies "latencies" to differentiate them from seeds.[42] *Seed* has the connotation of being the cause of something. *Latency* implies retaining the potential or energy of something. Although the mind that gives rise to seeds and latencies may be virtuous or nonvirtuous, seeds and latencies themselves are neutral.

Afflictions and Their Seeds

Afflictions arise in our minds in a manifest and active form—we become angry, jealous, greedy, or lazy—and we act motivated by these manifest afflictions. However, even though we haven't eliminated anger from our mindstreams completely, we aren't always angry. We may be sitting calmly but when someone criticizes us, our anger is triggered and becomes manifest. What connects the prior and later instances of anger? This is the function of the seed of anger. When manifest anger subsides, the seed of anger remains on our mindstreams. The seed provides for the continuity of anger in our mindstreams even when anger itself isn't manifest. The seed of anger is not anger; it is not an affliction, although it is the substantial cause for anger to arise again. Both anger and the seed of anger are afflictive obscurations and are not fully abandoned until we attain liberation or the eighth bodhisattva ground.

We cannot simultaneously experience two manifest mental states that are contradictory—we cannot be angry and loving at exactly the same moment. When we are loving, anger is not manifest in our minds, but we haven't totally eliminated anger from our mindstreams either. The seed of anger remains on our mindstreams when love is manifest, and it connects one instance of anger to the next.

Both innate and acquired afflictions have an aspect that is manifest and an aspect that is a seed. Manifest innate attachment arises in our minds from seeing an attractive object; it is a consciousness, whereas its seed—the potential set on the mindstream from a previous moment of attachment that can produce a future moment of attachment—is an abstract composite, an impermanent phenomenon that is neither form nor consciousness.

Manifest acquired afflictive obscurations are afflictions that are manifest in the mind due to learning incorrect ideas. If we read about a cosmic mind from which our minds originate at birth and dissolve back into at death, and then believe that exists, that wrong view is a manifest acquired affliction. The seed of that is a potential that can produce another moment of this incorrect belief in the future.

The seed of anger is not what psychologists call repressed anger. Having the seed of anger does not mean that there is low-grade anger in our minds all the time. Rather, it simply means that the potential to become angry again exists in our mindstreams, even though we are not angry now.

Similarly self-grasping isn't always manifest in our minds, but its continuity hasn't been eliminated; it is present in the form of a seed. When we encounter certain conditions—for example, someone falsely accuses us of bad behavior—this seed causes self-grasping to arise as a manifest mental state. In the same way, during the white appearance, red increase, black near attainment, and clear light of death of saṃsāric beings, self-grasping is not manifest although it is present as a seed. Because it has not yet been abandoned, self-grasping will reemerge in manifest form in our future lives.

There are also seeds for virtuous consciousness. These enable us to experience manifest faith, wisdom, concentration, and compassion today and again tomorrow, even though they were in seed form while we were asleep.

Reflection on the existence of the seeds of afflictions keeps us humble.

After working hard to subdue a particular affliction, we may think, "That one is taken care of. I don't need to continue working on it." But my (Chodron's) experience is that when we think like that and become a little smug, the affliction will once again surge up strongly when we least expect it. Because seeds of afflictions remain on our mindstream, complacency is ill advised, whereas humility brings the heedfulness necessary to stay on track in our practice.

The Pāli tradition speaks of underlying tendencies as connecting one instance of a root affliction with a later instance. It also explains that fetters and other defilements exist on three levels: (1) As underlying tendencies (P. *anusaya*), they are latent potencies in the mind. (2) As manifest fetters (P. *pariyuṭṭāna*), they actively enslave the mind. (3) As motivating forces (P. *vītikkama*), they motivate nonvirtuous actions of body and speech.

When we ordinary beings are not resentful, the underlying tendency of resentment still exists in our mindstreams. Someone criticizing us triggers this seed or underlying tendency and we become resentful; this is manifest resentment. If we leave our resentment unchecked and neglect to apply an antidote, it will increase and motivate us to say cruel words or plot how to harm someone. This is the motivating level of resentment.

A monk at the Buddha's time believed that fetters existed in a person's continuum only when they were manifest and active. If that were the case, the Buddha replied, then a newborn infant would not have the view of a personal identity because she doesn't even have the notion of a personal identity. But the underlying tendencies to the view of a personal identity are present in her mindstream. Similarly, a newborn does not have the notion of "teachings," yet the underlying tendency to doubt the teachings is in him. Infants and all other beings who have not attained stream-entry have the five lower fetters because they have the underlying tendencies for them. The commentary says that the underlying tendencies and the fetters are not distinct; a defilement is called an underlying tendency in the sense that it has yet to be abandoned and still resides in the mindstream; it is called a fetter in the sense that it binds us to cyclic existence (MN 64).

The higher training in ethical conduct helps us to restrain defilements before they can motivate destructive physical and verbal actions. The higher training in concentration suppresses the manifest level of defilements, although it alone cannot eradicate them because they still exist as underlying tendencies in the mind. Only an ārya's higher training in wisdom can eradicate the underlying tendencies completely.

Latencies of Afflictions

Latencies of afflictions are predispositions, imprints, or tendencies on the mindstream. Subtler than the seeds of afflictions, the latencies of afflictions do not give rise to manifest afflictions. They are cognitive obscurations that are possessed by all sentient beings, including arhats and pure-ground bodhisattvas (bodhisattvas of the eighth, ninth, and tenth grounds who have purified their continuums of afflictive obscurations). The latencies of self-grasping ignorance give rise to the appearance and "perception"[43] of inherent existence. Latencies of ignorance and of afflictions also obscure the mind from directly seeing the two truths simultaneously. The latencies of attachment and other afflictions cause arhats to behave in peculiar ways sometimes: they may spontaneously jump, speak harshly, or have unclear clairvoyance, even though they lack any afflictive motivation. This latency is more like habit. At buddhahood all cognitive obscurations as well as all latencies of afflictions have been eliminated forever, so that a buddha's body, speech, and mind are completely free from impediments and endowed with all excellent qualities.

Karmic Seeds and Latencies and Their Purification

Although the seeds and latencies of afflictions are different things with different functions, the seeds and latencies of karma are the same: they are the legacies of nonvirtuous actions and polluted virtuous actions that have the capacity to give rise to suffering and happiness in saṃsāra. Their fruits are ripening results, causally concordant behavioral and experiential results, and environmental results. Karmic seeds that cause rebirth in saṃsāra are true origins but are not afflictive obscurations. While they are not eliminated at arhatship, these seeds can no longer ripen because craving and clinging, the factors that stimulate their ripening, have been eradicated.

In the context of the ten paths of nonvirtue, the three that are done by mind—covetousness, malice, and wrong views—are afflictions, so when they cease they leave seeds of afflictions on the mind. The mental factor of intention that shares the same primary consciousness with those afflictions is karma, and that intention leaves seeds of destructive karma on the mindstream. The mental paths of virtue—noncovetousness, nonmalice, and correct views, which are not just the absence of covetousness and so forth, but mental factors that are the opposite of them—leave the seeds of those virtuous mental factors when they cease, and the intentions that accompanied them leave seeds of constructive karma.

In the chapter on fortitude in the *Supplement*, Candrakīrti speaks of the great adverse results that arise from one bodhisattva becoming angry at another. These range from the destruction of virtue created over thousands of eons, to suffering experiences, to obstructions preventing advancement to higher paths. Even when neither the angry person nor the person he is angry with are bodhisattvas, anger can destroy the roots of virtue. The *Questions of Upāli Sūtra* (*Upālipariprcchā Sūtra*) speaks of three levels: the roots of virtue being "diminished, thoroughly reduced, and completely consumed." "Diminish" means the increase of roots of great virtue dwindles, but the pleasant results are not destroyed. "Reduced" means that the pleasant results are minimal, and "completely consumed" indicates that the virtuous karma cannot ripen. With the last, the potency of the seed to bring pleasant results is destroyed, not the seed itself. These seeds of virtue are those from the collection of merit—created by generosity, ethical conduct, fortitude, and other compassionate actions. They are not seeds of virtue from the collection of wisdom, which are created by meditating on selflessness and emptiness, and by arranging for texts on these topics to be taught.

The *Ākāśagarbha Sūtra* says that transgressing the root bodhisattva precepts destroys previously created roots of virtue, and Śāntideva's *Compendium of Instructions* warns that spending time with benefactors with the motivation to receive gifts from them, bragging that we possess spiritual attainments that we lack, and abandoning the Dharma by giving incorrect teachings but saying they are the Buddhadharma also destroy our roots of virtue and impede our progress on the path.

The question arises: The *Teachings of Akṣhayamati Sūtra* (*Akṣayamatinirdeśa Sūtra*) says that just as a drop of water that falls in the huge ocean is not consumed until the ocean dries up, so too merit derived from actions motivated by bodhicitta and dedicated for awakening are not exhausted until awakening. If this is so, how can anger destroy this virtue?

The analogy of the drop of water in the ocean indicates that the merit of those actions is not exhausted when its effects arise; that merit will continue to bear fruit until awakening. Nevertheless, these roots of virtue may still be harmed by anger.

In the case of purifying nonvirtue, when we ordinary beings apply the four opponent powers, we impede the ripening of seeds of destructive karma by diminishing, reducing, or completely consuming their potency, as described above. Depending on the strength of the four opponent powers, the potency of the seed may decrease or the coming together of the cooperative conditions for the seed's ripening may be delayed. If purification is strong, the potency of the seeds—their negativity (*pāpa*)—is disabled, although those deactivated seeds remain on the mindstream, like burnt rice seeds that remain in the ground. The seed is there but it cannot bear a result even if suitable conditions occur. Purification by means of the wisdom directly realizing emptiness, which begins with the path of seeing, is the most powerful purification. It thoroughly destroys those seeds of nonvirtue.

Vaibhāṣikas and Sautrāntikas say that it is not possible to purify seeds of destructive karma completely; some result must be experienced. As proof, they recount a sūtra passage attesting that the Buddha experienced pain after stepping on a thorn due to a subtle remaining karmic seed. Similarly, they say that Maudgalyāyana's tragic death in which he was beaten by robbers was due to previous destructive karma, the seeds of which remained on his mindstream even after he attained arhatship. Cittamātrins and Mādhyamikas, however, assert that all seeds of destructive karma can be completely purified so that no suffering ever results from them.

Seeds and latencies are abstract composites; they are neither form nor consciousness. Of the five aggregates that are the basis of designation of a person, they are included in the fourth aggregate, the aggregate of miscellaneous factors. While the actions and afflictions that create seeds and latencies may be virtuous or nonvirtuous, the seeds and latencies themselves are neutral.

Having-Ceased

Most Buddhist schools explain the process by which karma gives rise to its results in terms of karmic seeds: affirmative phenomena that have been placed on the mindstream. They do this because they consider the *having-ceased* (*naṣṭa*) of an action to be a permanent phenomenon and, as such, unable to produce a result. Prāsaṅgikas, however, assert that it is the having-ceased of an action that connects the action with its results.

What is a having-ceased? During the time an action exists, it disintegrates in each moment. All Buddhist schools accept that the disintegration or ceasing (*vyaya*) of a thing is a function of the causes that gave rise to that thing. An action ceases or is ceasing, and when its ceasing is complete, it has ceased. At that time, the action is no longer happening in the present; it is past. For example, we have the intention to speak and our voice continues for a while; during that time the intention and our voice are ceasing. But when they both stop, they have ceased and are now past phenomena. Most Buddhist schools say that the having-ceased that follows the disintegration of a thing is permanent, uncaused, and therefore unable to produce an effect.[44] Nāgārjuna, however, says that just as the disintegration of an action—its act of ceasing—is a function of causes and conditions, so too is its having-ceased. The having-ceased of an action is a state of destruction that remains—the state of the action's having ended. This having-ceased has the potential to bring a result in the future. According to Prāsaṅgikas, a having-ceased is an impermanent phenomenon, which regenerates in each moment until it produces its result in the future.

In his commentary to Nāgārjuna's *Sixty Stanzas of Reasoning*, Candrakīrti explains why the having-ceased of an action is a conditioned phenomenon and a functioning thing. Just as the process of arising (*jati*)—the arising or production of a thing from its cause—is a conditioned phenomenon, in the same way, the arisen (T. *skyes pa*), which is the accomplished act of arising, is also a conditioned phenomenon. Therefore since the disintegration of a thing is a conditioned thing, the having-ceased, which is the complete act of disintegration, should also be a conditioned phenomenon. Being a conditioned phenomenon that arises due to an action, the having-ceased of that karma is able to connect that action to its result, which will occur in the future.

Both a karmic seed and a having-ceased remain when an action is completed. Since the action is impermanent, it ceases and is followed by a having-ceased. The action also itself gives rise to a seed, which has potency. Both the having-ceased and the karmic seed contribute to the arising of the karmic result.

Thus the potential of the physical karma of prostrating is passed on in two ways: as a latency or seed that is left by the mental factor of intention that motivated that physical action, and as a having-ceased of the perceptible form that is the physical action of prostrating. The second link of dependent origination, formative action, for the action of prostrating consists of both of those.

After an action has finished, its karmic seed is placed on the mental continuum. The having-ceased of a karmic action is present with the mental consciousness. However, we don't say it was *placed on* the mental consciousness. Both having-ceaseds of karmas and karmic seeds bear their results when the proper conditions have assembled.

What happens to the karmic seeds and having-ceaseds when an ārya is in meditative equipoise that directly realizes emptiness? At this time, her mental consciousness is unpolluted because it is totally absorbed in emptiness with no conceptual elaborations at all. An unpolluted mind cannot be the carrier of polluted karmic seeds and having-ceaseds. Buddhist tenet schools have different explanations, but Candrakīrti's is the most coherent. He distinguishes between the temporary and the long-term bases of seeds and latencies. The temporary basis is the mental consciousness. After the action has ceased, the seed is placed on the mental consciousness. The continual or long-term basis is the mere I—the conventional self that exists by being merely designated. This self is a mere convention; it carries the karmic seeds and so forth when an ārya is in meditative equipoise directly realizing emptiness. Although the mere I is not findable when searched for with ultimate analysis seeking its ultimate mode of existence, it still exists nominally. It goes from life to life, carrying with it karmic seeds as well as the seeds and latencies of afflictions. Just as the mere I, which is the basis of the seeds and latencies, cannot be found by ultimate analysis, neither can the latencies, seeds, and having-ceaseds. They, too, are empty of inherent existence yet exist nominally and dependently.

REFLECTION

1. What are karmic seeds and how do they function?
2. What are seeds of afflictions and what are latencies of afflictions? How do they differ?

Other Types of Latencies

Other types of latencies influence our experience as well. One type involves dreams, memories and mental objects. For example, we see a person during the day, and the latency of seeing him is placed on our mindstreams. Then at night we dream about that person. Similarly, memory is influenced by latencies; we see a flower and later remember it. In this case, the visual consciousness has placed a latency on our mindstreams. When we do meditation retreat, we may notice that as our minds become quieter, memories of people and events that we have not thought about in years surface. These are due to latencies.

Sense faculties also leave latencies on the mindstream that make it possible for new sense sources to arise in future lives. Beings born in the formless realm do not have physical forms and thus lack sense faculties. However, after they die from that realm and are born again in the desire realm, the latencies of the sense faculties that have been on their mindstreams become the substantial cause for their five sense faculties in the desire realm.

Latencies and Ideas in Other Religions and in Psychology

Those of us exposed to ideas in non-Buddhist faiths and in modern psychology often ask if latencies are comparable with notions in these other disciplines. What follows are some general thoughts on two ideas: original sin and the unconscious.

Original Sin

Some newcomers to Buddhism ask if our discussion of afflictions and karma being carried from one life to the next resembles the doctrine of original sin taught in other faiths. These teachings are very different. Original Sin is taught within a theistic framework. In brief, according to Augustine, God created the world and the first humans. Adam and Eve were disobedient, and subsequent generations of human beings inherited this sin through the act of procreation. Jesus was born to overcome human beings' innate tendency for evil and sin and to reconcile them with God. Cessation of sin depends on the great sacrifice Jesus made.

In contrast, in Buddhism there is no notion of a creator or an initial act of disobedience. Ignorance, afflictions, and saṃsāric rebirth have existed beginninglessly. They continue in the mindstream of an individual and are not inherited by his or her biological offspring. The Buddha held that sentient beings' basic nature is neutral and pure; it is not inherently defiled and sentient beings have the potential to become fully awakened. Afflictions and karmic seeds are adventitious and can be completely removed by the internal method of meditating with the wisdom realizing emptiness. Each of us must cultivate this wisdom ourselves; it is not something another being, however divine, can do for us.

In theistic religions, sentient beings can approach God but not become God. The Buddha said that by following the correct path, sentient beings can thoroughly cleanse all seeds and latencies of afflictions and karma from their mindstreams. Each of us has the potential to become a fully awakened buddha.

The Unconscious

Spoken about by Sigmund Freud just before the turn of the twentieth century, the unconscious is thought to be an area of the mind composed of feelings, ideas, animal-like instincts, fears, and hopes that are not allowed expression in conscious awareness. These things may manifest and express themselves in other ways, such as dreams, anxiety, psychosomatic illnesses, and phobias. Some unconscious material is inhibited or modified by the superego in the process of socialization, enabling us to live with others more harmoniously.

Carl Jung hypothesized the existence of a collective unconscious that consists of thoughts and feelings common to humanity. This unconscious material is often expressed in myths, legends, fairy tales, archetypes, and religious stories that contain common themes. The collective unconscious is sometimes seen as a storehouse of ancient wisdom passed on from generation to generation.

The preconscious is the area of the mind having thoughts and feelings that are below the level of immediate conscious awareness but that can come into conscious awareness through the focusing of attention. Do any of these psychological theories compare to the Buddhist notion of consciousness and the seeds and latencies on it?

The Buddhist explanation of mind does not contain an exact equivalent to the Western notion of the unconscious. In an attempt to draw some possible parallels, we may speak of the Buddhist view of different levels of consciousness—coarse and subtle. The Buddhist descriptions of underlying afflictions and latencies of afflictions may also have some resemblance to the Jungian idea of the unconscious. However, none of these precisely match either the psychoanalytic meaning of the unconscious or the more common use of the word *unconscious* to mean lack of conscious awareness, thought, or intention.

According to the Buddha, all phenomena are potentially knowable by our minds. Much of what psychology views as unconscious or preconscious material becomes fully conscious as our minds become clearer through meditation. As our mindfulness and introspective alertness increase, we see aspects of our minds—such as preconceptions, fears, assumptions, feelings, and emotions—that have been present but not previously perceived or acknowledged. Furthermore, advanced practitioners gain certain superknowledges (psychic powers) through cultivating single-pointed concentration and can directly perceive previous lives and other events not consciously known before. In this sense Buddhism might say that everything in our experience of this and previous lives is preconscious in that by focusing our attention and concentration in specific ways, it may be consciously known.

Virtue, Nonvirtue, Merit, and Roots of Virtue

The principal cause of happiness is virtue and the chief cause of suffering is nonvirtue. Being able to discern the difference between these two so that we can practice the former and abandon the latter is essential for making wise choices in life and for accomplishing the path to liberation and awakening. In general, virtue is that which brings an agreeable result and nonvirtue is that which brings a disagreeable result. Here virtue includes constructive intentions and actions. These leave seeds of virtue on the mindstream, and these seeds bring agreeable results.

While mental states and actions may be virtuous or nonvirtuous, the seeds of karma and latencies of afflictions are neutral. This is because virtue and nonvirtue are linked to our intention; an action becomes virtuous or nonvirtuous primarily due to our intention. Seeds and latencies, however, do not have that strong active intentional element and are therefore neutral. Thus we speak of the seeds of virtuous karma, for example, not the virtuous seeds of karma; we talk about the latencies of nonvirtuous afflictions, not the nonvirtuous latencies of afflictions.

Similarly, the pleasant or unpleasant ripening results of virtue and nonvirtue are neither virtuous nor nonvirtuous. Being born in a healthy human body is a result of virtue, but the body itself is ethically neutral. Possessing wealth is an agreeable result of the virtuous action of generosity but being wealthy itself is neither virtuous nor nonvirtuous.

What does virtue refer to? Asaṅga's *Compendium of Knowledge* speaks of five types of virtue:

(1) *Natural virtues* include the eleven virtuous mental factors—faith, integrity, consideration for others, nonattachment, nonhatred, nonconfusion, joyous effort, pliancy, conscientiousness, nonharmfulness, and equanimity. These are called natural virtues because their nature is virtuous; they naturally bring pleasing results.

(2) *Related virtues* are primary consciousnesses and mental factors that become virtuous because they are accompanied by virtuous mental factors. When compassion is present, the mental primary consciousness and the mental factors of intention, feeling, and so forth that accompany it become virtuous.

(3) *Subsequently related virtues* are seeds and latencies of virtue established by virtuous consciousnesses and mental factors, and virtuous actions; for example, the karmic seed created by the mind of generosity. Seeds and latencies are not actual virtues; this is an example of the name of the cause (the virtuous path of action) being given to the effect (the seeds and latencies of virtue).

(4) *Virtues due to motivation* are physical and verbal actions motivated by the naturally virtuous mental factors. The action of making a donation to a charity is a physical virtue when done with a generous motivation.

Vaibhāṣikas and Prāsaṅgikas assert that virtue includes both minds and forms. They consider virtues due to motivation—physical and verbal actions motivated by virtuous mental states—to be virtues. Since prātimokṣa precepts are form according to these two schools, the precepts are virtuous forms. According to Sautrāntikas, Cittamātrins, and Svātantrikas, only minds can be virtues.

(5) *Ultimate virtue* is emptiness because realizing it eradicates all obscu-

rations and enables virtue to flourish. Emptiness, however, is not an actual virtue because it is permanent and itself does not produce results.

This list of virtues is not exhaustive. Other virtues include, but are not limited to, a buddha's speech and the thirty-two signs and eighty marks of a buddha.

Even a moment of a natural virtue can have far-reaching results. When the mental factor of conscientiousness arises in the mind, the primary consciousness and mental factors associated with it all become virtuous. The physical and verbal actions done with that motivation are also virtuous. While the karmic seeds of those actions are neutral, they carry the potency for agreeable results to arise, and for that reason they are subsequently related virtues although they are not actual virtues.

Commensurate with the five virtues, there are five nonvirtues:

(1) Natural nonvirtues are mental factors such as attachment, anger, jealousy, and resentment that are nonvirtuous by nature.

(2) Related nonvirtues are the mental primary consciousness and mental factors that accompany a naturally nonvirtuous mental factor.

(3) Subsequently related nonvirtues are latencies left on the mind by nonvirtuous minds and mental factors. They are not actual nonvirtues but are ethically neutral.

(4) Nonvirtues due to motivation are physical and verbal actions done with a nonvirtuous motivation.

(5) Ultimate nonvirtue is, for example, saṃsāra, which breeds nonvirtue although it is not an actual nonvirtue.

In general, virtuous karma and merit are synonymous. In the context of saṃsāra, they are actions that have the ability to bring favorable results. Calling an action virtuous or meritorious emphasizes that it is psychologically healthy and ethically irreproachable. In terms of spiritual progress, virtuous actions enrich the mind, establishing the foundation for generating the realizations and excellent qualities of arhats, bodhisattvas, and buddhas. In the context of the two collections of merit and wisdom, merit is that which has the capacity to give rise to the form body of a buddha.

In general, the expression *root of virtue* refers to a virtuous mental factor, although it also seems to indicate seeds of virtuous karma. Śāntideva's *Engaging in the Bodhisattvas' Deeds* and Candrakīrti's *Supplement* contain extensive discussion about anger destroying the roots of virtue. When anger destroys the roots of virtue, or when wrong views or other heavy non-virtuous actions cut the root of virtue, it prevents future agreeable results from coming about even when suitable circumstances are present.

When human beings cut the root of virtue, it affects only the root of virtue related to the human realm; the root of virtue of the higher realms remains. They may still encounter fortunate conditions in the future and regain their root of virtue.

REFLECTION

1. Review the different types of virtue. Which are actual virtue and which are just called virtue? Make examples of each in your life.
2. Review the different types of nonvirtue. Which are actual nonvirtue and which are simply called nonvirtue? Make examples of each in your life.

6 | Karma, the Universe, and Evolution

True duḥkha includes sentient beings and our environment. In preceding chapters we discussed our unsatisfactory state as sentient beings and our life experiences as well as the true origins of these: ignorance, afflictions, and polluted karma. In this chapter we'll look more closely at how the true origins of duḥkha bring forth the environments in which we sentient beings dwell.

The Origin of the Universe

Similar to today, a vibrant topic of discussion among both religious and secular people in the Buddha's time centered on the origin and destruction of the universe. As recorded in the sūtras (MN 63), they asked: Was the universe eternal or not eternal, transient or permanent, finite or infinite? Did the universe have a beginning or was it beginningless? The Buddha refused to answer these questions because the people who asked them were thinking in terms of an inherently existent universe. No matter how the Buddha could have responded, they would have thought that either the universe existed inherently or did not exist at all. Because holding either of these views would have harmed them, the Buddha chose not to respond. At other times the Buddha refused to comment on the origin of the universe because it was not relevant to the alleviation of duḥkha and attainment of liberation. Abhidharma texts and the *Kālacakra Tantra*, however, commented on the evolution of the universe in conventional terms. Nowadays scientists research these same topics, leading to fascinating dialogues between Buddhists and scientists, some of which I have attended.

There are several approaches that could be taken regarding the origin of the universe: first we must investigate if it was created by a cause or if it arose causelessly. Most people find causeless or random production unacceptable because in our everyday lives we witness effects arising from causes. Furthermore, it would be difficult for anything to function and change if it lacked causes and conditions; permanent phenomena cannot interact with other things to produce something new.

Among those who accept that the universe arose due to causes, there are different assertions. Theistic religions such as Judaism, Christianity, Islam, and some branches of Hinduism speak of an external creator. Most scientists attribute the origin of the universe to the Big Bang, some asserting that one Big Bang began all existence, others saying there may have been several Big Bangs as different universes began. Non-theistic Sāṃkhya (a Hindu philosophical school) and some other traditions speak of a primal substance out of which everything was created. Buddhists speak of the interplay between the laws of nature and the law of karma and its effects.

Difficulties arise when we posit one original cause or event as the source of the universe with its mass, space, and time. If there were a single, initial cause for all existence—be it a cosmic substance, dense matter, or preceding Intelligence—what triggered that one cause to give rise to the universe with all of its complexity and diversity? Change—such as the production of a universe—involves a complex interplay of many factors that influence one another. Since even the existence of something small like a flower involves multiple causes and conditions, needless to say, this is the case with more complex entities such as the universe.

Because things depend on causes and conditions they change; whatever arises necessarily depends on the causes and conditions that produce it. This is the law of causality, a natural law of the universe that describes how things arise and produce results. Within this general law of causality, Buddhaghoṣa's commentary on the Dīgha Nikāya, *Sumaṅgala-vilāsinī*, speaks of five specific types of causality:[45]

1. *Inorganic causality* (P. *utu niyāma*) is the causality occurring with inorganic matter as described by physics, astronomy, and inorganic chemistry. It includes the causal functioning of subatomic particles as well as the causality involved with grosser matter such as the weather and aerodynamics.

2. *Biological causality* (P. *bīja niyāma*) involves organic forms—for example, the causality involved with genes, chromosomes, and biological processes in the plant and animal worlds.

3. *Psychological causality* (P. *citta niyāma*) deals with the complex interactions among various types of consciousnesses and mental factors—for example, how sensory cognizers occur, how mental consciousness arises in reaction to them, and how memory comes about.

4. *Karmic causality* (P. *kamma niyāma*) concerns volitional actions done by sentient beings and their karmic effects. Our actions have an ethical dimension that naturally influences the rebirth we take as well as our experiences, habitual actions, and environment.

5. *Natural phenomenal causality* (P. *dhamma niyāma*) concerns certain

natural phenomena such as the wondrous events that occur when a bodhisattva descends into his mother's womb in his last rebirth, attains awakening, turns the wheel of Dharma, and passes away (attains parinirvāṇa). These include events such as the earth quaking and a great light appearing in the world system. Such things occur *dhammatā*, or naturally.[46] The causality of the twelve links of dependent origination is natural phenomenal causality epitomized by the Buddha's words, "When that exists, this comes to be. From the arising of that, this arises. When that does not exist, this does not come to be. When that ceases, this ceases."

This causality is the natural order of things in the universe. Although the other four types of causality are actually types of natural phenomenal causality, only those causal relations that do not fall within those four are included in natural phenomenal causality.[47]

These five types of causality are explained to show that there is no external creator of the universe or of sentient beings. Rather, all things arise and cease continuously in dependence on their causes and conditions. While each of the five has its own sphere of operation, they are interconnected and influence one another.

Mind and the External World

Abhidharma texts speak of countless world systems, but I'm unsure if a world system is equivalent to a solar system, galaxy, or universe. In any case, Mahāyāna sūtras and the *Kālacakra Tantra* speak of vast world systems throughout infinite space. At any particular time, some world systems are arising, some abiding, some disintegrating, and others remaining dormant. In this view, there is no absolute beginning. There is simply the beginningless interplay of various factors that make world systems arise, abide, disintegrate, and remain dormant.

Buddhist thinkers speak of conditioned phenomena—things that are impermanent, composed of parts, and conditioned by other factors—as being of three types: form, mind, and abstract composites such as time. What is the relationship between form—the material building blocks and resultant compounded things in the external universe—and mind, with its thoughts, feelings, and intentions? When we speak of the development of a world system and the evolution of life in particular, what is the relationship between mind and form?

I will share my thoughts about this. These are by no means definitive conclusions but hopefully they will spark some curiosity among both those with scientific inclinations and those with spiritual dispositions.

The general Buddhist view is expressed by the First Dalai Lama in his commentary on the *Treasury of Knowledge* (EPL 556):

> If one asks: This manifold world which has been explained—the environment and the sentient beings living in it—where does it come from?
>
> It does not arise without cause or from a discordant cause because it arises occasionally. And it does not arise from [the creator god] Īśvara and so forth because it arises gradually. As it says this, if one asks, from what does it arise? The manifold world of the environment and the sentient beings living in it arise from karma.

The manifold world is comprised of the environment and the sentient beings living in it. The world did not arise without a cause because everything that functions must arise from causes. It did not arise from a discordant cause because a specific effect can arise only from the causes and conditions that have the ability to produce it. If causality were arbitrary, then anything could produce anything, and by studying Italian, we could learn to speak Chinese. The fact that something arises only at some times (occasionally) means that it arises only when all of its causes and conditions have come together. The world is not created from a creator such as Īśvara because if it were, it would arise all at once, whereas the world and the sentient beings in it evolved gradually. The source of the world and the sentient beings who inhabit it is karma—volitional actions originating in the minds of sentient beings.

Although Vasubandhu stated in the *Treasury of Knowledge*, "The manifold world arises from karma," he and other Abhidharma authors did not detail the exact process through which this occurs. The broad concept is that through the interdependence of material substances and sentient beings' karma, the world evolved in such a way that it could support the various life forms that live in it.

In a Sūtrayāna context, Candrakīrti noted in his *Supplement*, "From the mind the world of sentience arises. So too from the mind the diverse habitats of beings arise." The Cittamātra school understands this literally and developed a philosophical system that denies the existence of external objects and instead asserts that both the perceiving consciousness and perceived object arise from the same latency on the foundational consciousness. The Madhyamaka school disagrees. Although it refutes an objectively existent world "out there" that is unrelated to sentient beings' minds, it asserts external objects, saying that sentient beings' intentions create karma, which influences their resulting body-mind complex and their external habitat.

In Vajrayāna, the *Guhyasamāja Tantra* speaks about the inseparability of the subtlest mind and the subtlest wind (*prāṇa*). The subtlest wind is not the gross wind that blows leaves, nor is it the subtler energy, or *qi*, in our body. It is an extremely subtle wind or energy that is inseparable from the subtlest mind. The wind is the aspect of movement, the mind is the aspect of cognizance. This subtlest mind-wind is not within the range of what scientific instruments can measure. In general it is dormant throughout the lives of ordinary beings and becomes manifest only at the time of death or as a result of yogic practices that involve absorbing the coarser levels of wind and mind. From the perspective of highest yoga tantra, although the coarse mind and coarse form (the body) are different substances with different continuums, at the subtlest level of mind and form they are one nature—the subtlest mind-wind.

The *Kālacakra Tantra* speaks of the connection between the elements in our bodies and those in the external world and the analogous relationship between the movement of celestial bodies and changes within our bodies. Since our body and mind are related, these changes in the external and internal elements affect the mind. Conversely, the mind, especially its intentions (karma), influences our bodily elements and by extension the elements in the larger universe.

The *Kālacakra Tantra* explains that when a world system is dormant only space particles, which bear traces of the other four elements, are present. These elemental particles are more like attributes than distinct material substances. The material things in our environment are composed of these elements in varying degrees. As part of composite objects such as our bodies or a table, the earth element provides solidity, the water element fluidity and cohesion. The fire element gives heat and the wind element enables movement. The elements develop progressively in both the universe and our bodies: first space, then wind, fire, water, and earth sequentially. At the time of a human being's death, the elements absorb—they lose the power to support consciousness—in the reverse sequence.

Similarly, when a world system collapses and comes to an end the elements composing it absorb into each other in this reverse sequence—earth absorbs into water, water into fire, fire into wind, and wind into space. Unobservable by our physical senses and lacking mass, space particles are the fundamental source of all matter, persisting during the dormant stage between one world system and the next and acting as the substantial cause for the coarser elements that arise during the evolution of the next world system.

Space particles are not like the partless particles asserted by non-Buddhist schools that assert ultimate, partless, unchanging building blocks out of which everything is constructed. Nor are they inherently existent particles. They exist by being merely designated in dependence on the potency for the other four elements.

The external five elements are related to the corresponding inner five elements that constitute the body. These, in turn, are related to the subtlest wind that is one nature with the subtlest mind. The subtlest mind-wind is endowed with a five-colored radiance that is the nature of the five dhyāni buddhas and the five wisdoms. In this way, there is correspondence between the external world and the innermost subtlest minds of sentient beings. The five subtle elements in the body evolve primarily from the subtlest wind (one that is part of the subtlest mind-wind) of that sentient being. The five subtle elements in turn bring forth the coarse five elements in the body and in the external universe.

Thus from a tantric perspective, all things evolve from and dissolve back into this inseparable union of the subtlest mind-wind. The subtlest mind-wind of each individual is not a soul, nor does it abide independent of all other factors. The relationship between the mind, the inner five elements, and the five elements in the external universe is complex; only highly realized tantric yogis are privy to a full understanding of this.

The karma of the sentient beings who will be born in that universe are the cooperative conditions for that universe. When their karmic latencies begin to ripen, the space particles are activated, and they give rise to the wind element, the motion of pure energy. Fire, water, and earth elements sequentially and gradually arise after that.

I believe that the evolution from space particles into the manifold phenomena of a universe and those phenomena's devolution into space particles at the end of a universe could be related to the Big Bang theory. However, I don't think that there was one space particle in the center that exploded to produce everything. With further investigation, perhaps a correlation could be made between space particles and some theories of physics and astronomy.

The elements of an individual's body are related to his or her personal karma and subtlest mind-wind. The larger external universe is the environmental effect of the collective karma of the sentient beings who enjoy it. The collective karma of the sentient beings who dwell in a universe influence the way the coarse elements evolve to form that universe. In other words, the universe and sentient beings exist in dependence on each other. Sentient beings cannot exist without the environment in which they live and that environment cannot exist without the sentient beings whose karma played a role in its creation.

The relationship between the mind and the subtle elements is the domain of highly realized meditators with single-pointed concentration. According to scriptural sources and the experience of highly realized yogis, someone who has subdued his or her mind and developed a certain level of control over his or her inner elements can also control the external elements. This accounts for the stories we hear of people who can walk on water, fly in the sky (without boarding a plane!), and travel beneath the earth.

The Laws of Nature and the Law of Karma and Its Effects

The laws of nature and the law of karma and its effects operate in their own domain, although they intersect at key times. Not everything in sentient beings' lives and environments can be reduced to the functioning of either natural laws or karma. Natural laws function such that once particular processes are set in motion, they will produce certain effects. Karma enters the picture when sentient beings' intentions and their happiness and suffering are involved.

For the most part the natural laws of physics, chemistry, and biology that guide the interactions of external elements are involved in the development of our world system. However, sentient beings' minds, through the ripening of their karma, seem to exert influence at two points. The first is when the karma of the sentient beings who have the potential to live in a particular world system sparks the initial development of that world system. From the perspective of the scientific model, the collective karma of a huge number of sentient beings could influence the occurrence of the Big Bang. From the perspective of the model presented in the *Kālacakra Tantra*, the collective karma of all those sentient beings would stimulate the potencies of solidity, fluidity, heat, and motility existing in the space particles in between world systems so that coarse elements appear.

The second point at which karma could come into play is when the elements of a universe have evolved to the point where they can support sentient life. Here, karma could act as the instigating factor for previous inanimate forms to become the bodies of sentient beings—that is, mindstreams could enter these forms to produce sentient beings with bodies and minds. The evolution of various species would subsequently occur.

Another way to describe this process is in terms of substantial causes and cooperative conditions. Both are necessary whether we speak of natural laws or karmic law. A substantial cause is what actually transforms into the result; cooperative conditions are the causes that assist this process. For example, wood is the substantial cause of a table, and the people who built it as well as the nails that hold it together are cooperative conditions. Because everything that is produced must have previous causes that are concordant with it, I believe that the continuum of material existed before the Big Bang. This material was the substantial cause of the world system that developed after the Big Bang. Similarly, in the *Kalacakra Tantra* space particles existed before the formation of our world system; they were the substantial cause for all the material in this world system. Regardless of which model we accept, the karma of the sentient beings who will be born in that world system acts as a cooperative condition for these material elements to appear, coalesce, and form a world system. Karma could similarly enable them to become the bases for sentient life.

Karma and Our Present Environment

To review, there is a connection between the formation and evolution of the external world and the karma of sentient beings who will inhabit it. There is also a connection between the elements of the external world and those constituting our physical body. These, in turn, are related to subtler elements and subtler winds that themselves can be traced to the subtlest mind-wind. Karma—which primarily refers to sentient beings' intentions and the paths of action they motivate—may be the link between sentient beings' minds and the external world. Karma is related to the subtle winds in sentient beings' bodies, which in turn are related to the five inner elements. These correspond to the five external elements in the environment. Understanding the subtle winds spoken of in the tantric texts will help us understand this relationship. This is my opinion; more research is necessary.

As mentioned before, only a buddha can know the intricacies of karma, which include how karma affects the evolution of a world system and the sentient life in it. For us limited beings, it is hard to know where natural laws stop and the law of karma takes over, where the law of karma stops and natural laws take over, and where the two influence each other. For that reason, we should avoid making hard and fast distinctions regarding the interface of these two. Nevertheless, some general guidelines can be discerned.

In terms of the origin and development of a particular world system, there are two times when sentient beings' karma may exert an influence: at the very beginning of that world system when the coarse elements are arising, and later when the combinations of those elements are suitable to act as the bodies for sentient beings. In terms of the development of specific environments and climates in which sentient beings now live, karma could play a role in two ways. First, the karma of the people presently living in and experiencing a place—for example, Dharamsala, where I live—contributed to its development millions of years ago when it was forming. Only nowadays, in this lifetime, do they experience the effect. We may wonder: How could their karma have ripened so long ago before they were born here? An analogy is helpful. Before moving into a house, the future occupants design the floor plan and begin constructing it. Later, when the house is ready, they occupy it and experience that environment. Similarly, when this planet was forming, no sentient beings lived on it. But since there were sentient beings who would take birth here, their karma influenced the way the planet would evolve.

Second, a particular environment is influenced by the karma of the people who live in that place now but were not among the initial karmic contributors to the development of that climate and environment a long time ago. These sentient beings later accumulated karma similar to that of the initial karmic contributors and thus came to live in that place and experience that climate at this time. For example, after Dharamsala's specific climate had already come into existence, another group of people accumulated the karma that could produce this sort of climate. This group did not have a direct connection to the development of Dharamsala's climate thousands of years ago, but due to their actions, which were similar to the karma of the previous group of people, they came to live in this place. The karma of the first group actually contributed to the development of Dharamsala's climate and environment. The karma of the second group did not contribute directly but participated in it, since they live there. Both groups of people created the causes to experience that environment, but in different ways.

To use an analogy, many people start a business in Europe. Another person in the same field intends to seek employment in the United States. However, she happens to be in Europe and takes a job in the company established by the other people. Although she joins it later, she still contributes to the company's work.

Karma was not the only cause for Dharamsala's climate to develop the way it did; the laws of inorganic, physical causality were definitely involved. Nature has a certain autonomy that does not depend on karma. The tree we see over there grew from its seed. I doubt anyone's karma was involved in that. Similarly, the growth of some leaves today and others next week is due to the functioning of biological systems, not karma.

But this tree is in front of me and I can use and enjoy it. As soon as the tree is related to a sentient being and his or her happiness or suffering, the karma of that particular sentient being enters the picture.

Beautiful plants and colorful flowers grow in the garden where I live. They certainly are related to the karma of the sentient beings who use and enjoy them and who experience pleasure and pain in relationship to them. Human beings enjoy their beautiful colors and smell, bees imbibe nectar from the flowers, birds use the trees as their shelter, insects munch on the plants. The collective karma of all these beings contributed to the existence of these plants. This karma was created by the minds of the sentient beings involved. Nevertheless, since the plants consist of material substances, their growth depends on nature's biological laws. Karma does not transform into the water and fertilizer that make the plants grow.

Natural disasters such as earthquakes, hurricanes, and tsunamis are produced by the functioning of the laws of nature. Our karma does not make them happen. However, the fact that certain people are there when such events happen is due to their karma. A volcano explodes due to physical factors such as the build-up of pressure under the Earth's surface; this is not the result of karma. But the fact that some sentient beings are near that volcano and are injured or even die as a result of its explosion is related to the karma of those sentient beings. Other sentient beings, who did not create the karma to be harmed in that way, are not near the volcanic explosion.

Similarly, droughts and floods can be understood in terms of external causes, but insofar as they affect sentient beings, those beings' karma is involved. For example, a community of people that has intense and pervasive hatred may, in this or future lives, inhabit a place during a severe drought and famine. Their being present and experiencing suffering from this are effects of their karma. Similarly, people who consciously pollute the environment now create the karmic cause to suffer from living in a polluted environment in future lives.

Although we often speak of karma as actions created in previous lives, it also refers to the actions we do today. Our present motivations and choices directly affect the external world. We must not think that everything is due to our actions in previous lives and ignore the effects of our present actions. When we dump toxic wastes into our environment, we experience the result in this lifetime. When we do not share resources, the world becomes turbulent now. Our intentions and actions during this lifetime are causing global warming.

Karma, Instinctual Behavior, and Our Bodies

Both science and Buddhadharma agree that sentient beings have certain instinctual behaviors, but how they account for them varies. Science looks to genetic makeup for answers, while the Buddhist sage Bhāvaviveka said that calves instinctually look to their mother for milk because of latencies on their mindstreams from previous lives when they had acted in a similar way. One effect of karma is the tendency to do the action again, which accounts for many instinctual behaviors.

Nevertheless, certain instincts are related to the type of body a sentient being has. We are in the desire realm, where the bodily constituents of beings are such that desire is dominant. Thus we have many biological needs and desires, and our minds crave these.

Some animal species are vegetarian, others eat meat. This is not primarily due to karma, but to the physical conditions of their bodies—their genetic makeup and biological functions. However, the existence of these types of animal bodies on this planet is related to the general, collective karma of the sentient beings on this planet. The fact that a particular sentient being is born in a carnivore's body is a ripening result of that person's individual karma.

The functioning of the biological systems of an individual's body relates more to natural biological laws than to karma, although karma is involved when that person experiences pain or pleasure from his or her body. Our discomfort when we have a cold is due to our karma. Our catching a cold depends on the presence of the virus near us, sanitation in the area, the state of our immune system, and to some extent our karma. However, our hand being the nature of matter and our minds being the nature of clarity and cognizance are not due to karma. These are simply the nature of those phenomena.

The possibility of having a specific combination of genes in a fertilized egg is one in seventy trillion. Why a particular sentient being's mindstream is attracted to that particular zygote and is born in it is a result of his or her karma. My being born in this body is an effect of my karma, but my body itself is due to the sperm and egg of my parents. My height is due to my genes and diet, but my being born in a body with these genetic predispositions was influenced by my karma.

It is important to distinguish the role of karma vis-à-vis the general characteristics of a species and the experiences of an individual in that species. For example, it is doubtful that human beings having hair and fish having scales is related to karma. Human beings having hair is due to natural biological forces. However, my being born in a body with genes causing baldness is a result of my individual karma. Still, that the evolution of human bodies in general occurred the way it did—with the potential to be bald—was in part a function of the collective karma of the sentient beings who had created the causes to be born in these bodies, which includes me. As you can see, this is a complex topic! The extent to which the various systems of cause and effect—physical, biological, psychological, karmic, and so forth—are interrelated and influence one another is not easy to delineate.

Although Darwin's theory of evolution does not address the issue of what sentience is or how beings' mindstreams came to be associated with the various physical structures that are their bodies, it can explain the general physical evolution of the various forms of life on our planet. Buddhists would add that the karma of the sentient beings who will be born in those bodies influenced the types of sense organs and some of the features of the bodies in the various realms.

Some Buddhist scriptures and cultural legends describe other versions of evolution. According to the *Treasury of Knowledge,* the first human beings, whose minds were less afflictive than ours, had bodies made of light. But as their thoughts degenerated and they became greedy, their bodies became coarser and eventually were composed of material as they are now. Yet another view is the Tibetan legend that the Tibetan race came into being through the union of an ogress and a monkey. This is a compromise between the Darwinian theory that humans descended from apes and the scriptural view that the first humans had bodies of light!

More research is needed. I hope the above discussion will stimulate you to do further investigation and to understand the complexity of interdependence.

7 | Revolving in Cyclic Existence: The Twelve Links of Dependent Origination

THE PROCESS OF REBIRTH in saṃsāra is illustrated by the Wheel of Life. This painting of the samsaric cycle of existence has its origins in the time of the Buddha when the king of Vatsā, Udāyana, presented a jeweled robe to the king of Magadha, Bimbisāra. Bimbisāra consulted the Buddha about an appropriate gift to send in return, and the Buddha recommended a painting of the Wheel of Life that has the verses below written on it. Upon contemplating the Wheel of Life, King Udāyana attained realizations.

> Practicing this and abandoning that,
> enter into the teaching of the Buddha.
> Like an elephant in a thatch house,
> destroy the forces of the lord of death.
>
> Those who with thorough conscientiousness
> practice this disciplinary doctrine
> will forsake the wheel of birth,
> bringing duḥkha to an end.

The wheel consists of a series of concentric circles held in the mouth of the anthropomorphized lord of death, who symbolizes our impermanent nature. The center circle contains a pig, snake, and rooster, signifying the three poisons of ignorance, animosity, and attachment, respectively. Each animal has the tail of another in its mouth, indicating that they mutually reinforce each other, although in some paintings the tails of the snake and rooster are in the pig's mouth, showing that ignorance is the root of all afflictions.

The next circle has two halves: the left half (as we look at the painting) is light with happy beings ascending to fortunate rebirths; the right is dark with suffering beings descending to unfortunate rebirths. The imagery indicates that dependent on ignorance we create virtuous and nonvirtuous karma that lead to agreeable and disagreeable births.

These births are the five classes of being—devas (including asuras), humans, animals, hungry ghosts, and hell beings. They are shown in the next circle, which is divided into five sections. The outermost circle has twelve sections, each one illustrating one of the twelve links of dependent origination.

Above and outside the wheel clutched by the lord of death is the Buddha pointing to the radiant full moon: he shows us the path to nirvāṇa. The two verses cited above encourage us to follow this path to free ourselves from all duḥkha forever.

Dependent Arising

Dependent arising[48] is one of the most essential teachings of the Buddha. He expressed its overriding principle (MN 79:8):

> When this exists, that comes to be; with the arising of this, that arises. When this does not exist, that does not come to be; with the cessation of this, that ceases.

When the causes and conditions for something are assembled, that thing will arise. The Buddha employs this principle in a variety of circumstances, including his discussion of social turmoil and social benefit. However, since the Buddha's main concern was with sentient beings' bondage in saṃsāra and liberation from it, one of his main teachings on conditionality is the twelve links of dependent origination (*dvādaśāṅga-pratītyasamutpāda*). These twelve describe the causal process for rebirth in saṃsāra and the unsatisfactory experiences that ensue. They also show the way to attain liberation from this vicious cycle.

The twelve links are prominent topics for study and contemplation in both the Pāli and Sanskrit traditions. The Buddha spoke of them extensively in Pāli sūtras, especially in the *Connected Discourses on Causation* (*Nidānasaṃyutta,* SN 12), and in Sanskrit sūtras, particularly in the *Rice Seedling Sūtra* (*Śālistamba Sūtra*). An extensive explanation of dependent origination according to the Pāli tradition is found in chapter 17 of *The Path of Purification* as well as in Abhidharma texts. In the Sanskrit tradition extensive commentary can be found in Asaṅga's *Compendium of Knowledge* (*Abhidharmasamuccaya*). Chapter 5 of Maitreya's *Ornament of Clear Realizations* explains how to meditate on the twelve links in forward and reverse order, and chapter 3 of Vasubandhu's *Treasury of Knowledge* contains the Vaibhāṣikas' explanation of the twelve links. Chapters 24 and 26 of Nāgārjuna's *Treatise on the Middle Way* (*Mūlamadhyamakakārikā*) establish the conventional existence of the twelve links while refuting their inherent existence.

The Buddha presented dependent origination in a variety of ways. Sometimes he began with the twelfth link, aging or death, and worked backward (SN 12.2). This perspective begins with our present experience of aging and leads us to inquire as to how we arrived at it. Other times he began with ignorance and explained the links in forward order, culminating with aging or death (SN 12.1). In yet other sūtras, the Buddha began in the middle of the sequence and went either forward to aging or death or backward to ignorance (MN 11).

Although the Buddha did not explicitly teach emptiness when he taught the twelve links, he set out the basis on which we can understand it: everything that exists dependent on other factors is empty of having its own inherent nature, and everything that is empty exists dependent on other factors. Contemplating the first level of dependent arising—causal dependence—helps us to create the causes for higher rebirth by abandoning nonvirtue and practicing virtue. Contemplating a deeper level of dependent arising—dependent designation—leads us to realize emptiness and to attain liberation and awakening. Whether we seek a higher rebirth or highest goodness, understanding dependent arising is important and the teachings on it are precious.

Although the realization of the emptiness of inherent existence will free us from saṃsāra, we cannot dive into meditation on emptiness immediately. We must first eliminate coarse wrong conceptions, such as believing that our lives and our duḥkha are just random occurrences or that they arise from an external creator or from another incompatible cause. Contemplating causal dependence through the twelve links helps us to counteract these misnomers and to become familiar with dependent arising, the principal reason proving the emptiness of true existence. In the *Rice Seedling Sūtra*, the Buddha said:

> Monastics, he who understands this rice stalk can understand the meaning of dependent arising. Those who know dependent arising know the Dharma. Those who know the Dharma know the Buddha.

Dependent arising is an abbreviation for "dependent and related arising." In the context of the twelve links, *dependent* means that the arising of each link depends on the previous one. *Related* indicates that if one link does not exist, the next cannot arise; there is a relationship between the two links. Each set of twelve links contains the causes and results associated with one birth, although a complete set of twelve links may occur over two or three lifetimes. The twelve links are ignorance, formative actions, consciousness, name and form, six sources, contact, feeling, craving, clinging, renewed existence, birth, and aging or death. To fully understand each link, we need to understand its relation to both the link that precedes it and the link that follows it. The Buddha calls on us to contemplate: What is the origin of each link? What is its cessation? What is the path leading to that cessation?

In explaining the forward and reverse series of causation for both saṃsāra and liberation, the Buddha does not imply that any one link arises as a result of only the preceding link. Rather, a momentum builds up as the various factors augment and reinforce one another. In short, both saṃsāra and liberation depend on many interconnected causes and conditions.

How Cyclic Existence Occurs

When speaking of the twelve links, terminology is used in a specific way. For example, the link of ignorance refers to a specific instance of ignorance, not to all ignorance. The links of formative karma and consciousness refer to specific instances of these, not to all karma or all consciousnesses. Not all the types of craving and clinging described under the links of craving and clinging are instances of those two links.

The following explanation is from the Sanskrit tradition. A brief explanation of the Pāli tradition's perspective on a link is mentioned in cases where it differs or adds a unique perspective.

1. Ignorance (avidyā)

The ignorance that is the root of saṃsāra is beginningless. The Buddha said (AN 10.61–2):

> A first beginning of ignorance, monastics, cannot be discerned, of which it can be said, "Before that, there was no ignorance and it came to be after that." Though this is so, monastics, yet a specific condition of ignorance is discerned.

Although ignorance and cyclic existence are beginningless, in the evolution of a particular lifetime, ignorance is its initial cause. There are various explanations of what this ignorance is. Some say it is obscuration; others say it actively misapprehends how the person exists. Some say it observes the aggregates and conceives them to be a self-sufficient substantially existent person; others assert that it observes the mere I and grasps it to be an inherently existent person. Some associate the view of a personal identity with ignorance; others say they are unrelated mental factors.

According to the view held in common by all tenet schools and the Pāli tradition, first-link ignorance is the lack of understanding of the four truths of the āryas and of the three characteristics of conditioned phenomena—impermanence, duḥkha, and not-self—that leads to rebirth in saṃsāra. According to the Prāsaṅgikas, it is a moment of the innate ignorance grasping the person as inherently existent that leads to rebirth in saṃsāra.[49]

Vasubandhu, Asaṅga, and Dharmakīrti assert that the false conception of the self regards the aggregates and believes them to be a self-sufficient substantially existent person, whereas Prāsaṅgikas assert that the view of a personal identity observes the nominally existent I—the mere I—and grasps it to be inherently existent. Owing to the difference in their assertions about first-link ignorance, these masters have different assertions regarding what the wisdom realizing selflessness apprehends.

Vasubandhu and Asaṅga agree that first-link ignorance is an unknowing, a lack of clarity. However, Vasubandhu says that ignorance grasps the opposite of proper knowledge—in this case it grasps a self-sufficient substantially existent I—whereas Asaṅga asserts that ignorance does not grasp things as existing in a way opposite to how they exist. According to Vasubandhu, ignorance is similar to seeing a coiled rope at twilight: unable to see it clearly, we misconstrue it to be a snake. In the same way, due to the obscuring force of ignorance, how the aggregates exist is not clear and we suppose them to be a self-sufficient substantially existent person.

Vasubandhu's *Treasury of Knowledge* says, "Ignorance is like an enemy or a falsehood." An enemy is not just the lack of a friend, nor is it an unrelated object like a peach. It is the very opposite of a friend. Similarly, ignorance is not simply the lack of wisdom, nor is it an unrelated object. It is antithetical to wisdom.

Vasubandhu says that because the view of a personal identity is a form of intelligence—albeit an afflictive one—it cannot be ignorance. Ignorance accompanies the view of a personal identity, but the two are distinct mental factors. An innate affliction, ignorance is overcome only on the path of meditation, while the view of a personal identity is eliminated on the path of seeing. The primary mental consciousness that is accompanied by both ignorance and view of a personal identity has one facet that does not know the object accurately (ignorance), while simultaneously another facet apprehends the aggregates in a distorted manner and grasps them to be a self-sufficient substantially existent person (the view of a personal identity).

Asaṅga says that ignorance is like darkness that obscures seeing reality. It does not grasp the aggregates as existing in a contrary way, whereas view of a personal identity does. For this reason, he says view of a personal identity is not ignorance. He agrees that the view of a personal identity is a form of afflictive intelligence, but does not accept it as the mental factor of intelligence, because intelligence must necessarily be virtuous and the view of a personal identity is neutral.

Dharmakīrti says that the opposite of the wisdom realizing selflessness is the view of a personal identity, which he identifies with ignorance (PV). Ignorance observes the five aggregates and grasps them to be a self-sufficient substantially existent person.

> Here, the antidote, wisdom, is understanding the truth, the meaning of the selflessness of persons. Its opposite is the view of a personal identity, which grasps a self of persons.[50]

> All faults without exception arise from the afflictive view of self. That is ignorance.[51]

According to Prāsaṅgikas, the view of a personal identity and ignorance both grasp their object as existing inherently, and for that reason the view of a personal identity is a form of ignorance. First-link ignorance is the view of a personal identity; it is an innate self-grasping that has been present since beginningless time and gives rise to formative karma that projects a rebirth in cyclic existence. It is not acquired self-grasping that is due to familiarity with incorrect philosophies, nor is it the mental factor of ignorance, which is much broader and includes ignorance regarding karma and its effects. Ignorance grasps the inherent existence of persons and phenomena, whereas the view of a personal identity grasps the inherent existence of only our own I and mine. All beings except arhats, bodhisattvas on the eighth ground or higher, and buddhas have ignorance, but only ordinary beings—those below the path of seeing—have first-link ignorance. Āryas of the three vehicles who have not eradicated all afflictive obscurations have ignorance; however, it is not strong enough to produce karma that projects a saṃsāric rebirth and thus it is not first-link ignorance.

First-link ignorance is the specific moments of ignorance grasping inherent existence and the view of a personal identity that lie behind the motivation, performance, and completion of a virtuous or nonvirtuous karma powerful enough to project a rebirth in saṃsāra. It is not other moments of ignorance or other types of ignorance that occur in our lives. In short, first-link ignorance is the view of a personal identity that newly motivates its (that set of twelve links') second branch, formative action. This ignorance actively grasps the self as existing in a way it does not. It is the root of saṃsāra, the principal cause of rebirth in cyclic existence.

The notion of grasping inherent existence may seem abstract to us at first, but it is our frequent experience. When intense craving arises in us, the I appears to be independent of all other factors and we apprehend it as existing in this way. "*I* must have this!" When anger rules our minds, the self appears very solid, as if it existed under its own power. "That disturbs *me*!" The I seems to be somewhere within our bodies and minds, but also separate from them. This grasping is a troublemaker; it instigates and empowers afflictions that create karma, which ripen in lower rebirths. It also instigates polluted virtuous motivations, which bring higher rebirths, but still keep us bound in saṃsāra. It is a false view because when we examine how the I exists, we see it is not our minds, our bodies, the collection of body and mind, or something apart from them. The I exists by mere designation.

Vaibhāṣikas, Sautrāntikas, Cittamātrins, and Svātantrikas say first-link ignorance grasps a self-sufficient substantially existent person. This is the *root of saṃsāra* that must be eliminated to attain liberation. Cittamātrins and Svātantrikas also assert self-grasping of phenomena that must be eliminated to attain full awakening. They consider this to be the *ultimate root of saṃsāra*. For Cittamātrins the ignorance grasping a self of phenomena that is the final root of saṃsāra holds subjects and objects to be different entities and holds phenomena to exist by their own characteristics as the referents of their names. For Svātantrikas, the final root of saṃsāra is the ignorance grasping the true existence of all phenomena.

Prāsaṅgikas identify a subtler ignorance as the root of saṃsāra—the ignorance that grasps persons and phenomena to exist inherently. The view of a personal identity that grasps the I and mine is preceded by and dependent on the ignorance grasping the aggregates as inherently existent. Nāgārjuna says (RA 35):

> As long as the aggregates are grasped [as inherently existent],
> so long thereby does the grasping of I exist.
> Further, when the grasping of an [inherently existent] I exists,
> there is [formative] action, and from it there also is birth.

Grasping the aggregates as inherently existent gives rise to grasping the I that is merely designated in dependence on them to exist inherently. Based on the view of a personal identity that grasps our I as inherently existent, we create karma that projects rebirth in saṃsāra. Ignorance afflicts transmigrating beings because it obscures seeing the right view that directly perceives the emptiness of inherent existence.

How Ignorance Leads to the Creation of Karma

The *Treasury of Knowledge* speaks of two motivations for an action: (1) The *causal* or *initial motivation* (*hetu-samutthāna*) is the first motivation to act. It may occur a long time before the action is done. (2) The *immediate motivation* (*tatkṣaṇa-samutthāna*) occurs at the time of the action. Ignorance of the ultimate nature (ignorance grasping inherent existence) is the causal motivation for all polluted karma in general and for all formative actions that project rebirth in saṃsāra in particular.

When the immediate motivation, which occurs subsequent to the causal motivation, is an affliction such as attachment, anger, jealousy, or arrogance, the formative karma will be nonvirtuous. When the immediate motivation is virtuous—such as faith, integrity, or compassion—the formative karma will be virtuous. In short, first-link ignorance and the view of a personal identity are always neutral; the virtuous or nonvirtuous mental factors that arise after them determine the ethical value of the actions that follow.

As the initial motivation, first-link ignorance is the principal driving force that leads to formative karma. Distorted conceptions may arise after it—grasping the impermanent as permanent, what is duḥkha by nature as happiness, the unattractive as attractive, and the selfless as having a coarse self. Distorted attention that exaggerates the good or bad qualities of an object may also arise. Due to these distorted conceptions, the immediate motivation such as ignorance of karma and its effects coupled with other afflictions arise. With attachment we plan, connive, and manipulate to get the objects of our desire; we then lie or steal to make them ours. When our desires are thwarted, anger arises and develops into malice. We plan and act out retaliatory actions, mistakenly believing that anger protects us. Attachment and anger in the above examples are not a distinct link; some sages consider them part of the first link, others say they are the second link.

The causal motivation of first-link ignorance does not necessarily lead to nonvirtuous karma. When the immediate motivation is free from the ignorance of karma and its effects and is a virtuous mental state, the subsequent action will be virtuous. Examples are making offerings with faith, protecting life with compassion, and restraining from the ten nonvirtues.

The above is the technical description of causal and immediate motivations. Another way of using these terms is broader. Here *causal motivation* refers to the initial virtuous, nonvirtuous, or neutral thought to do an action sometime in the future, and *immediate motivation* is the intention at the time of doing the action.

In this case, both the causal and immediate motivations for an action are usually virtuous, nonvirtuous, or neutral, although sometimes they may differ. As part of our practice of training in bodhicitta, upon awakening each morning we generate contrived bodhicitta: "Today I will do all actions with the aspiration to attain full awakening to benefit all sentient beings." This is the causal motivation for all our actions that day. However, we often forget our altruistic intention, and the immediate motivation for many of our actions is attachment, animosity, jealousy, and so on. In this case, the immediate motivation determines the ethical value of the action, which is nonvirtuous. Nevertheless, generating bodhicitta in the morning is worthwhile because it lessens the strength of our destructive actions and reminds us to purify afterward. In addition, it plants seeds on our mindstreams so that one day we will have uncontrived, spontaneous bodhicitta. Sometimes the force of our compassionate motivation in the morning stays with us during the day, transforming many of our actions into virtue. High bodhisattvas' causal and immediate motivations for all actions are the same.

One action or mental state cannot be the cause of both saṃsāra and nirvāṇa. In general, any action that is instigated by ignorance is the cause of saṃsāra, even though the motivation may be virtuous, such as a similitude of the determination to be free from saṃsāra or the compassionate wish to help someone. Actions sustained by the power of the basis—referring to actions involving holy objects—are exceptions to this. Actions done with faith in the Three Jewels—such as making offerings, bowing, and meditating on their excellent qualities—are virtue concordant with liberation.

REFLECTION

1. Observe your thoughts during the day and identify the causal and immediate motivations for your actions.

2. Try to identify the ignorance of the ultimate nature. Then observe if misconceptions and instances of distorted attention arise.

3. Periodically during the day stop and examine your mental state: Is it vir-

tuous, nonvirtuous, or neutral? Is it creating the cause for happiness, suffering, or neither?

---

2. Formative Action (saṃskāra karman)

Formative actions afflict transmigrating beings because they plant polluted karmic seeds on the consciousness. Formative action is the intention (mental karma) or the physical or verbal action that is newly formed by first-link ignorance. It produces the mental and physical aggregates of a future birth in cyclic existence. In the context of the twelve links, formative action or karma refers specifically to volitional actions that bring rebirth as their result, not to all actions in general. These polluted virtuous and nonvirtuous intentions are expressed through the three doors of our bodies, speech, and minds in our deeds, words, and thoughts.

Formative actions are either virtuous or nonvirtuous; neutral mental states do not have the force to produce a rebirth because they lack a clear intention. The completion of the action produces a karmic seed that has the potency to bring a rebirth. This karmic seed is placed on the third link, causal consciousness. When nurtured by the eighth and ninth links—craving and clinging—the karmic seed will blossom into the tenth link, renewed existence, which in turn gives rise to the next birth. Both the seed and the resultant aggregates are ethically neutral.

Prāsaṅgikas say that in addition to the seed, the action also produces a having-ceased, a functioning thing that indicates the action happened and has stopped. Like karmic seeds, having-ceaseds are neutral. The having-ceased of an action and the karmic seed are activated by craving and clinging and lead to renewed existence.

Second-link formative action—our mental intentions and physical and verbal actions—is the direct cause of a future rebirth; it is a path of action with all four branches complete, which projects a fortunate or unfortunate rebirth. Other karmas that do not have all four branches or that are weaker complete that rebirth by influencing other conditions and events, such as our experiences, the environment we inhabit, and our habitual physical, verbal, and mental tendencies.

The term "formative action" may also be translated as "conditioning action," implying that it creates or composes something else, in this case a future rebirth. *Conditioning action* excludes unpolluted actions and neutral actions that are incapable of projecting a new birth with polluted aggregates.

Formative actions are of three types: demeritorious, meritorious, and invariable.

(1) *Demeritorious karma* is created under the influence of ignorance of ultimate truth and ignorance of karma and its effects; the motivation is one directed toward our own selfish happiness in this life. Created only in the desire realm, demeritorious karma leads to an unfortunate rebirth as a hell being, hungry ghost, or animal. Here the disadvantages of the eight worldly concerns become obvious. While it may be difficult to overcome our habituation to them, it is possible. By gradually steering our minds to more virtuous intentions, we will definitely decrease our misery now and in future lives.

(2) *Meritorious karma* is the virtuous karma created in the desire realm that leads to a fortunate rebirth in the desire realm. Such karma, created under the influence of first-link ignorance and virtuous mental factors, is created by Buddhists and non-Buddhists alike.

To create this meritorious karma, our motivation must be free from the eight worldly concerns that seek our selfish happiness of only this life. Our motive may be to live ethically and with kindness because those are our values. Someone who believes in rebirth may be motivated to take a higher rebirth with wealth and power. Although this is a worldly aspiration, it is free from attachment to the happiness of only this life and is a Dharma action and meritorious karma. Dharma practitioners who seek liberation or buddhahood want to have a series of higher rebirths in order to have a good basis to accumulate all the causes to fulfill their spiritual aims. Their actions done with that motivation are also meritorious.

(3) *Invariable karma* brings rebirth as a deva in the form or formless realms. These actions are created under the influence of first-link ignorance by a mind that has attained a form or formless realm meditative absorption that has not degenerated before the person dies.

Invariable karma leading to rebirth in the first three dhyānas where the feeling of happiness is present is motivated by a thought that is disinterested in lovely sense objects and primarily seeks the pleasurable feelings born from concentration. Someone who has reversed attachment for sense pleasure and grown tired of the bliss of the first three dhyānas seeks the feeling of equanimity. With this motivation she creates invariable karma that brings rebirth in the fourth dhyāna and the four formless realms. In these meditative states, the roughness of meditative bliss has been suppressed and the far-superior feeling of equanimity is experienced.

Invariable karma is so-called because it creates the cause to be born in that specific meditative absorption and no other. It may be the first, second, third, or fourth dhyāna of the form realm or a meditative absorption of infinite space, infinite consciousness, nothingness, or peak of saṃsāra (neither-discrimination-nor-nondiscrimination) in the formless realm. For example, a human being lacking Dharma realizations who develops the absorption of the second dhyāna and whose concentration has not degenerated before she dies will experience the craving and clinging of the second dhyāna at death. These will ripen that karmic seed, and she will be reborn in that very dhyāna, not in any other. In this sense that karma is invariable.

Each time we engage in an action supported by ignorance that has a clear intention and is either virtuous or nonvirtuous, we create the beginnings of a new set of twelve links. Which karmic seed and having-ceased ripen to bring the next rebirth depends on other factors such as the strength of the karma and our state of mind at the time of death. A new rebirth is not the sum total of all the karma we have ever created. Only one karma—or in some instances a few karma—determine the realm of our next rebirth.

How karma created to be reborn in the desire realm ripens may vary. The ripening of karma in the desire realm can be affected by the person's thoughts just before death, prayers of spiritual mentors, the circumstances of prospective parents, and occurrences in the *bardo* (the intermediate stage between death and the next life). If conditions change, upon a mini-death[52] in the bardo the karma that would bring rebirth as a dog may become inactive, and another karma that brings rebirth as a human being may ripen instead. Karma to be reborn as a human could ripen as rebirth in Amitābha's pure land if at the moment of death the person, either by her own power or by the influence of a spiritual friend, directs her mind toward Amitābha and his pure land.

Contemplating the first two links increases our renunciation of saṃsāra and motivates us to live ethically. We become more interested in learning about emptiness because the wisdom realizing the ultimate truth can eliminate the ignorance that is the root of saṃsāra and bring liberation.

REFLECTION

1. What are the different types of formative actions?
2. Trace the process of their arising from ignorance to afflictions to action. Make examples from your life.
3. As you go through the day, be aware that your actions that are complete with all four branches are creating causes for your future lives.
4. How does this awareness change how you think and what you do?

3. Consciousness (vijñāna)

Third-link consciousness is primarily to the polluted mental consciousness that has just joined to the next birth under the control of afflictions and karma. Third-link consciousness does not refer to all consciousnesses. It is not a sense consciousness, nor is it the consciousness of a buddha, pure-ground bodhisattva, or arhat, because they are no longer reborn under the power of afflictions and karma. Third-link consciousness afflicts transmigrating beings because it leads to the next rebirth.

The third link refers only to the mental consciousness of two specific moments:

(1) The *causal consciousness* is the moment of consciousness on which the karmic seed created by a formative action is placed. This consciousness is neutral and the seed of a virtuous or nonvirtuous karma infuses or "perfumes" it. The continuum of the causal consciousness carries the seed until the time it ripens as the new rebirth; at that time, it becomes the resultant consciousness.

(2) The *resultant consciousness* is the first, brief moment of mental consciousness at the beginning of a new life. In the next moment the fourth link, name and form, arises. In terms of most human lives, the resultant consciousness occurs at the moment of conception. We don't know if con-

ception occurs before the fertilized ovum implants in the uterus or at the time it does. It is also hard to say when the resultant consciousness occurs in cases of in vitro fertilization. However, it is clear that without the presence of a mental consciousness, the mere physical joining of a sperm and ovum will not become a human being.

What carries the karmic seeds until they bring their results is a widely discussed topic among Buddhist schools. In the context of the twelve links, the causal consciousness plays this role. The Vaibhāṣika, Sautrāntika, and Svātantrika schools assert the continuity of the mental consciousness to be the third-link consciousness. Unlike other Buddhist schools that assert six consciousnesses—visual, auditory, olfactory, gustatory, tactile, and mental—Cittamātra Scriptural Proponents assert eight consciousnesses, the previous six plus the afflictive consciousness and foundation consciousness (*ālayavijñāna*). The foundation consciousness, or storehouse consciousness, is the repository of all karmic seeds and assumes the role of the third-link consciousness. These Cittamātrins assert such a foundation consciousness because they say there must be a stable mind that carries karmic seeds from one life to the next. Also, there must be something that the word *I* refers to, something that is the person.

Prāsaṅgikas disagree, saying that in the long term the mere I carries the karmic seeds. They assert this because a nominally existent person exists when the action is created and when the action bears its result, so this mere I must be the basis for infusion of the karmic seed. The mere I is impermanent and cannot be found under ultimate analysis; there is nothing to point to and say "this is the person" other than the person that exists by mere imputation. Although the mere I carries the karmic seeds over a long period of time, the mental consciousness carries them temporarily. The mental consciousness cannot be the constant carrier because at the time a person directly realizes emptiness the mind is unpolluted, and polluted seeds cannot be associated with this unpolluted mind. Therefore the mere I carries the karmic latencies during this time.

Consciousness according to the Pāli Tradition

According to the sūtra explanation, third-link consciousness refers specifically to the consciousness that initiates the new life, the rebirth-linking consciousness (P. *paṭisandhicitta*) that follows the death consciousness and connects the mindstream from the previous life to the new life. This consciousness is illusory, like an echo, a light, a seal impression, or a shadow; it does not come here from the previous life yet it arises due to causes in previous lives.[53] The consciousness of the next life is not the same as the previous life's consciousness, nor it is totally unrelated. If they were identical, one could not cause the other. If they were totally unrelated, there would not be a continuum.

In the new life, consciousness simultaneously gives rise to the mental aspect of existence, which is called *name,* and animates the new physical *form*. In scientific terms, for a human rebirth, consciousness links with the fertilized ovum, making it become the body of a living being. Name consists of the five omnipresent mental factors of feeling, discrimination, intention, contact, and attention.[54]

In addition to this developmental perspective, consciousness conditions name and form whenever we cognize an object. The five factors of name depend on consciousness and cannot occur without it. Even in deep sleep, fainting, coma, or meditative absorption, consciousness is present, although it is a subtle type of consciousness that is not aware of the external world.

The Pāli Abhidharma explains that consciousness and name and form are *co-nascent,* meaning that they arise simultaneously like fire and its heat. In addition, consciousness and name and form are *mutual conditions* in that each conditions and supports the other, like two sticks leaning on each other to stand upright.

While the sūtras speak of six types of consciousness, emphasizing that each type of consciousness is responsible for cognizing its own corresponding object, consciousness also performs another role: it maintains the continuity of an individual's existence within any given life from birth until death and then beyond. It carries with it memories, karmic seeds, habits, and latencies, connecting different lives and making them a series such that future lives relate to previous ones.

4. Name and Form (nāma-rūpa)

Name and form afflict transmigrating beings because they hold the object of clinging, the body. *Name* refers to the four mental aggregates—feeling, discrimination, miscellaneous factors, and primary consciousnesses—and *form* is the body. The link of name and form exists during the time after the link of resultant consciousness and before the link of the six sources. Third-link consciousness is a condition for form because this body becomes a living body only when consciousness is present. When the "name" or mental aspect of this life ceases, the person's rebirth ends and the body remains a lifeless corpse. While the cognitive faculties remain after death, they cannot connect an object and preceding moment of consciousness to produce cognition because consciousness is no longer associated with the body.

The mental and physical aggregates—our minds and bodies—of this life are the polluted ripening result of karma. As such, they are produced by afflictions and karma. They are the basis of the duḥkha we experience in the present life, and because of attachment to them, afflictions arise, creating more karma that results in further rebirths.

In the case of human birth, fourth-link name and form refer to the five aggregates from the time just after conception until the time the five sense organs begin to develop. *Form* is the embryo that begins to grow in the womb. It consists of the four great elements—earth, water, fire, and air—and forms derived from them, such as color, smell, and so forth. The four great elements are metaphorical designations for the different qualities of matter. Earth is the solid aspect, the property of resistance and hardness. Water is the fluid and cohesive aspect that enables things to stay together. Fire is the quality of heat and energy, and air represents mobility, contraction, and expansion. Beings in the formless realm lack a body and have only the seed of form.[55]

Name refers to the four mental aggregates because they engage with objects with the help of names and terms. Just after conception only the mental and tactile consciousnesses arise because in the embryo only the mental and tactile faculties are present.[56]

Name and Form in the Pāli Tradition

Name (mentality) and form (materiality) are major aspects of our experience. *Form* is the four great elements forming the body. *Name* is a collective term for the other three mental aggregates (feeling, discrimination, and miscellaneous factors) and the five mental factors (contact, feeling, discrimination, intention, and attention) that accompany consciousness and are indispensable to making sense of and naming things in the world around us. When the object, cognitive faculty, and corresponding consciousness come together, *contact* is essential for any cognition. Once contact has occurred, *attention* functions to bring the mind to the object. Then *feeling, discrimination, and intention* arise as ways of experiencing and relating to the object. Although all five mental factors are present, the strength of each one will vary according to the mental state. When strong pain or pleasure is foremost, feeling is more prominent; when we are examining something and noting its characteristics, discrimination is stronger. When we are making plans and deciding what to do, intention is foremost.

Why are contact and feeling included in name when name is earlier in the causal sequence than the links of contact and feeling? Why are feeling, discrimination, and miscellaneous factors part of name as well as objects known by the mental source, which is part of the next link, the six sources? Different instances of these mental factors are spoken of in each link. While one instance of contact and feeling occur simultaneously with the link of name, another instance of contact follows name and form, and another instance of feeling follows that instance of contact. Similarly, one instance of the three mental aggregates may be included in name and form, while another instance is the object known by the mental source.

5. Six Sources (ṣaḍāyatana)

The fifth-link six sources are the six cognitive faculties that exist in the nature of the polluted ripening result (the five aggregates) during the time after the link of name and form has occurred and before the link of contact has come about. In the case of a human rebirth, the six internal sources—eye, ear, nose, tongue, body, and mental cognitive faculties—develop in the womb. They enable us to cognize the six external sources—visible forms, sounds, odors, tastes, tactile objects, and phenomena. The phenomena source (*dharmāyatana*) is objects of mental consciousness that are perceptible by mind but are not included in the first five external sources. It includes the aggregates of feeling, discrimination, and miscellaneous factors, and various subtle forms—such as dream objects and prātimokṣa ethical restraints—that cannot be known through the five physical senses.

The cognitive faculties are subtle sensitive forms located in the larger organs listed above, such as the eyeball. They function to connect an object and consciousness so that cognition of the object occurs. The six are called *sources* because they are the sources for the arising of the six consciousnesses.

If a sense faculty is injured and unable to function, the corresponding sensory function is also impaired. The body source is on the skin and inside certain areas of the body. It enables us to experience smooth and rough, hard and soft, and hot and cold, as well as hunger and thirst. The mental faculty is not form; it consists of the six consciousnesses that enable a later moment of mental consciousness to know objects.

The tactile and mental faculties are present from conception onward. The remaining four cognitive faculties come into being as the embryo develops. When the six cognitive faculties have formed this link is complete, and the new being has the potential to experience objects through the coming together of the object, cognitive faculty, and preceding moment of consciousness.

Sentient beings are born in four ways: by womb, egg, heat and moisture, and spontaneously. When beings such as devas and hell beings are born spontaneously, all cognitive faculties are complete, and they are fully equipped to interact with their environment.

A question arises: Do all twelve links pertain to rebirth in the three realms—desire, form, and formless? Vasubandhu's *Treasury of Knowledge* says that since beings in the form realm are spontaneously born and do not go through development in the womb, they lack the link of name and form because all their cognitive faculties are present at the time of conception. He also says that there is no occasion for the link of name and form or for five of the six sources for beings in the formless realm because they do not have bodies. Because they have only the mental source, they experience only ten links.

Asaṅga differs, saying all twelve links are present in births in all three realms. Name and form are partially present in the form realm, and in the formless realm, the link of name and form consists of only the mental consciousness. The link of six sources is partially present because the mental source exists although the sense sources do not.

The six sources afflict transmigrating beings because they complete name and form, thereby creating the potential for awareness of objects to arise.

The Six Sources according to the Pāli Tradition

The fifth-link six sources are the six internal cognitive faculties that join the object and the consciousness to produce contact, the sixth link. The way that the six sources arise from name and form can be understood in two ways: the development immediately after conception and the conditioning that occurs in any cognition.

Using the example of a human being, in *the developmental model* name and form refer to the psychophysical organism that was conceived in the mother's womb and is beginning to evolve. At the moment of conception the consciousness from the previous life enters the fertilized ovum. That is called "name and form taking place in the womb."

At this time, the consciousness from the previous life becomes the mental source, and with it arise the other three mental aggregates and the five omnipresent mental factors that constitute name. In this way, name becomes the condition for the mental sense source. The mental functioning of this newly conceived being is rudimentary.

After conception, the fertilized ovum becomes the body, which is made up of the four elements and form derived from the elements. As a tiny embryo, it has the tactile sense source (tactile faculty) and is capable of experiencing hardness, softness, smoothness, roughness, hot, cold, and so on. As the embryo develops, certain cells begin to specialize and the eye, ear, nose, and tongue sense sources arise. These are not the coarse physical organs but rather subtle sensitive material within them that is able to connect the object and consciousness to produce contact and cognition. In this way, form is the support of the six sense sources. If name and form are cut off—for example, in a miscarriage—the new human being ceases and the six sources do not develop.

Regarding the *conditioning that occurs in any cognition* in our daily lives, there is a complex interconnected web of factors that must come together as name and form for a particular sense source to exist and produce contact. In a visual cognition, the visual consciousness and the mental factors that make up name arise dependent on the eye source. That requires the existence of our eyeballs, which are made of the four elements and their derivatives. The eye source could not function if the body were not alive, and that requires the presence of consciousness and its accompanying mental factors. It is in that way that name and form condition the six sense sources.

Name—the mental aspect of living beings—depends on form—the body. The functioning of the body as a living organism depends on the presence of consciousness and the five omnipresent mental factors. Buddhaghoṣa says (Vism 18.36):

> They cannot come to be by their own strength,
> or yet maintain themselves by their own strength.
> Relying for support on other states,
> weak in themselves, and formed, they come to be.
> They come to be with others as condition;
> they are aroused by others as their objects;
> they are produced by object and condition,
> and each by something other than itself.
>
> And just as people depend upon
> a boat for traversing the sea,
> so does the mental "body" need
> the physical body for occurrence.
> And as the boat depends upon
> the people for traversing the sea,
> so does the physical body need
> the mental "body" for occurrence.
> Depending each upon the other,
> the boat and people go on the sea.
> And so do mind and body both
> depend the one upon the other.

Included in the mental source is the *bhavaṅga*, or subliminal consciousness. Spoken of in the commentaries and the Abhidhamma, but not the sūtras, the bhavaṅga is a passive, underlying stream of consciousness from which active consciousness arises. It occurs in the absence of any cognitive process and serves to connect all the active states of consciousness; however, it is not a permanent consciousness or self. It is included in the mental source because due to it, active mental consciousness arises. At the microscopic level of individual mind moments in the waking state, the mind could be going in and out of the bhavaṅga so quickly that we do not notice it. During sleep, the mind is in bhavaṅga for a longer time, emerging to dream and then returning to dreamless sleep with the bhavaṅga. The bhavaṅga is also present when fainting.

6. Contact (sparśa)

Contact is the polluted mental factor that, due to the convening of the three—the object, cognitive faculty, and consciousness—causes the object to be experienced as pleasant, painful, or neutral through its own capability and that exists after the link of six sources has occurred and before the link of feeling has come about. Contact afflicts transmigrating beings because it connects the object, cognitive faculty, and the consciousness, so that beings dualistically discriminate.

In general, a consciousness comes about because of three conditions: (1) The *observed object condition* (*ālambana-pratyaya*) is the object that causes a consciousness to be generated in its aspect—for example, in the aspect of blue or of a sound. (2) The *dominant condition* (*adhipati-pratyaya*) is the cognitive faculty that causes its corresponding consciousness to apprehend its corresponding object and no other. The dominant condition for sight—the eye faculty—enables a visual consciousness to apprehend color and shape, but not smell or taste. (3) The *immediately preceding condition* (*samanantara-pratyaya*) is the previous moment of consciousness that allows the next moment of consciousness to arise as something that cognizes objects.

When these three come together, contact arises. Because there are six objects (form, sound, smell, taste, touch, and phenomena), six cognitive faculties (eye, ear, nose, tongue, body, and mind), and six consciousnesses (visual, auditory, olfactory, gustatory, tactile, and mental), there are six types of contact. Contact acts as the basis for and leads to the feeling that exists in the next moment.

7. Feeling (vedanā)

Feeling is the polluted mental factor that experiences the object as pleasurable (happy), painful (suffering), or neutral through its own capability, by depending on its cause, the link of contact. *Feeling* here does not mean emotion; rather, it is the pleasant, unpleasant, or neutral experience that comes about just after any of our cognitive faculties contact an object and produce a consciousness cognizing that object. Feeling afflicts transmigrating beings because it experiences the polluted feelings of pleasure and pain.

While feeling is usually categorized as of three types—pleasure, pain, and neutral—or of five types—physical pleasure, mental happiness, physical pain, mental pain, and neutral—here in the explanation of dependent origination it is of six types: the feelings arising from eye, ear, nose, tongue, tactile, and mental contact. While many other mental factors, such as discrimination and intention, also arise in response to contact, the Buddha singled out feeling because it leads most directly to craving. This is evident in our lives: experiencing pleasure leads to craving for more pleasant feelings, experiencing pain sparks craving to be separated from such undesirable feelings, and experiencing neutral feeling prompts craving for it not to diminish. The latter especially applies to beings in the fourth dhyāna and above who have only neutral feeling and do not wish the peace it brings to cease.

Ignorance, karma, and causal consciousness project a rebirth that begins with the resultant consciousness and continues as the body develops during the links of name and form and the six sources, so that contact and feeling occur. Feeling is one of the chief ways that karma ripens: virtuous actions produce pleasant physical and mental feelings and nonvirtuous actions produce painful physical and mental feelings. On the one hand, feelings are the result of an evolutionary process beginning with ignorance and karma. On the other hand, they initiate a new chain of events because they instigate craving. Craving, which is also reflected in emotions such as attachment and anger, creates more karma. In this way, saṃsāra perpetuates itself.

If we observe our experience closely, we will notice how many feelings we experience, one after the other, during the day. We will also notice how reactive we are to those feelings. Our craving to have pleasure and to avoid pain is strong, affecting our moods and motivating most of our actions. The idea of experiencing pleasure from our morning cup of coffee or tea gets us out of bed in the morning. Seeking the happiness that comes from having money and possessions, we go to work. Craving to be free of pain, we defend ourselves against criticism and lash out at anything that hurts or even inconveniences us.

The space between feeling and craving is one of the places where the forward motion of dependent origination can be broken. Feelings naturally arise when contact with external objects or internal objects such as memories, ideas, and plans occurs. By being aware of feelings and noting them with introspective awareness, it is possible to prevent craving from arising in response to them. We practice observing feelings without reacting to them, observing where they come from, where they abide, and where they go. We study the seemingly instantaneous reactions we have to different feelings and how our craving for unpleasant feelings and craving to be free from unpleasant feelings control our lives.

Only feelings accompanied by ignorance cause craving. When ignorance has been eliminated, feelings are present but craving does not arise. Arhats, pure ground bodhisattvas, and buddhas also experience feelings, but since their feelings are not the result of a process initiated by ignorance, they are blissful.

The feelings experienced by an awakened one are inconceivable for us ordinary beings. During the Buddha's lifetime, a great drought and famine afflicted the land. The saṅgha received no alms, until one man who owned horses gave the monks some fodder to eat. The fodder tasted disgusting to the monks, but the Buddha ate it contentedly. One monk, overcome with sadness that the Buddha had to endure such foul food, said, "What a desperate situation that the Blessed One has only this vile fodder to eat!" The Buddha lovingly responded, "Please don't worry," and taking a small part of the fodder from his mouth, gave it to the monk to eat. Chewing it, the monk was astonished to taste what had become delicious divine food owing to its contact with the Buddha's senses.

REFLECTION

1. Observe your feelings with mindfulness and introspective awareness and identify pleasant, unpleasant, and neutral feelings.
2. Be aware that they arise after contact with an object.
3. Watch how instantly craving arises for pleasant feelings to continue and for unpleasant feelings to cease.
4. How do all these feelings, as well as the craving they provoke, affect your life? How do you respond to them?

5. Are there certain objects that it would be helpful for you to avoid temporarily so that you can work on reducing the craving that results from contact with them?

---

8. Craving (tṛṣṇā)

Craving is a mental factor that, by depending on the link of feeling, does not wish to separate from its object. Eighth-link craving occurs specifically while we are actively dying and is a form of attachment that arises strongly while the body weakens and the coarse consciousnesses still function. This craving does not wish to separate from our possessions, our dear ones, our body, and the ego-identity we have constructed during this life. Craving afflicts transmigrating beings by making the next rebirth closer.

In general three types of craving arise during the course of our lifetimes:

(1) *Craving for pleasant feeling* arises through the contact of our cognitive faculties with particular sense objects and does not want to separate from pleasurable feelings and the attractive objects and people that stimulate them. The Buddha compares giving in to craving to a person who drinks an exquisitely delicious drink knowing it contains poison. We become like laboratory rats who exhaust themselves tapping on a lever although they very rarely get a grain of rice for their effort.

(2) *Craving for existence* arises while dying because of terror that the continuity of the self will cease. Fearing that we will no longer exist, craving for saṃsāric aggregates surges.

(3) *Craving for nonexistence* desperately seeks separation from painful feelings. When the mind contacts an undesirable object, pain arises. This gives rise to craving for the pain to become nonexistent; we want to be released from the painful feeling and the object or person that triggered it. An extreme instance of this craving yearns for the self to become totally nonexistent at the time of death—a mistaken, nihilistic notion that could lead to suicide and bring devastating results.

The three types of craving are also described in relation to the three feelings: (1) craving not to be separated from pleasurable feelings, (2) craving to be separated from painful feelings, and (3) craving for neutral feeling not to diminish—that is, for neutral feelings not to degenerate into painful feelings.

In our daily lives, we can witness feeling giving rise to craving. We crave the pleasant feelings and the possessions, people, situations, talents, and opportunities that appear to generate them. We crave to be separated from anything that disturbs our peace, including ideas and policies we disagree with. Craving clearly demonstrates the unsatisfactory nature of cyclic existence—we always want something, are fearful of losing what we like, and are impatient to be free of what we don't like.

Once craving arises with respect to any of the three feelings, it swiftly leads to clinging to that feeling and to the object that seems to bring it. This, too, is easy to observe in our lives. We experience pleasure from being praised. Enjoying it, we crave more. When craving increases, clinging arises as we wish to hear more ego-pleasing words and to be with the people who say them.

From another perspective, craving is of six types: craving for visible objects, sounds, smells, tastes, tangibles, and phenomena. The latter are objects of mental consciousness and include conceptual appearances of the objects perceived by the five senses, thoughts, images, fantasies, ideas, feelings, and emotions. Craving is described in terms of its six objects because it arises from feeling, feeling from contact, and contact from the sense sources; each of those links is delineated as six in dependence on the six objects.

Developing mindfulness and wisdom to identify and counteract the different types of craving is essential. To do this, contemplate the various things you encounter and think about. Consider that they are merely fleeting conventions. They have no inherent essence. There is no "me," no "them." In this way, practice viewing all mental states and objects as transient. Let them go without attaching to them.

Beings who are free from craving experience whatever feelings arise in their minds with equanimity rather than with dissatisfied or fearful reactivity. Freedom from craving does not mean our lives become boring. Rather, there is now mental space for constructive aspirations—to develop wisdom, love, and compassion, and to benefit sentient beings—that are not influenced by ignorance.

Craving according to the Pāli Tradition

Craving for sense pleasure is described the same as in the Sanskrit tradition. *Craving for existence* seeks rebirth in any of the three realms. It accompanies the view of permanence (eternalism), which adheres to the notion of a permanent, unitary, independent self or soul that continues on, unchanged, after death. Most societies and religions throughout history have held an eternalistic view of one kind or another, and such a view is deeply ingrained in people who were taught as children that there is a permanent soul.

Craving for nonexistence accompanies the nihilistic view, which believes that when the body ceases to function after death, the self or person is totally annihilated. This view may arise in someone who falls into despair or cynicism and concludes that since death is inevitable and everything ceases at death, it is pointless to prepare for future lives or seek liberation. This view may also arise in someone who adheres to a materialistic doctrine that negates any existence after death. Thinking that total obliteration of existence is peaceful, such a person craves to cease completely at death.

All these forms of craving are manifestations of ignorance. A monk once asked the Buddha, "Who craves?" The Buddha replied that this question was not suitable. Rather than try to isolate a self that craves, it is appropriate to investigate, "What is the condition for craving?" Since craving arises dependent on feeling, we need to apply mindfulness, introspective awareness, and wisdom to our feelings, observing them as they are and doing our best not to react to them with any of the three types of craving.

REFLECTION

1. The space between feeling and craving is a weak spot in the twelve links. If we can learn to experience pleasant and painful feelings without reacting to them with craving, we can cease the production of formative karma.
2. Observe how easily and habitually each type of craving arises in response to a particular feeling.
3. Practice simply experiencing the feeling without craving for it to last longer or to cease immediately. Cultivate wise equanimity, not ignorant indifference, to feelings.

9. Clinging (upādāna)

Clinging is attachment that is the strong increase of craving. As it becomes increasingly evident that the aggregates of this life will be forfeited, craving gives rise to clinging—strong attachment for new polluted aggregates.

While a person is dying, he may have an illusory appearance of his next life and where he will be reborn. Even if someone will be born in an unfortunate realm, the illusory appearance of that place will be agreeable; he craves birth there, which leads to clinging to be born there. This nourishes the karmic seed previously placed on the causal consciousness, so that the karma is transformed into the link of renewed existence. Similarly, in terms of taking a fortunate rebirth, the dying person is attracted, for example, to an appearance of a precious human life. Craving and clinging arise for that, causing the seed of a virtuous karma to ripen and bringing the link of renewed existence for this fortunate rebirth.

This process occurs while a person is actively dying, while the mind still has coarse recognition and the person can recall things. From the perspective of the death process described in highest yoga tantra, craving and clinging occur prior to the white appearance, while the coarse mind is still functioning. When the coarse mental aggregates absorb, the mind is unable to remember virtue and nonvirtue, and the link of renewed existence has come about. In this way, clinging afflicts transmigrating beings because it prepares for the next life in saṃsāra.

Arhats have many karmic seeds that have the potential to bring a rebirth, but these cannot ripen because arhats have eliminated craving and clinging.

In the bardo someone who will be reborn as a human being sees the sperm and ovum of her parents, mistakenly believes the parents are in union, and craves and clings to be there. Clinging to the fertilized ovum, the person wants to be in that body and not to lose it. The consciousness enters the fertilized ovum, creating a mass that is conducive for the arising of the cognitive faculties.[57]

Clinging can nourish a karmic potency at other times of our lives. Frequently generating the aspiration to be reborn with a precious human life helps to nourish the karmic seeds on our mindstreams that will bring this about. Karmic seeds may be nourished by other means as well. If we have created the karma for a precious human life, all the other virtuous activities we do in life—making prostrations and offerings, studying and practicing the Dharma—help to nourish that potency. The craving and clinging that arise while we are actively dying are not a manifest thought, "I want this in the future," that is formed with effort. Craving and clinging are innate; ordinary beings experience them while they are dying whether or not they believe in rebirth.

In general, four types of clinging may arise during our lifetimes (MN 11.9):

(1) *Clinging to sense pleasures and desirable objects* arises easily for us beings in the desire realm and dominates our lives. One of our cognitive faculties contacts an object that sparks the experience of pleasure or happiness. Attachment arises followed by clinging to the pleasant feeling and the object that triggered it. Beings in the form and formless realms have suppressed clinging to sense pleasure, yet clinging to the intense bliss or peace of meditative absorption still arises in them.

Clinging to sensual pleasure lies behind most of the karma we human beings create. It motivates us to lie, cheat, backbite, and speak harshly to procure and protect the things we desire. It lies behind most of the scandals we read about. Besides harming ourselves and leading to unfortunate rebirths, it adversely affects others, even leading people to lose faith in those who occupy positions of authority and respect.

Some people who have the correct view of karma and its results want to enjoy sensual pleasures in future lives. They asked the Buddha how to attain heavenly rebirths or how to meet their spouse again in a future life. The Buddha taught ethical conduct, generosity, and kindness, which they happily practiced to attain their goal.

(2) *Clinging to views* clings to the view of extremes, the view holding wrong views as supreme, and wrong views, especially the wrong view disparaging karma and its effect, the existence of past and future lives, and so forth. Clinging to views easily leads to dogmatism, attachment to one's own religion, and denigration of other religions to the extent that one forces one's religious views on others either by verbal coercion or threats of violence.

(3) *Clinging to a doctrine of self* is the view of a personal identity that grasps the I and mine to exist inherently. Clinging to the self is the force behind our afflictions and lies behind most of our self-centered actions that create destructive karma. It arises throughout our lives and is especially powerful as we are dying. This clinging may also adhere to a permanent self

or soul or to a self-sufficient substantially existent I and mine. It may also motivate virtuous actions; some people keep ethical conduct because they want their eternal self to be born in a heavenly realm.

(4) *Clinging to rules and practices* arises as a result of holding wrong views about duḥkha and its causes. It causes us to have distorted notions of ethical conduct or the path to liberation. These include advocating extreme self-mortification by fasting for a long time, sitting in fire, and going naked in the cold. It may also lead to unethical actions such as sacrificing animals to have good fortune, thinking that the flawless performance of rituals causes liberation, or conflating meditative absorption with liberation.

These four types of clinging focus predominantly on distorted ideas and do not include all types of clinging.

Clinging according to the Pāli Tradition

Craving can also mean to thirst for something we do not yet have, and clinging can also imply holding on to what we already have. The three types of craving—for sensual pleasures, existence, and nonexistence—are generally directed toward what we do not yet have, while the four types of clinging—for sensual pleasure, views, doctrines of self, and view of rules and practices—are usually directed toward what we already hold.

The three types of craving and four types of clinging are related. Craving for sensual pleasure produces clinging to sensual pleasure. Craving for sensual pleasure may influence us to cling to certain views. Thinking that the purpose of life is simply to enjoy sensual pleasures could lead us to breach ethical conduct by stealing, lying, or having an affair. Craving for sensual pleasure in future lives could lead to holding the view of rules and practices, for example, believing that killing infidels will bring a heavenly rebirth with many sensual pleasures.

Craving for existence, which accompanies the eternalistic view, easily leads to clinging to a doctrine of self as well as clinging to views. Craving for nonexistence, which often accompanies the nihilistic view, could lead to clinging to views and to the view of rules and practices. For example, thinking that nothing exists after death, someone could think that it doesn't matter how they act as long as the authorities do not find out.

Clinging to wrong views, views of rules and practices, and view of a personal identity are abandoned at stream-entry when the fetters of doubt, view of rules and practices, and view of a personal identity are eliminated. Clinging to sense pleasure decreases when one becomes a once-returner and is abandoned when one becomes a nonreturner. Only arhats have abandoned all clinging.

REFLECTION

1. Identify moments of each of the four types of clinging in your experience.
2. How do they affect your life?
3. What ideas do you have for counteracting them?

---

10. Renewed Existence (bhava)

Renewed existence is the factor existing in the nature of the ripening aggregates (the body and mind of the future life) bound by afflictions, which is the potential of karma made stronger by craving and clinging. As a cause of birth, it refers not to the state a being will be born into but to the karmic force that leads to rebirth in that state. Renewed existence occurs the moment that all the causes for the future life have been completed in this life; it is the ripening of the karmic seed that is just about to produce the next life. The karma that projects the rebirth was the second link. It ceased and its continuation exists as a having-ceased and a karmic seed. Renewed existence is the fully nourished karmic seed and that karma's having-ceased that have the potential to produce a new birth in cyclic existence.

The link of renewed existence occurs in two stages. The *entering stage* is the fully nourished potency that is directed toward the next life. It occurs in the present life before death. The *entered stage* is the fully nourished potency during the bardo between two lives. There are three kinds of renewed existence corresponding to the three realms of saṃsāric existence: desire realm, form realm, and formless realm renewed existence.

Renewed existence is a case of giving the name of the result to the cause. For example, after planting a sprout, we say, "I planted a tree," giving the name of the resultant tree to the sprout that was its cause. Renewed existence is analogous to a seed (link 2) planted in a field (link 3) that is nourished by water and sunshine (links 8 and 9). The potential of the seed is now ready (link 10) to become a sprout (link 11).

Formative action and renewed existence are the same karma at different times. They differ in that formative action has not been activated by craving and clinging and is not immediately able to project another birth.

In terms of rebirth in the form and formless realms, a meditator must gradually prepare to attain the next higher meditative absorption of those realms. Each of the four dhyānas and the four formless absorptions have seven preparations (*manaskāra*)[58]—stages of contemplation that aid in attaining the next level of meditative absorption. Form realm renewed existence is the dhyāna that a meditator has attained in this life that will bring rebirth in that specific dhyāna in the next life. Formless realm renewed existence is the level of formless realm meditative absorption that a meditator has reached in this life that will propel her to be reborn in that specific formless realm in the next life.

While tenth-link renewed existence occurs while actively dying, in general there are four types of renewed existence, each of them occurring under the control of afflictions and karma: (1) *Renewed existence of birth* leads to the consciousness joining to the next birth under the control of afflictions and karma. (2) *Renewed existence of death* is the last moment of this life. (3) *Renewed existence of the bardo* occurs when the consciousness joins to the intermediate state under the control of afflictions and karma. At this time one has a subtle body similar to the body of the next birth. The bardo lasts the maximum of seven weeks and is considered part of the next life. (4) *Renewed existence of the previous time* begins the moment after the link of birth, lasts during the lifetime, and ends at death. Here *previous* means prior to death of that life.

Not only do ignorance and formative action bind us to saṃsāra, so do the craving, clinging, and renewed existence that occur while actively dying. These last three force the consciousness to join to the next body. In this way, afflictions and karma tie the merely designated self to cyclic existence. Wherever consciousness goes, the self goes, because consciousness is the principal basis of designation of the self.

Renewed existence afflicts transmigrating beings because it makes the resultant rebirth definitely occur.

Renewed Existence according to the Pāli Tradition

In the Pāli tradition also, renewed existence is the name of the result being given to the cause. *The Path of Purification* distinguishes two aspects of renewed existence. These are the same karma in different stages of ripening.

(1) *Karmically active renewed existence* is intention and the mental factors of covetousness and so forth conjoined with those intentions. The formative karma of meritorious, demeritorious, and invariable karma (link 2) is a condition giving rise to karmically active renewed existence, which is the karma that, as a condition for the next life, is ready to bring that new rebirth. It is of three types, corresponding to the three realms.

Nonvirtuous actions are desire realm renewed existence and lead to unfortunate rebirths as hell beings, hungry ghosts, and animals. Mundane virtuous actions such as the ten virtues are also desire realm renewed existence, but they bring rebirth as human beings and devas. Form realm renewed existence is any of the dhyānas that people have attained, mastered, and continued until the time of death. Formless realm renewed existence is any of the formless realm absorptions that are attained, mastered, and preserved until death. Form and formless realm rebirths last for eons, but when that karma is exhausted those beings take birth in less favorable circumstances.

(2) *Resultant rebirth renewed existence* is the four or five aggregates subject to clinging and projected by karma. This is the moment of rebirth as well as the entire existence in which we experience the many diverse results of our previous actions. Birth is the beginning of the resultant rebirth existence, aging is the continuation of that existence, and death is the end of that particular resultant rebirth existence.

During the time of the resultant rebirth existence, we sentient beings, through our choices and decisions and the actions that express them, create many new karmas that will lead to future rebirths in saṃsāra. Although these choices and decisions are influenced by our previous actions, they are not completely determined by them. We have the freedom to make responsible choices and to either nourish or counteract our tendencies toward various intentions.

In short, karmically active renewed existence is the causal karmic energy that projects a rebirth, and resultant rebirth existence is the resultant rebirth that is attained.

REFLECTION

1. Imagine your death and the dying process.
2. Based on how you have lived and on your habitual tendencies, what types of craving and clinging are likely to arise in your mind at this time?
3. What kind of thoughts and aspirations would you like to have while you are dying? Recall that these will influence which karmic seeds are nourished and become renewed existence.
4. How can you train in these thoughts and aspirations now so that your mind will be in a virtuous state then?

11. Birth (jāti)

Birth is the aggregates that exist in the nature of the ripening result bound by afflictions and joined to a new life in saṃsāra under the control of afflictions and karma. Ordinarily we think of birth as a baby coming out of the mother's womb, breathing on her own, and beginning her life. From a Buddhist perspective, birth is the first moment of the new life. For mammals this occurs when the consciousness joins with the fertilized ovum. The resultant consciousness—the second part of link 3—is the continuation of the mindstream of a being who has left its former body. This consciousness brings with it all the karmic seeds and latencies of afflictions that were present in the previous life. These will condition many aspects of the new being: which body with its specific genetic makeup he will take rebirth in, his upbringing and experiences, and his tendencies in the new life.

The link of birth lasts only a moment; from the second moment onward, aging or death occurs. Birth is the cause of aging and death. The Buddha makes the point that without being born, we would not age and die (DN 15.4):

> If, Ānanda, there were no birth at all, anywhere, of anybody or anything: of devas in the deva-state, of gandhabbas . . . , of yakkhas . . . , of hungry ghosts . . . , of humans . . . , of quadrupeds . . . , of birds . . . , of reptiles to the reptile state, if there were

> absolutely no birth at all of all these beings, then with the absence of all birth, the cessation of birth, could aging and death appear?—"No, venerable sir." Therefore, Ānanda, just this is the root, the cause, the origin, the condition of aging and death—namely, birth.

In society birth is usually seen as auspicious and people joyously welcome the birth of a child. We are blind to the inevitable result of birth—aging and death. When we train our minds to see the complete picture of life—birth, aging, sickness, and death—our aspiration will turn toward liberation.

As noted above, birth may occur in four ways: from the womb, egg, heat and moisture, and spontaneously. Hell beings, devas, and bardo beings are born spontaneously without having to go through a developmental process. Some hungry ghosts are born from the womb, others are born spontaneously. Animals are born from the womb, egg, and, as in the case of insects, from heat and moisture. There are instances of human beings being born in all four ways.

Rebirth afflicts transmigrating beings because it brings aging and death, which are the essential duḥkha of transmigrating beings.

Birth according to the Pāli Tradition

There is a debate, beginning with the early Buddhist schools and continuing to this day, about whether there is a period of time between the death of one life and the following rebirth. Although no clear statement is found in the Pāli sūtras, some passages suggest this. It makes sense that in some cases, time is necessary for the suitable immediate conditions to come together for a birth that accords with the ripening karma of renewed existence. If the parents of the next life are in different places at the moment someone dies, a period of time is needed for them to come together again.

Birth, aging, and death have different meanings according to the context. In the *Vibhaṅga*, the second book of the Pāli Abhidhamma, *birth* refers not to birth in one of the three realms but to the arising of a mind-moment. *Aging* refers to the impermanence intrinsic in all conditioned phenomena, not to gray hair, aches, and pains. Death is that mind-moment's cessation, not the upcoming separation of body and mind. Each presentation is valid and useful, but they should not be confused with each other or used to invalidate the other.

12. Aging or Death (jarāmaraṇa)

Aging and death are the result of birth. Aging is the body and mind that decay under the control of afflictions and karma. Death is the cessation of a similar type of mental and physical aggregates; it is the mind's separation from the body under the control of afflictions and karma. This link is called aging *or* death because some beings die before becoming aged. The Buddha says (SN 12.2):

> The aging of beings in the various orders of beings, their growing old, brokenness of teeth, grayness of hair, wrinkling of skin, decline of vitality, degeneration of faculties—this is called aging. The passing of beings from the various orders of beings, their perishing, breakup, disappearance, dying, completion of time, breakup of the aggregates, laying down of the carcass—this is called death.

Being under the influence of afflictions and karma, our bodies become ill, age, and die without choice. Contemplating this enables strong renunciation of saṃsāra's duḥkha to grow in our minds.

Aging can be spoken of in two ways: (1) *Progressive aging* occurs each moment of life, beginning the moment after conception. It is not the case that we grow up and aging starts at an amorphous future date. Rather, from the moment after conception onward, we are aging and nearing death. (2) *Deterioration* is aging with the discomfort and fear that accompany old age.

The *Sūtra on the Ten Grounds* (*Daśabhūmika Sūtra*) says:

> Death has two functions: (1) it causes a conditioned phenomenon to disintegrate, and (2) it brings about the cause of the continuation of ignorance.[59]

Death itself is a conditioned phenomenon, a result of birth. It causes a life to cease and, for ordinary beings, it enables ignorance and saṃsāric rebirth to continue.

Between aging and death is lamentation, sorrow, not getting what we seek, being separated from what is dear, encountering and being forced to endure what we do not like, being disillusioned when events do not occur as wished, and being unable to control the experiences and events we encounter in life. Reflecting on this closely, we begin to see cyclic existence for what it is: unreliable and repugnant.

The link of aging or death includes all our experiences of the duḥkha of pain and the duḥkha of change, which result from the preceding link, birth. This points to a deeper level of duḥkha—the pervasive duḥkha of conditioning, which is the underlying basis for all other duḥkha. Here, the eleventh link, taking birth under the control of ignorance and karma that entails assuming new polluted aggregates that are the basis for more duḥkha, is the primary meaning of pervasive, conditioned duḥkha.

Where does birth come from? From the preceding link, renewed existence. This comes from its preceding link, clinging. Clinging is the mind that seeks a new set of aggregates; it arises from craving, which does not want to separate from its object. Craving arises in response to pleasant, unpleasant, and neutral feelings that are experienced owing to contact—the coming together of the cognitive faculty, the object, and the consciousness. Contact comes from the sensory six sources—eye, ear, nose, tongue, body, and mental—and these arise from name and form, the five aggregates. Name and form arise from consciousness, which appropriates the new form. Third-link consciousness is the consciousness on which a karmic seed has been placed. It arises from formative action, which is produced by ignorance. The entire unsatisfactory sequence of the twelve links of dependent origination is rooted in ignorance. To be liberated from this cycle, we must generate the wisdom realizing emptiness that uproots this ignorance.[60]

REFLECTION

Beginning with ignorance, slowly contemplate each link and investigate:

1. What is the nature or meaning of this link?
2. What is its function?
3. What is its cause? How is it related to the preceding link?
4. What is its result? How is it related to the subsequent link?
5. What is the antidote that will stop this link?

8 | Dependent Origination: Cycling in Saṁsāra

HAVING LEARNED the meaning of each of the twelve links individually, we will now look at various descriptions of how they function together to produce rebirth in saṃsāra. This will help us to understand clearly our situation in cyclic existence and inspire us to be conscientious and mindful of our thoughts, words, and deeds so as to avoid creating causes for unfortunate rebirths. It will also energize us to engage in purification practices to prevent the seeds of destructive karma from ripening as unfortunate rebirths. Furthermore, it will arouse our enthusiasm to learn about, contemplate, and meditate on emptiness in order to free ourselves from cyclic existence. Then, when we think of sentient beings bound in the cycle of innumerable sets of twelve links, compassion and bodhicitta will grow in our hearts.

How the Twelve Links Produce a Life

In verse 2 of the *Heart of Dependent Origination* (*Pratītya samutpāda hṛdaya kārikā*), Nāgārjuna says (LC 1:322):

> The first, eighth, and ninth are afflictions.
> The second and tenth are karma.
> The remaining seven are duḥkha.

Of the twelve links, three—ignorance, craving, and clinging—are afflictions. Two—formative action and renewed existence—are karma. Seven—consciousness, name and form, six sources, contact, feeling, birth, aging or death—are suffering results. The three afflictions and the two actions are true origins of duḥkha and the seven results are true duḥkha.

Looked at from the broad perspective of continual rebirth in saṃsāra, each of these three groups causes the others, with no fixed order. Afflictions cause karma, which bring about duḥkha, unsatisfactory results. Included in these results are the mental aggregates, among which afflictions and karmic seeds are found. As Nāgārjuna says (RA 36):

> With these three paths mutually causing each other
> without a beginning, middle, or end,
> this wheel of cyclic existence
> turns like the wheel of a firebrand.

The twelve links of dependent origination are called links because they are connected and intertwined with each other. They follow one right after the other so quickly that, like a twirling firebrand, it is hard to tell where one set of twelve links stops and another begins. In fact, as we shall see, there are several descriptions of how a complete set of twelve links operates.

The links may be divided into projecting causes and effects and actualizing causes and effects: *Projecting causes* are links 1, 2, and 3a—ignorance, formative actions, and causal consciousness. *Projected effects* are links 3b through 7—resultant consciousness, name and form, six sources, contact, and feeling. *Actualizing causes* are links 8 through 10—craving, clinging, and renewed existence. *Actualized effects* are links 11 and 12—birth and aging or death.

According to the explicit teaching in the *Rice Seedling Sūtra*, the projecting causes and effects and actualizing causes and effects occur over three lifetimes. Let's call our present life, life B. In a preceding life, life A, the projecting causes—ignorance, formative action, and causal consciousness—created the potency on the consciousness that projected a new birth, called life B. In the present life, life B, the projected effects—resultant consciousness, name and form, six sources, contact, and feeling—occur. At the time of dying in life B, the actualizing causes—craving, clinging, and renewed existence—actualize the potency of another karmic seed on the mind. This results in life C, the actualized effects of our future life—birth, aging, and death.

Explicit Presentation

LINKS	RELATING TO WHICH LIFE	LIFE THEY OCCUR IN
Projecting causes 1–3a	B	A
Projected effects 3b–7	B	B
Actualizing causes 8–10	C	B
Actualized effects 11–12	C	C

There is no fixed time between lives A and B. Lives B and C are consecutive.

In the explicit presentation, the links from two different sets of twelve links are presented together. That is, two distinct sets of causality of two different lives are intertwined, with links 1–7 describing the evolution of life B and links 8–12 pertaining to the evolution of life C. For the production of life B, only links 1–3a are explicitly presented, and for the production of life C, only links 8–10 are explicitly presented. In actuality, both lives B and C have three projecting causes and three actualizing causes; the ones not explicitly mentioned are inferred. Similarly, only some of the resultant links for life B are explicitly mentioned (links 3b–7) and only some of the resultant links for life C are explicit (links 11–12). Here, too, the other resultant links are to be inferred for each life.

An example will help. An American man named John (life A) creates the projecting causes (links 1–3a) to be born as an Italian woman, Maria. In her life as Maria (life B), she experiences the projected effects of that karma (links 3b–7). As Maria is dying, the actualizing causes (links 8–10) to be reborn as a deva named Rooni ripen, and the deva Rooni (life C) is born and experiences their actualizing effects (links 11–12). One set of twelve links concerns the life as Maria, the other set has to do with rebirth as Rooni. Even though only links 1–7 are explicitly mentioned for Maria's life, links 8–12 in that set of twelve links is implied. Similarly, although only the actualizing causes and effects are mentioned for the set of twelve links of Rooni's life, the others are implied.

The Buddha explained the twelve links in this way to emphasize that the process of rebirth is continuous. While experiencing the effects of one life, the causes for another life are being created.

This presentation also emphasizes the unique functions of projecting causes and actualizing causes. *Projecting* means that those (projecting) causes are suitable to bring duḥkha after the actualizing causes come together and nourish them. *Actualizing* means that those (actualizing) causes make the potency of the karmic seed powerful enough to bring the result immediately.

In addition to the explicit presentation, Asaṅga set forth implicit presentations. In these, the order in which the four groups—projecting causes, projected effects, actualizing causes, and actualized effects—occur is not necessarily the order in which the twelve links are listed.

In the first implicit presentation, the cause of the new life (B) is begun in a previous life (A) with its projecting causes: ignorance prompted the creation of formative karma that has the power to bring rebirth, and that karmic seed was laid upon the causal consciousness. At the time of death of life A, the actualizing causes of craving and clinging nourished that seed and it transformed into renewed existence. In the very next life, all of the results—resultant consciousness, name and form, six sources, contact, feeling (projected effects), birth, and aging or death (actualized effects)—are experienced. Here the resultant consciousness and birth occur simultaneously, and in the very next moment, while name and form, six sources, contact, and feeling unfold, the link of aging or death is in process. In this way, a set of twelve links is completed in two consecutive lives.

Implicit Presentation 1

LINKS	RELATING TO WHICH LIFE	LIFE THEY OCCUR IN
Projecting causes 1– 3a	B	A
Projected effects 3b–7	B	B
Actualizing causes 8–10	B	A
Actualized effects 11–12	B	B

Lives A and B are consecutive.

In the second implicit presentation, the projecting causes created in life A ripen as life C, with life B occuring just prior to life C. Any amount of time may pass—one lifetime or eons of other lives—between lives A and C. At the end of one of these lives (B), craving, clinging, and renewed existence occur, and the karmic seed infused on the consciousness long ago is now about to bring a new birth. The projected effects and actualized effects occur together in the very next life (C).

IMPLICIT PRESENTATION 2

LINKS	RELATING TO WHICH LIFE	LIFE THEY OCCUR IN
Projecting causes 1–3a	C	A
Projected effects 3b–7	C	C
Actualizing causes 8–10	C	B
Actualized effects 11–12	C	C

There is no fixed time between lives A and B. Lives B and C are consecutive.

An Example

The teaching on the twelve links of dependent origination is complex and requires a great deal of contemplation. An example concerning the two implicit presentations will aid your understanding.

Pat arrives home from work and sees that her children left a mess in the kitchen. Tired from her job, she loses her temper and shouts at her children. This is the beginning of a set of twelve links. After Pat sees the mess, self-grasping ignorance/the view of a personal identity arises in her mind (link 1). This ignorance does not understand that the I is empty of inherent existence and instead grasps the I as inherently existent. In addition, self-grasping ignorance grasps her body and mind, her children, the mess in the kitchen, the chore of cleaning it up, and her unhappiness to exist inherently. Based on this, distorted attention that exaggerates the horribleness of the situation arises. This is immediately followed by anger and the intention to speak harsh words. Ignorance that does not understand the functioning of karma and its effects is also present, and because she is tired she does not consider either the long- or short-term effects of harsh words and does not apply the antidote to calm her mind. Harsh words fly out of her mouth, creating formative action (link 2), and a seed of destructive karma is laid on her mindstream. A having-ceased of the action of harsh words is also created (link 3a). This completes the projecting causes. The children scramble to clean the kitchen, and satisfied that shouting accomplished her purpose, Pat doesn't think to purify the paths of karma of malice and harsh words.

At the end of her life, as she is dying, Pat becomes angry and upset because the people around her are arguing and creating commotion. That mental state prompts craving and clinging (links 8 and 9) to nourish the seed of destructive karma created when she shouted at her children, priming it to bring a new rebirth (link 10). These are the actualizing causes. Her consciousness is drawn to the body of a screech owl and takes birth there (links 3b and 11). Aging or death (link 12) begins, as do the sequential links of name and form, six sources, contact, and feeling (links 4–7). These are the projected and actualized results of that set of links. Although like all sentient beings, Pat seeks only happiness, not suffering, owing to ignorance she created the cause for suffering. Since links 8–10 occurred at the end of Pat's life, that set of twelve links was completed in two lives as in implicit presentation 1.

Let's change the scenario slightly. Motivated by compassion Pat regularly volunteers at a hospital where she gladdens the hearts of people needing support and hope. This begins another set of twelve links and leaves the seed of virtuous karma on her consciousness. At the time of her death, she rejoices in her own and others' kind hearts and good deeds, and this virtuous mental state activates links 8–10 of the set of twelve links that began with her volunteer work. Her consciousness is attracted to take birth in the body of a human being and the projected and actualized results of that set of links occur.

Meanwhile, the karmic seed from harsh speech remains on her mindstream until in some future life its links 8–10 are activated and lead to an unfortunate birth. In that case, the set of twelve links associated with harsh speech occurs over three lifetimes, as in implicit presentation 2.

Many sets of twelve links can be in the works at one time, overlapping each other. While experiencing the resultant links of one set, the causal links of another set are being created. In Pat's case she was experiencing the link of aging from a set of twelve links that began in a previous life. When she became angry and shouted at her children, the links of ignorance, formative action, and consciousness of a new set of links began. Her volunteer work at the hospital started yet another set of twelve links. During her life many sets of twelve links begin depending on actions done with virtuous or nonvirtuous motivations. Each set has the potential to lead to a new rebirth, unless the karmic seed and having-ceased are impeded from ripening or she eradicates the afflictive obscurations that cause rebirth in saṃsāra. Here we get an inkling of what "bound in saṃsāra by afflictions and karma" means.

Do we choose our next rebirth? For us ordinary beings, the choice exists as we do each action in our daily lives and create new karmic seeds. It is not the case that in the bardo we calmly look down on Earth or other habitats and pick our future parents in order to learn certain lessons or repay karmic debts. Rather, just prior to death karmic appearances manifest in our minds. Due to emotional reactivity to these appearances, craving and clinging arise and nourish a karmic seed, and the mind seeks new aggregates in which to take birth. The bardo is a confusing time; anger, attachment, jealousy, fear, and self-grasping ignorance arise just like during life.

No one creates lessons for us to learn in our lives. Whether we learn from our experiences is up to us. Do we insist on blaming others for our difficulties or do we examine our own distorted conceptions, afflictions, and behavior, and apply the Dharma counterforces to transform them?

Ārya bodhisattvas, as well as some śrāvaka āryas, can guide their own minds at the time of death and determine where they will be reborn. The rebirths of ordinary people, however, are projected by their afflictions and karma, just as during life they are under the influence of afflictions and karma. Under these circumstances, we are not free to experience the happiness and peace that we seek.

REFLECTION

1. Review the process of how the twelve links produce a new rebirth according to the explicit and the two implicit presentations.
2. Make an example, using a formative action created under the influence of ignorance in your present life, of how a set of twelve links could unfold in the future.
3. How does this reflection affect your attitude toward life?

Flexibility

In all of the above situations, different elements of many sets of twelve links may occur during the present life. While we are experiencing the results of one set of twelve links, many new sets of twelve links are initiated with the creation of links 1–3a. While sometimes the projected and actualized effects occur soon after the projecting causes, in other situations a long interval may ensue. Cyclic existence is terrifying, for as we live out each saṃsāric existence, we ignorantly create the causes for many more.

Vasubandhu says that once the links of craving, clinging, and renewed existence occur, the bardo follows. There is no reversal of the process; it is not possible to accumulate new projecting karma in the bardo, and the links of birth and aging or death from that set of the twelve links will definitely occur (ADK):

> Once the intermediate state of a particular birth is actualized, it [the rebirth of that set of twelve links] will not waver.

Asaṅga has a different view (ADS):

> There is the possibility of the set [of twelve links] to waver because in the intermediate state there is the possibility of accumulating karma.

Pāli Tradition: How We Cycle

The Pāli commentaries, including the *Path of Purification*, explain the twelve links in terms of four groups, each with five links to illustrate the relationships of the twelve links with the different lifetimes in which they occur.

To explain the column "links": From our present life, life B, we look back and ask ourselves what factors were responsible for our present rebirth. Ignorance and formative actions occurred in a preceding life, life A. Through the maturation of formative actions conditioned by ignorance come the five resultant factors in this life (life B): consciousness, name and form, six sources, contact, and feeling.

The Pāli Tradition's Presentation

LIFE	LINKS	20 MODES AND 4 GROUPS OF 5
A	Ignorance (1) Formative actions (2)	Five past causes 1, 2, 8, 9, 10
B	Consciousness (3) Name and form (4) Six sources (5) Contact (6) Feeling (7)	Five present results 3, 4, 5, 6, 7
B	Craving (8) Clinging (9) Renewed existence (10)	Five present causes 8, 9, 10, 1, 2
C	Birth (11) Aging or death (12)	Five future results 3, 4, 5, 6, 7

In this life, when feeling occurs craving arises. That leads to clinging, which generates karmically active renewed existence. These three occurring in this life are the force that generates another rebirth—life C—in which birth, aging, and death are experienced. This corresponds to the explicit presentation in the *Rice Seedling Sūtra* explained above.

However, in any given life all these factors intermesh. So to understand how the twelve factors function in this life, we look to the last column with its twenty modes, which fall into four groups of five each.

(1) The group of the *five past causes*. In the previous life, life A, ignorance and formative actions were not the only causes for the present life; craving, clinging, and karmically active renewed existence were also present. These five are considered the five past causes that brought about the present life.

(2) The group of the *five present results*. The five past causes brought about the five present effects, links 3–7.

(3) The group of the *five present causes*. In this life, life B, there are five causes that will bring forth yet another rebirth—links 8, 9, 10, as well as 1 and 2. These same five factors that were five past causes of the present life become five present causes that will lead to a future rebirth, life C.

(4) The group of the *five future results*. Birth, aging, and death arise in the future life due to the five present causes. Links 3–7 are an expanded way of speaking of birth and aging or death.

In the above explanation, there are three connecting points: (1) Past causes connect with present results. This occurs between formative actions and consciousness. (2) Present results connect with present causes. This happens between feeling and craving. (3) Present causes connect with future results. This transition occurs between renewed existence and birth.

Of the twelve links, two are said to be roots of saṃsāra: Ignorance is the root extending from the previous life to the present one; craving is the root extending from the present life to the future life. As the basic unknowing that obscures the mind, ignorance is more fundamental than craving, but craving thrives on ignorance. Since identifying ignorance is more difficult than recognizing craving, we begin by subduing craving through restraining our senses and cultivating concentration. Then wisdom can arise and uproot ignorance.

As with many categories, the above distinctions serve explanatory purposes and are not fixed. Ignorance exists in all three lives, as does craving.

An Example from a Pāli Sūtra

In the *Greater Discourse on the Destruction of Craving* (MN 38), the Buddha gives an example of the twelve factors playing out in the life of an uninformed ordinary human being who is unaware that he is in saṃsāra and ignorant of the four truths. The Buddha then discusses the way to cut the cycle.

Conception in the womb requires three conditions, and if any one of them is missing, it does not occur. These are the sexual union of the mother and father, the woman being in the fertile time of her cycle, and the presence of a *gandharva* (P. *gandhabba*), a being who is ready to take rebirth and has a karmic affinity with these parents.[61] This karmic affinity is due to the first two links, (1) ignorance and (2) formative actions. The gandharva entering the newly fertilized ovum is called the "descent of consciousness." This consciousness (3) brings with it ignorance, afflictions, and the entire store of karmic seeds from previous lives.

At the time of conception, name and form (4) arise. Only the tactile and mental sources are present at that time, but gradually as the zygote becomes an embryo and then a fetus, all six sources come into being (5). After the baby is born, the six sources become active, contacting (6) and engaging with sights, sounds, smells, tastes, and tactile objects. Babies have rudimentary conceptual thought, which develops as the child learns language and is socialized and educated. As the child plays with toys and participates in games, his six cognitive faculties lead to contact with more agreeable, disagreeable, and neutral objects. This produces pleasant, painful, or neutral feelings (7), and the child craves (8) and clings (9) to have what brings him happiness and to be free of what brings suffering.

As the child becomes an adult and his toys are exchanged for more sophisticated means of entertainment, the six sources continue to contact the six objects, leading to many occasions of pleasant, painful, and neutral feelings. As a senior citizen, the objects of entertainment change again, but the process of the six sources leading to contact that produces feelings continues.

In all these occasions, pleasant and painful feelings lead to craving and clinging to have or to be separated from objects of the six senses. Attachment, anger, and other emotions arise one after the other in response to whatever he contacts. When he feels neither pleasure nor pain, he is bored and craves some excitement as an escape. Thus it is said "he delights in that feeling, welcomes it, and remains holding to it." Lacking mindfulness and introspective awareness regarding his own experience, he does not see any alternative and remains ignorant of the potential of his mind.

What does it mean to delight in a painful feeling? This indicates a person clings to the feeling with the thought "I" and "mine." His sense of I gets a boost through feeling uncomfortable. He may put himself in stressful or even dangerous situations to reinforce his sense that I exist. He may even create an identity out of his pain: "I am the person who was unfairly criticized."

Triggered by craving and clinging (8 and 9), he speaks, acts, or ruminates about the situation. This karmically active side of renewed existence (10) ripens in a new birth (11). Aging or death (12) begins immediately and "sorrow, lamentation, pain, grief, and despair come to be. Such is the origin of this whole mass of duḥkha." The process from contact onward to aging or death occurs repeatedly as a result of the six sources contacting objects of the six senses.

Seeing that this is our situation, a wise sense of danger arises, and we come to appreciate our precious human life and the opportunity it provides to counteract our situation in saṃsāra. We are grateful that the Buddha appeared in the world and taught the Dharma, which is "good in the beginning, good in the middle, and good in the end." Seeing the disadvantages of saṃsāra, we take refuge in the Three Jewels and choose to go forth into a life of Dharma. Abandoning the ten nonvirtues and practicing the ten virtues, we cultivate mindfulness and introspective awareness with respect to sense objects. Now, whenever our cognitive faculties contact their objects, we pause. While the arising of feeling is a natural result of previous conditions, we now see that a weakness in the process exists between feeling and craving. We have a choice regarding our response to pleasurable, painful, and neutral feelings. Instead of immediately letting the mind jump into craving, we remain mindful and equanimous.

Some practitioners who have attained serenity may use their concentration to temporarily suppress craving for sense objects. However, samādhi is not the final solution to saṃsāra, and subtle attachment to the blissful or equanimous feelings experienced in deep concentration may still exist. Seeing this, they cultivate insight. As the power of their unified serenity and insight increases, they employ wisdom to penetrate nirvāṇa and gradually eradicate defilements.

Other practitioners have a stronger aptitude for wisdom and rely on the power of reflection and examination to understand the unsatisfactory nature of sensual pleasures. Through this, they draw their minds back from entanglement with sense objects and with understanding they temporarily stop their minds from reacting to feelings with craving. On their own, reflection and examination do not go deep enough to uproot saṃsāra, but they calm the mind, allowing for the cultivation of serenity. These practitioners, like the previous ones, then unify serenity with insight and use wisdom to realize nirvāṇa and overcome all defilements.

Who Revolves in Cyclic Existence?

When outlining the twelve links in the *Rice Seedling Sūtra*, the Buddha said from ignorance arises formative action and from birth arises aging or death. He expressed the interconnection of the twelve links in this way to emphasize that there is no inherently existent person who experiences the twelve links. The links occur naturally as part of a causal process. The *Rice Seedling Sūtra* says:

> Nothing whatsoever goes from this world to the beyond. Nevertheless, from causes and conditions the effect of karma is manifested. It is just as in a clean mirror one sees the image of a face, but the image does not transfer into the mirror. Because the causes and conditions are complete, a face appears. Accordingly, there is not anyone who transfers from this lifetime at death; no one is born in another lifetime as well. Because the causes and conditions are complete, the effect of karma is actualized.

To this Nāgārjuna adds in the *Versed Commentary on the Rice Seedling Sūtra* (*Śālistamba Sūtra Kārikā*):

> Just as the distant moon appears in a small vessel of water,
> but is not transferred there, karma and its function exist.
> Likewise, at death nothing transfers from this life, but a being is born.
> If the causes and conditions are not complete, a fire does not burn;
> once they are complete the fire burns.
> So, from complete causes and conditions the aggregates [of a new] life arise.
> Just like the moon reflected in water, there is nothing that transfers from here at death,
> but a being is reborn.[62]

These moving passages point out that the person who transmigrates from one life to another is nothing more than a merely designated I. The rebirth process happens without a permanent, substantial self that is reborn. In fact, it would be impossible for rebirth to occur if there were an inherently existent self, because such a self would exist independent of all other factors and thus could not be influenced by causes and conditions and could not change. Since rebirth entails change, a permanent independent person could not be reborn. It is possible for rebirth to occur only if the I exists nominally, as a convention.

One moment of an oil lamp's flame doesn't transfer into the next moment, but a mere continuum goes on without interruption. Likewise, due to the coming together of causes and conditions, the mental continuum takes birth without a findable self that is reborn. When masters teach their disciples prayers by asking them to repeat the lines after them, the prayers are not transferred to the disciples, but they know the prayers just as the masters do. Just as a seal makes a clear impression on wax without anything transferring from the seal to the wax, so too does consciousness continue without a self that transfers from one life to the next.

Although we speak of a person revolving in cyclic existence—someone who creates karma, experiences its effects, and is the appropriator of the aggregates—this is a nominally existent self, not an inherently existent self. When the Buddha said that what arises through causes and conditions has no birth, he was referring to this uninterrupted process of causes and conditions that lacks any fixed beginning. No inherently existent aggregates or person goes from one life to the next. There are simply resultant factors that arise from causal factors. Both causes and results exist by mere designation; likewise the moment that a cause ceases and its result arises is merely designated by conception. As one impermanent, merely designated link ceases, another transient, merely designated link arises. In dependence upon this process, we say a person cycles in saṃsāra, but there is no soul or truly existent person who cycles in saṃsāra. There is simply the continuum of a merely designated person. Likewise the person who creates karma and attains nirvāṇa is like an illusion in that it cannot be pinpointed.

Not only can no inherently existent person who is reborn, practices the path, and attains liberation be found, but the aggregates and the twelve links themselves also lack inherent existence. Nāgārjuna tells us in his *Commentary on the Awakening Mind* (59, 60, 63):

> Starting with ignorance and ending with aging [or death],
> all processes that arise from
> the twelve links of dependent origination—
> we accept them to be like a dream and an illusion.
>
> This wheel with twelve links
> rolls along the road of cyclic existence;

outside this there cannot be sentient beings
experiencing the fruits of their deed . . .

In brief from empty phenomena
empty phenomena arise.
Agent, karma, effects, and their enjoyer—
the conqueror taught these to be [merely] conventional.

Although they are empty of inherent existence, the person, aggregates, and twelve links individually appear to be inherently existent to our minds that are polluted by ignorance. They resemble a dream and an illusion in that they appear falsely; they appear to have their own essence and exist from their own side, although they do not. These mistaken appearances come about due to the coming together of causes and conditions, just like a mirage appears on the road as a result of causes and conditions. The mirage exists and functions, although the water that appears to be there is a false appearance. Similarly, the person, aggregates, and links function although their appearance as inherently existent is false.

Just as inherently existent sentient beings bound in inherently cyclic existence do not exist, there are no inherently existent beings practicing the path and no inherently existent nirvāṇa to attain. Here, too, the agent, action, and object—the person practicing the path, the path itself, and nirvāṇa—lack any independent nature. The *Āryaratnakara Sūtra* says (OR 96):

The Tathāgata has said of those who go toward pacification
[nirvāṇa]
that no goer can be found.
They are proclaimed to be free from going.
Through their liberation, many sentient beings are liberated.

If we search for inherently existent āryas progressing toward nirvāṇa, we cannot find any. Their going on the path—their activity of practicing—also cannot bear ultimate analysis. Inherently existent liberation too cannot be found. Nevertheless, āryas practice the path, realize emptiness, purify their minds, and become free from the six realms of rebirth. When they have generated bodhicitta and attained full awakening, they are replete with the perfect qualities to lead others to nirvāṇa as well. While all these agents and actions do not exist from their own side, they exist and function on the conventional level. Although ultimate analysis refutes their inherent existence, it cannot destroy their nominal, illusion-like, veiled existence or their ability to function on the conventional level.

The Pāli tradition expresses the same thought. In speaking of the four truths, Buddhaghoṣa said (Vism 16.90):

> In the ultimate sense all the truths should be understood as void because of the absence of any experiencer, any doer, anyone who is extinguished, and any goer. Hence this is said:
>
> For there is suffering, but no one who suffers;
> doing exists although there is no doer;
> extinction [of saṃsāra] exists but no extinguished person;
> although there is a path, there is no goer.

Once a monk asked the Buddha, "Venerable Sir, what now is aging and death, and for whom is there this aging and death?" The Buddha responded that this is not a valid question because the monk presupposed a substantial self (SN 12.35). The commentary likens such a question to "a dish of delicious food served on a golden platter, on top of which a small lump of excrement is placed." While the question about aging and death is legitimate, asking it in terms of a substantial self contaminates the whole issue.

Someone who thinks the self and the body are the same falls to the extreme of nihilism by believing that both become nonexistent at death. If that were the case, there would be no need to practice the path because saṃsāra would end with death. Someone who thinks the self is one thing and the body is another falls to the extreme of absolutism by thinking that at death the self is released from the body and abides eternally. If the I were permanent and eternal, the path could not put an end to saṃsāra because something that is changeless cannot cease.

Not only did the Buddha refute a substantial self that is born, ages, and dies, he also denied that the body—and by extension the other aggregates—belong to such a person (SN 12.37):

> Monastics, this body is not yours, nor does it belong to others. It is old kamma, to be seen as generated and fashioned by intention, as something to be felt. Therein, monastics, the instructed ārya disciple attends carefully and closely to dependent arising itself thus: When this exists, that comes to be; with the arising of this, that arises. When this does not exist, that does not come to be; with the cessation of this, that ceases.

This body is not ours because there is not an independent person who possesses it. It does not belong to others either, because others also lack an independent self. Although the body is not literally karma, it is called *old karma* because previously created karma was its condition. This karma is intention; our volitional mental, verbal, and physical actions generated this body and life. When we contemplate dependent origination as ārya disciples do, we will understand the mere conditionality by which these things come into being and cease.

Buddhaghoṣa answers the question, "Who experiences the result of karma?" by first quoting an ancient Pāli verse and then explaining it (Vism 17.171–72):

> "Experiencer" is a convention
> for mere arising of the fruit [result].
> They say "it fruits" as a convention,
> when on a tree appears its fruit.

It is simply owing to the arising of tree fruits, which are one part of the phenomenon called a tree, that it is said "the tree fruits" or "the tree has fruited." Likewise, it is simply owing to the arising of the fruit consisting of the pleasure and pain called experience, which is one part of the aggregates called *devas* and *human beings*, that it is said, "A deva or a human being experiences or feels pleasure or pain." There is therefore no need at all for a substantial experiencer.

A substantial experiencer cannot be found: *experiencer* and *agent* are mere conventions. Thinking they are anything more than that is superfluous. We say "a human being experiences pleasure or pain" simply because that feeling has arisen in the feeling aggregate.

Āryas of the three vehicles who wisely understand dependent origination are free from doubt about the past, present, and future. They do not dwell on who they were in previous lives, or worry about whether they will exist in the future, and if so, as what. They do not fret about who they are, where they came from, and what will happen to them in the future. All these worries center on the idea of an independent self that persists in the past, present, and future. Those who understand dependent origination and how it functions in the past, present, and future know there is no need to posit a self that moves through these three time periods. They know that whatever occurs in the three times is simply due to conditionality—the fact that causes produce their effects and things come into being due to their respective causes and conditions. Factors in the past condition factors in the present. Causal factors are not the same as present factors, but they are not completely disconnected either. Through the transformation and ceasing of past factors, the present ones come into being. Through the present ones changing and ceasing, future factors will arise. All this occurs without a findable self who controls the process or who experiences it. There is no need for a persisting self to hold the stream of causes and effects together so that karmic seeds are carried to the next life.

If the description of the twelve links initially seems unfamiliar, that is because we have never seriously regarded our lives as conditioned events or thought of ourselves as conditioned phenomena that exist only because the causes for them exist. As we become familiar with the idea of dependent origination, this will become clearer. Although there is no substantial person to practice the path or attain nirvāṇa, a strong determination will arise in us to be free from cyclic existence, and this will propel us to cultivate the path of the āryas as the means to attain liberation.

REFLECTION

1. Review the explanation and quotations that refute the existence of an inherently existent person, self, or soul that is reborn.
2. Do you get a sense that there is not a permanent, fixed person that is you who goes from life to life?
3. Despite your not existing in that way, you still exist and function. The

absence of an inherently existent person and the conventional existence of a dependent person are complementary.

The Ultimate Nature of the Twelve Links

The Buddha spoke not only about the conventional functioning of the twelve links but also about their ultimate nature. The conventional twelve links describe the way that we are born repeatedly in cyclic existence and the way to reverse this process. The ultimate nature of the links and of the cycle of saṃsāric rebirth is empty of inherent existence. If the twelve links existed inherently, they could not form a causal chain where one link produces the next. The *Āryaratnakara Sūtra* says:

> How could something with inherent existence arise from another?
> Thus the Tathāgata has presented causation.

The links' causal dependence is the reason establishing the emptiness of inherent existence of saṃsāra and of a person who cycles in it. Speaking of causal dependence in the *Sūtra of the Enumeration of Phenomena That Is Called "Discerning the Divisions of Existence, and So Forth,"* the Buddha said:

> There are three defining characteristics of dependent arising: (1) no arising from a divine creator's thoughts, (2) arising from [multiple] impermanent cause(s), and (3) arising from a cause that has the capacity to give rise to that effect.[63]

Asaṅga echoed the Buddha's explanation of these three principles of causal dependence, saying: (1) The world did not come into being as a result of prior intelligence or an external creator. (2) It did not arise from a permanent cause. (3) It did not arise from a discordant cause. The *Rice Seedling Sūtra* adds two more characteristics: (4) it arises from existing causes, and

(5) it arises from selfless causes. Nāgārjuna said in *Versed Commentary on the Rice Seedling Sūtra*:

> External dependent arisings arise
> neither from self, nor from other,
> nor from both, nor from time as a [permanent] agent.
> Similarly, they are not created by Īśvara or another deity.
> They are neither products of a principal nature, nor are they
> causeless.
> They come from a succession of causes and conditions
> that stem from beginningless time.[64]

The twelve links produce one rebirth after another without the intercession of an external force, such as a creator deity, a universal mind, or a cosmic substance from which everything is derived. Ju Mipham says in *Sword of Wisdom for Thoroughly Ascertaining Reality* (*Shes rab ral gri don rnam nges*):

> These appearances around us are generated
> through the process of dependent arising.
> Just as a lotus never appears in the sky,
> so we will never see anything independent.
>
> The completion of a collection of causes
> carries out the function of inducing an effect.
> The entire identity of each diverse effect
> depends upon its particular causes.
>
> Therefore, by knowing what is and is not the case
> for causes and effects
> we can avoid one thing and pursue another.

If the twelve links existed inherently—independent of all other factors—they would not be dependent on one another, because independent and dependent are mutually contradictory. Something must be one or the other, it cannot be both. Because things exist dependently, we can attain the peace we seek by avoiding the causes of suffering and creating the causes of happiness.

Nāgārjuna examined the relationship between causes and their results. How does an effect arise from a cause? Are the two independent of each other or related? His seminal work, *Treatise on the Middle Way,* begins with an analysis of arising:

> Neither from itself nor from another,
> nor from both,
> nor without cause
> does anything anywhere ever arise.

We will fully unpack this verse and its implications in a later volume, but for now we can begin to question how arising—the production of an effect by a cause—occurs. If it occurs independently, according to Nāgārjuna there are four alternatives:

(1) The effect already exists in the cause in a manifest or unmanifest way. One version of *arising from self* is that one cosmic substance contains all of creation in an unmanifest form such that the arising of various phenomena is simply the appearance or manifestation of what is already there. In that case, a fully formed sprout would already exist in a seed.

(2) The effect arises from causes that are inherently *other* than it. While the seed and the sprout are different, they are not inherently different; they are related as cause and effect. Asserting that the cause and effect both exist inherently is problematic because a dependent relationship between the two would be impossible. If cause and effect were unrelated, roses could grow from daisy seeds.

(3) Things arise from *both* self and other. This combines elements of both the above and contains the faults of both.

(4) Things arise *causelessly* means that all things and events arise randomly, there being no relationship between what existed previously and what exists later. Holding such a view is tantamount to saying that a sprout grows without a cause.

The texts unpacking the reasoning that refutes these four erroneous views and establishes the emptiness of true existence of all phenomena often use seeds and sprouts as examples. However, the important issue is, how does duḥkha arise and how is it ceased? When we wake up in a bad mood, where did our bad mood come from? Did it appear without any cause? Is it someone else's fault? Was it already present in our minds in an unmanifest form? Is it God's will? Or did it arise dependent on its own causes and conditions, in which case it does not exist independently, with its own self-enclosed essence.

When we initially begin studying these reasonings, we may wonder why the great masters go into such great depth analyzing how sprouts grow when that is perfectly obvious to anyone who has a garden. But when we start to examine this process, what initially seems obvious begins to blur as we recognize our misconceptions and see that they are based on ignorance. Although we feel and believe that everything, ourselves included, has an independent essence that makes it what it is, it is impossible for things to exist this way. They are empty of an independent essence; they do not exist from their own side, nor are they self-powered.

Nevertheless, things arise and function dependent on other things. Sprouts grow from seeds; formative action arises due to ignorance. All these things and events exist conventionally when we don't analyze, but when we research for an independent essence in them, we cannot find it. So it is with the twelve links. Their being empty of inherent existence does not interfere with their dependent functioning on the conventional level. Each link arises from its preceding link and in turn gives rise to its subsequent link. The five causal links produce the seven resultant links. A person cycles in saṃsāra but cannot be found when we ask, "Who is the person who cycles in saṃsāra, really?" Tsongkhapa says (OR 70):

> Therefore, conventionally the nonexistence of the four extremes with respect to arising and the existence of arising are not contradictory.

As a dependent phenomenon, our duḥkha exists only because its causes and conditions exist. Cyclic existence and its unsatisfactory circumstances are not predestined; they are not due to fate or to the will of a creator deity. They are malleable and can be overcome by ceasing their causes. In *Praise to the Supramundane* (*Lokātītastava* 19) Nāgārjuna praises the Buddha:

Sophists maintain that duḥkha is self-created,
that it is created by another, and both,
and that it arises causelessly.
You have taught that it is dependently arisen.

REFLECTION

1. Review the three characteristics of dependent arising the Buddha described.
2. Consider how those three characteristics apply to the existence of a material object, such as your residence.
3. Consider how they apply to the existence of people—yourself, your friends, and your relatives.
4. Review how nothing can arise from a cause that is itself, from something inherently different from it, from both, and without a cause.

9 The Determination to Be Free

ANY PRISON INMATE can quickly and easily list the faults of being incarcerated: the physical dangers they face in prison, the confinement in their cells, the boredom, the ill treatment from guards and other inmates, and so on. Those with a strong determination to be free will be in contact with their attorney, make use of the law library, attend vocational courses and classes on anger management, and draw up a release plan so they can succeed after being released. Similarly, when those of us in saṃsāra clearly know the faults of rebirth by the twelve links, we will have a strong determination to be free. Seeking liberation, we will learn its characteristics and the causes to attain it. Then we will go about creating those causes and persevere until we attain genuine freedom and peace.

The Benefits of Meditating on the Twelve Links

The Buddha taught the twelve links not only to show the evolution of saṃsāric rebirth but also to lead us to a deep understanding of causal dependence and emptiness, and their compatibility.

Meditating on dependent origination—that each link is produced dependent on the preceding one—is meditation on causal dependence, which helps us to avoid the two extremes of absolutism and nihilism. None of the links arises independent of other factors or due to a permanent cause; each link is dependent on the specific causes and conditions that brought it about. Understanding this counteracts the extreme of absolutism, thinking that the links exist inherently or that saṃsāra arises due to a permanent creator. Furthermore, when each link ceases, it does not become totally nonexistent; it gives rise to subsequent links. Understanding this eliminates the view of nihilism, thinking that there is no continuity of saṃsāra or that saṃsāra can occur without a cause.

Reflection on dependent origination clears away a host of wrong views. Identifying that ignorance and actions in this life create the causes for future lives eliminates the wrong view that there are no previous or future lives. Seeing the variety of realms we may be born into ceases the incorrect idea that aside from the types of living beings we already know about, no others reside in the universe. The fact that formative actions bring fortunate or unfortunate rebirths dispels misguided notions that our actions have no effects or that virtue produces suffering and nonvirtue leads to happiness. Furthermore, because results arise from their concordant causes, not randomly, there is no purpose to justify, rationalize, or deny our harmful actions. They will always lead to suffering. Knowing this inspires us to be more mindful of our motivations and actions and to purify misdeeds.

In addition, we see that the causes of duḥkha exist within us, so relief from duḥkha must also be accomplished within our own mind. No miraculous drug can stop the cycle of rebirth, nor can cryonics conquer death. The only way to the deathless state—nirvāṇa—is by eliminating the causes of saṃsāric rebirth.

Contemplating each link individually accentuates its unsatisfactory nature. Cyclic existence is beginningless, and unless we make effort to cease it, its continuity will be endless. Now while we have the opportunity, we must develop a strong aspiration for liberation and live our lives according to this deep, heartfelt aspiration. What sense is there in seeking worldly pleasure when attachment to it simply leads to endless rebirth? As Togme Zangpo asks us in *Thirty-Seven Practices of Bodhisattvas*, "When your mothers who've loved you since time without beginning are suffering, what use is your own happiness?" There has to be more to life; there has to be a way to realize reality, arrive at a state of lasting peace, and benefit all beings as well. This accords with Togme Zangpo's response: "Therefore to free limitless living beings develop the altruistic intention [bodhicitta]." Inspired to make our lives meaningful, we put energy into generating bodhicitta and realizing the ultimate nature of reality.

Thinking about the beginninglessness of saṃsāra pulls us out of fixation on our own, often petty, problems—the molehills we make into mountains that preoccupy so much of our mental energy. Considering the larger perspective of many lives, the vast variety of life forms in this universe, and the numerous sufferings we and other sentient beings endure instigates compassion for all sentient beings. Our obsession with our happiness of only this life fades, and the aspiration for full awakening gives our lives greater meaning.

It is said that each of us has been born in every life form and done every activity in cyclic existence infinite times. What, then, is truly important to do in this very moment? Since saṃsāric pleasures arise due to causes and vanish when the causal energy is consumed, clinging to them does not make sense. Seeing that I and mine are dependent phenomena releases the tightness of having to prove or defend ourselves. We can relax and let go of trying to control everything and everyone around us. Instead, we will derive inner satisfaction from creating the causes for well-being, liberation, and full awakening. Such are the benefits of contemplating dependent origination.

Invigorating a Dry Dharma Practice

Some practitioners lament that they do not progress in their practice as rapidly as they would like. Many factors may be at play: having unrealistic expectations of quick attainments, being very self-critical, lacking sufficient study so we do not know how to practice properly, or living far away from a teacher and supportive Dharma community. The remedy for these hindrances is to approach the Dharma with a relaxed, cheerful attitude, rely on spiritual teachers, and study the teachings.

Other factors may also be at play, such as the three types of laziness: (1) postponing study and practice in favor of sleeping and lounging around, (2) being distracted from Dharma activities by involvement with meaningless works aimed only at the happiness of this life, or (3) feeling discouraged due to a self-defeating attitude or lack of self-confidence.

The first two types of laziness stem from attachment to the happiness of only this life. To overcome these, meditation on impermanence and death is recommended so that we appreciate our precious human life and use it wisely. Meditation on the defects of saṃsāra is also helpful in this regard. Without seeing these defects clearly, we may want to use the Dharma to make our saṃsāra more comfortable—for example, by employing Dharma methods to lessen our anger. Although this is helpful and reduces the destructive karma we create owing to anger, it alone will not lead to liberation. Looking into our minds, we may find that at some level, we see cyclic existence as a rather pleasant and familiar situation. Although we may intellectually know the six disadvantages of cyclic existence, three types of duḥkha, and eight unsatisfactory conditions, in our hearts we still think happiness can be found in cyclic existence—especially in beautiful objects, attractive people, social status, good looks, praise, and money and possessions. We remain attached to that type of happiness and forget that superior states of fulfillment and bliss are available if we make the effort to attain them.

To overcome distorted views and attachment to the joys of cyclic existence, we must meditate deeply and consistently on the disadvantages of saṃsāra as explained in the first truth and on the origins of duḥkha as detailed in the second truth. Some people are not eager to do analytic meditation on these topics. They prefer to visualize deities, engage in breathing meditation to develop concentration, recite mantras, or meditate on love. Of course these meditations are worthwhile, but without a genuine aspiration to be free from cyclic existence and attain liberation, these meditations lack energy and long-term effects. There is the danger that we do them simply to feel good, relieve stress, improve our relationships—all goals that are worthwhile but are limited in scope because they don't look beyond this life.

We need to make our minds strong and courageous. While looking at the defects of cyclic existence may initially be startling or unpleasant, the sobering effect it has on our minds enables us to make wise choices and propels us toward sincere and continuous practice. By seeing that nothing of lasting purpose, pleasure, or worth exists in cyclic existence, our interest will naturally turn to the Dharma and we will be eager to transform our minds.

Sustained reflection on the opposite of four distorted conceptions helps us to generate the aspiration for liberation. Contemplating the impermanent nature of all saṃsāric pleasure, we understand that things such as financial security, relationships, and reputation are not fixed and stable as we had assumed. Seeing them as transient, we will accept them for what they are, use and enjoy them, but will not be sidetracked from Dharma practice by attachment to them.

Contemplation on the unattractive nature of our own and others' bodies will relieve anxiety about our physical appearance and the effects aging will have on it. It also helps to release the fear we have about separating from this body at the time of death and dampens unrealistic notions about sexual relations. We'll learn to relate to our bodies in a more practical way, keeping them clean and healthy—eating nourishing food, taking medicine when necessary, and avoiding substances that harm them—so that we can continue practicing the Dharma.

Meditation on the fact that whatever is produced by afflictions and karma cannot provide genuine happiness and peace helps us to relate to people and things in our environment in a more down-to-earth manner. Our unrealistic expectations will be waylaid, and we will be able to accept things for what they are rather than lament that they aren't completely satisfying. When we recognize that saṃsāric happiness is deceptive and inferior, our craving for it will relax and our minds will turn to liberation, true peace, and bliss.

Reflecting that all the people and phenomena that seem so real do not exist as independent, self-enclosed units with semipermanent personalities expands our view. We'll understand that the way things appear to exist from their own side is deceptive. They are dependent on other factors and empty of all the false modes of existence that our ignorance projects on them. Since there are no inherently evil people, we won't be so upset and angry and will maintain an optimistic attitude knowing that people can and will change. Aggravating situations in our daily lives will seem less dire, and our minds will be more peaceful. Dharma practice will become much easier, and with joyous effort we will be able to transform our minds without labored difficulty.

The third type of laziness is discouragement, which comes from thinking that we are incompetent, the path is too difficult, or the resultant awareness is too high to attain. I (Chodron) believe that this a big hindrance to people in contemporary Western society. Rooted in the view of a personal identity and the self-centered attitude, it makes us give up on ourselves before we even make any effort. Whether it comes from being taught original sin, being pressured to excel, or constantly comparing ourselves to others and never measuring up to our own satisfaction, this discouragement poisons our approach to the path. Examining and shedding our erroneous thoughts about the meaning of success, learning about buddha nature, and developing deep self-acceptance are antidotes to discouragement.

How can we accept ourselves when we are full of faults and have created so much destructive karma? First, we have to ease up on self-criticism and extend some kindness and compassion to ourselves. This enables us to accept ourselves for who we are at present, knowing that we can improve in the future. We recognize that in previous lives we created a tremendous amount of merit because we now have precious human lives with all the conducive conditions to progress on the path. In addition, we have the potential to become buddhas—a potential that can never be taken away or destroyed—and each of us has our own unique talents and gifts that we can contribute to the world.

Can a Leper Find Happiness?

Māgandiya was a wanderer who believed that experiencing a rich variety of sensual pleasures was the source of growth and should be pursued with great enthusiasm (MN 75). To help him assess if his view was correct, the Buddha described his own sensual, luxurious life in the palace during his youth and then explained that he came to understand the origin, disappearance, gratification, danger, and escape of sensual pleasures and relinquished craving for them.

The *origin* and *disappearance* of sensual pleasures refers to their transient nature—they are continuously arising and disintegrating, never remaining the same for even one moment and are thus unable to give long-term happiness. To explain gratification, danger, and escape, the Buddha gave the example of an attractive person (MN 13). *Gratification* is the pleasure we experience by looking at, hearing, smelling, touching, and thinking about the person. But this gratification cannot be sustained, and the *danger* is that the person will age and become frail, with broken teeth, white hair, age spots, and wrinkles. Eventually that person will fall gravely ill and die, the corpse being assigned to the charnel ground. Disappointment in sensual objects is assured. *Escape* is giving up desire and lust for them, wisely disentangling ourselves from those afflictions and objects that bind us to misery.

Having seen the origin, disappearance, gratification, danger, and escape with respect to sensual pleasures, the Buddha explained to Māgandiya that he chose to leave the palace, become a monastic, and adopt a simple lifestyle of sensual restraint. He did not envy those delighting in sensual pleasures, "because there is a delight apart from sensual pleasures, apart from nonvirtuous states, which surpasses divine bliss." He thereby cultivated concentration based on the fourth dhyāna and attained arhatship with its inner peace and bliss. The joy he then experienced in no way compared with the insufficient pleasure derived from sensual objects.

The Buddha then spoke of a leper seeking happiness and relief from the unpleasant physical feelings of his disease. He gave some analogies that, ghastly as they are, accurately describe the leper's situation as well as the situation of those of us addicted to wonderful sights, sounds, smells, tastes, tangibles, and thoughts (MN 75.13):

> Suppose there is a leper with sores and blisters on his limbs, being devoured by worms, scratching the scabs off the openings of his wounds with his nails, cauterizing his body over a burning charcoal pit. Then his friends and companions, his kinsmen and relatives bring a physician to treat him. The physician prepares medicine for him, and by means of that medicine the man is cured of his leprosy and becomes well and happy, independent, master of himself, able to go where he likes. Then he might see another leper with sores and blisters on his limbs, being devoured by worms, scratching the scabs off the openings of his wounds with his nails, cauterizing his body over a burning charcoal pit. What do you think, Māgandiya? Would that man envy that leper for his burning charcoal pit or his use of medicine?

The lesions on a leper's body are home for worms. Their crawling in his flesh irritates him, and the itching is so terrible that he scratches the scabs off his wounds, giving more area for the worm infestation. In another attempt at relief, he cauterizes the wounds on his body. Scratching and burning his flesh provide some satisfaction, but it lasts only a short while and then the painful itching arises again, more intensely than before.

Similarly, we beings in the desire realm—overcome by the dissatisfaction of unfulfilled craving, tormented by and seeking relief from the itching brought on by craving to get more and better of whatever we find attractive—try to satisfy our desires. But like the leper, this worsens our situation because everything we get serves to increase the craving. It's like drinking salt water: at first our thirst decreases, but then it returns more voracious and unbearable than before.

Just as someone cured from leprosy would not envy the happiness a leper gets from scratching his scabs and burning his wounds, arhats never envy the pleasure of beings in the desire realm.

The Buddha then related that after the leper was cured, two strong people dragged him to a charcoal pit as he wailed in fear and pain. "Is it only now that the fire is painful to touch, hot, and scorching, or previously too, when he was a leper, was the fire like that?" the Buddha asked Māgandiya. Māgandiya replied that it was hot, scorching, and painful before, only due to his illness the leper's senses were impaired and he experienced the fire that was painful to touch as pleasurable. The Buddha explained that so too, beings who are devoured by craving for sensual pleasures, who burn with the fever of craving for more and better sensual experiences, have impaired faculties that cause them to believe that sensual pleasures, which are in fact painful, bring the highest delight. In fact, they would be much happier and less tormented by disappointment and dissatisfaction if they could see the origin, disappearance, gratification, danger, and escape of sensual pleasures and release craving for them.

This corroborates recent studies that found that money does not equal happiness. The Inuit of Greenland and the Maasai in Kenya report being just as happy as those on the Forbes 500 list of richest Americans. To conclude, the Buddha counseled Māgandiya:

> The greatest of all gains is health,
> nibbāna is the greatest bliss,
> the eightfold path is the best of paths,
> for it leads safely to the deathless [nibbāna].

At first Māgandiya misunderstood the meaning of health to be physical health. But once the Buddha explained that nirvāṇa, the cessation of craving and clinging, is the highest health, Māgandiya was overjoyed and requested monastic ordination. Practicing sincerely, he soon became an arhat.

REFLECTION

1. Contemplate the example of a leper seeking happiness. Then reflect that uninstructed worldly people live in a similar manner.
2. Apply this example to yourself.
3. Generate the determination to be free from cyclic existence and cultivate compassion for all other sentient beings.

Compassion for Ourselves and Others

Courage and clear-mindedness are necessary to see cyclic existence for what it is—a deceptive cycle of misery. The aspiration for liberation from saṃsāra is a reflection of the compassion we have for ourselves. When we recognize that all other sentient beings are in the same predicament, compassion for them will also arise. Compassion gives us inner strength as we practice diligently to cease the causes of saṃsāra.

Puchungwa (1031–1106), a Kadampa geshe in Tibet, cultivated this compassion by contemplating duḥkha, its origin, its cessation, and the path to that cessation according to the perspectives of the three levels of practitioners. *Initial practitioners*, who focus on avoiding an unfortunate rebirth and attaining a fortunate one, reflect that under the influence of the ignorance of karma and its effects, they create nonvirtuous formative karma. When nourished by craving and clinging, the karmic seed matures into renewed existence and the seven resultant links of an unfortunate rebirth ensue. Seeing this process, initial-level practitioners will work to abandon the ignorance of karma and its effects, create virtuous karma, and purify previously created nonvirtue.

Middle-level practitioners contemplate the twelve links in terms of all saṃsāric rebirths. They focus on the process that brings fortunate rebirths—

ignorance giving rise to polluted virtuous formative karma, and so on. But they go a step further and understand that staying in cyclic existence—even if they have peaceful rebirths in the form and formless realms—is unsatisfactory. They want to eliminate the root of saṃsāra, first-link ignorance. Aware of another weak spot in the chain, that between feeling and craving, they practice experiencing pleasant, painful, or neutral feelings—even the feeling of bliss and equanimity in the form and formless realms—without reacting with craving for pleasure to continue or for pain to stop. Generating the aspiration for liberation from all of saṃsāra, they practice the three higher trainings of ethical conduct, concentration, and wisdom.

Advanced-level practitioners—and Geshe Puchungwa was one of these—contemplate the twelve links from the perspective of other sentient beings revolving uncontrollably in cyclic existence. With compassion for all the diverse sentient beings, they generate bodhicitta, engage in the bodhisattvas' deeds, and cultivate the wisdom realizing emptiness in order to become a buddha, one who has full wisdom, compassion, and power to lead others to awakening.

Cultivating compassion by considering that other sentient beings cycle in saṃsāra by means of the twelve links is a powerful way to subdue anger and resentment. When we reflect that others are trapped by their ignorance and subjected to the three types of duḥkha, hating them seems ludicrous. How can we possibly wish suffering on people who are already bound in the tortuous cycle of saṃsāra?

Sentient beings are conditioned phenomena; they are not fixed, inherently existent personalities. There is no "solid" person to feel malice toward and no benefit from wishing someone ill. Rather, with compassion and wisdom, let's do what we can to help them attain true freedom. As verses chanted daily in Tibetan monasteries after the midday meal say:

> May all those who offered me food attain happiness of
> total peace.
> May all those who offered me drink, who served me,
> who received me, who honored me,
> or who made offerings to me attain happiness that is
> total peace.

> May all those who scold me, make me unhappy, hit me,
> attack me with weapons, or do things up to the point of
> killing me
> attain the happiness of awakening.
> May they fully awaken to the unsurpassed,
> perfectly accomplished state of buddhahood.

REFLECTION

1. Think of someone whom you care about deeply and reflect that they cycle in saṃsāra under the control of afflictions and karma. Let compassion arise.
2. Think of someone whom you do not like or who has harmed you. Recognize that this person too cycles in saṃsāra under the control of afflictions and karma. Let compassion arise for them.
3. Recall that if they were free from duḥkha, their ways of thinking and behaving would be entirely different than they are now.

The Demarcation of Generating the Determination to Be Free

How do we know our antipathy toward saṃsāra is a genuine determination to be free? Tsongkhapa says in *The Three Principal Aspects of the Path*:

> By contemplating in this way, when you do not generate even for an instant the wish for the pleasures of cyclic existence, and when you have day and night unceasingly, the mind aspiring for liberation, you have generated the determination to be free.

When generated, the aspiration for liberation brings an enduring shift in perspective that alters how we see and relate to our lives and to the world around us. This determination to be free from saṃsāra involves relinquishing our obsessive attachment for saṃsāric pleasures and the duḥkha it brings and focuses our attention on attaining nirvāṇa, the state beyond sorrow, and making that the aim of our lives.

Generating the determination to attain liberation from saṃsāra is essential to cultivate compassion. After seeing the defects of our own saṃsāra, we shift our focus to others, contemplating that they face the same undesirable situation. Compassion—the wish for someone to be free from duḥkha and its causes—arises as a result.

Bodhisattvas fear rebirth in saṃsāra under the control of afflictions and karma and seek to be free from it. But, having firm compassion for others and strong resolve to benefit them, they willingly take rebirth in saṃsāra. Sūtra statements such as "bodhisattvas should not become disenchanted with saṃsāra" do not mean that bodhisattvas should indulge in saṃsāric pleasures. Rather, they urge bodhisattvas to have such strong joyous effort that they will never give up benefiting sentient beings trapped in saṃsāra. Even if bodhisattvas experience overwhelming difficulties when benefiting others, they persevere without succumbing to fear of duḥkha or disenchantment with sentient beings. Taking on the misery of others, bodhisattvas do not dread physical or mental pain. Knowing that their actions to benefit others enable them to fulfill the collection of merit—an essential factor to attain full awakening—bodhisattvas joyfully take many rebirths in saṃsāra. This is the meaning of the passage in the *Sūtra of the Tathāgata's Inconceivable Secret* (*Tathāgatācintya-guhya-nirdeśa Sūtra,* LC 1:328):

> Bodhisattvas, thinking of the maturation of living beings, view cyclic existence as beneficial. Accordingly, they do not view great nirvāṇa as beneficial to the maturation of beings.

If bodhisattvas do not renounce their own saṃsāra and continue to take rebirth under the control of afflictions and karma, their ability to benefit others will be extremely limited. Unable to accomplish their own goal of full awakening, they cannot help other sentient beings accomplish their spiritual goals. To fulfill both the purpose of themselves and others, bodhisattvas seek nonabiding nirvāṇa, in which they will be free from saṃsāra as well as their own personal peace of nirvāṇa. Bhāvaviveka says in *Heart of the Middle Way* (*Madhyamaka-hṛdaya-kārikā*, LC 1:330):

> Since bodhisattvas see the faults of cyclic existence, they do not remain here.
> Because they care for others, they do not remain in nirvāṇa.
> In order to fulfill the needs of others, they resolve
> to remain in cyclic existence.

Inspired by bodhisattvas' compassion and courage, may we do the same.

10 | Seeking Genuine Peace

Each of us wants happiness and not duḥkha. But among the various types of happiness, which is best? The Buddha answered (AN 2.65, 67, 68):

> Monastics, there are these two kinds of happiness. What two? Sensual happiness and the happiness of renunciation . . . Of these two kinds of happiness, the happiness of renunciation is foremost.
>
> Monastics, there are these two kinds of happiness. What two? The happiness with defilements and the happiness without defilements . . . Of these two kinds of happiness, the happiness without defilements is foremost.
>
> Monastics, there are these two kinds of happiness. What two? Worldly happiness and spiritual happiness . . . Of these two kinds of happiness, spiritual happiness is foremost.

Here "renunciation," "happiness without defilements," and "spiritual happiness" refer to liberation. The Buddha steers us to a higher and more commendable type of happiness, the peace that goes beyond saṃsāra, the joy of nirvāṇa and full awakening. While we may experience many kinds of happiness in our present human rebirth, all of these pale in comparison to the joy and peace of nirvāṇa. Because the pleasures of this life are immediate and appeal strongly to our senses, some people have difficulty gaining confidence in the peace of nirvāṇa. To give up craving for sense pleasures requires an understanding of their defects and of the benefits of nirvāṇa. The more we understand these, the more our minds will naturally turn away from cyclic existence to liberation.

But we don't have to wait until we attain liberation or awakening to experience Dharma happiness. Each time we release attachment, anger, and other afflictions in our daily lives, Dharma happiness, peace, and confidence take their place. Experiencing this Dharma happiness here and now gives us a small glimpse of the peace of nirvāṇa.

We began the section on the twelve links of dependent origination with the Buddha's succinct statement on causality and conditionality:

> When this exists, that comes to be;
> with the arising of this, that arises.
> When this does not exist, that does not come to be;
> with the cessation of this, that ceases.

The first two lines tell us that saṃsāra comes about due to a causal process, which we have explored in the previous two chapters. The last two lines inform us that nirvāṇa—the cessation of saṃsāra and its origins—can be attained through eliminating ignorance, the fundamental cause of saṃsāra. When the causes and conditions of saṃsāra do not exist, the resultant state of duḥkha will not arise. With the "remainderless fading away and cessation of ignorance," the new creation of all the other links will cease, just as when the first domino in a row is hit, the others tumble down as well. What brings the cessation of ignorance? According to the common Buddhist view, it is the eightfold path, especially the wisdom or true knowledge that understands the four truths and nirvāṇa. According to the Prāsaṅgikas' unique view, it also entails the direct, nonconceptual realization of the emptiness of inherent existence of all persons and phenomena. The process of gaining this wisdom is a gradual one, which itself depends on many causes and conditions.

The "Ye Dharmā" Dhāraṇī

A *dhāraṇī*—an intelligible phrase that encapsulates the essence of a teaching—that is frequently recited by followers of both the Pāli and Sanskrit traditions is the "Essence of Dependent Arising Dhāraṇī." In Sanskrit it reads:

> *Ye dharmā hetu prabhavā hetun, teṣāṃ tathāgato hyavadat, teṣāṃ ca yo nirodha, evaṃ vādī mahāśramaṇa.*
>
> All phenomena arise from causes. Those causes have been taught by the Tathāgata. And their cessation too has been proclaimed by the great renunciant.

Before becoming a follower of the Buddha, Śāriputra encountered the arhat Aśvajit and asked him to explain the essence of the Tathāgata's teaching to him. Aśvajit recited these words, and fully understanding their meaning, Śāriputra immediately became a stream-enterer. He later recited them to his friend Maudgalyāyana, who attained the same realization. They and five hundred of their followers then approached the Buddha and requested to become his disciples.

Fearlessly, and with complete self-confidence, the Buddha did not hesitate to proclaim four statements: He is fully awakened. He has destroyed all pollutants. He has correctly identified all obscurations. He knows that the Dharma, when practiced correctly, leads to the destruction of duḥkha. The Buddha taught the *ye dharmā* dhāraṇī by means of these four self-confidences or fearlessnesses.

All phenomena arise from causes indicates that each link of dependent origination comes into being dependent on the preceding ones. This emphasizes that true duḥkha—the seven resultant links—arises from true origins—the three links that are afflictions and the two that are karma. Here the Buddha instructs everyone who seeks liberation to abandon true origins; he says this by means of the third self-confidence, by which he has correctly identified the obscurations to liberation.

Those causes have been taught by the Tathāgata indicates that the Buddha has taught the counterforce to saṃsāra—the true path, a consciousness that directly perceives the selflessness of persons and phenomena. He states this in reliance on the fourth self-confidence, that he knows the way leading to the complete destruction of duḥkha.

And their cessation too indicates that by practicing true paths we will attain the final true cessation that is the eradication of true duḥkha and true origins. The Buddha states this by means of the second self-confidence, knowing that he has eradicated all pollutants.

Has been proclaimed by the great renunciant means that the Buddha has actualized true paths and true cessations and thus has completely perfected what to practice and what to abandon. He does this by means of the first self-confidence, being able to state with complete assurance that he is awakened with respect to all phenomena.

This short dhāraṇī contains great meaning because it incorporates the four truths, the eightfold path, a buddha's truth body that is the perfection of abandonment and realization, and a buddha's form body that acts to benefit all beings with the four self-confidences. A profound understanding of this dhāraṇī will enable us to attain the four bodies of a buddha.

PHRASE IN DHĀRAṆĪ	RELATIONSHIP TO FOUR TRUTHS	SELF-CONFIDENCE
All phenomena arise from causes.	True duḥkha arises from true origins.	Third: The Buddha correctly identified the obscurations to liberation.
Those causes have been taught by the Tathāgata.	True path.	Fourth: The Buddha knows the way leading to the complete destruction of duḥkha.
And their cessation too . . .	True cessation.	Second: The Buddha knows that he has eradicated all pollutants.
has been proclaimed by the great renunciant.	True paths and true cessations have been actualized.	First: The Buddha knows that he is awakened with respect to all phenomena.

Forward and Reverse Orders of the Afflictive and Purified Sides of the Twelve Links

The twelve links of dependent origination can be spoken of in terms of affliction—how cyclic existence continues—and purification—how cyclic existence ceases. Both the afflictive and purified presentations have a forward and a reverse order. The *forward order of the afflictive side* emphasizes the origins of duḥkha: with ignorance as condition, formative action arises; with formative action as condition, consciousness arises; and so forth, up to with birth as condition, aging and death arise. The *reverse order of the afflictive side* emphasizes the resultant true duḥkha: aging and death are produced in dependence on birth; birth is produced in dependence on renewed existence, and so on, up to formative action is produced in dependence on ignorance.

The purified forward and reverse sequence indicates the method for quelling saṃsāra and attaining liberation. The *forward order of the purified side* says: by ceasing ignorance, formative action ceases. By ceasing formative action, consciousness ceases, and so on until aging or death ceases. This sequence emphasizes the true paths that cease ignorance, thus stopping the other links from arising.

The *reverse order of the purified side* begins with the last link, aging or death, and investigates how to cease it. That is done by ceasing birth. Birth is ceased by ceasing renewed existence and so on back to ceasing ignorance. Looking at the twelve links in this way emphasizes true cessation: that all the links can be ceased and nirvāṇa attained.

ORDER OF TWELVE LINKS OF DEPENDENT ORIGINATION	NOBLE TRUTH THAT IS SHOWN	UNDERSTANDING AND ASPIRATION ARISING FROM MEDITATION
Reverse order of afflictive dependent origination: aging or death arise due to birth . . .	True duḥkha.	Understanding the nature of duḥkha, we desire to be free from it.
Forward order of afflictive dependent origination: with ignorance as condition, formative action arises . . .	True origin.	Understanding the origins of duḥkha, we aspire to abandon them.
Reverse order of purified dependent origination: aging or death are ceased by ceasing birth . . .	True cessation.	Understanding that duḥkha can be ceased, we want to actualize that cessation.
Forward order of purified dependent origination: by ceasing ignorance formative actions cease . . .	True path.	Understanding that true paths cease ignorance, we desire to cultivate them.

The question then arises: How do we cease the ignorance that is the origin of cyclic existence? We beginners must first develop a robust understanding of karma and its effects and bring that into our lives so that it influences our daily choices and actions. Then with a motivation aspiring for either liberation or full awakening, we seek the antidote that will demolish saṃsāra's root, first-link ignorance. Nāgārjuna says (MMK 26.10):

> The root of cyclic existence is [formative] action;
> therefore the wise one does not act.
> Therefore the unwise is the agent.
> The wise one is not, because he sees reality.

The first line points to formative actions, the second link, as the root of saṃsāra. Usually the fundamental root of saṃsāra is identified as ignorance, but here the root is said to be formative action because it is the source of consciousness entering into a new body. The distinction between the wise and the unwise lies in whether or not someone has realized the emptiness of true existence. Wise ones—āryas of all three vehicles—do not create formative actions because they have realized emptiness directly. Not having yet gained the direct realization of emptiness, unwise ordinary beings accumulate karma that propels new rebirth in cyclic existence.

In saying "the wise one does not act," Nāgārjuna does not mean they do nothing at all. If that were the case, they would never complete the path. Rather, the wise do not engage in activities motivated by their own self-centered, saṃsāric desires. But in terms of creating the causes and conditions for liberation or awakening, they do as much as possible.

This leads to further investigation of the last two of the four truths, true cessations and true paths. Nāgārjuna says (MMK 26.11–12):

> With the cessation of ignorance
> [formative] action will not arise.
> The cessation of ignorance occurs through
> exercising wisdom in meditating on suchness [emptiness].
>
> Through the cessation of this and that,
> this and that will not manifest.

That which is only a mass of duḥkha
will thus completely cease.

The wisdom realizing emptiness is the true path that ceases first-link ignorance. In the second verse, "this and that" refer to first-link ignorance and second-link formative action. By ceasing ignorance, there is no fuel for formative action to arise. In this way, the entire chain of twelve links that is a mass of constantly recurring misery ceases, and nirvāṇa, true freedom, is obtained.

The key that ceases first-link ignorance is the wisdom realizing the emptiness of inherent existence. The Buddha and great sages taught many reasonings to refute inherent existence and establish emptiness. A famous one is refuting the four extremes of arising. Nāgārjuna introduces it (RA 37):

Because this wheel [of saṃsāra] is not obtained from self, other,
or from both, in the past, present, or future,
[one who knows this] overcomes the grasping of I
and thereby karma and rebirth.

Cyclic existence—our five polluted aggregates—does not arise from itself in the sense that it does not exist already inside its causes waiting to manifest. Saṃsāra also does not arise from causes that are inherently different from it. Nor does it arise from both self and other together, or without a cause. Because there is no inherently existent origin of saṃsāra, an absolute beginning to a set of twelve links cannot be found in the past, present, or future. Those who realize the dependent nature of saṃsāra and the person who cycles in it can overcome the ignorance grasping inherent existence. By overcoming the root cause of saṃsāra, the entire cycle of rebirth discontinues and nirvāṇa is attained. As Nāgārjuna says (RA 365):

Having properly realized that in this way
beings are actually unreal, having no basis [for rebirth],
or any appropriation [of new aggregates],
one attains nirvāṇa like a fire whose causes have ceased.

REFLECTION

1. Review the forward and reverse orders of afflictive dependent origination. Generate the aspiration to be free from saṃsāra.
2. Review the forward and reverse orders of purified dependent origination. Have conviction that it is possible to free yourself from saṃsāra.

Transcendental Dependent Origination (Pāli Tradition)

Dependent arising, the lack of independent existence, and impermanence go hand in hand. The present is different from but related to the past. Impermanent things do not exist under their own power; they arise due to causes that preceded them. The present is the continuation of the past and is conditioned by the past. Present things and events have their own unique functions, and in the next moment they give way to a new moment that becomes the present.

We often think of impermanence as something negative: we are separated from what we like. However, because things are impermanent and conditioned, they can also change for the better. Transcendental dependent origination clarifies this and, in doing so, encourages us to practice the path leading to liberation and to knowledge of the destruction of all pollutants (*āsravakṣaya*, *āsavakkhaya*).

This theme is expressed in the forward and reverse orders of purified dependent origination. In addition, a few sūtras in the *Numerical Discourses* as well as the *Proximate Cause Sutta* (*Upanisā Sutta*, SN 12.23) present dependent origination in a dynamic way where one virtuous factor produces another, culminating in knowledge of the destruction of all pollutants. This emphasizes that spiritual evolution involves not just eradicating problematic factors but also enhancing constructive ones.

The presentation of transcendental dependent origination according to the Pāli tradition is expounded in the *Proximate Cause Sutta*. This presentation highlights the goal: knowledge of the destruction of all pollutants. The steps for arriving at that goal are then traced backward. Knowledge of the destruction of all pollutants has a proximate cause: liberation. Liberation has a proximate cause: dispassion. Dispassion's proximate cause is disenchantment. Disenchantment's is knowledge and vision of things as they really are. The proximate cause of knowledge and vision of things as they really are is concentration. Concentration's proximate cause is bliss, bliss's is pliancy, pliancy's is joy, joy's is delight, and delight's is faith.

At this juncture, the Buddha makes an interesting turn and cites duḥkha as the chief condition for faith: without duḥkha, we would not turn to the Buddhadharma for relief and would not generate faith in it. This is the point where we cross from mundane to transcendental dependent origination. The Buddha then says birth is the proximate cause for duḥkha and traces the sequential series of causes back to first-link ignorance. He goes forward again from ignorance to birth, then to suffering, and then crosses to the transcendental links beginning with faith and going through to the destruction of all pollutants. Meditating back and forth from ignorance to knowledge of the destruction of all pollutants has a powerful effect on our minds and shows us that we saṃsāric beings can attain liberation.

TRANSCENDENTAL DEPENDENT ORIGINATION (FORWARD ORDER):	
1.	Faith (P. *saddhā*)
2.	Delight (P. *pāmojja*)
3.	Joy (P. *pīti*)
4.	Pliancy (tranquility, P. *passaddhi*)
5.	Bliss (P. *sukha*)
6.	Concentration (P. *samādhi*)
7.	Knowledge and vision of things as they are (P. *yathābhūta-ñāṇadassana*)
8.	Disenchantment (P. *nibbidā*)
9.	Dispassion or fading away (P. *virāga*)
10.	Liberation (P. *vimutti*)
11.	Knowledge of the destruction of all pollutants (P. *āsavakkhayañāṇa*)

1. Duḥkha is the proximate cause for faith.

Our lives are fraught with frustration and duḥkha. Not knowing a healthy way to deal with our stress, misery, and confusion, we usually seek to distract ourselves from it, spawning a culture of addiction to sense objects: drugs and alcohol, food, sex, entertainment, shopping, sports, news, and so on. Alternatively, we react to duḥkha with self-pity, digging ourselves deeper into despair. Although we sometimes deal with our pain in a healthy way by building up fortitude, resoluteness, and using our talents and intelligence, ignorance still obscures us from seeing that duḥkha permeates our lives. No matter how much we succeed in changing the external world to make it what we want it to be, we cannot bring our bodies, minds, or the external world completely under our control. Deep inside, a spiritual malaise remains and a small voice within us says, "There must be another way."

Acknowledging this malaise spurs us to seek answers beyond what we already know. Here we have to thank the illness, injury, breakup of a treasured relationship, loss of a job, or internal dissatisfaction and anxiety for spurring us to look more deeply at the human situation.

Duḥkha alone will not cause faith to arise. We must encounter a reliable and true teaching that shows us the way out of our situation. We must investigate the teaching, teacher, and followers using our intelligence and reasoning. When we conclude they are reliable and trustworthy, we take refuge in the Three Jewels. Our faith is not blind or coerced. Based on inferential reliable cognizers and reliable cognizers based on authoritative testimony, our faith and confidence will be stable.[65]

2. Faith is the proximate cause for delight.

Through learning and contemplating the Dharma, we come to adopt the Buddhist worldview. This worldview does not demand submission to an external creator, nor does it justify suffering as something that is good for us. The worldview of the four truths looks squarely at our situation so that we know duḥkha, abandon its origin, realize its cessation, and cultivate the path. Relief arises because at last we have found a reliable path. Delight, which is a weak kind of joy, arises because we have met the ārya's eightfold path, which now lies in front of us. Our hearts swell with virtuous aspirations and we dive into practice, commencing with the higher training in ethical conduct. Living ethically and purifying our past misdeeds, we experience freedom from guilt and self-recrimination. The low self-esteem that plagued us due to our mistaken actions evaporates, and our self-confidence increases because we now make wise decisions rooted in compassion and restraint from self-indulgence.

3. Delight is the proximate cause for joy.

On the basis of following ethical conduct, we now engage in meditation. While some people prefer to begin with insight meditation, in general it is recommended to tame the coarse afflictions first by generating serenity. In the eleven factors of transcendental dependent origination, joy, pliancy, bliss, and concentration are part of the higher training in concentration. Knowledge and vision of things as they are, dispassion, and disenchantment pertain to insight meditation and the higher training in wisdom.

Cultivating serenity requires effort, fortitude, and perseverance. As the mind becomes more concentrated, joy arises, uplifting and refreshing the mind and bringing strong interest and delight in the object of meditation. The commentaries talk of five degrees of joy that develop as the mind approaches single-pointedness: (1) minor joy can make the hair on our bodies stand on end, (2) momentary joy flashes through the body with an intensity likened to lightning, (3) showering joy is like waves of ecstasy breaking over the body[66] or flowing through the mind, (4) uplifting joy gives the body a feeling of lightness, and in some cases can make the body levitate, and (5) pervading joy fills the entire body. The first four precede the attainment of the first dhyāna, and the fifth occurs in the first dhyāna.[67]

4. Joy is the proximate cause for pliancy.

Although joy brings great pleasure, it agitates the mind. It may also bring subtle fear of losing the ecstasy and cause the meditator to cling to the experience of ecstasy. The restlessness, anxiety, and clinging interfere with deep concentration, so as meditators progress they come to regard the ecstasy as a hindrance to be pacified. As joy calms down and becomes less exuberant, pliancy—the subsiding of distress and unserviceability—becomes more prominent. Pliancy is of two types: mental pliancy applies to the consciousness aggregate, and physical pliancy applies not to the body but to the mental factors in the aggregates of feeling, discrimination, and miscellaneous factors that accompany the consciousness. Pliancy subdues the excited disturbance caused by joy, eliminates rigidity and sluggishness, makes the mind more flexible so that it can be used to actualize higher stages of the path, and brings incredible stillness in the mind.

5. Pliancy is the proximate cause for bliss.

Due to the stillness brought by pliancy, bliss, which was present before, now becomes prominent. Joy is a mental factor belonging to the fourth aggregate, whereas bliss is a type of pleasant feeling. Joy is comparatively coarse; bliss is more subtle. Joy is compared to the gladness a weary, thirsty traveler feels upon hearing of an oasis nearby, and bliss to the happiness he experiences after he has bathed, satisfied his thirst, and lies down to rest in the shade of trees. In the present stage, joy is present, but due to pliancy it has been toned down and bliss is dominant.

Bliss here refers to the bliss experienced with access concentration, which is prior to the first dhyāna. Access concentration arises when the five hindrances have been suppressed and the counterpart sign—the radiant inner object of meditation—arises. Although subduing the hindrances began with faith and delight, now they have been suppressed more firmly so that the mind can remain concentrated and free from constant disruption. The meditator has much greater control of his or her mind. The bliss of being released from the hindrances, even temporarily during access concentration, is compared to the relief and joy someone feels upon being freed from slavery.

6. Bliss is the proximate cause for concentration.

As the bliss of access concentration expands, it permeates the mind and the hindrances to the unification of the mind vanish. At this point the mind enters into absorption or full concentration, dhyāna. In general, concentration is a mental factor present in many mental states, including both access and absorption. It functions to unite the mind on a single object and to enable the consciousness and its accompanying mental factors to operate in harmony, making them steadier and more focused. While concentration has been increasing all along while cultivating serenity, in the dhyānas it becomes especially strong. The mind becomes very still, like a still lake on a cloudless night that clearly reflects the trees and moon. No discursive thought disturbs the mind's stillness.

During access concentration the dhyānic factors—investigation, analysis, joy, bliss, and one-pointedness—are strong enough to suppress the five hindrances, but not to place the mind in full meditative absorption. With the attainment of the first dhyāna, the dhyānic factors are strong enough to do this. Now the mind is so concentrated that any feeling of separation from the meditation object vanishes. From the first dhyāna, a meditator can proceed sequentially to attain the second, third, and fourth dhyānas, and then to the four formless absorptions, which are very refined states of mind in meditative absorption.

7. Concentration is the proximate cause for knowledge and vision of things as they really are.

Although it is an important precursor for wisdom, concentration alone is not sufficient to free us from cyclic existence. Despite its bliss and tranquility, concentration has only suppressed the coarse defilements. Other defilements still remain in the mind, dormant and ready to spring up whenever conditions allow. The ignorance of the four truths that is the root of saṃsāra as well as the other pollutants and fetters that depend on it must still be abandoned. To do this, insight and wisdom are essential, so now concentration is used to generate knowledge and vision of things as they really are, which is a form of insight that knows and sees the five aggregates as they actually are—their nature, arising, and passing away.

A mind in which the hindrances have been suppressed through concentration is needed to be able to see reality clearly. Just as a woodcutter needs not only a sharp ax but also clear eyesight so he can strike the same point repeatedly and fell the tree, similarly meditators require the steadiness and clarity that concentration provides to direct their wisdom to the analysis of conditioned phenomena.

The knowledge and vision of things as they really are liberates us. The Buddha said (SN 12.23), "The destruction of the pollutants is for one who knows and sees, I say, not for one who does not know and does not see." Knowledge and vision are not intellectual but are a knowing and seeing that are so vivid that it is as if we were perceiving something with our eyes. Its initial cultivation may depend on conceptual knowledge, which helps to dispel mistaken notions. However, once the coarse misconceptions are dispelled and right view is established, we must go beyond conceptual knowledge to effect the very deep changes that lead to liberation.

Since all our experiences consist of a combination of the five aggregates, essential to the cultivation of wisdom are mindfulness and introspective awareness placed on the five aggregates. Although every experience and cognition can be broken down into the five aggregates, our ignorant, non-analytical mind takes the aggregates as a uniform whole. This leads to the view that there is a permanent, substantial self. This view of a personal identity as being a self is the outer shell surrounding ignorance, and to eliminate it we must continually break our experience down into the five aggregates, see their nature, their arising, and their passing away.

A very peaceful and concentrated mind has difficulty engaging in the intense analysis that is now required. Thus the meditator emerges from the deep concentration of a dhyāna and studies each factor of that dhyānic state, identifying it as one of the five aggregates. She then examines the causes and conditions giving rise to each factor and each aggregate. This brings awareness that there is simply an ever-changing flow of physical and mental events that is devoid of a controlling self. She understands conditionality because each event arises when its causes and conditions exist and ceases when its causes and conditions cease. None of the factors or aggregates exist on their own, independently, and none of them require a supervisory self to function.

This awareness of conditionality leads to the examination of the arising and passing away of each physical and mental event. Noticing the coming into existence and the vanishing from existence of form, feelings, discriminations, miscellaneous factors, and consciousnesses reveals their impermanence. They not only arise and cease due to conditions, but conditions cause them to arise and cease in each nanosecond.

Changing in every brief moment, the five aggregates are unsatisfactory because they are incapable of bringing us stable happiness. The five aggregates cannot be the core of a real self because they are impermanent and unsatisfactory both individually and as a collection. The clear seeing of the three characteristics of conditioned phenomena—impermanence, duḥkha, and no self—is the knowledge and vision of things as they really are.

8. Knowledge and vision of things as they really are is the proximate cause for disenchantment.

Knowledge and vision of things as they really are is weak insight; disenchantment is strong insight. To progress from the former to the latter, a meditator now focuses his attention on the momentary passing away of the aggregates—their disintegration and cessation. Repeated mindfulness on the vanishing of what he thinks is the source of happiness and security sparks disenchantment and disappointment. The things that he believed would protect him and bring him joy are now seen as they are—farces and deceptions—and the mind wisely turns away from them. This process of disenchantment is similar to that of a child who realizes without a doubt that Santa Claus does not exist and stops waiting for Santa to come on Christmas Eve. Disenchantment is not depressing; it is simply losing interest in the transient, unsatisfactory, and selfless external world with its kaleidoscope of illusory sensual delights that leave us exhausted. We now turn inward to wisdom.

He realizes that until now he has filtered and evaluated every experience through the distorted lens of mine, I, and my self. Whereas he previously believed this was truth, he now sees mine, I, and my self are conceptual fabrications imputed by ignorance and knows without a doubt that believing them to be true is the source of duḥkha. He knows the aggregates are not mine, these I am not, these are not my self, and he begins to mentally set down the burden that was never his to begin with. The Buddha says (SN 22.59):

> Therefore, monastics, any kind of form whatsoever, any kind of feeling . . . discrimination . . . miscellaneous factor . . . consciousness whatsoever, whether past, future, or present, internal or external, coarse or subtle, inferior or superior, far or near should be seen as it really is with correct wisdom thus: This is not mine, this I am not, this is not my self.
>
> Seeing thus, monastics, the instructed ārya disciple experiences disenchantment toward form, feeling, discrimination, miscellaneous factors, and consciousness. Experiencing disenchantment, he becomes dispassionate. Through dispassion [his mind] is liberated. When it is liberated, there comes the knowledge: "It is liberated." He understands, "Birth is destroyed, the holy life has been lived, what had to be done has been done, there is no more coming to any state of being."

Here we see the progression that outlines the upcoming steps of dispassion, liberation, and knowledge of destruction.

9. Disenchantment is the proximate cause for dispassion.
Disenchantment with conditioned phenomena results from understanding their nature. It is based on accurate knowledge and insight and is not emotional rejection, fear, or escapism. Understanding the conditioned prepares us to realize the unconditioned. With disenchantment, a meditator detaches herself from conditioned phenomena. With knowledge that there is an actual state of lasting happiness that can be attained, she is determined to attain it. She continues relinquishing craving and clinging to conditioned things and does not take up any new attachments. This process of mental "spring cleaning" sees the gratification and danger of conditioned things and now seeks an escape—a path to freedom—from them.

Insight becomes deeper and more penetrative until a breakthrough is reached and she sees nirvāṇa. This is dispassion, path wisdom that is the first supramundane (*lokottara*, *lokuttara*) factor in transcendental dependent arising. While the eight previous factors are called members of transcendental dependent arising, they are in fact still mundane (*laukika*, *lokiya*) because their objects are conditioned phenomena, in particular the five aggregates. While these factors are indispensable steps to arrive at the supramundane path, they themselves are not supramundane.

10. Dispassion is the proximate cause for liberation.
The commentary on the Saṃyutta Nikāya explains:

> Seeing with correct wisdom (P. *sammappaññāya*) is path wisdom together with insight. The mind becomes dispassionate at the moment of the path and is liberated at the moment of the fruit.

The mind becomes dispassionate when it sees nirvāṇa with correct wisdom and insight. This marks entrance into the supramundane path of stream-enterer. When the first three fetters—view of a personal identity, doubt, and view of rules and practices—have been abandoned, the fruit of stream-enterer is attained. In this way, dispassion as the path is the condition for liberation as the fruit. The path and fruit sequence begins with stream-entry, continues with once-returner and nonreturner, and culminates in arhatship. Each path is a time of reducing or eliminating fetters, and each fruit is a time of knowing and enjoying the reduction or abandonment of those fetters. The mind is peaceful and delights in its newfound freedom.

There are two aspects to full liberation. One is freedom from the ignorance and defilements experienced during this lifetime. The mind is now immune to attachment, animosity, and confusion, and any last traces of these poisons have been eliminated so that they can never arise again. This nirvāṇa is visible here and now; it is nirvāṇa with remainder. The Buddha says (AN 3.55):

> When a person is impassioned with sensual desire . . . depraved through animosity . . . bewildered by confusion, overwhelmed and infatuated by [sensual desire, animosity, and] confusion, then he plans for his own harm, for the harm of others, for the harm of both; and he experiences in this mind suffering and grief. But when sensual desire, animosity, and confusion have been abandoned, he neither plans for his own harm, nor for the harm of others, nor for the harm of both; and he does not experience in his mind suffering and grief. In this way, nibbāna is directly visible, immediate, inviting one to come and see, leading onward, to be personally experienced by the wise.

The other aspect of liberation is freedom from rebirth after the breakup of the present body. At arhatship, the peace in the mind is immense, for the mind is no longer controlled by defilements. Arhats rest with the security that comes from knowing that all future existence in saṃsāra has ceased.

Liberation—the fruit of arhatship—is the freedom from all pollutants that comes at the end of this chain of four paths and four fruitions. The path has been completed; there is nothing more to be abandoned or added.

11. Liberation is the proximate cause for knowledge of the destruction of all pollutants.

Each path, which reduces or abandons certain fetters, is immediately followed by its own fruit, which enjoys the reduction or abandonment of those fetters. That is followed by a reviewing knowledge (P. *paccavekkhaṇa ñāṇa*) that ascertains what has just occurred. It reviews the fetters that have been abandoned by that path and those that still remain. The reviewing knowledge after attaining the fruit of arhatship certifies that all fetters, pollutants, and defilements as well as any underlying tendencies toward them have been eradicated and that none remains.

At the time of the path of arhatship, the four truths are known as they actually are. This knowing eradicates any remaining defilements. At the time of the fruit of arhatship, the remaining defilements have been eradicated and the mind is freed. Following this, the reviewing knowledge arises that understands that this has occurred and that the mind is liberated from defilements. The Buddha describes the sequence (MN 39.21):

> He understands as it actually is: "This is duḥkha" . . . "This is the origin of duḥkha" . . . "This is the cessation of duḥkha" . . . "This is the way leading to the cessation of duḥkha" . . . "These are the pollutants" . . . "This is the origin of the pollutants" . . . "This is the cessation of the pollutants" . . . "This is the way leading to the cessation of the pollutants."
>
> When he knows and sees thus, his mind is liberated from the pollutant of sensual desire, the pollutant of existence, and the pollutant of ignorance. When it is liberated, there comes the knowledge: "It is liberated." He understands: "Birth is destroyed, the holy life has been lived, what had to be done has been done, there is no more coming to any state of being."

An arhat sees the final cessation of duḥkha and defilements very clearly and there is no doubt in his or her mind that this has occurred.

Two ascertainments are involved in this retrospective cognition. The *knowledge of destruction* knows that all the fetters have been uprooted and no longer remain. The *knowledge of nonarising* knows that they can never arise again. Together these are called the knowledge and vision of liberation (P. *vimutti ñāṇadassana*). Arhats experience freedom from defilements and enjoy the certitude that defilements can never arise again. This brings an incredible confidence and ease in the mind; arhats never experience anxiety or uncertainty. Having fully understood that there is no self or anything belonging to a self anywhere at all, they are the masters of their minds.

While the knowledge and vision of liberation is not always manifest in an arhat's mind, it remains there under the surface and can manifest as soon as she looks at the state of her mind. The Buddha analogized this to someone whose hands and feet have been amputated. Whatever he is doing, his limbs have been cut off, and the instant he turns his mind to it, he knows this is the case. Similarly, someone who has destroyed all pollutants is always free from them, and the instant he looks at his mind, he knows that this is the case.

Karma in Saṃsāra and Beyond

Karma is of many varieties; discerning them is helpful to our practice. Of the *polluted karma* of saṃsāra, there is virtuous, nonvirtuous, and neutral karma.

Virtuous polluted karma is created by ordinary beings—everyone who is not an ārya. It ripens as happiness in saṃsāra and does not directly lead to liberation. It is of two kinds as mentioned above: (1) *Meritorious karma* is created by beings in the desire realm and brings a good rebirth or other happy circumstances in the desire realm. (2) *Invariable karma* is created by beings in the desire, form, or formless realms; it causes rebirth in the form or formless realms.

Nonvirtuous or nonmeritorious karma, when created by ordinary beings, propels unfortunate rebirths and other undesirable events in saṃsāra. When created by stream-enterers and once-returners, it does not propel a rebirth. Śrāvaka āryas who are not arhats may still experience suffering in their lives due to seeds of previously created nonvirtuous karma on their mindstreams. Ārya bodhisattvas, owing to the power of their wisdom and compassion, do not experience physical or mental suffering.

Neutral karma brings neither happy nor suffering results. Created by beings in all three realms, it is not powerful enough to propel rebirth in cyclic existence.

Unpolluted karma is created by āryas who are not buddhas. It does not propel rebirth in saṃsāra. Together with the latencies of ignorance, it produces the mental bodies of ārya bodhisattvas and arhats and leads to liberation and buddhahood. Buddhas do not create karma but engage in spontaneous awakened activities that benefit sentient beings.

When we closely examine our intentions, we may be surprised to find that many of them seek the happiness of only this life. The appearances of this life are so vivid to our senses that naturally the minds of us ordinary beings gravitate toward them. Even if we believe in future lives, in our daily lives we often are not mindful that our actions create the causes for our future rebirths and our experiences in them. This limited perspective obscures the great opportunity our precious human lives provide to gain spiritual realizations. Although we may still create virtuous karma that will result in a fortunate rebirth with a motivation focused on this life, such a motivation impedes us from attaining liberation or full awakening. To expand the intentions behind our daily actions, it is important to enlarge our worldview to include future lives, liberation, and awakening.

All ordinary beings—including those from the supreme dharma stage of the path of preparation of all three vehicles downward—accumulate karma that propels rebirth in saṃsāra under the influence of ignorance and view of a personal identity.[68] Their motivations that see the disadvantages of saṃsāra and genuinely aspire for liberation, and virtuous karma similar to the wisdom analyzing selflessness, are contrary to first-link ignorance and are remedies for the craving for rebirth. They lead to the eradication of craving and the attainment of the ārya path, and in this sense they are not actual true origins. However, since they are similar to true origins in that they are not free from grasping true existence, this karma is included under true origins. The *Compendium of Determinations* (*Viniścaya-samgrahaṇī*) says (LC 1:305):

> By nature they are not directed toward rebirth in saṃsāra. However, they approximate the physical, mental, and verbal good conduct that leads to rebirth. Consequently, you should understand that on this account they are included under the truth of the origin.

Antipathy toward all forms of duḥkha, sincere aspiration to attain liberation, bodhicitta, and the mind similar to the correct view are excellent steps along the path. But to create unpolluted karma that leads directly to liberation and awakening we must generate the ārya path by realizing emptiness directly. Only then do our actions become unpolluted and direct causes for liberation.

For us ordinary beings, the only karma we create that is not typical true origins of duḥkha are actions depending on the power of the field—that is, by interaction with holy objects, places, and people. Tsongkhapa says (LC 1:305–6):

> You might not have acquired, through extensive meditative analysis of the faults of cyclic existence, the remedy that eradicates the craving for the wonders of cyclic existence. You might also not have used discerning wisdom to properly analyze the meaning of selflessness, and might not have become habituated to the two bodhicittas [conventional and ultimate], in which case your virtuous activities—with some exceptions on account of the field's power—would constitute typical origins [of duḥkha], and hence would fuel the process of cyclic existence.

Nevertheless, contact with holy objects creates seeds of powerful virtuous karma. In *Letter to a Friend* (*Suhṛllekha*) Nāgārjuna says that even if someone sees the form of the Tathāgata in a mural and reacts to it with an afflictive attitude, he still creates karma to have visions of buddhas and buddha lands in the future. Buddhas and bodhisattvas are such powerful fields for accumulating merit because they have dedicated their lives to benefiting sentient beings for as long as saṃsāra endures. Due to the incredible virtue of their aspirations, any contact with them becomes virtuous in the long term. When we make offerings or prostrations to them, bodhisattvas rejoice in our virtue and dedicate their merit to be able to benefit us. Even when people harm them, bodhisattvas pray to be able to teach them the Dharma and lead them to awakening.

Although creating merit with holy objects is important, it is not sufficient for the attainment of spiritual realizations. We must cultivate all the steps on the path—the three higher trainings, the three principal aspects of the path, and the path of Tantrayāna—to gain full awakening.

11 | Freedom from Cyclic Existence

THE SIXTEEN ATTRIBUTES of the four truths spoken of in chapter 1 tell us that true cessation, as exemplified by nirvāṇa, has four aspects: (1) It is the *cessation* of the continuum of afflictions, their seeds, and the karma that causes rebirth. (2) It is true *peace*, the state of total tranquility that is completely free from all afflictive obscurations. (3) It is *magnificent* because we have reached ultimate satisfaction. (4) It is *freedom* because we have definitely emerged from cyclic existence.

Nirvāṇa is our goal, and the true path to attain it that is held in common by all Buddhist traditions constitutes the Dharma Jewel. The word *Dharma* has many meanings, depending on the context. In *Dharma Jewel*, it means to hold or prevent us from falling into duḥkha. From this perspective, even the path of the initial practitioner is the Dharma in that it prevents us from falling into the suffering of unfortunate rebirths. More broadly, Dharma holds or prevents us from experiencing all kinds of duḥkha; this is the role of true paths and true cessations, which together constitute the Dharma Jewel.

In general true paths consist of the three higher trainings in ethical conduct, concentration, and wisdom, which include the eightfold path. More specifically, the wisdom directly realizing emptiness is the counterforce that eliminates first-link ignorance and directly brings liberation. One moment of this wisdom is not sufficient to remove all deeply entrenched afflictions that have disturbed the mind from beginningless time. Because continual habituation with this wisdom is necessary, we need to cultivate single-pointed concentration (*samādhi*) and serenity (*śamatha*) that can focus on emptiness in a sustained manner free from distraction.

This concentration must be free of two principal faults: laxity and restlessness, which prevent us from focusing with stability and clarity on the object of meditation for long periods of time. The mental factors of mindfulness and introspective awareness are crucial to overcome laxity and restlessness, and these two mental factors are initially cultivated in the training of ethical conduct. To abide in pure conduct, we must hold our precepts with mindfulness and closely monitor the actions of our body, speech, and mind with introspective awareness. Having developed some degree of mindfulness and introspective awareness by observing ethical conduct, we can then employ these two to identify and suppress laxity and restlessness and to deepen concentration. With strong concentration, wisdom becomes a stable and powerful counterforce to eradicate ignorance. In short, all three higher trainings assist one another and all three are necessary to attain liberation.

Stages Leading to Liberation and Full Awakening

Attaining spiritual realizations occurs over time. Learning the stages leading to liberation and full awakening gives us an idea of the process of spiritual transformation we will undergo and the practices that will bring about the desired spiritual progress. There are many similarities in the paths and fruits of śrāvakas, solitary realizers, and bodhisattvas; there are many differences in them as well.

Before even entering one of the three vehicles—śrāvaka, solitary realizer, and bodhisattva—we must have a correct and stable understanding of the Buddhist worldview, purify our minds, and create much merit. Each vehicle has five paths: the paths of accumulation, preparation, seeing, meditation, and no more learning. Practitioners enter the śrāvaka path of accumulation when their aspiration to attain liberation remains stable day and night. Practitioners enter the bodhisattva path of accumulation when bodhicitta spontaneously arises in relation to any and all sentient beings.

In all three vehicles, practitioners go from the path of accumulation to the path of preparation when they have attained the union of serenity and insight on emptiness. This is still a conceptual realization, but through repeated practice they remove the veil of conceptuality and realize emptiness directly. At this point they attain the path of seeing and become āryas.

Stream-enterers, the first level of śrāvaka āryas, are on the path of seeing and have eliminated acquired afflictions. Afflictions may arise in their minds and they may create destructive karma. However, this karma is not strong enough to project rebirth in saṃsāra, so they no longer begin new sets of twelve links. They still have the seeds of projecting karma of many other sets of twelve links on their mindstreams, and when these are activated by craving and clinging, they take rebirth. Although they are not liberated from cyclic existence, they are not fully under its sway in the way ordinary beings are. Stream-enterers can no longer be reborn in unfortunate realms, although they still experience suffering and sickness when born as humans.

Continuing to practice, stream-enterers gradually reduce layers of afflictions. When sensual attachment and malice have been subdued to a certain degree, they become once-returners, so-called because they will take only one more rebirth in the desire realm. Once-returners may still create destructive karma, although it is weak.

Ordinary beings are attached to the self, and while dying the fear that they will no longer exist arises, followed by craving for saṃsāric aggregates. This precipitates the bardo state. Attachment to self may arise in stream-enterers and once-returners, but investigating it with wisdom, they cast it out. It does not arise in nonreturners.

Once-returners continue their practice, and when the five lower fetters—view of a personal identity, doubt, view of rules and practices, sensual desire, and malice—are eliminated, they become nonreturners, so-called because they are never again born in the desire realm. Since destructive karma is created only in the desire realm, nonreturners no longer create it. Like stream-enterers and once-returners, nonreturners are still reborn under the power of afflictions and karma. When they abandon all afflictive obscurations completely, they attain the śrāvaka path of no more learning and become arhats—those who have attained liberation and are totally free from cyclic existence.

Although arhats no longer create new karma to be born in saṃsāra, the potency of previously created karmic seeds that could bring a saṃsāric rebirth remains intact. However, because they have eliminated all afflictions, those seeds are not nourished by craving and clinging and do not produce new rebirths.

Karmic seeds of completing karma remain on arhats' mindstreams and these may ripen. The most famous example of this occurred to Maudgalyāyana, one of the Buddha's chief disciples. Many lifetimes ago, he had killed his parents. Although he had been born in the hell realm as a ripening result of that deed, the fruit of that karma had not yet been exhausted. Some non-Buddhists knew that Maudgalyāyana was foremost among the Buddha's disciples in terms of his supernormal powers and would use those powers to bring people to the Buddhadharma. Jealous of the Buddha and his followers, they directed some thugs to kill Maudgalyāyana. Maudgalyāyana wished to spare them the nonvirtuous karma of killing an arhat and so tried to use his supernormal powers to escape. Due to the karmic seeds remaining from having killed his parents, his supernormal powers failed; the thugs beat him severely and left him for dead. Maudgalyāyana crawled to the Buddha, paid final homage to him, and passed away. Although he experienced physical pain from the beating, he was not upset or angry.

While arhats are alive, intentions arise in their minds, but they do not leave any traces. The *Dhammapada* compares the action of arhats to the flight of birds across the sky (92–93):

> Those who do not hoard [anything] and are wise regarding food,
> whose object is emptiness, the unconditioned, freedom—
> their track cannot be traced,
> like the path of birds in the sky.
>
> Those whose pollutants are destroyed and who are unattached to
> food,
> whose object is emptiness, the unconditioned, freedom—
> their path cannot be traced,
> like the path of birds in the sky.

While alive, arhats are free from saṃsāra although they still have the saṃsāric aggregates—especially the bodies they took at birth, which are ripening results of polluted karma. Their bodies are true duḥkha, so their nirvāṇa is called "nirvāṇa with remainder (of the polluted aggregates)." When they die, all karmic seeds vanish on their own without a remedy being applied, although the latencies of afflictions still remain on their mindstreams. Leaving the five polluted aggregates and taking mental bodies (T. *yid lus*) that are not made of atoms, arhats now have a nirvāṇa without remainder. They remain meditating in peaceful nirvāṇa for eons, until the Buddha wakes them and encourages them to become fully awakened buddhas. They then generate bodhicitta, take birth by the power of prayers and aspirations, and enter the bodhisattva path.

Bodhisattvas on the paths of accumulation and preparation are born in saṃsāra owing to ignorance. From the path of seeing onward they are āryas and take birth according to their compassionate wishes and intentions and no longer experience birth, aging, sickness, or death under the power of afflictions and karma. By the force of their fervent compassionate intentions and stainless altruistic prayers, they may choose to take birth in a particular family or country to benefit the beings there. When doing so, they appear to experience everything ordinary beings do, yet their experience is very different from ours because of the intensity of their realization of emptiness supported by bodhicitta. Because they have not yet eradicated all afflictive obscurations, these ārya bodhisattvas are said to be *in* saṃsāra, but not *of* saṃsāra.

When sharp faculty bodhisattvas attain the path of seeing, due to the force of their great resolve and bodhicitta, their bodhicitta transforms into the bodhicitta that is the purity of the extraordinary great resolve. From the path of seeing onward, bodhisattvas also gain a mental body that arises from unpolluted karma—the intention to assume such a body—and the subtle latencies of ignorance. This body is not one entity with the mind, but it is said to be in the nature of mind, because like the mind, it is not made of atoms and lacks physical impediment. It is unpolluted and free of physical pain, although until bodhisattvas attain the eighth ground it is not free from the pervasive duḥkha of conditioning.

To benefit us ordinary beings, these ārya bodhisattvas take or emanate a form similar to ours and show the aspect of sickness, aging, death, and so forth. These bodies are not true duḥkha.

If they manifest in the animal, hungry ghost, or hell realms to benefit sentient beings there, they are not beings of that realm; they are merely assuming that appearance. Bodhisattvas who practice Tantra actualize an impure illusory body and then a pure illusory body, even when they still have a polluted human body. The actual or ultimate unpolluted body is attained at buddhahood.

Ārya bodhisattvas progress through the ten bodhisattva grounds that occur on the paths of seeing and meditation. Until they reach the eighth ground, afflictions may still manifest in their minds, but they don't remain long and do not function as afflictions usually do in that they do not disturb the mind. Ārya bodhisattvas create only unpolluted karma.

Unless they had previously become śrāvaka arhats, ārya bodhisattvas are not liberated from saṃsāra until the beginning of the eighth bodhisattva ground. At this time, they have purified all afflictive obscurations and become pure ground bodhisattvas. Since cognitive obscurations still remain on their mindstreams, they must exert subtle effort to motivate their physical and verbal actions done to benefit of others. During the three pure grounds, they gradually abandon cognitive obscurations, and at the Mahāyāna path of no more learning when the cognitive obscurations have been fully pacified, they become buddhas who spontaneously and effortlessly act for others' welfare until saṃsāra ends.

Some ordinary beings are born in pure lands such as Sukhāvatī, Amitābha Buddha's pure land, as a result of special virtuous karma and sincere virtuous aspirations and prayers to take rebirth there. Birth in Amitābha's and Akṣobhya's pure lands is not taken under the power of afflictions and karma and is not in the twelve links. The bodies of ordinary beings born there are not true duḥkha. Although many beings born in those pure lands still have self-grasping and other afflictions, these do not arise in manifest form, so they do not create karma for rebirth in unfortunate realms. Because they practice the path diligently, they no longer create karma for rebirth in saṃsāra and attain full awakening in the pure land.

REFLECTION

1. Review the stages of the path to liberation for those following the Śrāvaka Vehicle.

2. Review the stages of the path to full awakening followed by those in the Bodhisattva Vehicle.

3. Get a sense of your potential. Realize that you can progress through these paths and stages and attain the peaceful results.

The Two Obscurations

The minds of ordinary sentient beings are veiled by two types of obscurations: afflictive obscurations and cognitive obscurations. The former principally prevent liberation from saṃsāra; the latter are mainly obstacles to full awakening. The state of having eliminated afflictive obscurations is nirvāṇa, or liberation. The state of having additionally removed cognitive obscurations is full awakening, nonabiding nirvāṇa, and buddhahood.

Afflictive obscurations (*kleśāvaraṇa*) are coarse and subtle self-grasping ignorance and its seeds and the three poisons of confusion, attachment, and animosity and their seeds. In short, afflictions and their seeds constitute afflictive obscurations.

Cognitive obscurations (*jñeyāvaraṇa*) are more subtle and difficult to remove from the mindstream. Compared with afflictive obscurations, which are like onions in a pot, cognitive obscurations are like the smell that remains after the onions have been removed. Cognitive obscurations are the latencies of self-grasping ignorance, the latencies of the three poisons, the mistaken dualistic appearances that arise from them, and the defilement (*āvaraṇa*) of apprehending the two truths as different entities. All of these are abstract composites, not consciousnesses (although some contest this point).

The word *appearance* does not adequately indicate the meaning of the Tibetan word *snang ba*, which can refer to either appearance or perception. By saying "appearance of inherent existence," we may mistakenly think that the obscuration is external to our minds—that phenomena from their side appear inherently existent—whereas the obscuration is associated with our minds—we "perceive" inherent existence, which does not exist at all. Please keep this in mind when we talk about the appearance of inherent existence.

The aspect of the mind that continues to have the mistaken appearance of inherent existence is called "manifest cognitive obscuration," while the latencies left from the afflictions that cause these appearances are called "factors of a seed." The latencies are subtle tendencies (T. *bag la nyal*). By their power, the mind continues to have the appearance of inherent existence.

Mistaken dualistic appearances are the aspect of the mind that continues to have the mistaken appearances of all internal and external phenomena as existing inherently. This aspect of the mind obscures all six consciousnesses—the five sense consciousnesses and the mental consciousness. Both ordinary beings and āryas who are not in meditative equipoise on emptiness have these mistaken dualistic appearances. The only consciousness in sentient beings' continuums that lacks them is āryas' exalted wisdom in meditative equipoise on emptiness.

Within the appearance/perception of inherently existent objects, one part exists and one part does not. A flower exists, but its being inherently existent does not. The flower is not a cognitive obscuration, but its appearing to be inherently existent is. When the mind is freed from this mistaken appearance, conventionally existent things do not cease to exist; rather, they no longer appear inherently existent.

The *defilement of apprehending the two truths as different entities* prevents seeing all phenomena—veiled truths and their emptiness—simultaneously. Since arhats and pure ground bodhisattvas have this defilement, they cannot simultaneously cognize the two truths. They must alternate consciousnesses: their meditative equipoise on emptiness sees only emptiness; veiled truths, which are the substrata—that is, they are the objects that are empty—do not appear to that mind focused on emptiness. When they arise from their meditative equipoise on emptiness in the time of subsequent attainment, they know conventionalities but cannot perceive their emptiness directly. Because this defilement has been eradicated in buddhahood, buddhas can directly and simultaneously know the two truths.

Latencies of attachment and other afflictions also cause arhats to have dysfunctional behaviors of body and speech (*dauṣṭhulya*) that are breaches of discipline. Arhats may inadvertently jump around owing to the latency of attachment. They may spontaneously call someone a name owing to the latency of anger. Their clairvoyance may be unclear owing to the latency of ignorance. These infrequent occurrences are not due to any negative intention or ignorance on arhats' part, for they have eliminated all afflictions. Candrakīrti's *Autocommentary to the "Supplement"* says:

> Although arhats have abandoned afflictions, they have the latencies, due to which they will jump as they did when formerly they were monkeys . . . Those latencies are overcome only in omniscience and buddhahood, not in others.[69]

The same idea is also found in later Pāli commentaries. They explain that although arhats have eliminated all obscurations due to afflictions, they still have latencies of afflictions, which can induce conduct that is a breach of decorum. This is because unlike the Buddha, arhats have not eliminated the obstruction to all-knowing and thus do not know all existents. The commentary to the *Udāna* says:

> A *vāsanā* [latency] is a mere capacity to behave in certain ways similar to the behavior of those who still have defilements; it is engendered by the defilements that have been harbored in the mind from beginningless time, and remain in the mental continuum of the arhat even after the defilements have been abandoned, as a mere habitual tendency. The vāsanās are not found in the mental continuum of a buddha, who removes the defilements by abandoning the obstruction to all-knowing, but they are found in the minds of hearers and solitary realizers.[70]

An example is the bhikkhu Pilindavaccha. Although he was an arhat and had eradicated conceit and contempt, he continued to address fellow bhikṣus as outcastes. This occurred owing to the force of predispositions (latencies) established by his habitual behavior as a brahmin during five hundred previous lives.

Some schools speak of non-afflictive ignorance. To Vaibhāṣikas, this mainly impedes attaining all-knowing and consists of the four causes of non-knowingness: (1) non-afflictive ignorance of the profound and subtle qualities of a buddha, (2–3) ignorance due to the distant place or time of the object, and (4) ignorance of the nature of the object, such as the subtle details of karma and its effects. According to Prāsaṅgikas, non-afflictive ignorance refers to the latencies of ignorance and is not a consciousness.

Nirvāṇa

All Buddhists seek nirvāṇa, but what is it? In general, nirvāṇa is a state or quality of mind. It is not an external place, nor is it something reserved for a select few. Nirvāṇa is attainable by each and every sentient being.

Nirvāṇa is the ultimate nature of our minds—the emptiness of the mind that has been totally cleansed of obscurations. Wisdom directly realizes the emptiness of all phenomena, including the emptiness of the mind itself. This wisdom gradually purifies the mind of defilements. As it does so, the emptiness of that mind, which is one nature with that mind, is also purified. The purified state of the emptiness of the mind that is free from afflictive obscurations is an arhat's nirvāṇa; the purified state of the emptiness of the mind that is free from both afflictive and cognitive obscurations is the nonabiding nirvāṇa of a buddha.

All produced things naturally cease because momentary disintegration is part of their nature; their cessation doesn't depend on some other cause or condition that is a counterforce. However, the true cessation that is the severance of afflictions does not occur in that way; it is not the natural disintegration of a thing when its causal energy ceases. True cessations come into existence due to wisdom, a counterforce that has been deliberately cultivated. Wisdom destroys ignorance such that it can never arise again; it severs the continuity of ignorance completely. By meditating on the reasonings that refute inherent existence and establish the lack of inherent existence, we generate the ārya path, the wisdom that directly realizes emptiness. This wisdom apprehends the opposite of ignorance. Whereas ignorance apprehends phenomena as inherently existent, wisdom apprehends them as empty of inherent existence. In this way, wisdom uproots ignorance and its seeds. By the cessation and nonarising of ignorance, all other afflictions cease as well. Formative actions also cease, as do the remaining links.

There is debate whether nirvāṇa is a nonaffirming negative—a simple negation that doesn't imply anything—or an affirming negative—a statement that negates one thing while implying a positive phenomenon. An example of the former is "The I is empty," where nothing positive is implied.

An example of the latter is "The I that is empty," which asserts a positive phenomenon—the I—while negating it being inherently existent.

Some people say nirvāṇa is an emptiness, the lack of inherent existence that never existed. This is a nonaffirming negative, a permanent phenomenon, and an ultimate truth. Others say nirvāṇa is the extinguishment of the afflictions, which did exist. It is an ultimate truth but not an emptiness. Here is how I see it. Nāgārjuna said (RA 42cd):

> Nirvāṇa is said to be the cessation of the notions of things and non-things.

Nirvāṇa is the extinction of afflictions means not only that afflictions (things) have been extinguished but also that there are no inherently existent afflictions (non-things) in nirvāṇa. This beginningless absence of inherently existent afflictions is emptiness, an ultimate truth.

The absence of afflictions that is nirvāṇa, a true cessation, is a nonaffirming negative. The afflictions can never again arise because their causes have been completely eradicated. If nirvāṇa were an affirming negative, a having-ceased of the afflictions rather than their total extinguishment, then the afflictions could arise once again. This is because the having-ceased of impermanent phenomena such as the afflictions can produce a result. However, in nirvāṇa, the afflictions and their causes can never again reappear. Nirvāṇa is the emptiness of the mind that is totally purified of afflictions. Nothing else is being affirmed.

Nirvāṇa is the state beyond sorrow, *sorrow* referring to saṃsāra, its duḥkha, and origins. Alternatively, *sorrow* alludes to inherent existence, and nirvāṇa being beyond sorrow indicates that it is the emptiness of inherent existence.

Four types of nirvāṇa are spoken of: natural nirvāṇa (*prakṛti-nirvṛta*), nirvāṇa with remainder (*sopadhiśeṣanirvāṇa*), nirvāṇa without remainder (*nirupadhiśeṣanirvāṇa*), and nonabiding nirvāṇa (*apratiṣṭha-nirvāṇa*).

Natural Nirvāṇa

Natural nirvāṇa is the ultimate nature of a mind that is primordially pure and devoid of inherent existence; it is the mind's emptiness of inherent existence. Candrakīrti says in *Clear Words*:

> Since only emptiness has the character of stopping all elaborations, it is called *nirvāṇa*.

Emptiness itself is free from the elaborations of inherent existence. It appears in the way it exists to the main consciousness perceiving it; that is, to the wisdom directly realizing emptiness, emptiness appears without any elaboration of inherent existence at all. The mind has always been empty of inherent existence; this emptiness is called *natural nirvāṇa*, and by repeatedly realizing it we can attain the nirvāṇa that is the cessation of all duḥkha and its origins.

Natural nirvāṇa is not actual nirvāṇa—nirvāṇa that is the passing beyond the sorrow of saṃsāra. However, as emptiness, natural nirvāṇa acts as the basis that allows for the attainment of actual nirvāṇa. As the primordial nature of the mind, it is a quality of the mind, so attaining nirvāṇa does not entail procuring an external quality. Rather it involves recognizing a quality of the mind that is already present. When the mind is polluted, it is unawakened, and when it is purified it is awakened. Its empty nature is present in both instances. Because the mind lacks inherent existence, it can be freed from all pollutants that are based on grasping inherent existence.

In a more general way, natural nirvāṇa refers to emptiness. Everything around us—as well as the four truths and the basis, path, and result—are empty of inherent existence. In this way, all phenomena can be said to possess natural nirvāṇa or emptiness. However, only sentient beings can attain the nirvāṇa that is free from obscurations, because that nirvāṇa is the emptiness of the purified mind.

Nirvāṇa with and without Remainder

According to the Svātantrikas and below, *remainder* in the terms *nirvāṇa with* and *without remainder* refers to the ordinary aggregates, which are true duḥkha because they arise under the control of ignorance and polluted karma. Śrāvaka arhats first attain nirvāṇa with remainder, because at the time they eliminate all afflictive obscurations and attain liberation, they still have their ordinary bodies.[71] When they die and shed those bodies, there is nirvāṇa without remainder because the continuity of the polluted aggregates has ceased.

Vaibhāṣikas and Sautrāntikas, who do not accept one final vehicle—that is, they do not believe that all sentient beings can attain buddhahood—assert that at the time of nirvāṇa without remainder, when an arhat passes away, his or her continuum of consciousness ceases although the nirvāṇa without remainder exists.[72] Prāsaṅgikas, Svātantrikas, and Cittamātra Reasoning Proponents who assert one final vehicle—that all sentient beings will eventually attain buddhahood—say that the continuum of consciousness exists even after arhats leave their polluted bodies. At this time they are born in the Sukhāvatī pure land; there they have nirvāṇa without remainder because no suffering aggregates remain and they instead have a mental body. While these arhats still have the five aggregates, they are not polluted aggregates because they were not taken under the control of afflictions and polluted karma.

In Sukhāvatī, these arhats stay in meditative equipoise on emptiness for eons. In time, the buddhas will wake them from their meditative equipoise, teach them the Mahāyāna doctrine, and cause them to follow the bodhisattva path to full awakening. These arhats then generate bodhicitta and enter the bodhisattva path of accumulation. Unlike bodhisattvas who initially enter the bodhisattva path of accumulation and practice for three countless great eons to attain awakening, these arhats who later become bodhisattvas require a much longer time to attain awakening because the habituation of seeking only their own liberation is very strong. In the process of practicing the bodhisattva path, they often spend long periods of time in meditative equipoise on emptiness because they are captivated by the bliss of personal peace. It is difficult for them to generate great compassion and the great resolve that takes the responsibility for the welfare of all sentient beings.

Prāsaṅgikas have a unique meaning for nirvāṇa with and without remainder. *Remainder* refers to the appearance of inherent existence and the dualistic appearance of subject and object. Nirvāṇa without remainder is the final true cessation when arhats have completely overcome the afflictive obscurations and attain nirvāṇa, the passing beyond sorrow, where sorrow indicates the afflictive obscurations. This occurs during meditative equipoise on emptiness. This nirvāṇa is free from the remainder of dualistic appearance and the appearance of inherent existence. Later, upon arising from meditative equipoise on emptiness, arhats again experience the false appearance of inherent existence due to cognitive obscurations. This is nirvāṇa with remainder of the appearances of inherent existence and of subject-object duality.

Nonabiding Nirvāṇa

Nonabiding nirvāṇa is the purified aspect of the ultimate nature of a mind that is forever free of both afflictive and cognitive obscurations. It is called *nonabiding* because a buddha does not abide in either saṃsāra or in the personal nirvāṇa of a śrāvaka arhat. All Buddhist practitioners agree that saṃsāra is clearly undesirable and want to be free from it. For bodhisattvas, who wish to attain full awakening to best work for the welfare of sentient beings, the personal nirvāṇa of an arhat is limited because arhats spend eons in blissful meditative equipoise on emptiness while sentient beings continue to suffer in saṃsāra. Bodhisattvas seek the nirvāṇa of a buddha, a nirvāṇa that lacks the impediments of both saṃsāra and personal nirvāṇa. Nonabiding nirvāṇa, possessed only by buddhas, is free from the two extremes of saṃsāra and personal nirvāṇa.

Nonabiding nirvāṇa is also the nature dharmakāya of a buddha. It is the emptiness of a buddha's mind, the purified state of the natural buddha nature. Nonabiding nirvāṇa possesses two purities: natural purity and purity from adventitious defilements. Its natural purity is its primordial emptiness of inherent existence; its purity from adventitious defilements is the aspect of true cessation.

Pāli Tradition: Nirvāṇa

In the Nālandā tradition, there is debate whether nirvāṇa is the cessation of something that once existed (the afflictions) or a state in which nothing existent was removed—an emptiness that is naturally free from inherent existence—and we now realize that emptiness. Most sages agree it is the latter. Pāli sūtras and commentators also speak of nirvāṇa in a variety of ways. In some cases, nirvāṇa refers to the elimination of the five aggregates subject to clinging; nirvāṇa is the state of cessation in which true duḥkha and the true origin of duḥkha have been eradicated. In other situations, nirvāṇa is spoken of as reality, the object of meditation of āryas' meditative equipoise.

Nirvāṇa as the Cessation of Duḥkha and Its Origin

In the Buddha's description of his own awakening, he says (MN 26.18–19):

> Then, monastics, being myself subject to birth, having understood the danger in what is subject to birth, seeking the unborn supreme security from bondage, nibbāna, I attained the unborn supreme security from bondage, nibbāna; being myself subject to aging, having understood the danger in what is subject to aging, seeking the unaging supreme security from bondage, nibbāna, I attained the unaging supreme security from bondage . . . [the passage continues with sickness, death, sorrow, defilement, in place of birth] . . . the knowledge and vision arose in me: "My deliverance is unshakeable; this is my last birth; now there is no renewal of being."
>
> I considered: "This Dhamma that I have attained is profound, hard to see and hard to understand, peaceful and sublime, unattainable by mere reasoning, subtle, to be experienced by the wise." But this generation delights in worldliness, takes delight in worldliness, rejoices in worldliness. It is hard for such a generation to see this truth, namely, specific conditionality, dependent arising. And it is hard to see this truth, namely, the stilling of all formations [aggregates], the relinquishing of all attachments, the destruction of craving, dispassion, cessation, nibbāna . . ."

"This Dhamma" refers to the four truths. "Specific conditionality, dependent arising" refers to the true origins of duḥkha, and "the stilling of all formations, the relinquishing of all attachments, the destruction of craving, dispassion, cessation, nibbāna" is the standard expression of nirvāṇa in the sūtras. It is the extinguishment of the aggregates (formations), which are true duḥkha, and of all attachment and craving, which are true origins of duḥkha. The reference to true origins implies the truth of duḥkha and the reference to true cessation implies the true path. In nirvāṇa all four truths have been realized.

In some sūtras, nirvāṇa is said to be the eradication of attachment, anger, and ignorance (SN 38:1):

> Friend Sāriputta, it is said, "Nibbāna, nibbāna." What now is nibbāna?"
>
> [Sāriputta]: "The destruction of sensual desire, the destruction of animosity, the destruction of confusion: this, friend, is called nibbāna."

This meaning fits in well with the etymological explanation of nirvāṇa. Literally, *nibbāna* indicates extinguishment. In Pāli, the word is formed from the negative particle *ni* and *vana,* which refers to craving. Thus nibbāna is the destruction or absence of the craving that propels repeated rebirths in cyclic existence. In Sanskrit, *nir* means "out" and *va* means "to blow." Here *nirvāṇa* indicates that ignorance, the root of cyclic existence, and craving, the affliction that links one life to the next, have been blown out and extinguished. In this sense, nirvāṇa is the absence of something that once existed.

Nirvāṇa as the Object of Meditation

Some sūtras in the Pāli tradition present nirvāṇa as the object of meditation of a supramundane path, where it refers more to a negation or lack of something that never existed. The Buddha says (AN 3.47):

> There are, O monastics, these three characteristics that define the unconditioned [nibbāna]. What three? No arising is seen, no vanishing is seen, no changing while it persists is seen.

Unlike conditioned phenomena that arise and pass away, nirvāṇa—the unconditioned—is free from such fluctuation. Having no arising, nirvāṇa is not produced from causes and conditions. It never vanishes or ceases because of causes and conditions, and while it exists, it does not change or transform into something else. Here nirvāṇa is presented as a simple negation of attributes that never existed in it. The Buddha describes nirvāṇa (Udāna 8.4):[73]

> One that is dependent [on craving and views] has wavering. One that is not dependent has no wavering. There being no wavering, there is calm. There being calm, there is no yearning. There

> being no yearning, there is no coming or going [birth and death]. There being no coming or going, there is no passing away or arising [succession of deaths and rebirths]. There being no passing away or arising, there is neither a here nor a there [this world or another world] nor an in-between-the-two. This, just this, is the end of duḥkha.

In another sūtra, the Buddha says (Ud 8.1):

> There is, monastics, that base where there is neither earth, nor water, nor heat, nor air; neither the base of the infinity of space, nor the base of the infinity of consciousness, nor the base of nothingness, nor the base of neither-discrimination-nor-nondiscrimination; neither this world nor another world, neither sun nor moon. Here, monastics, I say there is no coming, no going, no standing still, no passing away, and no being reborn. It is not established, not moving, without support. Just this is the end of duḥkha.

And in another sūtra from the Udāna, he says (Ud 8.3):

> There is, monastics, an unborn, unbecome, unmade, unfabricated. If, monastics, there were no unborn, unbecome, unmade, unconditioned, no escape would be discerned from what is born, become, made, fabricated. But because there is an unborn, unbecome, unmade, unfabricated, therefore an escape is discerned from what is born, become, made, fabricated.

Here nirvāṇa is a distinct phenomenon that has nothing to do with matter or with even the deepest samādhis in saṃsāra. Nirvāṇa is a negation—no coming, no going, not made, and so forth—without anything being posited in their stead. Because nirvāṇa exists, saṃsāra can be overcome; nirvāṇa is not total nonexistence. The language the Buddha uses in the above two passages reminds us of Nāgārjuna's homage in his *Treatise on the Middle Way*:

> I prostrate to the perfect Buddha,
> the best of all teachers, who taught that
> that which is dependent arising is
> without cessation, without arising,
> without annihilation, without absolutism,
> without coming, without going,
> without distinction, without identity,
> and peaceful—free from fabrication.

The *Abhidhammattha Saṅgaha* explains nirvāṇa (CMA 258):

> Nibbāna is termed supramundane and is to be realized by the knowledge of the four paths. It becomes an object of the paths and fruits, and is called nibbāna because it is a departure from craving, which is an entanglement.

Nirvāṇa is the object of only a supramundane path—the supreme, ultimate mind cognizing the supreme, ultimate object. Nirvāṇa is spoken of as having three aspects (CMA 260): (1) Because nirvāṇa is empty of ignorance, animosity, and attachment and because it is empty of the conditioned, it is *emptiness* (P. *suññata*). (2) Because it is free from the signs of ignorance, animosity, and attachment and is free from the signs of conditioned things, it is signless (P. *animitta*). (3) Because nirvāṇa is free from the hankering of ignorance, anger, and attachment and because it is not wished for by craving, it is wishless (P. *appaṇihita*).

Ānanda once asked Śāriputra if a monk could attain a samādhi in which he does not perceive any mundane phenomenon such as the four elements, the formless absorptions, this world and the world beyond, yet still be percipient. Śāriputra points to his experience of a state of samādhi in which this occurs (AN 10.7):

> "Nibbāna is cessation of becoming, nibbāna is cessation of becoming"—one such perception arose in me and another such perception ceased. Just as when a fire of twigs is burning, one flame arises and another flame ceases, even so, "Nibbāna is cessation of becoming, nibbāna is cessation of becoming"—one such

> perception arose in me and another such perception ceased. On that occasion, friend, I perceived that nibbāna is the cessation of becoming.

Śāriputra indicates that nirvāṇa is the object of his perception. The commentary explains that he entered a samādhi of the fruition attainment of an arhat, which is an attainment in which the mind of the arhat is absorbed on nirvāṇa as an object. It is not cessation of discrimination and feeling or the attainment of cessation in which there is no discrimination or feeling, because Śāriputra is conscious. In this samādhi an arhat may focus on one aspect of nirvāṇa—for example, peaceful. It seems that Śāriputra is focusing on nirvāṇa and the cessation of becoming—that is, the absence of any active karma that could bring rebirth.

Buddhaghoṣa refutes a number of misconceptions about nirvāṇa (Vism 16:67–74). The first is that nirvāṇa is nonexistent. Nirvāṇa exists because it is apprehended by the supramundane path. The fact that the limited minds of ordinary beings cannot perceive it does not render it nonexistent. If nirvāṇa were nonexistent, practicing the path would be futile and attempting to realize nirvāṇa would be useless.

Buddhaghoṣa also refutes the assertion that nirvāṇa is simply the disintegration of defilements and the ceasing of existence. If nirvāṇa were the destruction of craving, it would not be the unconditioned, because the destruction of craving is a conditioned event. Nirvāṇa is called the destruction of craving because realizing it brings the destruction of craving. However, it is not the destruction of craving because the destruction of craving is produced by causes; it has a beginning and an end, whereas nirvāṇa has no beginning or end and is definitely unconditioned. "It is uncreated because it has no first beginning," Buddhaghoṣa says. There is no cause that brings about its arising; it is not made of matter.

The commentaries engage in many debates such as these, so there must have been a variety of viewpoints and a lot of discussion in India and Sri Lanka about what characterized nirvāṇa. We see the sūtras give two senses of nirvāṇa: It is the *goal*—a blissful state free from duḥkha and its origins—that can be experienced in this life. It is also the *object to be meditated on*—the unconditioned, the unborn, the unmoving that transcends all conditioned things.

Pāli commentators propose several ways to bring these two together and show that they are compatible. One is that nirvāṇa is metaphorically said to be the destruction of attachment, animosity, and confusion, but in actuality it is the unconditioned element that is seen by the attainment of the supramundane path and fruit. The realization of this unconditioned element has the effect of cutting away and finally eliminating attachment, animosity, and confusion. Because those defilements are destroyed in dependence upon seeing nirvāṇa, nirvāṇa is called the destruction of attachment, animosity, and confusion, although it is not the destruction of those three poisons.

While nirvāṇa is realized in time by a person, it does not come into existence through the act of being realized. As the unconditioned element, nirvāṇa always exists; it is the unborn, unoriginated, unchanging, deathless. Because nirvāṇa exists, the eradication of defilements is possible. The cultivation of the ārya path brings realization of the unconditioned, and this realization cuts off the defilements. The meditator who has reached the extinction of defilements gains access to a special meditative attainment in which he or she can abide directly experiencing the bliss of nirvāṇa in this very life.[74] The object that is seen by that meditative attainment is the unborn, unceasing, unconditioned.

The experience of nirvāṇa is beyond our ordinary cognitive processes. To give us a rough idea of nirvāṇa, the Buddha sometimes presents analogies and synonyms. For example, the Buddha referred to nirvāṇa as the truth, the far shore, the subtle, the very difficult to see, the unaging, the stable, the undisintegrating, the unmanifest, the unproliferated, the peaceful, the deathless, the sublime, the auspicious, the secure, the destruction of craving, the wonderful, the amazing, the unailing, the unailing state, the unafflicted, dispassion, purity, freedom, nonattachment, the island, the shelter, the asylum, the refuge, the destination, and the path leading to the destination (SN 43:13–44).

The consciousness of an arhat realizing nirvāṇa is described (DN 11.85):

> Where consciousness is signless, boundless, all-luminous,
> that's where earth, water, fire, and air find no footing.
> There both long and short, small and great, fair and foul—

there name and form are wholly destroyed.
With the cessation of consciousness this is all destroyed.

This consciousness is one where worldly phenomena such as the four elements and concepts such as "long" and "short" find no footing: they do not become totally nonexistent, but they do not appear to this mind of meditative equipoise focused on nirvāṇa. The ordinary mind of name and form that perceives sense phenomena is cut off.

Some people understand the last line to indicate that at arhatship, consciousness is totally ceased. However, it can also mean that with the temporary cessation of this dualistic mind, all appearances of veiled phenomena cease in the face of (in the experience of) profound meditative equipoise.

There are similarities as well as differences in the description of nirvāṇa in the Pāli and Sanskrit traditions. In the Pāli tradition, nirvāṇa is the unconditioned, in contrast to saṃsāra, which is conditioned. Nirvāṇa is completely separate and doesn't have anything to do with the saṃsāric world governed by dependent arising. Nirvāṇa, which is reality, is also distinct from selflessness, which is a characteristic of saṃsāric phenomena.

In the Sanskrit tradition, nirvāṇa is an emptiness, and emptiness is equivalent to selflessness and ultimate reality. Emptiness is also compatible with dependent arising, which includes dependent designation. Being empty and existing by mere designation are characteristics of both saṃsāra and nirvāṇa. In addition, because phenomena arise dependently, they are empty of inherent existence.

Nirvāṇa and Liberation

Although liberation and an arhat's nirvāṇa often seem to be the same, in some contexts they may be somewhat different. In the Sanskrit tradition, *liberation* (*vimukti,* T. *rnam par grol ba*) may refer to liberation itself or to the path leading to liberation. Liberation itself is true cessation—nirvāṇa—and is unconditioned. The path to liberation is a conditioned phenomenon. It is spoken of in the context of five heaps—ethical conduct, concentration, wisdom, liberation, and liberating wisdom. Here liberation is in the nature of the aspiration for liberation, and liberating wisdom is in the nature of the wisdom that liberates. Both are elements of the liberating path that leads to cessation. *Mokṣa* (T. *thar pa*) is a true cessation that is the abandonment of afflictive obscurations. It is also translated as "liberation" and refers to nirvāṇa.

In the Pāli tradition, liberation (P. *vimutti*) and nirvāṇa differ in that nirvāṇa is what is realized in the experience of liberation. Nirvāṇa is unconditioned, whereas liberation is a conditioned event. In transcendental dependent origination, liberation has the proximate cause of dispassion and is the proximate cause of knowledge of the destruction of all pollutants. In contrast, nirvāṇa is "unborn, unconstructed, unmade, unconditioned." It is ever-existent and does not arise through causes and conditions. Liberation is the release of the mind from the defilements, especially the three pollutants. To give an analogy: nirvāṇa is like a building and liberation is the act of entering it; or nirvāṇa is like the area beyond the finish line and liberation is the act of crossing that line.[75]

Bodhi

Bodhi is generally translated as "awakening" or "enlightenment," the final goal of our spiritual practice. A buddha's awakening is a state in which all defilements of the mind have been abandoned and all excellent qualities and realizations have been completed. The basis for attaining awakening is the essentially pure nature of mind—the natural purity of the mind—which is present in all of us. When the pure nature of the mind is obscured by afflictions, we are not awakened; when afflictions, their seeds, and their latencies have been completely purified, we are awakened. Thus awakening has to do with the nature of our minds.

In the Perfection of Wisdom sūtras, the essential pure nature of the mind is called *natural nirvāṇa*. These sūtras also say, "The mind is devoid of mind because the nature of the mind is clear light." Both of these passages indicate that the nature of the mind does not exist inherently. The emptiness of ordinary beings' minds has not been cleansed of obscurations; āryas have attained a certain degree of purity; the nature of buddhas' minds is completely pure. In *Praise to the Sphere of Reality* (*Dharmadhātu-stava*), Nāgārjuna says (DS 2):

> When that which forms the cause for all saṃsāra
> is purified along the stages of the path,

this purity itself is nirvāṇa;
precisely this, the dharmakāya, too.

Here *the cause for all saṃsāra* could be understood as the unpurified aspect of the emptiness of inherent existence of the mind, according to Sūtrayāna, or as the unpurified subtlest clear light mind, according to Tantrayāna. Through cleansing that "cause," nirvāṇa is attained. That nirvāṇa can be characterized as the truth body, specifically the nature truth body of a buddha, which is the final true cessation and the emptiness of the perfectly purified mind. The nature truth body is one nature with the wisdom truth body, the omniscient mind of a buddha. Here, the nature truth body is the meaning of *bodhi*.

12 | The Mind and Its Potential

Once we have recognized the unsatisfactory nature of saṃsāra and identified its causes, the questions arise: Is liberation possible? If so, how do we attain it? To answer these, we must understand our mind, which is the basis for saṃsāra and nirvāṇa.

The Mind's Potential

As sentient beings—beings with minds that are still obscured—we have great potential, our greatest potential being to become fully awakened buddhas, omniscient beings who have the wisdom, compassion, power, and skillful means to be of the greatest benefit to all.

A natural quality of mind is its ability to cognize objects. This capacity to be aware of and to know objects is already present; it does not have to be newly cultivated. Nevertheless, various obstructions can inhibit the mind from cognizing objects. When these are eliminated, the mind will have no difficulty knowing all phenomena.

One type of obstruction is physical matter; a wall obstructs us from seeing what is beyond it. When the wall is removed, our visual consciousness can see what is there. A second obstruction is distance and size: the object is too far away or too small for our cognitive faculties to come in contact with it. To some extent telescopes and microscopes have helped alleviate this difficulty. In these cases, we can know the object not because the mind has become clearer and better able to apprehend the object but because the object is brought within the range of our operable cognitive faculties.

A third difficulty concerns the cognitive faculties that are the bases of consciousness. The visual consciousness is able to perceive only visible forms, not sounds or other sense phenomena, because it is dependent on the eye faculty. If a healthy eye faculty is absent, the visual consciousness cannot perceive visible forms.

The type of brain a being has also influences what that being can perceive. A mental faculty dependent on an animal brain and one dependent on a human brain have different ranges of objects they can know. Due to the complexity of the brains of these two beings, the mental faculties and consciousnesses depending on them differ in what they can perceive and understand.

Furthermore, a mind proliferating with wrong views and overwhelmed with disturbing emotions is too distracted and preoccupied to turn its attention to other objects. The range of what such afflictive mental states can know becomes very limited. A calm mind can be more astute.

A further difficulty in knowing objects is that some objects are so subtle, profound, or vast that the ordinary mind is unable to cognize them. To know these objects, single-pointed concentration and/or wisdom that is freed from wrong conceptions is needed.

Another type of obstruction is subtle defilements on the mind that produce false appearances. These prevent us from attaining buddhahood, the state of omniscient mind. When these subtle defilements are removed, the mind will naturally perceive all phenomena. The main obstructions to omniscience are the latencies of afflictions, the subtle appearance of inherent existence that they produce, and the defilement preventing seeing the two truths simultaneously. After the wisdom realizing ultimate reality eliminates the afflictive obscurations, it must cleanse the cognitive obscurations from the mind. When every last defilement is removed, the mind is totally purified and its excellent qualities are fully developed. This is the state of buddhahood in which the capabilities of the mind have no limits. The effectiveness of a buddha's activities depend not on the abilities of that buddha but on the receptivity of sentient beings.

Bhagawan, or "endowed victor," is one epithet of the Buddha. The Buddha is endowed with all excellent qualities and is victorious in overcoming the four māras—the polluted aggregates, afflictions, death, and distraction to external objects. Since the mind has the natural capacity to be aware and to understand, when all obscurations have been removed, it will be able to directly perceive all phenomena. A buddha's omniscient mind is able to realize simultaneously both veiled and ultimate truths with a single consciousness.

REFLECTION

1. Review the various factors that obstruct the mind's knowing phenomena.
2. Contemplate that all of these can be eliminated.
3. Rest in the awareness of the potential of your mind to become omniscient.

Is Liberation Possible?

To review, disturbing emotions and wrong views are called afflictions because when they arise in the mind they afflict us and disturb our mental peace. In addition, they motivate us to do actions that disturb and afflict the peace of others. Fortunately, these afflictions can be removed, enabling us to attain liberation, a true state of peace that does not fluctuate according to external circumstances. Several factors make liberation possible.

(1) *The basic or true nature of the mind is pure.* The basic nature of the mind is clear like water. Dirt in a glass of water isn't the nature of the water and can be removed. No matter how murky the water may be, its essential quality of clarity is never lost. This basic conventional nature (*svabhāva*) of the mind is clear and cognizant. It is the basis upon which awakening can be attained, and as such it is the ultimate source of our confidence that awakening is possible. Inanimate objects such as stones and trees cannot attain awakening because they lack the qualities of clarity and cognizance that only a mind possesses.

(2) *The afflictions are adventitious*; they are not part of the nature of the mind. Dharmakīrti says (PV 2.208ab):

> The nature of the mind is clear light;
> the defilements are adventitious.

Afflictions have not penetrated into the basic nature of the mind. The fact that afflictions are not always present in the mind indicates that every instance of the mind's clarity and cognizance is not associated with afflictions. Sometimes our minds are peaceful and calm. Afflictions may arise and after a while pass away. If they were inherently part of the true nature of the mind, they would always be present and it would be impossible to eliminate them. But this is not the case.

The purest form of mind is the fundamental innate clear light mind. In ordinary beings this subtle clear light mind is neutral; it has never been and can never become nonvirtuous. However, by engaging in special yogic practices, it can be transformed into a virtuous state. From this perspective, too, we see that defilements are not inherent in the nature of the mind.

(3) *It is possible to cultivate powerful antidotes*—realistic and beneficial mental states—that eradicate the afflictions. Saying that defilements are adventitious means that when suitable conditions are present, the defilements can be removed from the basic nature of the mind. It does not mean that at one time afflictions did not exist and later came into existence. Rather, afflictions are beginningless and have continuously obscured our minds until now. They can be ceased completely when the proper antidote is applied. In *Praise to the Sphere of Reality* (DS 20–21), Nāgārjuna compares the mind to asbestos cloth that is filled with dirt. When put into fire, the dirt will burn, but not the cloth. Similarly, the fire of the wisdom realizing emptiness will destroy defilements, but the clear light mind will remain unscathed.

Afflictions are rooted in the ignorance that misapprehends reality. Ignorance grasps phenomena as inherently existent, whereas reasoning proves that in reality phenomena are empty of inherent existence. Since ignorance does not rest on a valid foundation, it can be overcome by the wisdom realizing emptiness. When ignorance is severed from its root, the afflictions that depend on it are also eradicated and can never return. Excellent qualities such as compassion cannot be undermined by wisdom because they rest on a valid foundation. Dharmakīrti affirms (PV1.220–21):

> All flaws, being susceptible to decrease and increase, have counterforces (*vipakṣa*); hence due to having inculcated the counter-

> forces through habituating oneself to them, at some point the pollutants should be eliminated.
>
> The nature of the mind is such that it is free of pollutants and by nature it [a mind that has realized emptiness] has a real [undistorted] object. As such, it cannot be counteracted by what is opposite to it because, even if one were to attempt to do so, the mind is naturally inclined toward its nature.

REFLECTION

1. Reflect that the basic or true nature of the mind is pure and untainted.
2. Consider that the afflictions that plague your mind and cause so many disturbances in your life are adventitious; they are not embedded in the nature of the mind.
3. Reflect that it is possible to cultivate powerful antidotes to each and every affliction and obscuration.
4. Conclude that the possibility to attain liberation exists within you and that, given your precious human life with all conducive factors for practicing the path, you have the ability to attain liberation and full awakening.

Excellent Qualities Can Be Cultivated Limitlessly

In *Commentary on Reliable Cognition*, Dharmakīrti explains why it is possible to cultivate the mind's excellent qualities limitlessly and to transform our ordinary mind into a buddha's fully awakened mind. Three factors make this possible.

(1) *The clear and cognizant nature of the mind is a stable basis for the cultivation of excellent qualities.* It is firm and continual; there is nothing that can cease it. For example, if we continuously boil water, it will dry up and nothing will remain. There is no basis for limitlessly boiling water. Excellent

qualities cannot be cultivated limitlessly on an unstable basis such as the physical body because it falls ill, ages, and eventually dies. However, the clear light mind is a stable and continuous basis for cultivating excellent qualities. The more we train in excellent qualities, the more those qualities will be enhanced limitlessly until they are fully perfected in the state of buddhahood.

(2) *The mind can become habituated to excellent qualities that can be built up cumulatively.* Excellent mental qualities can be built up gradually without having to begin anew each time we focus on developing them. A high jumper cannot develop his or her ability limitlessly. Each time the bar is raised, he or she must cover the same distance he jumped before, plus some more. The mind's nature is different. The energy from cultivating a quality one day remains, so that if that same quality is cultivated the next day, it builds on what was previously accomplished without having to reestablish it. We do not need to exert the same degree of energy to get to the same level on the second day, and that same effort will serve to increase that excellent quality. Of course this requires consistent training on our part, otherwise our spiritual "muscles" will atrophy. But if we practice regularly, our energy can be directed to enhancing the excellent qualities continuously until the point where they become so familiar that they are natural and spontaneous.

(3) *Excellent qualities can be enhanced, but never diminished, by reasoning and wisdom.* Constructive attitudes and emotions have a valid support in reasoning and wisdom. They can never be harmed by the wisdom realizing reality. Compassion, faith, integrity, generosity, concentration and all other excellent qualities can be cultivated together with wisdom and are enhanced by wisdom. For this reason, too, they can be cultivated limitlessly.

REFLECTION

1. Reflect that the clear and cognizant nature of the mind is a stable basis for the cultivation of excellent qualities.
2. Remember that the mind can become habituated to excellent qualities, which can be built up cumulatively.
3. Contemplate that excellent qualities can be enhanced, but never diminished, by reasoning and wisdom.

4. Understanding these points, feel confidence arise in yourself that, with effort and training, your mind can be transformed into the mind of a buddha.

Afflictive Mental States and the Nature of the Mind

One moment of an affliction such as anger has two facets: the clarity and cognizance of the primary consciousness, and the mental factor of anger that pollutes it. When a mind of anger is manifest, these two cannot be separated. Does that mean that the clear and cognizant nature of the mind is defiled at that time?

According to Sūtrayāna, from the viewpoint that the primary consciousness and the mental factor of anger are concomitant in that single mental event, it is said both are defiled. However, this is not the whole picture, because anger can be extracted. When it is counteracted, the clear and cognizant consciousness remains. This consciousness is not defiled and its continuity can go on to awakening, since clarity and cognizance are also the nature of the awakened mind. The consciousness that is clear and cognizant is said to be pure, while the mental state of anger, which cannot continue on to awakening, is afflictive and adventitious.

Within Tantrayāna, both Dzogchen and the New Translation schools speak of the subtlest mind, which may be called *rigpa* or the primordial clear light mind. In the Dzogchen system, rigpa is said to pervade all states of mind, whether they are coarse—such as the consciousnesses manifest during our everyday lives—or subtle—such as the subtlest clear light mind that arises after the coarse consciousnesses have absorbed, for example, while dying or during special tantric meditations. Rigpa is undefiled, and because it pervades all mental states, the clear and cognizant aspect of those consciousnesses is undefiled.

Both sentient beings and buddhas possess the primordially pure awareness of rigpa, and from that perspective there is no difference between them. However, there is a great difference between having and not having the two obscurations, so sentient beings must still practice the path because defilements do not vanish by themselves.

From the Dzogchen perspective, when an afflictive mental state such as hatred or jealousy is manifest, the rigpa or clear light mind that pervades that coarse mind is not defiled. There is still the potential for rigpa to shine forth. This is the source of statements in the Dzogchen literature that resemble Nāgārjuna's assertion in *Praise to the Sphere of Reality*: "Within afflictions, wisdom abides." Here "wisdom" refers to the cognitive component of that mind—its clarity and cognizance—not to actual wisdom. That cognitive component is called wisdom because it is the cause for wisdom to arise in the future.[76] The meaning is that amidst the afflictions, this undefiled, clear, cognitive component, or rigpa, exists.

In the New Translation schools of Tantrayāna, this primordially pure mind is called the clear light mind. Similar to rigpa, it continues from our present unawakened state to full awakening. But unlike rigpa, which is manifest while the coarse consciousnesses are functioning, the innate clear light mind is said to manifest only when the coarse consciousnesses—which include the afflictions—have absorbed at the time of death or due to special tantric meditative practices.

Dzogchen and the New Translation systems agree that when the coarser levels of mind are manifest, the subtlest mind is also present. As long as there is a being, a person, it is present. They differ on the issue of whether it is active or dormant while the coarse minds are functioning. Dzogchen says that rigpa is active and manifest at that time, and the New Translation schools say that the subtlest clear light mind is dormant.[77] Dzogchen teaches a method whereby one can experience rigpa even while the coarse consciousnesses are functioning. The New Translation schools rely on dissolving the coarse consciousnesses and the winds that are their mount by means of special tantric meditation exercises to make manifest the subtlest clear light mind. Both agree on the necessity of accessing this subtlest mind because, when used to realize emptiness, it swiftly eradicates obscurations.

The Equality of Saṃsāra and Nirvāṇa

From the perspective of their ultimate nature, all the afflictive phenomena of saṃsāra and all the purified phenomena of nirvāṇa are equally empty. This is the context of the expressions the "equality of saṃsāra and nirvāṇa," "unity of saṃsāra and nirvāṇa," "one taste of all phenomena," and similar phrases found in sūtras and tantras. Nāgārjuna mentioned this in *Treatise on the Middle Way*, Haribhadra spoke of it in his commentary to *Ornament of Clear Realizations*, and Tsongkhapa explained it in his *Elucidation of the Five Stages of Guhyasamāja*.

From the perspective that the emptiness of the mind is called natural nirvāṇa and that this emptiness of the mind exists while we are in saṃsāra, it is said that saṃsāra and nirvāṇa are not different. The ultimate nature of saṃsāra and nirvāṇa is the same; it is the "one taste" of emptiness. In this context, it is said that if one realizes the nature of saṃsāra, one actualizes nirvāṇa.

Since saṃsāra and nirvāṇa are different entities conventionally, they may be called "the manifold." In that their ultimate nature is the same taste—emptiness—it is said that the one taste is manifold and the manifold has one taste. This means that emptiness is the nature of all the manifold phenomena of saṃsāra and nirvāṇa, and all these manifold phenomena have the same ultimate nature, the emptiness of inherent existence. In other words, from the perspective of the substratum—the objects that have this empty nature—phenomena are many and varied. But from the perspective of their final nature, they share the one taste of emptiness.

Understanding that saṃsāra and nirvāṇa are equal in being empty of true existence is important for ordinary unawakened people who grasp both saṃsāra and nirvāṇa as truly existent. When such people view saṃsāra and nirvāṇa, they don't just see them as bad and good on the conventional level but also grasp them as inherently so. Such grasping diminishes our confidence in being able to free ourselves from saṃsāra and actualize nirvāṇa. This is because our minds not only highlight the faults of saṃsāra but also see them as fixed and unchangeable, as if they could never be abandoned. Similarly, we see nirvāṇa as independently good and thus too exalted for us to actualize.

Understanding that saṃsāra and nirvāṇa are of one taste counteracts the grasping that binds us to saṃsāra. Seeing both of them as empty of true existence, we become confident that however many faults saṃsāra has, they can all be eliminated, and that all the excellent qualities of nirvāṇa can be actualized. It is a matter of stopping the causes for saṃsāra and creating the causes to attain nirvāṇa.

Saying "saṃsāra and nirvāṇa are equal" does not mean that being in saṃsāra is the same as being in nirvāṇa or that we need not try to cease saṃsāra and attain nirvāṇa. Conventionally, saṃsāra and nirvāṇa are different; the bases of their emptiness are different. A mind in saṃsāra is one trapped in duḥkha by afflictions and karma; a mind in nirvāṇa is one that has generated the true path and actualized the final true cessation. Although saṃsāra and nirvāṇa are said to be equal from the viewpoint of their ultimate nature, emptiness, on the conventional level each has its own distinctive features. Saṃsāra is to be abandoned and nirvāṇa is to be actualized.

Some people may glibly say, "Saṃsāra and nirvāṇa are the same. Good and bad don't exist; awakening is beyond such dualistic distinctions," and on that basis, they ignore ethical conduct. This may sound well and good, but the moment their stomach hurts or they are criticized, these people scream, "This is bad! Stop it!" To avoid such dilemmas, it is important to study and correctly understand the meaning of some of the enticing phrases in the scriptures.

Levels of Mind

Both Sūtrayāna and Tantrayāna speak of different levels of mind. In Sūtrayāna, the principal factor distinguishing various levels of mind is the depth of single-pointed concentration. Beings in the desire realm have coarse states of mind; those in the four form realms and four formless realms have progressively subtler and more refined states of mind corresponding to their progressively deeper states of concentration. The subtlest mind is that of the peak of saṃsāra (neither-discrimination-nor-nondiscrimination). This mind is considered coarse compared with the subtlest mind presented in Tantra.

In highest yoga tantra, the levels of mind are differentiated by the physical condition of the body. When the sense faculties are active, the sense consciousnesses function; they are the coarsest level of mind. The dream state is a little subtler because at that time the sense faculties do not function, although the brain is still active and the eyes move during REM sleep. Deep sleep and fainting are even subtler. The subtlest level of mind, which can function apart from the physical body, manifests at the time of death. This fundamental innate clear light mind (T. *gnyug ma lhan cig skyes pa'i 'od gsal gyi sems*) is accompanied by a very subtle wind, which is its mount. This subtlest mind and subtlest wind are one entity but nominally different; that is, one cannot exist without the other although they can be spoken of separately.

The term *clear light* (*prabhāsvara*) has various meanings, depending on the context. In the Sūtra Vehicle, it refers to (1) the clear and cognizant nature of the conventional mind, which is the *subject clear light* (here, saying the mind is clear light implies that the afflictive obscurations and cognitive obscurations are adventitious and do not exist in the nature of the mind), and (2) the emptiness of the mind, which is the *object clear light*, the ultimate nature of the mind.

In both Sūtra and Tantra, the subject clear light is the awareness that cognizes the object clear light. However, the subject clear light mind spoken of in Tantra is far subtler. This innate clear light mind (*lhan cig skyes pa'i 'od gsal gyi sems*) is a special mind because it is the source or basis of all phenomena of saṃsāra and nirvāṇa. This subtlest mind continues from one life to the next. It is not a soul or self; it changes moment by moment and is empty of inherent existence. At death the coarser levels of mind absorb into the innate clear light mind, and after rebirth, the coarser consciousnesses reemerge from the basis of the innate clear light mind. When these coarser levels of consciousness exist, constructive and destructive thoughts and emotions arise and karma is created. The result of afflictive thoughts and actions is saṃsāra; the result of thoughts and actions purified by the realization of emptiness is nirvāṇa. The presence of ignorance or wisdom determines whether this mind is in saṃsāra or nirvāṇa.

It is said that the innate clear light mind is the creator in that it is the source or basis of saṃsāra and nirvāṇa. This indicates that phenomena do not arise causelessly nor are they created by an external creator. To make an analogy: Owing to the climate in a particular place, plants and animals come to exist there. From that perspective, we say the climate of a place creates the living things there because it acts as their basis. Similarly, because the innate clear light mind exists, all the phenomena of saṃsāra and nirvāṇa become possible.

Saying that the clear light mind is the source of all phenomena in saṃsāra and nirvāṇa is a general statement; it does not mean that the subtlest mind-wind is the substantial cause for phenomena in saṃsāra and nirvāṇa. Nor does it mean that all phenomena arise from my clear light mind or your clear light mind. Furthermore, it is not the same as the Cittamātrin assertion that all phenomena are the nature of the mind, which refers to their unique tenet that an object and the consciousness perceiving it arise from the same substantial cause, a latency on the foundation consciousness.

Saying that the clear light mind is the source of all phenomena in saṃsāra and nirvāṇa means that all phenomena exist in relation to the mind. All phenomena exist by being merely designated by mind. This conclusion is arrived at because all other possibilities—such as objective existence and existence from its own side—are untenable.

The *Kālacakra Tantra* explains that the ultimate goal, buddhahood, is based on the subtlest clear light mind. The coarse levels of mind cannot be transformed into the omniscient mind of a buddha. Only the subtlest mind-wind, which is beginningless and endless, can continue to buddhahood. By employing the special practices of highest yoga tantra to neutralize the coarser levels of mind, the defilements present with the coarser levels of mind dissolve, and subtler states of mind arise. When accompanied by wisdom, these progressively subtler levels of mind have more power to effect change and purify the mind. When the subtlest mind-wind is activated, made blissful, and used to realize emptiness directly, it is extremely effective in rooting out the deepest and most entrenched obscurations. When all obscurations have been removed, this innate clear light mind becomes a buddha's omniscient mind, the wisdom truth body of a buddha. Its emptiness becomes the nature truth body, and the subtlest wind transforms into a buddha's form bodies—the enjoyment and emanation bodies by which a buddha benefits sentient beings. The key to the tantric path is learning how to make manifest the subtlest mind-wind and use it to accumulate merit and wisdom and attain full awakening.

This begins with gaining a comprehensive understanding of the entire Buddhist path from beginning to end, and then generating the three principal aspects of the path: the aspiration for liberation, bodhicitta, and the correct view of emptiness. When properly prepared in this way, we then receive empowerment into highest yoga tantra, abide with the tantric ethical restraints, and meditate on the generation and completion stages. This causes the winds to enter, remain, and dissolve in the central channel, at which time all coarser levels of mind cease and the subtlest mind-wind is activated. This is made blissful and used to realize emptiness. The stage of *example clear light* (T. *dpe'i 'od gsal*) is attained when this subtle blissful mind-wind realizes the object clear light—emptiness—via a conceptual appearance. When it cognizes emptiness directly, the stage of *actual clear light* (T. *don gyi 'od gsal*) is attained. Someone who has this attainment will become a buddha in that very life.

The discussion of clear light relates to the topic of buddha nature—the potential of each and every sentient being to become a fully awakened buddha—to which we now turn.

13 | Buddha Nature

All Buddhist traditions accept that excellent qualities can be cultivated and that defilements can be forever eliminated from the mind. What is the basis upon which this occurs? Each tradition describes it somewhat differently.

The Mind's Potential according to the Pāli Tradition

Although the term *buddha nature* is not used in the Pāli scriptures to describe the mind's potential to attain liberation, the Buddha identified certain characteristics that reveal spiritual practitioners' inclinations toward liberation. Characteristics such as having modest desire and a sense of contentment signify that a person is a genuine spiritual practitioner aiming for liberation. Practitioners endeavor daily to cultivate these virtuous characteristics that indicate their potential to gain realizations.

In the sūtra *Luminous*, the Buddha spoke of the clear nature of the mind that is tainted by adventitious defilements that can be removed (AN 1.51–52):

> This mind, O monastics, is luminous, but it is defiled by adventitious defilements. The uninstructed worldling does not understand this as it really is; therefore for him there is no mental development.
>
> This mind, O monastics, is luminous, and it is freed from adventitious defilements. The instructed ārya disciple understands this as it really is; therefore for him there is mental development.

Ārya Disposition according to the Vaibhāṣikas and Sautrāntikas

The tenet schools put forth assertions about the disposition (trait, lineage, T. *rigs*) that accord with their general presentation of the basis, path, and result of practice. For Vaibhāṣikas, the ārya disposition (T. *'phags pa'i rigs*) is the mental factor of nonattachment that acts as a cause for its own resultant ārya path. Since Vaibhāṣikas emphasize craving as a formidable cause of cyclic existence, it makes sense that they assert nonattachment as both the antidote to craving and the disposition in sentient beings that has the potential to bring the realizations of the ārya path and liberation.

Contentment with what we have and lack of greed for what we do not have are the source of āryas' pristine wisdom. While nonattachment in the mindstream of an ordinary person is polluted in that it is associated with ignorance, when it is associated with an ārya's pristine wisdom, it is unpolluted. Guṇaprabha's *Sūtra on the Code of Ethical Conduct* (*Vinayasūtra*) explains that āryas with the disposition have four qualities: (1–3) They are satisfied with whatever food and drink, shelter, and robes they have. (4) They take joy in meditation and in overcoming what is to be abandoned.

The first three qualities are the means to actualize the ārya path, and the last is the actual cause to generate the realizations of the ārya path that bring true cessation. The first three are also the means to exhaust the sense of I and mine, while the last is the means to exhaust ignorance. Everyone seeking liberation or full awakening cultivates these four qualities in order to attain their goal.

According to Sautrāntikas, the disposition is the potential or seed for the arising of the unpolluted mind (T. *zag med sems kyi nus pa*), the pristine wisdom of the āryas. All sentient beings have this potential because all of them at one time or another have experienced happiness. Since happiness is the result of virtue, everyone has virtue and thus has the potential for the unpolluted mind. This potential is nourished through learning, reflecting, and meditating on the Dharma in the present life. However, if someone's roots of virtue are cut by his engagement in extremely destructive actions, this seed cannot grow and may even be destroyed.

In general, Vaibhāṣikas and Sautrāntikas assert that only sentient beings who will become wheel-turning buddhas—buddhas that initially teach the Dharma in a time and place where it is absent—will attain full awakening. All other sentient beings will attain arhatship. At the time they have completely abandoned all afflictive obscurations, arhats attain nirvāṇa with remainder—the remainder being their polluted bodies produced by afflictions and karma. When they pass away from that life and shed their polluted bodies, they attain nirvāṇa without remainder. At this time, the polluted aggregates no longer remain and the continuity of the mental consciousness is severed, which precludes their entering the Bodhisattva Vehicle.

Buddha Nature according to the Cittamātra School

In Mahāyāna literature, buddha nature, or buddha disposition (*buddha-gotra*),[78] is discussed from three perspectives: the Cittamātra, Madhyamaka, and Vajrayāna. All three speak of the naturally abiding buddha disposition and the transforming buddha disposition.

According to Cittamātrins, as explained by Asaṅga in the *Compendium of the Mahāyāna* (*Mahāyānasaṃgraha*), buddha disposition is the latency, seed, or potency that has existed since beginningless time and has the potential to give rise to the three bodies of a buddha. A conditioned phenomenon, the buddha disposition is the seed of unpolluted pristine wisdom (T. *zag med ye shes kyi sa bon*). Saying the buddha disposition is a latency fits in well with the Cittamātra school's assertion that everything arises as a result of latencies on either the foundation consciousness or the mental consciousness. When this latency of the unpolluted pristine wisdom has not yet been nourished by learning, reflecting, and meditating, it is called the naturally abiding buddha disposition, because it is beginningless. When the same latency has been nourished by learning, reflecting, and meditating on the Dharma, it is called the transforming buddha disposition. It is the same latency, the difference being whether or not it has been activated by means of Dharma practice.

Initially, as the *naturally abiding buddha disposition*, it is a simple latency that has three characteristics: (1) It has existed since beginningless time and continues from one life to the next uninterruptedly. (2) It is not newly created but is naturally present. (3) It is carried by the foundation consciousness according to the Cittamātra Scriptural Proponents and by the mental consciousness (the sixth consciousness) according to the Cittamātra Reasoning

Proponents. This is so because sensory consciousnesses are unstable and only intermittently present.

When the naturally abiding buddha disposition is awakened and transformed by means of learning, reflecting, and meditating, it brings the realization of the ārya path and, at that time, it is called the *transforming buddha disposition*. In particular, when meditation on great compassion has progressed to the point where the great resolve that takes responsibility to work for the welfare of all sentient beings arises, the Mahāyāna disposition has been awakened.

Citing the *Sūtra Unravelling the Thought* (*Saṃdhinirmocana Sūtra*), Cittamātra Scriptural Proponents assert three final vehicles—the Śrāvaka and Solitary Realizer Vehicles that culminate in arhatship and the Bodhisattva Vehicle that brings full awakening. The doctrine of three final vehicles states that once śrāvaka and solitary realizer practitioners attain arhatship, they will abide in meditative equipoise on emptiness forever and will not later enter the Mahāyāna and attain the full awakening of buddhahood. The Cittamātra Scriptural Proponents base this on their belief that there are five types of disposition (lineage)—śrāvaka, solitary realizer, bodhisattva, indefinite, and severed. Here "disposition" connotes a source of excellent qualities, and each sentient being has the latency for one of the five dispositions. This latency is an internal predisposition that exists naturally in each sentient being's foundation consciousness that inclines him or her toward a particular spiritual path.

People display certain signs that are indicative of their buddha disposition. Those with the śrāvaka disposition have strong determination to be free from saṃsāra; they avoid nonvirtue and purify destructive karma, are moved by teachings on the four truths, and live ethically. They take prātimokṣa precepts with the aspiration for their own liberation and dedicate all the merit from their practice for this goal.

Those having the solitary realizer disposition have few afflictions and weak compassion, so they dislike busyness and prefer solitude. Teachings on the twelve links of dependent origination touch them deeply and they meditate primarily on this. Like śrāvakas, they purify destructive karma, create constructive karma, and have strong determination to be free from saṃsāra. Their motivation and dedication are directed toward the liberation of a solitary realizer arhat.

Those with the bodhisattva or Mahāyāna disposition are naturally empathetic and compassionate. They purify and abandon nonvirtue, create virtue, and take prātimokṣa and bodhisattva precepts with the aspiration to attain the full awakening of a buddha. Seeking to work for the welfare of sentient beings, they practice the six perfections and have fortitude to engage in the bodhisattvas' deeds. Their motivation and dedication is for the attainment of buddhahood.

Persons of these three dispositions are definite in their path. They will not change vehicles but will proceed to the attainment of their own vehicle.

At present, it is uncertain which vehicle those of indefinite disposition will enter. Depending on the spiritual mentor they meet and the Buddhist teachings they learn in the future, they will develop an inclination toward one vehicle or another.

Those whose lineage is severed (*icchantika*) have engaged in extremely destructive actions or strongly adhere to pernicious wrong views. They have little merit, great negativity, and lack integrity and consideration for how their actions affect others. Not wishing to abandon nonvirtue and lacking insight into the unsatisfactory nature of saṃsāra, they have no interest in liberating themselves or others. Even if they dabble in the Dharma, their motivation is one seeking the pleasures of saṃsāra. Having cut their roots of virtue, they are in a state where, either temporarily or perpetually, they cannot attain liberation or awakening.[79]

This perspective on the buddha disposition and on three final vehicles is supported by Cittamātra tenets: Because a being's disposition is truly existent, it cannot change into the disposition of another vehicle. Since it can bring only the result of its respective vehicle, there must be three final vehicles.

Our buddha disposition may be impeded from manifesting when great attachment or strong afflictions overwhelm our minds and when we are too busy to be interested in spiritual practice or don't see the faults of the afflictions. Thinking our actions lack an ethical dimension and experiencing hindrances such as illness, poverty, or strong karmic obstructions also prevent our disposition from developing.

Certain activities can stimulate our buddha disposition: Learning and reflecting on teachings, living in an environment that is conducive to practice, and abiding near our spiritual mentor or sincere practitioners.

Generating the aspiration for virtuous qualities, restraining our senses, abandoning nonvirtue, receiving monastic ordination, purifying obscurations, and so on also invigorate our buddha disposition.

Relying on the *Lotus Sūtra* (*Saddharma Puṇḍarīka Sūtra*) and the *Tathāgatagarbha Sūtra*, Cittamātra Reasoning Proponents and all Mādhyamikas assert one final vehicle: all sentient beings can enter the Bodhisattva Vehicle and attain buddhahood. The *Sublime Continuum* by Maitreya and Asaṅga's commentary on it speak of four types of people whose buddha nature is defiled in that they are not yet ready to enter the Bodhisattva Vehicle, engage in the two collections, and progress on the path to full awakening: worldly people who are infatuated with saṃsāric pleasures, non-Buddhists who hold wrong views, śrāvakas, and solitary realizers. They also discuss the specific obscurations that block these sentient beings and explain their antidotes. Here Asaṅga writes from a Madhyamaka viewpoint that holds that all sentient beings have the buddha nature.

Buddha Nature according to the Madhyamaka School

The topic of buddha nature (*gotra*) is found in the Perfection of Wisdom sūtras, *Ornament of Clear Realizations*, *Sublime Continuum* (*Ratnagotravibhāga*, *Uttaratantra*) by Maitreya and its commentary by his disciple Asaṅga, *Bodhisattva Grounds* (*Bodhisattva Bhūmi*), and other Mahāyāna texts. The *Tathāgatagarbha Sūtra* and *Nirvāṇa Sūtra* speak of buddha essence (*garbha*), using a more essentialist language. As a Mādhyamika, I prefer presentations that lack the essentialist meaning. Like Ngok Lotsawa, who translated the *Sublime Continuum* into Tibetan, in the Sūtrayāna context I believe buddha essence primarily refers to the emptiness of the mind.

The *Sublime Continuum* defines buddha nature as phenomena that have the possibility to transform into any of the buddha bodies. It is of two types—the naturally abiding buddha nature (*prakṛtisthagotra,* T. *rang bzhin gnas rigs*) and the transforming buddha nature (*samudānītagotra,* T. *rgyas 'gyur gi rigs*). Both exist in all sentient beings whether or not they are on a path.

The *naturally abiding buddha nature* is the emptiness of the mind that is yet to abandon defilements and that is able to transform into the nature dharmakāya of a buddha. Sakya Paṇḍita described it as the unchanging nature of the mind. In *Treatise on the Middle Way* Nāgārjuna notes that whatever is the nature of a tathāgata is the nature of sentient beings (22.16).

> Whatever is the essence of the Tathāgata,
> that is the essence of the transmigrator.
> The Tathāgata has no essence.
> The transmigrator has no essence.

This empty nature of the mind is beyond the three times (past, present, and future), beyond the realms of cyclic existence, and beyond constructive and destructive karma. Neither virtuous nor nonvirtuous, it can act as the basis for both saṃsāra and nirvāṇa. The *Eight-Thousand-Line Perfection of Wisdom Sūtra* (*Aṣṭasāhasrikā Prajñāpāramitā Sūtra*) says:

> Thus that which is the reality of all things
> is not past nor future nor present.
> Whatever is neither past, future, nor present
> is utterly free from threefold time,
> cannot be transferred nor objectified
> nor conceptualized nor cognized.

The existence of the naturally abiding buddha nature—the emptiness of inherent existence of ordinary beings' minds—means that mental defilements can be eliminated. Why? If phenomena existed inherently, they would be independent of everything else and thus would be unable to function, influence one another, or change. The fact that the ultimate nature of the mind is empty of inherent existence indicates that the mind can change.

In addition, all defilements are rooted in fundamental ignorance, the erroneous mental factor that grasps all phenomena as possessing an inherent reality. This erroneous grasping gives rise to attachment, anger, and all other afflictions and supports virtuous polluted mental states as well. From these spring our actions or karma, which cause us to take continual rebirth in cyclic existence. Cultivating insight into the true nature of reality, emptiness, initiates the process of undoing this causal chain. With the development of the wisdom that directly perceives reality—emptiness or suchness—this ignorance can be overpowered and completely eradicated from the mind. The defilements are not embedded in the ultimate nature of the mind. They too lack inherent existence, so when the antidote of the wisdom directly realizing emptiness is applied to them, they can be removed from the mind.

On the basis of recognizing the naturally abiding buddha nature—natural nirvāṇa, or the emptiness of the mind—we can attain the nirvāṇa that is the total pacification of mental defilements. A buddha's nirvāṇa is nonabiding nirvāṇa, the full purification of the naturally abiding buddha nature.

In some texts the emptiness of the mind is called a cause of buddhahood in the sense that meditation on emptiness purifies the mind of defilements and leads to buddhahood. However, emptiness is not an actual cause because it is a permanent phenomenon that does not change or bring results.

The *transforming buddha nature* is the seed for the unpolluted mind. It consists of conditioned phenomena that can transform into a buddha's wisdom truth body. The transforming buddha nature includes neutral mental consciousnesses[80] as well as virtuous mental factors, such as love, compassion, wisdom, and faith, and other virtuous mental states, such as bodhicitta, that are progressively developed as a bodhisattva progresses through the ten bodhisattva grounds. The transforming buddha nature also includes consciousnesses that form the collection of wisdom—the principal cause of the wisdom truth body—and the mind visualizing ourselves as a deity, which is a cause for a buddha's form body. It is possible to increase these virtuous qualities and mental states limitlessly because their base, the clear light mind, is stable and because no antidote exists that can eliminate them. At the time we become buddhas, our naturally abiding buddha nature will become the nature truth body of a buddha, and our transforming buddha nature will become the wisdom truth body of a buddha.

Which of the seven types of awareness can be included in transforming buddha nature? Wrong awarenesses, such as resentment, self-grasping ignorance, and the mind that fantasizes being a star athlete without creating the causes, are not buddha nature. Inattentive awarenesses are not buddha nature because they don't correctly know their object. Correct assumptions, doubt inclined to the correct conclusion, inferential cognizers, correct mental direct perceivers, and subsequent reliable cognizers are transforming buddha nature. The five paths of the śrāvakas, solitary realizers, and bodhisattvas are transforming buddha nature, as are the ten bodhisattva grounds.[81] The emptiness of inherent existence of all these minds is the natural buddha nature.

In short, any neutral or virtuous mind that is not free from defilement and can transform into a buddha's wisdom dharmakāya is part of the transforming buddha nature. Mental consciousnesses accompanied by manifest afflictions cannot be transforming buddha nature because they are eliminated on the path.

As neutral or virtuous states of mind, the transforming buddha nature consists of impermanent phenomena. As the emptiness of the mind, the naturally abiding buddha nature is permanent. These two buddha natures are one nature. Although they are not exactly the same, one cannot exist without the other. Only the emptiness of neutral and virtuous consciousnesses can be the naturally abiding buddha nature because only the neutral or virtuous consciousnesses that are their bases are the transforming buddha nature.

Because the afflictions are empty of inherent existence, awakening is possible. However, the emptiness of the afflictions is not buddha nature. Since the afflictions are eliminated on the path and cannot be transformed into any of a buddha's bodies, their emptinesses will similarly cease and cannot become the nature truth body.

Some people speak of inanimate phenomena—rocks, trees, and so forth—as having buddha nature. I believe that they are referring to the fact that these phenomena are empty of inherent existence. Only sentient beings have buddha nature. That we can generate the determination to be free from saṃsāra, bodhicitta, and wisdom indicates that the buddha nature is within us. Because inanimate phenomena lack mind, they cannot generate these virtuous mental states and do not possess buddha nature.

Someone may wonder: Since the emptiness of the mind of a sentient being and the emptiness of the mind of a buddha are the same in being the emptiness of inherent existence, does that mean that sentient beings already have the qualities of buddhas or that they are already buddhas? No, it does not, because the minds that possess that emptiness differ. Tsongkhapa explains in *Illumination of the Thought*:

> It is said, "The buddha nature is that which serves as the cause of āryas' qualities when observed; thus, here the absurd consequence [that all sentient beings would have the qualities of āryas] is not entailed." The mere presence of the nature of phenomena (*dharmadhātu*) does not mean that one abides in the buddha nature in terms of the path. When one observes and meditates on the nature of phenomena through the path, it comes to serve as the special cause of āryas' qualities. At that time one's buddha nature is regarded as special.[82]

Emptiness is the "cause" of the wonderful qualities of āryas when we perceive it directly and use that realization to cleanse our minds of defilements. The fact that we have the naturally abiding buddha nature—the empty nature of the mind—does not mean that we have already realized it with a true path—a reliable cognizer that realizes emptiness directly. Only a direct realization of the empty nature of the mind will bring about an ārya's qualities. When this realization arises in our mind, the emptiness of our minds—our buddha nature—will be regarded as special.

The emptiness of inherent existence of our minds is a permanent phenomenon. It does not change moment by moment, as do conditioned phenomena. While emptiness in general is eternal, when we speak about the emptiness of a specific thing, that emptiness may not always exist. For example, the emptiness of a glass ceases when that glass shatters. An emptiness is posited in relation to an object that is empty; it is one nature with that object—the emptiness of the mind exists in dependence on the mind. The emptiness of an ordinary being's mind exists as long as that ordinary being does. Because that mind has defilements, its emptiness is together with defilement. When portions of the mind's defilements have been removed by the true path, the mind becomes an ārya's mind and its emptiness is the emptiness of an ārya's mind. When ordinary beings realize emptiness directly and become āryas, the emptiness of the ordinary being's mind no longer exists; now there is the emptiness of an ārya's mind. These two emptinesses are both the absence of inherent existence, and to an arya's mind in meditative equipoise on emptiness, they are undifferentiable.

While it is true that sentient beings' minds are empty of inherent existence and that defilements are adventitious, we cannot say that sentient beings' buddha nature is the same as a buddha's nature truth body that has the twofold purity—being naturally pure of inherent existence and being newly purified of all adventitious defilements. That is because sentient beings' minds are still together with defilements.[83]

No matter in which realm a sentient being abides, the naturally abiding buddha nature is always there. It does not decrease or increase. Gold may be buried in the ground for centuries, but it is still gold and it is always possible to access it. The gold may be covered with dirt, but it doesn't become the dirt. If dirt were its nature, it could never become clean. But because the dirt only obscures it, the gold can be cleansed so that its natural radiance can be seen. Similarly, the emptiness of our defiled mind is always there; when we realize emptiness, that wisdom cleanses the defilements from our minds, and in doing so, the emptiness of our minds will also be cleansed. Even though our minds have always been naturally pure of inherent existence, at that time we will have the additional purity of being free from all adventitious defilements.

Without the two kinds of buddha nature, there would be no way for the awakened activities of the Buddha to enter into us. Our minds would not be receptive to the Buddha's influence or to the teachings; nothing in our minds could germinate by coming into contact with these. Buddha nature is the basis of cultivation of the Mahāyāna; it is what enables our minds to be affected and transformed by the teachings. The fact that the Buddha taught the Dharma indicates that sentient beings have the potential to become Buddhas. If we didn't, it would have been useless for the Buddha to deliver 84,000 teachings.

Buddha Nature according to Tantra

Highest yoga tantra points to buddha nature in a unique way: it is the subtlest mind-wind that is empty of inherent existence and whose continuity goes on to awakening. All sentient beings have this subtlest mind-wind. In ordinary beings, it becomes manifest only at the time of the clear light of death and goes unnoticed.

While the subtlest mind-wind is neutral in the case of ordinary beings, through special yogic practices it can be brought into the path and transformed into a virtuous state, a yogic state. Sentient beings' subtlest mind serves as the substantial cause for the wisdom dharmakāya—the omniscient mind of a buddha—and the true cessation and emptiness of a buddha's mind is the nature dharmakāya. The subtlest wind that is its mount is the substantial cause for the form bodies of a buddha—the enjoyment and emanation bodies. The *Hevajra Tantra* says:

> Sentient beings are just buddhas,
> but they are defiled by adventitious stains.
> When these are removed, they are buddhas.

The first line indicates that sentient beings have the substantial cause for buddhahood, the subtlest mind-wind. It does not mean that sentient beings are buddhas, because someone cannot be both a sentient being and a buddha simultaneously. Through the practice of special techniques in highest yoga tantra, the continuum of this subtlest mind-wind can be purified and transformed into the three bodies of a buddha.

Nine Similes for Tathāgatagarbha

By using nine similes, the *Tathāgatagarbha Sūtra* gives us an inkling of the buddha nature that has always been and will continue to be within us. Maitreya's *Sublime Continuum* and its commentary by Asaṅga explain these similes that point to a hidden richness inside of us—a potential that we are usually unaware of. Contemplating the meaning of these similes generates great inspiration and confidence to practice the path.

All afflictive and cognitive obscurations are condensed into nine obscurations spoken of in the nine similes. By applying the appropriate antidotes, all of these can be removed and full awakening attained.

From beginningless time, the basic nature of the mind has been immaculate and has never been mixed with stains or afflictions. But it has been covered by these nine obscurations. As we progress on the path, the transforming buddha nature develops, the mind becomes purer, and the obscurations are gradually eliminated. When all obscurations have been removed such that they can never return, the purified mind becomes the wisdom dharmakāya and its emptiness becomes the nature dharmakāya. Maitreya says (RGV 1:80–81):

This [tathāgatagarbha] abides within the shroud of the afflictions,
as should be understood through [the following nine] examples:

Just like a buddha in a decaying lotus, honey amidst bees,
a grain in its husk, gold in filth, a treasure underground,
a shoot and so on sprouting from a little fruit,
a statue of the Victorious One in a tattered rag,
a ruler of humankind in a destitute woman's womb,
and a precious image under clay,
this [buddha] element abides within all sentient beings,
obscured by the defilement of the adventitious poisons.

1. The buddha essence is like a beautiful buddha image in an old, ugly lotus. When the petals close around a buddha image, we see only the old lotus and not the beautiful buddha image. Not knowing the image is there, we never think to open the petals and take it out. Similarly, the seeds of attachment obscure our buddha essence. While all beings who are not arhats are obscured by the seeds of attachment, this simile applies particularly to ordinary sentient beings in the form and formless realms. Although they have temporarily suppressed the coarse manifest afflictions of the desire realm by entering into deep states of meditative absorption, the seeds of afflictions still remain in their mindstreams. Ordinary beings in the form and formless realms are specified because āryas may also take rebirth in these realms. However, they have already eliminated some portion of the seeds of afflictions.

We beings in the desire realm, too, have the seed of attachment. When it explodes and becomes full blown, we have no awareness of our buddha essence, which is the source of all hope and confidence. Instead we become totally engrossed in the objects of our attachment. Just as the beautiful and fragrant lotus withers and becomes decrepit after a few days, the people and things we cling to age and decay. While they initially bring us happiness, later we become bored and cast them aside, as we would a withered flower.

A person with clairvoyance can see the buddha image inside the lotus and will open the flower and remove the buddha image. Similarly, the Buddha sees the buddha essence in each sentient being, even those in the hells, and thinks, "Who will liberate these beings from their obscurations, especially their attachment?" Because the Buddha has great compassion and is free from all defilements, he will guide us to discover the beautiful buddha image—the wisdom dharmakāya—hidden by our attachment.

2. The buddha essence is like honey with a swarm of bees surrounding it.
The honey is like the ultimate truth—the emptiness of inherent existence. Just as all honey has the same taste, the ultimate nature of all phenomena is the same. Bees not only conceal the honey but also angrily sting someone who tries to take it, harming themselves as well as their enemy. Similarly, we cannot see our honey-like buddha essence because it is obscured by the seeds of hatred, anger, resentment, and vengeance. This obscuration pertains specifically to ordinary beings in the form and formless realms who do not experience manifest anger, but still have the seeds of anger in their mental continuums. We beings in the desire realm have the seeds of anger as well as coarse manifest anger. These seeds not only prevent us from seeing our buddha essence but also enable the destructive emotions related to anger and animosity to manifest in our minds, mercilessly stinging ourselves and those around us.

An insightful person knows that despite the bees around it, the honey itself is pure and delicious. She devises a skillful way to separate the bees from the honey, and then enjoys the honey as she wishes. Tasting honey, like realizing the emptiness of the mind, always brings joy. Similarly, the Buddha sees the buddha essence in each sentient being and with skillful methods, such as the teachings of the three turnings of the Dharma wheel, frees it from defilements.

3. The buddha essence resembles a kernel of grain in its husk.
The husk obscures the grain. For the grain to become edible food, the husk must be removed. In the same way, the seed of ignorance obscures our minds so that we cannot realize the ultimate truth. As above, this obscuration applies particularly to ordinary beings in the form and formless realms, but those of us in the desire realm have it as well. The seed of ignorance makes self-grasping ignorance and the ignorance of karma and its effects manifest in our minds. By means of the above three seeds of the three poisons, sentient beings create karma that brings rebirth in saṃsāra.

Just as the grain cannot be eaten when inside the husk, the deeds of a buddha cannot be displayed while the buddha essence is in the husk of defilements. A wise person knows how to remove the husk and prepare the grain so that it becomes nourishing food. In the same way, the Buddha guides sentient beings to remove their defilements, and the buddhas they will become will provide spiritual sustenance for others.

4. The buddha essence resembles gold buried in filth.

If someone accidentally drops some gold in a pile of filthy refuse at the side of the road, we don't know it is there let alone think to take it out, clean it, and use it. Similarly, while our gold-like buddha essence is not mixed with defilements, the filth of the manifest coarse three poisons prevents us from seeing it. Manifest coarse afflictions are the chief obscuration hindering beings in the desire realm. They provide the condition through which we are reborn especially in the desire realm. Led here and there by powerful emotions that arise suddenly and dominate our minds and by strong wrong views that we stubbornly cling to, we do not even consider the buddha essence that has always been there. Like the filth, manifest coarse attachment, animosity, and ignorance are repugnant. We dislike ourselves when they rule our minds, and others are likewise repulsed by our behavior.

The gold is pure—it can never become impure—but we cannot see it or use it as long as it is sunk in the filth. Similarly, the emptiness of the mind can never be infiltrated by the afflictions, but it cannot shine forth when obscured by the troublesome manifest afflictions.

A deva who possesses the clairvoyant power of the divine eye sees the gold, tells a person where to find it, and instructs him to make the gold into something worthy of being gold. Similarly, the Buddha sees the empty nature of our minds, teaches us how to purify it, and instructs us how to transform our minds into the minds of buddhas. These first four similes pertain specifically to ordinary beings who have not yet realized emptiness.

5. The buddha essence is like a treasure under the earth.

Like a magnificent treasure buried under the earth in a poor person's yard, the buddha essence is obscured by the latencies of the afflictions. This obscuration pertains especially to śrāvaka and solitary realizer arhats, who have eliminated the coarse manifest afflictions and their seeds, but whose minds are still obscured by the latencies of afflictions, especially the latency of ignorance, that prevent them from becoming fully awakened buddhas. While these arhats have realized emptiness and overcome afflictions, the ground of the latencies of afflictions are the condition through which arhats obtain a mental body and abide in the pacification of saṃsāra that is an arhat's nirvāṇa. After these arhats generate bodhicitta, they follow the bodhisattva paths and grounds. In doing so, when the ground of these latencies is removed, they will attain the ultimate true cessation, nonabiding nirvāṇa.

A treasure buried under the house of a poor family can free them from poverty, but they do not know it is there, even though it is right under them. The treasure does not say, "I'm here. Come and get me." Our naturally abiding buddha essence is like a treasure that has existed in our minds beginninglessly. This emptiness of the mind does not decrease or increase, it does not call out to us saying, "I'm here." But when the Buddha tells us about it, we learn how to uncover it, freeing it from even the ground of the latencies of ignorance that prevent full awakening.

6. The buddha essence resembles a tiny sprout hidden within the peel of a fruit. Beans have tiny sprouts inside but we cannot see them until the fruit and its peel have been shed. Similarly, for the path of seeing to be actualized, the objects of abandonment by the path of seeing must be destroyed. This simile applies particularly to ordinary beings on the paths of learning as well as Fundamental Vehicle āryas who are not yet arhats. Until they attain the path of seeing, the acquired afflictions, which are the objects to be abandoned by that path, obscure their buddha essence. While on the path of seeing, these learners have overcome the acquired afflictions but still have the innate afflictions and their seeds.

The transforming buddha essence is like a sprout that has the potential to grow into a huge tree that will offer shade for many people on a hot day. Just as the sprout needs good conditions to grow, we rely on the conditions of the collections of merit and wisdom to nourish the transforming buddha essence. Great compassion, wisdom, reverence for the Mahāyāna teachings and their goal, a great collection of merit, and samādhi are nourishing conditions that assist the transforming buddha essence to become the wisdom dharmakāya.

7. The buddha essence is like a buddha statue covered by a tattered rag.
The innate afflictions and their seeds—the objects to be abandoned on the path of meditation—resemble a buddha image wrapped in a tattered rag. The dismantling of the afflictions began on the path of seeing, and now, on the path of meditation, they are in tatters and ready to be discarded completely. Similarly, ordinary beings and āryas on the learning paths (āryas who are not yet arhats) are still obscured by the innate afflictions and their seeds, but they are weak and will soon be overcome. Nevertheless, while present, they obscure the buddha essence.

A deva sees a buddha statue under a dirty cloth and explains to a person who wants to have a buddha statue that it is there and she should retrieve it. In the same way, the Buddha sees that the ultimate nature of his own mind—emptiness—is the same as the emptiness of the minds of all sentient beings, even animals, hungry ghosts, and hell beings. This beautiful nature is covered by the remnants of the eighty-four thousand afflictions. To free it from these, the Buddha teaches the Dharma. The nature dharmakāya is like a precious statue. Just as the whole statue comes out at once when the rag is removed, the nature dharmakāya appears in its entirety when the mind is freed from all defilements.

8. The buddha essence resembles a baby who will become a great leader in the womb of a poor, miserable, forlorn woman.
In her womb a woman bears a baby who will be a great leader and do much good in the world. Not knowing that her child will one day be able to protect her, she knows only her present suffering. Similarly, ārya bodhisattvas on the impure grounds—grounds one through seven—have amazing potential that they are as yet unaware of owing to the womb-like confines of the afflictive obscurations. When they emerge from these on the eighth ground, their pristine wisdom becomes even more powerful, like the baby who has grown into a great leader.

Cyclic existence is like the homeless shelter in which this poor, miserable woman lives. There she is reviled by others and sinks into despair because she has no refuge or protector. Her child, as a great ruler, will soon be able to care for her, but she does not know this. Similarly, we do not realize that our ultimate protector is inside of us. But when the emptiness of our minds is revealed and becomes the nature dharmakāya, our problems are forever pacified. When we later actualize the enjoyment body, we will be like a wealthy monarch who can protect all beings in the land.

9. The buddha essence is like a golden buddha statue covered by a fine layer of dust.

The buddha essence of the pure-ground bodhisattvas—grounds eight through ten—is still covered by a thin layer of cognitive obscurations that impedes their full awakening—the latencies of the defilements that bring about the appearance of inherent existence and prevent directly seeing

NINE SIMILES FOR THE TATHĀGATAGARBHA

	SIMILE FOR THE OBSCURING FACTOR	OBSCURING FACTOR	SIMILE FOR THE OBSCURED
1.	Lotus	Seeds of attachment that brings rebirth in the form and formless realms	Buddha image
2.	Bees	Seeds of anger	Honey
3.	Husk	Seeds of ignorance that brings rebirth in the form and formless realms	Kernel of grain
4.	Filth	Manifest afflictions of attachment, animosity, and confusion that bring rebirth in the desire realm	Gold
5.	Earth	Ground of the latencies of ignorance that create unpolluted karma[84]	Treasure
6.	Skin of fruit	Acquired afflictions, objects to be abandoned on the path of seeing	Sprout
7.	Tattered rag	Innate afflictions and their seeds, objects to be abandoned on the path of meditation	Buddha statue
8.	Womb of a destitute woman	Afflictive obscurations	Baby who will become a universal monarch
9.	Fine layer of clay dust	Cognitive obscurations	Golden buddha statue

Note: Each simile is correlated with an obscuration and the particular sentient beings who possess it. While other sentient beings may also possess that obscuration, it is the outstanding obscuration—the immediate the two truths simultaneously. Like a magnificent, golden buddha statue that was cast in a mold and now is covered by only a layer of fine clay dust remaining from the mold, their buddha essence will soon be fully revealed when the vajra-like concentration at the end of the continuum of a sentient being removes the last remaining obscurations from the mindstream, allowing the buddha essence to be fully revealed.

An expert statue maker recognizes the preciousness of the gold statue covered by clay dust and cleanses it to reveal its pure beauty for everyone to enjoy. Similarly, the Buddha sees our buddha essence and guides us on the

Nine Similes for the Tathāgatagarbha (continued)

OBSCURED PHENOMENON	PERSON SPECIFICALLY OBSCURED BY THIS OBSCURING FACTOR
The buddha nature that can become the truth body	Ordinary beings in the form and formless realms
The ultimate truth, the emptiness of inherent existence of the mind	Ordinary beings in the form and formless realms
Naturally pure buddha essence	Ordinary beings in the form and formless realms
The emptiness of the mind	Ordinary beings in the desire realm
Naturally abiding buddha essence that can become nonabiding nirvāṇa, the nature dharmakāya	Śrāvaka and solitary-realizer arhats
Transforming buddha essence that can become the wisdom dharmakāya	Ordinary beings who have entered a path, śrāvaka and solitary realizers, āryas who are not arhats
Naturally pure buddha essence that will become the nature dharmakāya	Ordinary beings who have entered a path, learning āryas
Buddha essence that will bring forth the enjoyment body of a buddha	Bodhisattvas on the 7 impure grounds (1–7)
The buddha essence that will bring forth the emanation bodies of a buddha	Bodhisattvas on the pure grounds (8–10)

hindrance—that those particular sentient beings must overcome to progress on the path. The particular sentient beings pointed out in one simile may also possess the obscurations mentioned in another.

path to reveal it, so that we will be able to manifest emanation bodies. These emanation bodies will appear in various forms according to the karma of the sentient beings who can benefit from them. By these means, the buddha we will become will compassionately instruct and guide sentient beings according to their disposition.

REFLECTION

1. Contemplate each simile one by one.
2. Consider how it applies to you, the people you know, and all beings around you.
3. Seeing that each sentient being is impeded by obscurations that limit happiness and cause misery, let compassion arise for each and every sentient being.
4. With strong compassion, cultivate bodhicitta and determine to become a buddha in order to lead all beings to actualize their buddha essence.

Three Aspects of the Tathāgatagarbha

Maitreya asserts that each sentient being has the buddha essence and can attain buddhahood (RGV 1.27).

> Because a perfect buddha's body is pervasive,
> because suchness is without differentiation,
> and because a [buddha] lineage exists, all embodied [beings]
> are always in possession of a buddha essence.

He gives three reasons for stating that all sentient beings have the buddha essence and can attain full awakening: (1) *The buddhas' bodies are pervasive* so sentient beings can engage with the awakening activities of the buddhas. (2) *The suchness (natural purity) of the buddhas' minds and of sentient beings' minds cannot be differentiated* because both are the emptiness of inherent existence. (3) *Sentient beings possess the transforming buddha nature* that can develop all of a buddha's excellent qualities and transform into the three buddha bodies. These reasons, confirmed by the nine similes, indicate the following three aspects of the tathāgatagarbha.

1. The tathāgatagarbha has the nature of the dharmakāya of self-arisen pristine wisdom.

The tathāgatagarbha possessing the nature of the dharmakāya refers to the clear light nature of the tathāgatagarbha being called the dharmakāya. This is another case of giving the name of the result (dharmakāya) to the cause (tathāgatagarbha). Although the emptiness of the mind is permanent and is not an actual cause, it is called a cause because it is the foundation on which the dharmakāya is attained. The first three similes describe this.

The tathāgatagarbha is pervaded by the awakening activities of the dharmakāya. This means that sentient beings have the potential to be engaged with and influenced by the buddhas' awakening activities that will guide them to awakening.

Within this first aspect of the buddha essence, the dharmakāya, there are two parts: (1) The *dharmakāya of realizations* is the undefiled empty nature of a buddha's mind that is realized by that buddha's wisdom dharmakāya. This emptiness is the actual dharmakāya and refers specifically to the dharmadhātu that is totally free from defilements and has the nature of clear light. It is what is perceived and experienced by the wisdom dharmakāya of a buddha. (2) The *dharmakāya of the teachings* leads to the realization of this empty nature. These teachings consist of the profound teachings of the definitive sūtras that explain the ultimate truth, and the interpretable teachings of the provisional sūtras that explain various veiled truths—such as the person, aggregates, grounds and paths—that are taught in accordance with the dispositions and interests of various disciples. The dharmakāya of the teachings is called the dharmakāya although it is not the actual dharmakāya. The actual dharmakāya is experienced by a buddha. The teachings are the conditions to attain this dharmakāya.

Just as the buddha image hidden in the closed lotus in the first simile cannot be seen, the wisdom dharmakāya—the ultimate, supreme meditative equipoise on emptiness—is not perceivable in the world. The honey (simile 2) resembles the profound teachings on the ultimate truth. Just as all honey shares the same taste of sweetness, all phenomena have the same "taste" of being empty of inherent existence. The grain (simile 3) corresponds to the vast teachings on the method side of the path. Just as the grain needs to be removed from its husk and cooked to become edible food, the vast teachings are provisional and require interpretation.

The definitive and interpretable teachings and the profound and vast teachings are given to disciples of all three dispositions—śrāvakas, solitary realizers, and bodhisattvas—as well as to sentient beings who are temporarily of uncertain disposition. This latter group consists of individuals who will later become disciples with one of the three dispositions, depending on the teachers they meet and the teachings they receive. By hearing, reflecting, and meditating on both the vast and profound teachings, sentient beings will attain the actual wisdom dharmakāya.

The chief way in which buddhas' awakening activities engage with and influence sentient beings is by means of the buddhas' speech—the teachings they give. This ability of the buddhas' awakening activities to influence sentient beings is always present, and in this sense sentient beings are pervaded by the awakening activities of the dharmakāya.

2. The tathāgatagarbha has the nature of emptiness, suchness.

The tathāgatagarbha—the emptiness of sentient beings' minds—cannot be differentiated from the aspect of the natural purity of the dharmakāya. The gold buried in filth (simile 4) illustrates the emptiness of the mind. Just as pure gold does not change into a base metal, the emptiness of the mind does not change into something else. Like pure gold, the tathāgatagarbha is pure and faultless. The ultimate nature of sentient beings' minds and the ultimate nature or natural purity of the tathāgatas' minds cannot be differentiated in that both are emptiness. They appear the same and cannot be distinguished to the face of the meditative equipoise directly perceiving emptiness. In this sense it is said that the suchness of the Tathāgata is the essence of sentient beings.

3. The tathāgatagarbha has the nature of the buddha lineage or disposition.

This disposition culminates as the three bodies of a buddha, thus accomplishing buddhahood. Encompassing the remaining five similes, this disposition has two parts: (1) The *buddha disposition that has existed begin-*

ninglessly resembles a treasure under the ground (simile 5). Just as no one put the treasure there and its beginning is unknown, the naturally abiding buddha nature has existed beginninglessly. (2) The *transforming buddha disposition that has the potential* resembles a sprout (simile 6). Just as a tiny sprout, upon meeting the conditions that nourish it, will gradually grow into a tree, the transforming buddha disposition has the potential to accomplish buddhahood and the three buddha bodies when it encounters the right conditions, such as learning, reflecting, and meditating on the Dharma.

The buddha statue covered by tattered rags (simile 7) represents the beginningless, naturally abiding buddha disposition. Just as a beautiful, precious statue shines forth when the impediment of the tattered rags is removed, the beginningless purity of the mind—its emptiness of true existence—is revealed when all adventitious defilements have been forever banished owing to the collection of wisdom. At this point the naturally abiding buddha disposition is called the nature dharmakāya of a buddha.

The transforming buddha disposition blossoms owing to the accumulation of merit. When it is fully evolved, it becomes the enjoyment and emanation bodies of a buddha. Just as a future great leader who is now in his mother's womb (simile 8) will come to enjoy majesty, the enjoyment body enjoys the majesty and wealth of the Mahāyāna Dharma. Similar to a golden buddha statue emerging from the dust that surrounds it (simile 9), emanation bodies, which represent the actual dharmakāya, appear in whatever forms are most conducive to subduing the minds of sentient beings.

In our practice, our buddha disposition is initially awakened through listening to and reflecting on the Dharma, especially teachings on the value and purpose of bodhicitta and the two methods of generating it. Upon generating bodhicitta, we have the strong aspiration to attain the three buddha bodies. To accomplish this, we engage in the bodhisattva deeds—the six perfections and the four ways of maturing disciples—and fulfill the collections of merit and wisdom. Cultivating the collection of wisdom leads to gaining the pristine wisdom directly perceiving the ultimate nature of all phenomena. When this wisdom is developed further and used to fully cleanse all obscurations from our mindstreams, our naturally pure buddha nature becomes the nature dharmakāya—the suchness of the mind that has the two purities: the natural purity of inherent existence and the purity from adventitious defilements. The cultivation of the collection of merit, done through practicing the method aspect of the path, leads to our transforming buddha nature becoming the two form bodies—the enjoyment body and the emanation body. In this way, the three bodies of a buddha are actualized and our pristine wisdom perceives all existents throughout the universe.

Three Aspects of the Buddha Disposition

1. The clear light nature of the tathāgatagarbha that will become a buddha's dharmakāya in the future.
    - The dharmakāya of realizations: the undefiled empty nature of a buddha's mind that is realized by that buddha's wisdom dharmakāya; buddha image (1).
    - The dharmakāya of the teachings that are the conditions to attain it.
    - Profound teachings of the definitive sūtras on the ultimate truth; honey (2).
    - Interpretable teachings of the provisional sūtras on veiled truths; grain (3).

2. The tathāgatagarbha's empty nature (suchness) that cannot be differentiated from the emptiness of a buddha's mind; gold (4).

3. The tathāgatagarbha that has the buddha lineage and accomplishes the state of a buddha.
    - Beginningless buddha nature; treasure (5).
    - Transforming buddha nature that has the potential to accomplish buddhahood; sprout (6).
    - When purified, the beginningless, naturally abiding buddha disposition becomes the nature dharmakāya of a buddha; statue (7).
    - When the transforming buddha disposition is fully evolved, it becomes the enjoyment body of a buddha; the future great leader in his mother's womb (8).
    - The emanation bodies of a buddha; golden statue (9).

In summary, in his commentary to the *Sublime Continuum*, Asaṅga says:

> The similes taught in the *Tathāgatagarbha Sūtra* explain that the mind, which has existed without beginning in all realms of sentient beings, is empty by nature and therefore the afflictions are adventitious. Being empty by nature, this beginningless mind is inseparable from the innate development of the qualities of awakening.[85]

A Puzzle

Maitreya admits that some aspects of buddha nature are difficult for ordinary beings to understand (RGV 1.25).

> [The buddha nature] is pure and yet has affliction.
> [Awakening] is not afflictive and yet is purified.
> Qualities are totally indivisible [and yet not manifest].
> [Awakening activity] is spontaneous and yet without any thought.

Here are several puzzling points.

- From beginningless time buddha nature has been pure and free from defilements, yet it still has afflictions and defilements.
- The awakened mind is pure, yet it needs to be purified.
- The emptiness of buddhas' minds and sentient beings' minds are indistinguishable in that both are pure and empty of inherent existence, yet one belongs to buddhas and the other to sentient beings.
- Buddhas' awakening activity is spontaneous, yet it occurs without conscious motivation.

Initially these four statements may seem contradictory, but seen from the proper perspective, they cease to be paradoxical. The explanations below clarify their meaning. We must think carefully to understand the explanations correctly; doing so will bring important and essential insights.

- Buddha nature is completely pure; the defilements are adventitious. They obscure the buddha nature but are not its essential nature.
- The awakened mind has no defilements, but prior to becoming a buddha, the mind's nature is covered by defilements. It is like gold hidden by stains. The gold is still gold, but its luster and beauty cannot be seen. Similarly, when the mind is immersed in defilements, the potential to develop a buddha's qualities remains; it is part of the mind's nature. However, this potential is covered and cannot yet function as the actual qualities of a buddha. Love and compassion are present in the unawakened mind; they cannot be forever extricated from the mind. But when anger overwhelms the mind, the seed of love is not apparent, although it is still there.
- In terms of their ultimate nature, both buddhas' minds and sentient beings' minds are empty of inherent existence, and any difference in these emptinesses cannot be discerned by the wisdom directly realizing emptiness. However, on the conventional level, the two minds are different: one is a mind with obscurations, the other is a mind that is completely free from obscurations.
- Buddhas' awakening activities are effortless; they occur spontaneously, without purposefully cultivating a motivation. A buddha is free from conception and has become so habituated with compassion over many eons that no motivation or thought is needed for that buddha's awakened activities to radiate out in the most flawless and suitable way according to the disposition of each sentient being. This is inconceivable to us unawakened beings because our virtuous deeds require deliberate effort.

As we practice the path, sometimes discouragement fills our minds. If we observe closely, we will see that discouragement is simply a mass of distorted conceptions that we believe to be true. Instead of following these proliferating perverted thoughts, if we challenged their validity we would easily see they are false. One distorted conception is particularly pernicious; it believes that buddha nature does not exist and thus eliminating duḥkha and attaining awakening is not possible. Maitreya banishes this noxious thought (RGV 1.34):

If the buddha nature were not present,
there would be no remorse over suffering.
There would be no longing for nirvāṇa,
or striving and devotion toward this aim.

If sentient beings truly lacked the possibility to be awakened and were doomed to irreversible saṃsāric suffering, no one would ever regret being in saṃsāra or long to be free from duḥkha and attain nirvāṇa. No one would aspire for full awakening or make effort toward that goal. This clearly is not true; the life stories of the Buddha and other realized beings disprove this. We see within ourselves the wish to be free from saṃsāra's duḥkha, the yearning for freedom from the grip of afflictions and karma. While we may not make as much effort as we would like toward this aim, we do take steps in this direction. This is based on trust that there is an alternative to saṃsāra and that an awakened state exists.

REFLECTION

1. Contemplate the four puzzling points above and then reflect on the explanations that resolve them.
2. Feel your own yearning for spiritual awakening and your aspiration to free yourself from the obscurations that bind you. Realize that these indicate the existence of the buddha nature. Respect that aspect of yourself and determine to nourish it.

14 | Going Deeper into Buddha Nature

VOLUME I of this series, *Approaching the Buddhist Path*, introduced the three turnings of the Dharma wheel and briefly described the presentation of true cessation and true path in each. I would now like to review and then expand on this topic and its relationship to buddha nature.

The Three Turnings of the Dharma Wheel and Buddha Nature

The first turning of the Dharma wheel presents the overall structure of the Buddhist worldview based on the four truths. The second turning of the Dharma wheel contains a more detailed explanation of the third and fourth truths and presents the emptiness of inherent existence and the bodhisattva path. The essence of the third truth—true cessation—is understood in the context of the emptiness of the mind. The fourth truth—true path—is the wisdom realizing that emptiness.

We can see a progression. The first turning of the Dharma wheel discusses selflessness (*anātman*) in a general way. Having described the nature or identity of each truth and the way to engage with it, the Buddha explained the resultant understanding of each truth. Here he said that true cessation is to be actualized but there is nothing to actualize. This statement has deep implications. The Buddha wants us to understand emptiness, true cessation, and the unborn nature of phenomena.

In the second turning, the Buddha clarified that the precise meaning of selflessness is the emptiness of inherent existence (*śūnyatā*), the unborn nature. He also described the wisdom realizing this unborn nature. Here he called it "objectless" or "nonobjectifying" wisdom because it has ceased the apprehension of any objectifiable basis or inherent existence in persons and phenomena.

The Perfection of Wisdom sūtras—which were taught in the second turning—and the *Ornament of Clear Realizations*, a commentary by Maitreya on those sūtras, explain *tathāgatagarbha*—buddha essence—from the perspective of it being the ultimate nature of the mind, the emptiness of the mind.

The third turning of the Dharma wheel delves deeper: The purified aspect of the emptiness of the mind is true cessation, but what mind is the basis of that emptiness? The ordinary mind we have at present, which is the basis of all our afflictions, is not that mind. Our sense consciousnesses also cannot be that basis, because they are not stable and continuous. Nor can afflictive minds such as ignorance be that basis because the continuity of ignorance is not present at buddhahood and thus the emptiness of ignorance is also absent then.

The mind that is the basis for true cessation must be a pure mind—pure in that afflictions have not entered into its nature. That mind must be beginningless and endless because its continuum must go without interruption to buddhahood and become a buddha's mind. This mind is the clear light mind that can become a liberating path—the subject clear light realizing the object clear light, the emptiness of the mind. This is the tathāgatagarbha presented in the third turning. While the second turning speaks of tathāgatagarbha primarily as the object, emptiness, the third turning presents it as the subject, the clear light mind that can realize emptiness, which is also the basis of that emptiness.

In this way, the second turning of the Dharma wheel gives a thorough account of emptiness—the third truth, true cessation—while the third turning presents a thorough explanation of the fourth truth, true path. Here the Buddha introduces the clear light mind, a mind that has always been and will continue to be pure. However, he does not explain how to access and realize that mind. Where can we find a deeper explanation of the clear light mind and the method to actualize it? This is the key that opens the door to Tantra. A disciple who wants to learn about this mind in more depth cannot find the explanation in Sūtra, so she is automatically drawn to Tantra.

Of the four classes of tantra, the first three are preparations for the fourth, the highest yoga tantra (*mahānuttarayoga tantra*), which contains the real meaning of Tantra. The highest yoga tantra provides a clear explanation about how to access the fundamental innate clear light mind, utilize it, and transform it into a virtuous mental state, a true path that realizes emptiness. The development of this wisdom mind culminates in the state of union, the state of full awakening described in Tantra.

From this perspective Nāgārjuna's *Commentary on Bodhicitta* can be seen as a commentary on the third turning because it unpacks the meaning of a verse from the *Guhyasamāja Root Tantra*:

> Devoid of all real entities;
> utterly discarding all objects and subjects
> such as aggregates, elements, and sense sources;
> due to sameness of selflessness of all phenomena,
> one's mind is primordially unborn;
> it is in the nature of emptiness.[86]

Similarly, Nāgārjuna's *Praise to the Sphere of Reality* comments primarily on the subject matter of the third turning, the subject clear light mind, but hints at the meaning of clear light mind as explained in Tantra. It says (DS 20–21):

> Just as asbestos cloth[87]
> that is filthy with all kinds of dirt,
> when put into fire,
> the filth is burnt but not the cloth.
>
> Similarly, it is the case with the clear light mind,
> which has defilements produced by attachment;
> the fire of pristine wisdom burns the defilements
> but not that clear light [mind].

When fireproof asbestos cloth is put in fire, the stains on it burn until they disappear completely, but the cloth remains untouched. Likewise, when the ordinary mind of sentient beings, the clear light mind, is exposed to the realization of emptiness, the stains on the mind—attachment and so forth—are removed but the clear light mind remains.

True cessation ultimately refers to the emptiness of the subtlest clear light mind that has become an awakened mind. Although this is not explicitly stated in the third turning, the clear light mind mentioned in the third turning ultimately refers to the clear light mind of highest yoga tantra. Here we see that the three turnings of the Dharma wheel are not disconnected teachings on different topics. Each turning is closely linked to the previous one; it builds on and unpacks the meaning of the previous turning in more depth and detail. In this way, the Buddha, a skillful and wise teacher, gradually leads us to deeper understandings. Similarly, each turning hints at deeper explanations found in the future turnings.

To summarize, in the context of the three turnings, from the Sūtra perspective buddha nature is of two types: (1) The emptiness of the mind—the object that is perceived—as explained in the Perfection of Wisdom sūtras in the second turning. (2) The mind that is the basis of that emptiness. This undefiled mind has existed beginninglessly and will transform into the liberating paths that perceive this emptiness. Saying this mind is clear light means that the defilements are not an inherent property of this mind.

As the third turning leads us to understand, the emptiness of the mind is the natural buddha nature, and the basis of this emptiness is the transforming buddha nature. Both are buddha nature according to the Sūtra explanation. Furthermore, there is an extremely subtle mind that is the clear light mind and the seed of wisdom. It, too, is buddha nature. The full explanation of this mind and how to access it is presented in Tantra, specifically in highest yoga tantra.

A Link between Sūtra and Tantra

This way of describing the buddha nature as both the object, emptiness, and the subject, mind, is confirmed by the Seventh Dalai Lama in his *Commentary on the "Pristine Wisdom on the Verge of Transcendence Sūtra"* (*Atyayajñāna Sūtra*). He explains that the pristine wisdom on the verge of transcendence refers to both the pristine wisdom realizing the ultimate nature as one approaches nirvāṇa and the pristine wisdom realizing suchness that is at the heart of the practice that one must engage in at all times, including at the point of death. In his commentary, the Seventh Dalai Lama quotes the sūtra:

> If you realize the nature of your mind, it is wisdom. Therefore cultivate thorough discrimination not to seek buddhahood elsewhere.

What is the nature of that mind? He says it has three characteristics: (1) The nature of that mind is such that it is devoid of all conceptual elaborations (it is empty of inherent existence). (2) Since the ultimate nature of all phenomena is undifferentiable, the nature of that mind is all-pervading. (3) The nature is not polluted by any adventitious conceptualizations (afflictions).

He then turns to the tathāgatagarbha, saying that it exists in the mental continuum of each sentient being. Tathāgatagarbha refers to three factors:

(1) *The factor that allows for the buddhas' awakening activity to interact with sentient beings* (T. *nges legs kyi 'phrin las 'jug tu yod pa'i chha*). This factor is called the "essence or seed (*garbha*) of buddhahood" because it allows for sentient beings to enjoy and benefit from the buddhas' awakening activities, which are fruits of their awakening. It is the aspect of the mind that is receptive and has the capacity to receive the buddhas' various awakening activities and influence. This is the potency that exists in sentient beings that allows for the buddhas' awakening activity to interact with sentient beings and stimulate their progress on the path.

(2) The *factor of the sphere of reality*—namely, the mind's emptiness of inherent existence (T. *sems rang 'zhin gyis stong pa'i chhos nyid gyi chha*). This factor is the emptiness of the mind that is not free from defilements. It is called "the essence of buddhahood" because the nature of the Buddha's dharmakāya and the nature of sentient beings' mind are the same in terms of not being inherently polluted by afflictions. In terms of the mind being empty of existing from its own side, there is no difference between a buddha and a sentient being. In that way, sentient beings share the buddhas' nature.

(3) The *factor that is the seed that serves as the basis for the actualization of the three buddha bodies* (T. *sku gsum 'grub byed kyi nyer len sa bon gyi chha*). This factor is called the "essence of buddhahood" because from this cause the resultant three buddha bodies emerge. This is the subject clear light mind described in the third turning, which transforms into the three buddha bodies. Usually a seed is an abstract composite, but in this case it refers to a mind. Here the tathāgatagarbha is a conditioned phenomenon,

the clear light mind that will become a buddha's mind. This clear light mind has existed beginninglessly, will continue endlessly, and is the basis of the emptiness of the mind. Why is it called clear light? Clear light implies that the actual nature of the mind is undefiled. The stains that presently cover the mind are adventitious; they have not entered into the nature of the mind and are not an inherent part of the clear light mind. As Maitreya said (RGV 1.62):

> This clear and luminous nature of mind
> is as immutable as space. It is not afflicted
> by desire and so on, the adventitious defilements
> that spring from false conceptions.

The clear light mind is not permanent, but the fact that the afflictions are adventitious does not change. In the sense of the clear light mind being a continuity, nothing new is created at awakening; the obscurations and defilements have simply been eradicated. At this point, this mind, which has existed since beginningless time and whose nature is undefiled, becomes the omniscient mind.

Because the Seventh Dalai Lama is ostensibly speaking in terms of Sūtra, the buddha nature he speaks of is the clear light mind described in Sūtrayāna. Looking deeper, I believe that he is actually referring to the fundamental innate clear light mind that has been present in sentient beings since beginningless time and goes on endlessly. The continuity of this mind will attain awakening. Because a clear exposition of the fundamental innate clear light mind that acts as the seed of the three buddha bodies is not found in Sūtra, a practitioner must seek it in Tantra, especially in highest yoga tantra, which contains an extensive explanation of the fundamental innate clear light mind that has existed beginninglessly and continues on until awakening. Without saying it directly, the Seventh Dalai Lama is directing us to the tantric explanation of the innate clear light mind. In this way, the sequence of the three turnings of the Dharma wheel leads us from the basic teaching of the four truths, to in-depth explanations of the third and the fourth truths, and then eventually to the highest yoga tantra.

Dzogchen and Mahāmudrā usually refer to a subtle mind, rigpa or the clear light mind, as the buddha nature. Among Gelukpas, in Sūtrayāna buddha nature is usually discussed from the perspective of the *Ornament of Clear Realizations*, where it refers to the emptiness of the mind, not to the subtlest clear light mind itself, as Tantra speaks of it. However, here, commenting on a sūtra, the Seventh Dalai Lama, who is a traditional Gelukpa, also describes the buddha nature in a way similar to that of Dzogchen and Mahāmudrā.

REFLECTION

1. When the sūtra says, "If you realize the nature of your mind, it is wisdom. Therefore cultivate thorough discrimination not to seek buddhahood elsewhere," what does it mean?
2. What are the three characteristics the Seventh Dalai Lama points to as the characteristics of that wisdom mind?
3. What is the sequence of teachings in the three turnings of the Dharma wheel that lead us to the tantric explanation of the fundamental innate clear light mind?

Nothing Is to Be Removed

A verse is found in the *Ornament of Clear Realizations* and the *Sublime Continuum*, both written by Maitreya. The *Ornament* is a commentary on the Perfection of Wisdom sūtras from the second turning; the *Sublime Continuum* is a commentary on the *Tathāgatagarbha Sūtra* from the third turning. Speaking of buddha nature, this verse says (RGV 1.155):

> Nothing whatsoever is to be removed;
> not the slightest thing is to be added.
> Perfectly view the perfect [truth];
> seeing the perfect will liberate completely.

If the meaning of this verse were the same in both texts, there would be unnecessary repetition. To avoid that complication, the verse should be interpreted differently in each text. According to Abhayākaragupta (d. 1125), one of the great Indian commentators on the *Ornament*, from the viewpoint of the Perfection of Wisdom sūtras, the verse refers to the tathāgatagarbha from the perspective of the object, the empty nature of the mind. In this context, the element within sentient beings from which nothing needs to be removed and nothing needs to be added—something the discovery of which will lead us to nirvāṇa—is the emptiness of the mind. There is nothing to remove from the mind's emptiness because inherent existence has never existed. There is nothing to add to it because it is the ultimate nature of the mind. It is perfect, and seeing it perfectly—seeing it directly without any conceptual overlay—will cleanse the mind of obscurations and bring awakening. The object, emptiness, is flawless and perfect, and the way of perceiving it is also flawless and perfect. When one actually perceives emptiness in this way with an uninterrupted path, in the very next moment one will attain a liberated path. Nāgārjuna echoes this. Referring to the Buddha, he says (LS 23):

> There is nothing that you have brought forth;
> there is nothing that you have negated.
> You have comprehended that suchness,
> as it was before, so it is afterward.

The wisdom realizing emptiness does not remove something from the emptiness of the mind that was previously present. Nor does it bring a new reality to the mind. As the *Descent into Lanka Sūtra* (*Laṅkāvatāra Sūtra*) says, "Whether the Tathāgata appears in the world or not, reality forever abides." Buddha nature—understood as the emptiness of the mind—is always present and does not change. The only difference is that wisdom now realizes this ultimate nature of the mind.

According to the *Sublime Continuum*, the verse refers to the clear light mind being the buddha nature. The clear light mind is the basis that has many attributes, such as its being pure from the beginning and not newly created. Its being pure from the beginning is described in the first line: because afflictions are not an inherent part of the clear light mind, there is nothing whatsoever to remove from it. Its not being newly created is explained in the second line: it is not the case that once the clear light mind was absent and then it was freshly created. Thus there is nothing to add to it because the clear light mind is eternal. But what does viewing this clear light mind perfectly mean? According to Sūtra, how can nonconceptual experience of the clear light mind liberate us?

The *Sublime Continuum* says that the ultimate nature is to be self-revealed: there is no need to use reasoning to understand it; one's own experience will reveal it. Gyaltsab maintains that this ultimate nature refers to the emptiness of the mind, as it does in the *Ornament*. If that is the case, what does saying it is self-revealed mean? How can ultimate reality reveal itself? Interpreting the ultimate nature mentioned here to be the clear light mind connects to the Dzogchen and Mahāmudrā meditations on the mind. By stopping memories of the past and plans for the future, the clear and cognizant nature of the mind can be directly perceived. If one abides in this state and has a prior correct realization of emptiness, then the coarse levels of mind dissolve and the subtlest innate clear light mind—rigpa in Dzogchen—manifests; it reveals itself. Combining this mind with our previous familiarity with emptiness liberates us from afflictions and defilements.

The Capacity Giving Rise to the Three Kāyas

What is the relationship between the transforming buddha nature and the third factor of the tathāgatagarbha as set forth by the Seventh Dalai Lama—the factor that is the seed that serves as the basis for the actualization of the three buddha bodies? Take the example of a rosary and the beads that form it. When we think of a rosary, we think of one thing that is a continuum. That is similar to buddha nature as presented by the Seventh Dalai Lama. When we think of the individual beads, we focus on the particular components of the rosary. The beads are analogous to the various consciousnesses that can be the buddha nature. At one time it is bodhicitta, at another time it is the mind realizing emptiness, at yet another time it is the mind restraining from nonvirtue, and so on. The Seventh Dalai Lama is not referring to these specific mental states; he is emphasizing the continuum, the common feature shared by all of them. This common feature is the mental primary consciousness; this is the tathāgatagarbha. Some of the instances of this continuum may grasp true existence, and from that perspective they are not buddha nature. But from the perspective of that mind still being clear light—that which is clear and cognizant, whose obscurations are adventitious—it is the buddha nature.

Looking deeper, this third factor of tathāgatagarbha cannot refer to the transforming buddha nature. Why not? According to Sūtra, the transforming buddha nature is any mind that is not freed from defilements, whose continuity goes on to awakening and that serves as the basis for the emptiness that is the naturally abiding buddha nature. The naturally abiding buddha nature is the emptiness of the mind that is not yet freed from defilements. The seed having the capacity to give rise to the three kāyas must be a pure state of mind that is not defiled. This can only be a very subtle mind that has existed since beginningless time and will go on endlessly. The explanation of this primordial clear light mind is found in great depth only in highest yoga tantra, not in the Sūtra teachings that speak of the transforming buddha nature.

A Buddha's Nature Dharmakāya

To review, in Tantra the fundamental innate clear light mind of sentient beings has never been mixed with defilements. This innate, ever-present mind has two qualities—it is the subtlest mind, and it has existed beginninglessly, exists endlessly, and will go on to awakening. When coarser levels of mind appear out of this subtlest mind, afflictions manifest. But when the coarser levels of mind—including the white appearance, red increase, and black near attainment—absorb and cease, only the beginningless and endless clear light mind remains. At that time it is not possible for afflictions to arise. This indicates that the coarse minds are adventitious—they are not stable and enduring—while the innate clear light mind is eternal. This primordial clear light mind is the basis from which an individual's saṃsāra evolves and it is also the basis from which the qualities of nirvāṇa come about.

The primordial clear light mind differs from the clear light mind described in Sūtra, which is together with afflictions in that afflictions manifest in it even though those afflictions are not an inherent part of that mind. However, afflictions are never able to manifest in the primordial clear light mind presented in Tantra because this mind manifests only after the coarser levels of mind and wind have ceased, at the time of death or by means of special yogic techniques.

In the Perfection of Wisdom sūtras, the nature body of a buddha (*svābhāvikakāya*) is said to be an unconditioned, permanent phenomenon—the emptiness of inherent existence of the awakened mind. The wisdom dharmakāya of a buddha is a conditioned, impermanent phenomenon that is the continuation of the clear light mind described in Sūtra. In Tantra, the primordial clear light mind is called the "composite nature body of a buddha." Although the emptiness of the awakened mind—the nature body in common to Sūtra and Tantra—is a permanent phenomenon, the existence of a composite nature body is unique to Tantra because only Tantra speaks of the primordial clear light mind. Calling the primordial clear light mind at buddhahood the composite nature body emphasizes that nothing is newly created at buddhahood. This mind has been there all along, but now all the defilements, which were never an inherent part of it, are completely gone.

From the perspective of it cognizing all veiled and ultimate truths simultaneously, the purified primordial clear light mind of a buddha is called the omniscient mind, the wisdom dharmakāya. From the perspective of its existing from beginningless time and now becoming the purified basis of the emptiness that is the unconditioned nature body, it is called the composite nature body. The Seventh Dalai Lama refers to it as the "seed that has the capacity to give rise to the three kāyas of a buddha." Although "seed" usually refers to an abstract composite, here it is a mind that serves as the basis for the three buddha bodies. This innate, primordial, ever-present mind also transforms into the wisdom dharmakāya. Thus in Tantra, the composite nature body and the wisdom dharmakāya of a buddha are the same mind seen from different perspectives.

In summary, Sūtra speaks of two buddha natures. One is the naturally abiding buddha nature; the other is the transforming buddha nature. The naturally abiding buddha nature is the emptiness of the mind that is not free from defilements. The transforming buddha nature is the mind that is the basis of that emptiness as well as any other neutral or virtuous qualities of mind that continue on to buddhahood.

If an intelligent person who is inclined toward Tantra hears of the third factor of tathāgatagarbha as explained by the Seventh Dalai Lama—the seed having the capacity to give rise to the three kāyas—she will understand that there is some aspect of her own mind that is a composite phenomenon and the buddha nature. What is that? It cannot be the defiled coarse mind because that mind does not continue to awakening. It must be a subtle mind that is hinted at but not explained extensively in Sūtra. She turns to Tantra, where there is a lengthy and explicit presentation of this mind. In this way, she enters Tantrayāna.

Pristine Wisdom Abiding in the Afflictions

There is an area of potential confusion about tathāgatagarbha that we must take care to avoid. It stems from such statements as "Within afflictions, wisdom (*jñāna*) abides," found in Nāgārjuna's *Praise to the Sphere of Reality*. *Jñāna* usually refers to āryas' pristine wisdom that directly realizes emptiness. Does this mean that afflictions are in fact wisdom? If so, are we already buddhas?

Statements such as this need to be understood correctly. Here *jñāna* refers not to āryas' wisdom realizing emptiness but to the clear light nature that can transform into the wisdom of the resultant state. Jñāna is the aspect of the mind—found even in an afflictive mind—that can become the wisdom realizing emptiness. The cause—the clear light mind of sentient beings—will eventually become the result—a buddha's pristine wisdom—and for this reason the clear light mind of sentient beings is called *wisdom* even though it has yet to become that wisdom. How is that aspect of the mind transformed into the nonconceptual wisdom directly realizing emptiness? By means of learning, reflecting, and meditating on the Dharma. This wisdom is generated in dependence on or in relation to the clear light mind.

Giving the cause the name of the result is reminiscent of Nāgārjuna's discussion of the three kāyas (buddha bodies) in the ordinary state, on the path, and at the resultant level. The expression "three kāyas in the ordinary state" does not mean that the three resultant kāyas are already present in us in our ordinary state. Rather, in the ordinary state we possess the basis upon which we can actualize the three kāyas. This basis is given the name of the result.

Similar ways of speaking are found in other scriptures. In *Treasury of Dharmadhātu* (T. *chos dbyings mdzod*), Longchenpa says that what is primordially awakened becomes reawakened. Some people take such passages literally, thinking that we are already buddhas. But if that is the case, then we are very strange and disgraceful buddhas! Longchenpa's statement echoes the notion of natural nirvāṇa found in Madhyamaka texts. Natural nirvāṇa refers to the mind's emptiness of inherent existence. This ultimate nature of the mind is pure and clear light; the defilements have not penetrated into it. Because this nature is naturally untainted, it is possible to remove the defilements that obscure it. While natural nirvāṇa is not the nirvāṇa of liberated beings, it serves as the basis upon which actual nirvāṇa can be attained. This is similar to the meaning of Longchenpa's statement that what is the primordially awakened becomes reawakened.

Nāgārjuna's statement that wisdom exists in the afflictions is made from the Sūtra point of view where wisdom refers to the continuity of the mental consciousness. According to Dzogchen and Mahāmudrā, the wisdom that is present in the afflictions is much subtler and refers to the innate clear light mind. They say this wisdom is a noncomposite phenomenon. Dodrubchen Jigme Tenpai Nyima (1865–1926), the Third Dodrup Rinpoche, explains that *noncomposite* in this context does not have its usual meaning of permanent and unconditioned. Rather, wisdom is said to be noncomposite because it has existed beginninglessly and is not newly created by causes and conditions. In the same way, the *Sublime Continuum* refers to the buddhas' activities as permanent because they have existed beginninglessly and will exist eternally. Here "permanent" means eternal and unending; it doesn't mean unchanging or unconditioned.

Gyaltsab Darma Rinchen has another view. He says that the term "wisdom" in this statement is not to be understood literally. Rather it refers to the emptiness of the mind, which is noncomposite, permanent, and always present.

I believe the Dzogchen and Mahāmudrā interpretations are more applicable when trying to understand the presentation in the *Sublime Continuum*. There is not much difference between the Seventh Dalai Lama's view of buddha nature and that of Dzogchen and Mahāmudrā. However, Dzogchen and Mahāmudrā speak from the viewpoint of highest yoga tantra and thus they identify the innate ever-present clear light mind as buddha nature, whereas the Seventh Dalai Lama speaks from the Sūtra viewpoint that points to Tantra.

Causal Clear Light Mind

The causal clear light mind can be spoken of from the perspective of both Sūtra and Tantra. Sūtra speaks of the continuity of the mental consciousness, which is present at all times. The jñāna that abides in the afflictions refers to the continuum of this mental consciousness. While the continuum of the mental consciousness is not actual pristine wisdom, it will become this wisdom as we progress through the paths and grounds to buddhahood.

Highest yoga tantra differentiates two types of mind—the temporary, adventitious consciousnesses and the innate ever-present clear light mind. When all the coarser levels of mind—including the white appearance, red increase, and black near attainment—have dissolved, the subtlest innate clear light mind becomes manifest. Only this mind remains. The fact that all the other minds have dissolved indicates that they are adventitious, while the subtlest innate clear light mind, which has existed since beginningless time and continues on endlessly to awakening, persists.

From the viewpoint of highest yoga tantra, the clear and cognizant nature of the mind that is the fundamental innate clear light mind underlies all consciousnesses. But we should not equate clarity and cognizance in general with the fundamental innate clear light mind. All consciousnesses are clear and cognizant because that is the definition of consciousness. The fundamental innate clear light mind is the subtlest mind. The coarser minds of the waking state are derivatives of this everlasting mind. Although they have a clear and cognizant nature, they are not this subtlest innate mind.

Neither the continuum of the mental consciousness spoken of in Sūtra nor the fundamental innate clear light mind spoken of in Tantra is a soul or inherently existent self. Both are empty of inherent existence.

What Continues to Awakening?

Who is the person that goes from being an ordinary being to an ārya to a buddha? To answer this, we speak of the *general I*—the continuity of the merely designated I from one life to another—and the *specific I* of each lifetime that constitutes that continuity. The specific I of each lifetime is designated in dependence on the aggregates of that life. Since our physical and mental aggregates change from one lifetime to the next, the I designated in dependence on them also changes. In one lifetime we may be Susan, in the next John. In one lifetime we may be a monkey, in another a human being, and in yet another a deva. These are the specific Is of those three lifetimes.

The general I or person that goes from one life to the next is designated in dependence on the series of specific Is. The Buddha spoke of the general I when he said, "In my previous life I was a king, in the present life I am Śākyamuni Buddha." The person or I that exists continuously in the past, present, and future without interruption is the general I. That general I encompasses the monkey of one life, the human in the next, and the deva in the life after that. The monkey, human being, and deva are the specific persons of those individual lives. They are born and die; the general I goes from saṃsāra to full awakening.

When speaking of the self that exists in the three times, we are not referring to a subtle self or a coarse self—no distinction like that is made. It is simply the general I. Likewise, without making any distinction in terms of subtle or coarse, we say there is a general mental consciousness that exists in the three times.

Although the general mental consciousness goes from one life to the next and on to awakening, the specific mental consciousnesses of the sentient beings in that continuum do not. The consciousness aggregate of the monkey is not the substantial cause of the consciousness aggregate of the human being in the next rebirth. However, the last moment of the consciousness of one life is the substantial cause for the first moment of the consciousness of the next life. In this way, it is said that the continuity of the mental consciousness goes on to awakening. However, this mental consciousness is not a truly existent self or soul.

As discussed above, because afflictions such as ignorance are eradicated on the path and do not go on to awakening, they cannot be considered buddha nature. Although afflictions do not continue on to awakening, the clear and cognizant characteristic of the afflictions does. Here it is helpful to understand two kinds of continuities: (1) a *continuity of type* in which the cause and the result share similar characteristics, and (2) a *continuity of substance* in which one thing is the substance that transforms into another thing.

For example, a log burns and becomes ashes. The ashes are the substantial continuity of the log because the material of the log turned into the ashes.

The ashes are not the continuity of type of the log because the log and the ashes do not have similar characteristics. Applying this to the question of afflictions continuing to awakening: the awakened mind is not the continuity of type of afflictions. Afflictions are polluted, they are the true origin of duḥkha. The awakened mind is unpolluted and is not the true origin. The two do not share the same characteristics. However, the clear and cognizant nature of the awakened mind is in the substantial continuity of the clear and cognizant nature of the afflictions.

From one perspective, it seems that if the mind grasping inherent existence changed objects and apprehended emptiness, it would be a virtuous mind. In that case, from the viewpoint of substance—clarity and cognizance—ignorance and wisdom would be in the same substantial continuity. But from the viewpoint of their characteristics, ignorance and the wisdom realizing emptiness are total opposites. The ignorance grasping true existence does not go to awakening; it is a totally distorted consciousness that cannot improve or become virtuous. In fact, when the antidote of wisdom realizing emptiness is applied, ignorance degenerates and becomes nonexistent. But when we look just at the clear and cognizant nature of ignorance, we can say that it can be purified and its purified continuum goes on to awakening.

Dzogchen and Mahāmudrā

According to Sūtra, meditation on the clear and cognizant nature of the mind or on the transforming buddha nature alone will not eradicate afflictions. However, it does lead us to have more confidence that afflictions are not an inherent part of the mind and therefore that becoming a buddha is possible. This, in turn, leads us to question: What defiles the mind and what can eliminate these defilements completely? Seeking the method to purify the transforming buddha nature, we will cultivate the wisdom realizing the emptiness of inherent existence and eradicate ignorance.

According to Dzogchen and Mahāmudrā, meditation on the clear and cognizant nature of the mind could lead the coarse winds to dissolve and the subtlest clear light mind to become manifest. When this happens, practitioners who have previously cultivated a correct understanding of emptiness then incorporate that understanding in their meditation and use the innate clear light mind to realize emptiness and abolish afflictions.

It is important to understand the *Sublime Continuum* correctly from a Dzogchen and Mahāmudrā point of view. Some people take it literally, leading them to incorrectly believe that primordial wisdom is permanent, inherently existent, independent of any other factors, and does not rely on causes and conditions. They then make statements such as, "If you unravel this secret, you will be liberated." Dodrup Jigme Tenpai Nyima (1865–1926) and his disciple Tsultrim Zangpo (1884–c.1957), who were great Dzogchen scholars and practitioners, said that the mere presence of this primordial wisdom within us alone cannot liberate us. Why not? At the time of death, all other minds have dissolved, and only the primordial mind remains. Even though it has manifested in all the infinite number of deaths we have experienced in saṃsāra, that has not helped us attain buddhahood. These two sages say that in order to attain buddhahood, it is necessary to utilize the primordial wisdom to realize emptiness; only that will liberate us. This is consistent with Tsongkhapa's view.

Some commentaries on Dzogchen and Mahāmudrā say: This wisdom that abides in the afflictions is the true wisdom, and on this basis every sentient being is already a buddha. Although we have been buddhas from beginningless time, we have to be awakened again. The wisdom that we have now is the omniscient mind of a buddha, and the three bodies of a buddha exist innately in each sentient being. Sentient beings have a basis of essential purity that is not merely emptiness but is endowed with three aspects. Its entity is the dharmakāya—the mode of abiding of pristine wisdom; its nature is the enjoyment body—the appearance aspect of that mind; and compassion is the emanation bodies—its radiance or expression. In short, they say that all three buddha bodies are present, fully formed in our ordinary state, but since they are obscured we are not aware of their presence.

Such statements taken literally are fraught with problems. While some people are partial and unfair in their criticism and refute misconceptions in only some traditions, Changkya Rolpai Dorje (1717–86) was unbiased and pointed out incorrect interpretations in all four Tibetan traditions, including his own Geluk tradition. In his *Song of the Experience of the View*, he says, "I say this not out of disrespect to these masters, but perhaps they have had less exposure to rigorous philosophical investigation of the great treatises and were unable to use certain terminology appropriately." That is, the difficulty in their assertions lies in a broad use of terminology that is not grounded in the authority of the great treatises. Of course, Changkya's comments do not apply to Dzogchen and Mahāmudrā masters such as Dodrup Jigme Tenpai Nyima and his teacher Awa Pangchu, who have done serious philosophical study and examination of the great treatises and who ground their understanding of Dzogchen in them. Their interpretations and writings are excellent.

All four Tibetan traditions teach practices that search for the mind—where it came from, where it goes, what its shape and color are, and so forth. Speaking of this shared practice, Changkya said that after searching in this manner, we find that the mind is not tangible, lacks color and shape, and does not come from one place or go to another. Discovering this, meditators experience a sensation of voidness. However, this voidness is not the emptiness of inherent existence that is the ultimate reality of the mind; it is the mere absence of the mind being a tangible object. Although someone may think this voidness is ultimate reality and meditate in that state for a long time, this is not meditation on the ultimate nature of the mind.

There are two ways to meditate on the mind. The first is as above, examining whether the mind has color, shape, location, tangibility, and so forth. This leads to the sense that the conventional nature of the mind lacks these qualities. The second is meditation on the ultimate nature of the mind, in which we examine the mind's ultimate mode of existence and discover its emptiness of inherent existence. People who confuse these two ways of meditating on the mind and think that the mind's absence of tangibility, color, and so forth is the mind's ultimate nature may criticize masters such as Dignāga and Dharmakīrti for their precise expositions on debate, logic, and reasoning, saying these only increase preconceptions. Gungtang Konchog Tenpai Dronme (1762–1823), another master who was impartial in his critical analysis of Tibetan Buddhist traditions, said he found this amazing.

Some people believe there is no need for reasoning or investigation on the path, that simply by having faith and receiving the blessing of a guru primordial wisdom will arise. In this light, I have been very happy to see the establishment of more shedras—academic institutes—that teach the classical philosophical texts from India and Tibet.

Some Westerners similarly do not value Dharma study and investigation, perhaps because Buddhadharma is relatively new in the West. Without a comprehensive understanding of the Buddhadharma, people tend to seek the easiest and shortest path to awakening, a path that does not require giving up their attachments. Such an attitude exists among Tibetans as well. Tsongkhapa said that many people think that the Buddha's qualities are wonderful, but when a spiritual mentor explains through reasoning and scriptural citations how to attain them, they become discouraged and say, "Who can actually achieve such realizations?"

Are We Already Buddhas?

In the *Tathāgatagarbha Sūtra*, the Buddha explained that each sentient being possesses a permanent, stable, and enduring tathāgatagarbha that is a fully developed buddha body (*kāya*) replete with the thirty-two signs of a buddha. Questions arise: If an already realized buddha existed within us, wouldn't we be ignorant buddhas? If we were actual buddhas now, what would be the purpose of practicing the path? If we were already buddhas and yet still needed to purify defilements, wouldn't a buddha have defilements? If we had a permanent, stable, and enduring essence, wouldn't that contradict the teachings on selflessness and instead resemble the self or soul asserted by non-Buddhists? Mahāmati expressed these same doubts to the Buddha in the *Descent into Lanka Sūtra*:

> The tathāgatagarbha taught [by the Buddha in some sūtras] is said to be clear light in nature, completely pure from the beginning, and to exist possessing the thirty-two signs in the bodies of all sentient beings. If, like a precious gem wrapped in a dirty cloth, [the Buddha] expressed that [tathāgatagarbha]—wrapped in and dirtied by the cloth of the aggregates, constituents, and sources; overwhelmed by the force of attachment, animosity, and ignorance; dirtied with the defilements of conceptualizations; and permanent, stable, and enduring—how is

> this propounded as tathāgatagarbha different from the non-Buddhists propounding a self?[88]

Some Tibetan scholars accept the teaching on a permanent, stable, and enduring buddha nature literally, saying it is a definitive teaching. Sharing the doubts expressed above by Mahāmati, Prāsaṅgikas say this is an interpretable teaching. They say this, not on a whim, but by examining three points.

(1) *What was the Buddha's final intended meaning when he made this statement?* When speaking of a permanent, stable, and enduring essence in each sentient being, the Buddha's intended meaning was the emptiness of the mind, the naturally abiding buddha nature, which is permanent, stable, and enduring. Because the mind is empty of inherent existence and the defilements are adventitious, buddhahood is possible.

(2) *What was the Buddha's purpose for teaching this?* The Buddha taught a permanent, stable, enduring essence complete with the thirty-two signs, in order to calm some people's fear of selflessness and to gradually lead non-Buddhists to the full realization of suchness. At present, these people, who are spiritually immature, feel comfortable with the idea of a permanent essence. The idea of the emptiness of inherent existence frightens them; they mistakenly think it means that nothing whatsoever exists. They fear that by realizing emptiness, they will disappear and cease to exist. To calm this fear, the Buddha spoke in a way that corresponds with their current ideas. Later, when they are more receptive, he will teach them the actual meaning. This is similar to the way skillful parents simplify complex ideas to make them comprehensible to young children.

(3) *What logical inconsistencies arise from taking this statement literally?* Accepting this teaching on a permanent, stable, and enduring buddha nature at face value contradicts the definitive meaning of emptiness and selflessness explained by the Buddha in the Perfection of Wisdom sūtras. In those sūtras, the Buddha set forth many reasonings that refute this view. Furthermore, if this statement were accepted literally, the Buddha's teachings would be no different from those of non-Buddhists who assert a permanent self.

The emptiness of inherent existence—which is the ultimate reality and the natural purity of the mind—exists in all sentient beings without distinction. Based on this, it is said that a buddha is present. But the ultimate reality of a buddha does not exist in sentient beings. While buddhas and sentient beings are the same in that the ultimate nature of their minds is emptiness, that ultimate reality is not the same because one is the ultimate reality of a buddha's mind—the nature dharmakāya—and the other is the ultimate reality of a defiled mind. If we said that the nature dharmakāya existed in sentient beings, we would have to also say that the wisdom dharmakāya, which is one nature with it, existed in sentient beings. That would mean that sentient beings were omniscient, which certainly is not the case! Similarly, if the abandonment of all defilements existed in ordinary sentient beings, there would be nothing to prevent them from directly perceiving the natural purity of their minds. They would directly realize emptiness. This, too, is not the case.

Some people say the dharmakāya with the two purities—the natural purity and the purity of the abandonment of all defilements—exists in the mindstreams of sentient beings, but because sentient beings are obscured, they don't perceive it. If that were the case, then whose mind is purified and who attains the freedom that is the purity of all defilements? If sentient beings already possess the dharmakāya, there is no need for them to practice the path and purify their minds, because from beginningless time their minds have been free of adventitious defilements.

The assertion that a buddha complete with the thirty-two signs exists within the continuums of all sentient beings echoes the theistic theory of an eternally pure, unchanging self. If the thirty-two signs were already present in us, it would be contradictory to say that we still need to practice the path to create the causes for them. If someone says that they are already in us in an unmanifest form and they just need to be made manifest, that resembles the Sāṃkhya notion of arising from self, because even though existing, this buddha would need to be produced again in order to be made manifest. Nāgārjuna and his followers soundly refuted production from self.

The sūtra continues with the Buddha's response:

> Mahāmati, my teaching of the tathāgatagarbha is not similar to the propounding of a self by non-Buddhists. Mahāmati, the tathāgatas, arhats, the perfectly completed buddhas indicated

> the tathāgatagarbha with the meaning of the words *emptiness, limit of complete purity, nirvāṇa, unborn, signless, wishless*, and so forth. [They do this] so that the immature might completely relinquish a state of fear regarding the selfless, [and to] teach the nonconceptual state, the sphere without appearance.[89]

Here we see that the Buddha skillfully taught different ideas to different people, according to what was necessary at the moment and beneficial in the long term to further them on the path. We also learn that we must think deeply about the teachings, exploring them from various viewpoints and bring knowledge gained from reasoning and from reading other scriptures to discern their definitive meaning.

The purpose of learning about buddha nature is to understand that the mind is not intrinsically flawed and that, on the contrary, it can be perfected. It is not just that the mind can be transformed; there is already part of the mind that allows it to be purified and perfected. Understanding this gives us great confidence and energy to practice the methods to purify and perfect this mind of ours so that it will become the mind of a fully awakened buddha.

REFLECTION

1. What does it mean to say that pristine wisdom abides in the afflictions?
2. Are we already wise buddhas but just don't know it? Do buddhas have afflictions?
3. The Buddha said there is a permanent, stable, and enduring buddha nature in each of us. What was his final intended meaning in saying this?
4. What was his purpose for teaching this?
5. What logical inconsistencies arise from taking this statement literally?

Awareness of Our Buddha Nature Eliminates Hindrances

Maitreya said (RGV 1.158):

> [The sūtras of the second turning of the Dharma wheel] state in numerous places that all knowable [phenomena] are in all ways empty like a cloud, a dream, or an illusion. Why is it then, that in [the sūtras of the third turning of the Dharma wheel] the Buddha, having said this, declared that the buddha nature is present within beings?

Maitreya tells us that although the sūtras of the second turning characterize the buddha nature by giving the examples of an illusion and so forth to illustrate the emptiness of the mind, he will explain buddha nature slightly differently in the *Sublime Continuum*. This is a clue implying that he will emphasize the clear light mind being the buddha nature. This may cause some people to doubt: "The Buddha taught emptiness extensively in the second turning, saying that was the buddha nature. Why in the third turning would he speak about buddha nature being the clear light mind that has beginninglessly been completely pure in sentient beings? Is there a contradiction between the second and third turnings?"

Maitreya explains that the Buddha spoke of buddha nature being the clear light mind in order to help us sentient beings overcome five factors that hinder us from developing bodhicitta, realizing emptiness, and attaining buddhahood.

(1) *Discouragement* makes us believe that awakening cannot be attained. Because we don't know that the buddha nature exists in us, cynicism and a lack of confidence prevent us from generating bodhicitta. Even before beginning, we give up and don't make an effort.

(2) Having *arrogant contempt for those we consider inferior* comes from not knowing that the buddha nature exists in others. With derision we judge and disparage others, abandon love and compassion, and abstain from engaging in the bodhisattva practices.

(3) *Distorted conceptions* incorrectly hold that adventitious defilements are truly existent, exist in the nature of the mind, and are impossible to eradicate. These wrong views superimpose true existence on things that are

empty of true existence. They arise from not knowing the existence of the buddha nature in all sentient beings and interfere with our cultivation of the wisdom correctly realizing reality.

(4) *Denigrating the true nature* is to deny the existence of buddha nature or to think the buddha nature has not been present beginninglessly. This misconstrued deprecation repudiates the potential that exists within each sentient being and inhibits realizing the excellent qualities that are inseparable in nature from the buddha nature.

(5) *Self-centeredness* makes us biased toward the self, quenching the equanimity that sees self and others as equally valuable. Egocentrism obliterates the thought that buddha nature exists equally in ourselves and others. Preoccupied with our own concerns, we are unable to generate the love and compassion that regard ourselves and others as equal. This, in turn, interferes with generating bodhicitta.

Understanding buddha nature counteracts these five faults. When we sentient beings hear about buddha nature, (1) joy, not discouragement, arises in our minds because we know duḥkha can be overcome; (2) in place of contempt arises respect for the Buddha and sentient beings who have this great potential; (3–4) analytical wisdom that correctly views reality abolishes superimpositions and denigration of the actual nature, replacing it with liberating wisdom; and (5) great love for all sentient beings overcomes confining self-preoccupation by opening our hearts to others. In short, eliminating these faults clears the way to generating bodhicitta and engaging in the six perfections, especially meditative stability and wisdom, which are essential to overcome the two obscurations.

In this way, Maitreya clarifies that the description of buddha nature in the *Sublime Continuum* does not contradict that of the second turning but speaks of it from a different perspective. He also elucidates the purpose for teaching the tathāgatagarbha in the third turning: it is to help sentient beings overcome the five faults and have enthusiasm and determination to practice the path and attain full awakening.

Notes

1. *Upādāna* means clinging, the aggregates being *subject to clinging.* This connotes that the aggregates are objects of our clinging and are brought about by clinging. *Upādāna* may also be translated as *appropriated*, connoting that the aggregates have been "taken" by the person.
2. In Buddhism *permanent* means unchanging. Permanent phenomena are not dependent on causes and conditions. *Impermanent* means changing from one moment to the next.
3. The way nirvāṇa is described here in the Pāli tradition—as a permanent, unconditioned, and unborn reality that allows for the eradication of defilements—sounds similar to the Madhyamaka description of emptiness in the Sanskrit tradition.
4. This refers to the fourfold classification of nirvāṇa. See chapter 11. According to the Prāsaṅgikas, *natural nirvāṇa* is emptiness. *Nirvāṇa without remainder* is true cessation in the continuums of arhats of the three vehicles that is qualified by the vanishing of the manifest appearance of true existence. *Nirvāṇa with remainder* is true cessation in the continuums of arhats of the three vehicles that is together with the manifest appearance of true existence. This occurs in the postmeditation time of arhats who are not buddhas. *Nonabiding nirvāṇa* is true cessation in which the two obscurations have been extinguished, and it is possessed only by buddhas. The lower tenet systems explain nirvāṇa with and without remainder differently.
5. See His Holiness the Dalai Lama and Thubten Chodron, *Buddhism: One Teacher, Many Traditions* for an explanation of the sixteen attributes according to the Pāli tradition.
6. *Self* has two distinct meanings, depending on the context: (1) the person, someone who is a sentient being or a buddha, and (2) inherent existence, as in self-grasping ignorance.
7. Māra is the personification of hindrances and obscurations.
8. See the first four chapters of Āryadeva's *The Four Hundred* for a thorough description of the four distorted conceptions and their antidotes.
9. In both the Pāli and Sanskrit traditions, the three higher trainings of ethical conduct, concentration, and wisdom—which include the eightfold path—are

generally specified as the path to liberation. Alex Wayman notes that the four distorted conceptions and four attributes of true cessations correspond to the four distorted conceptions and four attributes of true paths. These, in turn, relate to the three higher trainings. (1) True paths lead to true cessations, which together counteract the distorted conception that nirvāṇa does not exist because true paths do not exist. (2) The higher training of concentration is a *suitable* path that leads to *peace* because it calms and focuses the mind. (3) The higher training in ethical conduct is the *accomplishment* leading to *magnificence* because realizing the nature of the mind promotes nonharmfulness. (4) The higher training in wisdom is the *way to deliverance* because it leads to *irreversible freedom*. See Alex Wayman, "The Sixteen Aspects of the Four Noble Truths and Their Opposites," *Journal of the International Association of Buddhist Studies* 3, no. 2 (1980), 73.

10. In general, when the meditative concentrations of both the form and formless realms are referred to together, they are called meditative absorptions. However, technically, *dhyāna* refers specifically to the levels of concentration in the form realm and *samāpatti* to those in the formless realm.
11. For a more detailed explanation, see Lati Rinpoche, Denma Locho Rinpoche, Leah Zahler, and Jeffrey Hopkins, *Meditative States in Tibetan Buddhism* (Somerville, MA: Wisdom Publications, 1983), 23–47.
12. Classes 29 to 25 are the Five Pure Abodes (*Śuddhāvāsa*).
13. Some say this is a separate division of the fourth dhyāna, making eighteen dhyānas; others say it is within the Great Fruit Land.
14. The Pāli tradition does not include the Increasing Merit or Cloudless in the fourth dhyāna; it does include the Unconscious Beings. Some Sanskrit versions include the Unconscious Beings, making eighteen form realm gods; others do not.
15. *Śubha* can also be translated as "pure" or "auspicious."
16. See AN 4.123 for a fuller description of the form realm.
17. The Pāli Abhidhamma says they also lack the sense of touch.
18. The *Treasury of Knowledge* explains why the Realm of Thirty-Three Devas is so-called: "There are eight wealth gods, eleven wrathful gods, twelve sun gods, and the two young sons of Ashvini. Due to there being these thirty-three principal [gods,] it is called so, or, alternatively, due to there being thirty-three residences of the gods, such as Excellent Dharma (*Sudharma*), the meeting place of the gods, and so forth, it is called so."
19. Pāli sūtras do not speak of asuras as a separate realm, but consider them as having an unfortunate rebirth. They mention asuras who are neighbors of the devas in the Land of the Thirty-Three, but often fight with them. Some Pāli commentators say asuras are in the hungry ghost realm.
20. In some texts, the order of hungry ghosts and animals is reversed.
21. The Dalai Lama, *The Meaning of Life from a Buddhist Perspective*, trans. and ed. Jeffrey Hopkins (Boston: Wisdom Publications, 1993), 7.
22. See also Artemus Engle, *Inner Science of Buddhist Practice* (Boston: Snow Lion Publications, 2009), 125–34.
23. Candrakīrti's *Commentary on Āryadeva's "Four Hundred"* (*Catuḥśatakaṭīkā*).

24. The following list shows different contexts in which the term "ignorance" is used; it is not a standard textual enumeration.
25. *Gratification* is the pleasure experienced by contact with the aggregates. *Danger* is the decay of the aggregates that leaves us disappointed. *Escape* is giving up desire for the aggregates, wisely freeing ourselves from the afflictions that bind us to duḥkha.
26. A primary consciousness has several mental factors that *accompany* or are *concomitant* with it, meaning that they share five similarities: they have the same basis, observed object, aspect, time, and entity. In this case, ignorance is a mental factor accompanying the primary mental consciousness and thus shares these five similarities with it. See *The Foundation of Buddhist Practice*, chapter 3.
27. P. *sīlabbata-parāmāsa*. The term has several different translations. In Pāli *parāmāsa* means "misapprehension." It seems the corresponding Sanskrit term may be spelled similarly to the term meaning "supreme," and thus the Tibetan term is often translated as "holding bad rules and practices as supreme."
28. "Eternalism" in Buddhist philosophy is not the same as the eternalism that is a philosophy of time.
29. Tibetan Buddhism calls these sixty-two "bad views," but does not speak of them in the context of the mental factor of wrong views. Tsongkhapa discusses these in *Illumination of the Thought* (*Dgongs pa rab gsal*).
30. This is sometimes translated as "shamelessness," referring to the lack of the good kind of shame that feels badly about our poor behavior.
31. MN 148.28 speaks of three underlying tendencies: attachment to sensuality, anger, and ignorance. MN 64.3–6 speaks of five underlying tendencies: view of a personal identity, doubt, view holding bad rules and practices, sensual desire, and malice. These five are also the five lower fetters. The *Jñānaprasthāna*—the last text in the Sarvāstivādin Abhidharma—explains ten underlying tendencies that are the same as the ten root afflictions in the Sanskrit tradition.
32. See Padmanabh S. Jaini, "*Smṛti* in the Abhidharma Literature and Development of Buddhist Accounts of Memory of the Past," in *In the Mirror of Memory: Reflections on Mindfulness and Remembrance in Indian and Tibetan Buddhism*, ed. Janet Gyatso (Albany: State University of New York Press, 1992), 47–60. Also see Collett Cox, "The Sarvāstivādin Path of Removing Defilements," in *Paths to Liberation: The Marga and Its Transformations in Buddhist Thought*, ed. Robert E. Buswell Jr. and Robert M. Gimello (Honolulu: Kuroda Institute / University of Hawaii Press, 1992), 70–72.
33. Origin and disappearance refer to their transient nature. Gratification is the attraction or enjoyment we have, danger is the unpleasant consequences that come from afflictive involvement, and escape is the freedom we wish to attain.
34. The *Treasury of Knowledge* contains two other categories of defilements that overlap with these twenty. The *ten full entanglements* (*pāryavasthāna*) are: (1–2) Lack of integrity and inconsideration for others interfere with ethical conduct. (3–4) Jealousy (being mentally upset by another's success) and miserliness (possessiveness that opposes giving Dharma, possessions, and skills) are inconsistent

with benefiting others. (5) Restlessness is agitation. (6–7) Regret and lethargy are inconsistent with concentration. (8) Sleep is the gathering in of the mind that leaves one incapable of controlling the body. Sleep and regret are full entanglements only when they are afflictive. In the *Compendium of Knowledge* regret and sleep are listed as variable mental factors because they may accompany virtuous mental states. (9) Wrath includes all types of anger directed at sentient beings and inanimate objects (except malice and harmfulness). (10) Concealment is hiding disgraceful behavior.

The *six stains* (*mala*) are: (1–2) Pretension (misleading others) and deceit (crookedness of mind that leads to acting in a distorted manner) are forms of dishonesty. (3) Haughtiness is smug complacency. (4) Spite is holding firmly to disgraceful behavior and not accepting good advice. (5) Resentment is continued animosity. (6) Harmfulness is cruelty that injures others with weapons or harsh words.

35. According to Asaṅga, the definitions of pretention and deceit are reversed.
36. Bhikkhu Bodhi differentiates these two, saying that the auxiliary affliction of arrogance is a manifest affliction, whereas the underlying tendency of arrogance is an unmanifest potential or seed that will become a manifest affliction when provocative circumstances are encountered. Personal correspondence.
37. After speaking of the pollutants, Vasubandhu addresses the floods (*ogha*) and yokes (*yoga*), saying they are four in number: attachment, existence, ignorance, and views. They are called *floods* because they carry us away to rebirth in saṃsāra. They are called *yokes* because they tie us to rebirth in saṃsāra. He does not include views as a pollutant because the pollutants establish us in saṃsāra, whereas views alone, without being associated with other afflictions, are not sufficient to do this.
38. View of extremes holds the aggregates to be either eternal or nonexistent. According to the Vaibhāṣika and Sautrāntika schools, when one attains nirvāṇa without remainder, the aggregates cease to exist, so there is no person who actually possesses this type of nirvāṇa because without the aggregates, a person cannot exist. Since one part of view of extremes holds the aggregates to be nonexistent and accords with the above way of defining nirvāṇa without remainder, this view is neutral, not nonvirtuous.
39. See *The Foundation of Buddhist Practice*, chapter 3.
40. Here we note a difference between true origins, which include karma, and afflictive obscurations, which do not. True origins are the source of all types of duḥkha; afflictive obscurations are what must be overcome to attain liberation. Once afflictions are overcome, the karma causing rebirth can no longer ripen.
41. The Pāli tradition does not set out five paths, as does the Sanskrit tradition. It speaks of seeing and meditation, but not the path of seeing or the path of meditation.
42. Cittamātrins have a complex presentation of seeds and latencies and how they produce both the object and the consciousness cognizing it. This explanation will be saved for a later volume in the series.
43. The Tibetan word *nang wa* can be translated as either "appearance" or "perception." "Appearance of inherent existence" makes it seem that the problem is on the object's side—that phenomena appear inherently existent. However, the problem

is actually on the subject's side—the mind is obscured and perceives things as if they were inherently existent. But "perceive" is not exactly the right word either, because it implies direct perception, and inherent existence also appears to conceptual consciousnesses.

44. Vaibhāṣikas are an exception to this. Their position differs from that of the Prāsaṅgikas with whom we are now concerned.
45. These were described while commenting on the meaning of *dhammatā*, the nature of things, in DN 14.
46. This and other examples from DN 14 are commonly given in the ancient commentaries. More research needs to be done on the meaning of dharma causality. Bhikkhu Bodhi speculates that it may include the causality of progressing on the path, with one realization being the cause of the next.
47. See Leti Sayadaw, *The Niyama-dipani: The Manual of Cosmic Order*, http://mahajana.net/texts/kopia_lokalna/MANUAL04.html.
48. *Pratītyasamutpāda* is translated as "dependent origination" when speaking about the twelve links and as "dependent arising" when speaking of the broader sense in which all phenomena are dependent and therefore empty of true existence.
49. The length of a moment varies according to the context from the tiniest nanosecond to the length of time to complete something to a lifetime. Here it refers to the length of time it takes for first-link ignorance to cause second-link formative action.
50. Geshe Lhundrup Sopa, with David Patt, *Steps on the Path to Enlightenment: A Commentary on Tsongkhapa's Lamrim Chenmo*, vol. 2, *Karma* (Boston: Wisdom Publications, 2005), 326.
51. Chim Jampalyang, *Ornament of Abhidharma: A Commentary on Vasubandhu's Abhidharmako'sa*, trans. Ian James Coghlan (Somerville, MA: Wisdom Publications, 2019), 411.
52. The bardo may last up to forty-nine days. If a new rebirth has not been found, at the end of each week there is a mini-death at which time it is possible for a new karma to ripen.
53. Pāli Abhidhamma commentaries say that in the moment just after the cessation of the rebirth-linking consciousness, the same type of consciousness apprehending the same object continues uninterruptedly when there is no cognitive process, until the arising of death consciousness. This consciousness is called the life-continuum. According to a more detailed explanation, the bhavaṅga follows immediately after the rebirth-linking consciousness and is a product of the same karma that produced the rebirth-linking consciousness. The bhavaṅga is a deep, underlying consciousness that accounts for the continuity of mind coming from the living being in the previous life. It is not a continuous consciousness, an independent consciousness, or a permanent self; it arises and passes away in each micro-moment. During the lifetime, the bhavaṅga arises whenever there isn't a cognitive process, maintaining the continuity of mind. At the end of life, the life-continuum becomes the death consciousness. After death, the rebirth-linking consciousness and so forth of another set of twelve links occur. In this way,

the mindstream (P. *cittasantāna*) flows on from conception until death and from death to the new birth, revolving like the wheel of a cart (CMA 228).

54. In other contexts "name" includes consciousness and refers to the mind as a whole.
55. This is from the Sūtra viewpoint. From the Tantric perspective, beings in the formless realm still have a very subtle body—the subtlest wind that is one nature with the subtlest mind.
56. This is according to Chim Jampalyang's commentary on the *Treasury of Knowledge*.
57. See LC 1:311–12.
58. These seven are the mental contemplations of a mere beginner, individual knowledge of the character, belief, thorough isolation, withdrawal or joy, analysis, and final training. Sometimes an eighth contemplation, the mental contemplation of the result of final training, is listed. This is the actual dhyāna or meditative absorption.
59. Daniel Cozort, *Unique Tenets of the Middle Way Consequence School* (Ithaca, NY: Snow Lion Publications, 1998), 182.
60. The Pāli tradition prescribes the eightfold path as the remedy to cyclic existence.
61. Among the eighteen early schools the Sarvāstivāda, which later became influential in Tibet, asserted an intermediate state between one life and the next. The Theravāda commentarial tradition rejected this, saying that the consciousness separates from one body and in the very next moment the rebirth consciousness takes place in the new existence. Nevertheless, there is mention in the Pāli sūtras of the "being to be reborn," or *gandhabba* (MN 38.26 and MN 93.18). The Pāli sūtras do not explain the meaning of gandhabba, but treat it as if the listeners already understood its meaning. Buddhaghoṣa explained a gandhabba as a being who is going to be reborn—that is, the consciousness of a being who has passed away that is in a condition suitable for taking rebirth. In the case of a human birth, the gandhabba will be born as the child of two parents with whom it has a karmic connection.

    In other contexts, gandhabba refers to semi-divine spirits inhabiting forests and plants or to a type of celestial musician.
62. Geshe Yeshe Tabkhye, "Dependent Arising, the King of Reasons Used to Distinguish the Ontological Status of All Things," trans. Geshe Damdul Namgyal and Joshua W. C. Cutler, unpublished manuscript. This essay on dependent arising acts as an introduction to Kamalaśīla's commentary on the *Rice Seedling Sūtra*, which Geshe Thabkhe translated into Hindi.
63. The sūtra's Tibetan title is *Yod pa nyid la sogs pa'i bye brag rnam par 'byad pa zhes bya ba'i chos kyi rnam grangs kyi mdo*. The sūtra passage is cited in *Vasubandhu's Explanation of the Divisions of the First Factor of Dependent Arising* (DK, vol. *chi*, 5a, 4.xz; the citation is from Geshe Thabkhe's unpublished manuscript, "Dependent Arising").
64. Excerpt from Geshe Thabkhe's unpublished manuscript, "Dependent Arising."
65. See *The Foundation of Buddhist Practice*, chapter 2, for an explanation of reliable and unreliable awarenesses.
66. There is discussion regarding to what extent this joy is physical, because input from the five senses is subdued as concentration deepens.

67. Usually joy is said to accompany the first dhyāna, although here it arises before the attainment of access concentration, which is prior to the first dhyāna.
68. An exception is someone who followed the śrāvaka or solitary realizer path to arhatship, later entered the Mahāyāna, and is on the bodhisattva path of accumulation or preparation.
69. Jeffrey Hopkins, *Maps of the Profound* (Ithaca, NY: Snow Lion Publications, 2003), 692.
70. John Ireland, *The Udāna and the Itivuttaka* (Kandy: Buddhist Publication Society, 2007), 200.
71. A difficulty arises in speaking of nirvāṇa with remainder in this way. In the lifetime that they attain liberation, arhats may be beings in the desire, form, or formless realm. Clearly those in the desire and form realms have polluted bodies. Arhats in the formless realm have only four mental aggregates, so we cannot say their bodies are polluted. Saying their mental aggregates are polluted is awkward because their mindstreams are temporarily free from afflictions owing to their deep concentration. Thus it is a bit difficult to posit an illustration or an example of the polluted aggregates of formless-realm arhats. On the other hand, it is difficult to say that they have *no* polluted aggregates, because they have nirvāṇa with remainder in their continuums.
72. Espousing three final vehicles, Cittamātra Scriptural Proponents do not assert that arhats directed exclusively to their own personal peace enter the Mahāyāna. However, they say that an arhat whose liberation is transformed can enter the Mahāyāna and attain buddhahood. He makes this transition from nirvāṇa with remainder; it cannot occur from nirvāṇa without remainder because the continuity of mind has ceased at that time.
73. This and the two citations below from the Udāna were translated by Thanissaro Bhikkhu.
74. Pāli commentaries say that all āryas from stream-enterers on up can gain access to this state. However, some people say that there doesn't seem to be evidence for this position in the sūtras: according to the sūtras, arhats alone can enter this samādhi.
75. Bhikkhu Bodhi, personal correspondence, August 6, 2017.
76. This is another case of the name of the result being given to the cause. His Holiness gave another example: A commentary to the *Ornament* refers to great compassion as the Bhagawati—the one who is completely subdued—indicating the Buddha. In fact, great compassion is neither full awakening nor the one who is completely subdued. Rather, the name of the result—Bhagawati—is being given to the cause—compassion—because great compassion is an essential cause of buddhahood.
77. Questions that spark much debate arise: What does it mean for a consciousness to exist or be present? If the clear light mind exists but is not active while the coarse consciousnesses are manifest, is it present? There are two main views. According to one view, if a consciousness is present, it needs to be manifest. In this case, the clear light mind is present only when the coarse consciousnesses have subsided and it is manifest. But in that case, the clear light mind would not exist continuously, so how could it be the basis for saṃsāra and nirvāṇa?

According to the other view, a consciousness need not be manifest in order to be present. It may also be present in a dormant form. In this case, the clear light mind is present even when someone is going about their daily life and the coarse consciousnesses are active.

This brings up a further question: For a consciousness to exist, it must have an object, so if the innate clear light mind exists and is present while the coarse consciousnesses are manifest, what is its apprehended object? When the coarse levels of mind are active, they are dominant and are cognizing their apprehended objects. In that case, the subtler mind would be inactive and not apprehend anything. Lacking an apprehended object, how can we say that consciousness exists? On the other hand, that consciousness is the basis for saṃsāra and nirvāṇa, so how can it not exist continuously? This is a thorny topic!

Everyone agrees that when the coarse levels of mind have been absorbed, the innate clear light mind is manifest. In ordinary beings, this occurs primarily at the time of death. This subtlest clear light mind is free from afflictions because they were absorbed when the coarse minds and winds ceased functioning during the dying process. As such, unlike the coarse states of mind, this clear light mind can never be nonvirtuous or afflictive, and through tantric practice it may be transformed into virtue. This is one reason why Tantra is said to be profound.

78. Several other terms are also used in the discussion of buddha nature. In some circumstances they are used interchangeably, in others they have a slightly different meaning. In addition to the above terms, other terms include *buddha essence* (*tathāgatagarbha*, T. *bde bzhin gsegs pa'i snying po*) and *element of sentient beings* (*sattvadhātu*, T. *sems can gyi khams*), or simply *element*. *Gotra* (T. *rigs*), which is translated as *nature* or *disposition*, as in *buddha nature* or *buddha disposition*, may also be translated as *lineage*, *trait*, or *family*.
79. The Cittamātra Scriptural Proponents is the only Mahāyāna tenet school asserting that not all sentient beings can attain full awakening. Some people postulate that speaking of icchantikas is done to warn practitioners not to become lax or negligent.
80. There are different views about whether the five sense consciousnesses are included in the transforming buddha nature. Some sages say they are not, because alone the sense consciousnesses do not have the ability to accomplish the path—they are neither stable nor continuous. Only the mental consciousness can practice and realize the path. The mental consciousness leads the sense consciousnesses, which alone are blind with respect to emptiness. Others say that because the sense consciousnesses go with the mental consciousness to awakening they are part of buddha nature. The mental consciousness generates bodhicitta and realizes emptiness, so the sense consciousnesses also attain awakening.
81. These are the stages that spiritual practitioners actualize as they progress toward their spiritual goal.
82. Tsong-kha-pa Lo-sang-drak-pa, "Extensive Explanation of (Chandrakīrti's) 'Supplement to (Nāgārjuna's) "Treatise on the Middle"': Illumination of the Thought," trans. Jeffrey Hopkins, unpublished manuscript.

83. Both Cittamātrins and Mādhyamikas agree that afflictions are adventitious, but they differ in explaining how they are adventitious. This affects their explanations of the clear light mind. Cittamātrins say the clarity and cognizance that are hallmarks of the conventional nature of the mind constitute the buddha nature. Because mental factors come and go while the nature of the mind remains clear and cognizant, they say the afflictions are not an inherent property of the mind. Nāgārjuna and the Prāsaṅgikas assert that because the mind is primordially pure of inherent existence, the afflictions derived from self-grasping ignorance are not an inherent property of mind. In short, whereas the Cittamātrins explain the undefiled nature of the clear light mind from the viewpoint of its conventional nature, Nāgārjuna does so from the viewpoint of its ultimate nature.
84. The ground of the latencies of ignorance is subtle motivational effort that instigates physical, verbal, and mental actions and is the cause of unpolluted karma. Created only by āryas, unpolluted karma produces the mental bodies of śrāvaka and solitary realizer arhats and of ārya bodhisattvas.
85. Gyaltsap Darma Rinchen, "The Tathāgata Essence," trans. Gavin Kilty, unpublished manuscript, 170.
86. Unnumbered introductory verse, translated by Geshe Thupten Jinpa, 2007.
87. This cloth, also called "stone wool," is woven asbestos. It is cleaned by placing it in fire, which burns the dirt, leaving a sparkling clean cloth.
88. William Magee, "A Tree in the West: Competing Tathāgatagarbha Theories in Tibet," *Chung-Hwa Buddhist Journal* 19 (2006), 482.
89. Magee, "A Tree in the West," 482.

Glossary

abstract composites (*viprayukta-saṃskāra*). Impermanent phenomena that are neither forms nor consciousnesses.

access concentration. Serenity, which arises when the five hindrances have been suppressed.

affirmative phenomenon. A phenomenon realized by means of not eliminating an object of negation.

affirming negative (*paryudāsapratiṣedha*, T. *ma yin dgag*). A negative where, upon an awareness eliminating a negated object, another phenomenon is suggested or established.

afflictions (*kleśa*). Mental factors that disturb the tranquility of the mind; these include disturbing emotions and wrong views.

afflictive obscurations (*kleśāvaraṇa*). Obscurations that mainly prevent liberation; afflictions and their seeds.

aggregates (*skandha*). The four or five components that make up a living being: form (except for beings born in the formless realm), feelings, discriminations, miscellaneous factors, and consciousnesses.

apprehended object (*muṣṭibandhaviṣaya*, T. *'dzin stangs kyi yul*). The main object with which the mind is concerned—that is, the object that the mind is getting at or understands. Synonymous with *engaged object.*

arhat. Someone who has eliminated all afflictive obscurations and attained liberation.

ārya. Someone who has directly and nonconceptually realized the emptiness of inherent existence.

ātman. A permanent, unitary, independent self, as asserted by non-Buddhists.

awakening (*samyaksaṃbodhi*). Buddhahood; the state in which all obscurations have been abandoned and all excellent qualities developed limitlessly.

bardo (*antarābhava*). The intermediate state between one life and the next.

basis of designation. The collection of parts or factors in dependence on which an object is designated.

bodhicitta. A main mental consciousness induced by an aspiration to bring about the welfare of others and accompanied by an aspiration to attain full awakening oneself.

bodhisattva. Someone who has spontaneous bodhicitta.

buddha nature (buddha disposition, T. *sangs rgyas kyi rigs*). A phenomenon that is suitable to transform into a buddha's exalted body; sentient beings' potential to become fully awakened.

causal or initial motivation (*hetu-samutthāna*). The first motivation to do an action.

causally concordant behavioral result. Karmic result in which our action is similar to an action we did in a previous life.

causally concordant experiential result. Karmic result in which we experience circumstances similar to what we caused others to experience.

causally concordant result. The karmic result that corresponds to its cause. It is of two types: the result similar to the cause in terms of our experience and the result similar to the cause in terms of our habitual behavior.

Cittamātra (*Yogācāra*). A Buddhist tenet system that asserts the true existence of dependent natures but does not assert external objects.

clear light (*prabhāsvara*). The clear and cognizant nature of the conventional mind is the subject clear light. The emptiness of the mind is the object clear light.

cognitive faculty (*indriya*). The subtle material in the gross sense organ that enables perception of sense objects; for the mental consciousness, it is previous moments of any of the six consciousnesses.

cognitive obscurations (*jñeyāvaraṇa*). Obscurations that mainly prevent full awakening; the latencies of ignorance and the subtle dualistic view that they give rise to.

collection of merit (*puṇyasaṃbhāra*). The practices of generosity and so forth—the method aspect of the path—motivated by bodhicitta and informed by the wisdom realizing emptiness that bears the result of buddhahood.

conceived object (T. *zhen yul*). The object conceived by a conceptual consciousness; synonymous with the *apprehended* or *engaged object* of a conceptual consciousness.

conceptual appearance (*artha-sāmānya*). A mental image of an object that appears to a conceptual consciousness.

conceptual consciousness (*kalpanā*). A consciousness knowing its object by means of a conceptual appearance.

conceptual fabrications. False modes of existence and false ideas imputed by the mind.

conceptualizations (*vikalpa viparyāsa*). Distorted concepts such as thinking impermanent things are permanent.

consciousness (*jñāna*). That which is clear and cognizant.

continuity of substance. A continuity in which one thing is the substance that transforms into another thing.

continuity of type. A continuity in which the cause and the result share similar characteristics.

conventional existence (*saṃvṛtisat*). Existence.

conventional reliable cognizer (T. *tha snyad pa'i tshad ma*). A reliable cognizer of conventionalities. It does not have the ability to perceive ultimate truths.

conventional truths (*saṃvṛtisatya*). That which is true only from the perspective of ignorance grasping true existence. They are not seen as true by an arya's meditative equipoise on emptiness. Synonymous with *veiled truths*.

cyclic existence (*saṃsāra*). The cycle of rebirth that occurs under the control of afflictions and karma.

death (*maraṇabhava*). The last moment of a lifetime when the subtlest clear light mind manifests. The moment after the consciousness leaves the body is the bardo.

definitive sūtra (*nītārtha sūtra*). Sūtras that mainly and explicitly teach ultimate truths.

demeritorious karma. Second-link nonvirtuous formative actions that create the cause for unfortunate rebirths.

dependent arising (*pratītyasamutpāda*). This is of three types: (1) causal dependence—things arising due to causes and conditions, (2) mutual dependence—phenomena existing in relation to other phenomena, and (3) dependent designation—phenomena existing by being merely designated by terms and concepts.

desire realm (*kāmadhātu*). One of the three realms of cyclic existence; the realm where sentient beings are overwhelmed by attraction to and desire for sense objects.

deva. A being born as a heavenly being in the desire realm or in one of the meditative absorptions of the form or formless realms.

dhāraṇī. An intelligible phrase that encapsulates the essence of a teaching.

dharmakāya. See *truth body*.

dhyāna. Meditative stabilization in the form realm; full concentration where not only are the five hindrances suppressed but also the mind is in full meditative absorption.

direct reliable cognizer (*pratyakṣa-pramāṇa*). A nondeceptive awareness that knows its object—an evident phenomenon—directly, without depending on a reason.

disenchantment (P. *nibbidā*). Lack of interest in and detachment from phenomena conditioned by ignorance, which frees the mind from attachment.

dispassion (fading away, P. *virāga*). The path wisdom that first directly sees nirvāṇa.

distorted attention (distorted conceptions, *ayoniśo manaskāra,* T. *tshul min yid byed*). Attention that exaggerates or deprecates the characteristics of an object so that it is not known correctly. It induces conceptual proliferation (*prapañca, papañca*).

duḥkha. Unsatisfactory experiences of cyclic existence.

Dzogchen. A tantric practice emphasizing meditation on the nature of mind, practiced primarily in the Nyingma tradition.

eight worldly concerns (*aṣṭalokadharma*). Material gain and loss, disrepute and fame, blame and praise, pleasure and pain.

emanation body (*nirmāṇakāya*). The buddha body that appears as an ordinary sentient being to benefit others.

emptiness (*śūnyatā*). The lack of inherent existence and true existence.

enjoyment body (*saṃbhogakāya*). The buddha body that appears in the pure lands to teach ārya bodhisattvas.

environmental result (adhipatiphala). The result of karma that influences what environment we live in.

existent (*sat*). That which is perceivable by mind.

extreme of absolutism (eternalism, permanence, existence, *śāśvatānta*). Believing that a permanent, unitary, independent self exists or that phenomena exist inherently.

extreme of nihilism (*ucchedānta*). Believing that our actions have no ethical dimension; believing that nothing exists.

five actions of immediate retribution (*ānantaryakarman*). Killing one's mother, father, or an arhat; wounding a buddha; and causing a schism in the saṅgha.

five lower fetters. View of a personal identity, doubt, view of rules and practices, sensual desire, and malice.

form body (*rūpakāya*). The buddha body in which a buddha appears to sentient beings; it includes the emanation and enjoyment bodies.

form realm (*rūpadhātu*). The saṃsāric realm in which beings have bodies made of subtle material. Attainment of various states of concentration without the determination to be free from saṃsāra causes rebirth there.

formless realm (*ārūpyadhātu*). The saṃsāric realm in which sentient beings do not have a material body. Deep meditative absorption without the aspiration for liberation from saṃsāra causes rebirth there.

four distorted conceptions (distorted attention, *ayoniśa manaskāra*, T. *tshul min yid byed*). Thinking (1) what is impermanent is permanent, (2) what is duḥkha by nature is happiness, (3) the unattractive and foul are attractive, and (4) what lacks a self has one.

four māras. Polluted aggregates, afflictions, death, and distraction to external objects.

four seals (*caturmudrā*). Four views that make a philosophy Buddhist: all conditioned phenomena are transient, all polluted phenomena are duḥkha, all phenomena are empty and selfless, nirvāṇa alone is true peace.

four truths of the āryas (*catvāry āryasatyāni*). The truth of duḥkha, its origin, its cessation, and the path to that cessation.

fundamental innate clear light mind (T. *gnyug ma lhan cig skyes pa'i 'od gsal gyi sems*). The subtlest consciousness that has existed beginninglessly, will exist endlessly, and will go on to awakening.

Fundamental Vehicle. The path leading to the liberation of śrāvakas and solitary realizers.

gandharva (P. *gandhabba*). (1) A being (in the bardo) to be born, (2) a celestial musician.

grasping inherent existence (*svabhāvagraha*). Grasping persons and phenomena to exist truly or inherently. Synonymous with *grasping true existence*.

grasping true existence (true grasping, *satyagrāha*). Grasping persons and phenomena to exist truly or inherently.

gratification, danger, and escape. Gratification is the pleasure experienced by contact with the aggregates. Danger is the decay of the aggregates that leaves us disappointed. Escape is the freedom we wish to attain.

having-ceased (*naṣṭa*). An impermanent phenomenon that is an affirming negative and follows the ceasing or disintegration of a thing that is the past of that thing. The having-ceased of a karma has the potency to bring forth the results of that action.

hell being (*nāraka*). A being born in one of the unfortunate classes of beings who suffer intense physical pain as a result of their strong destructive karma.

highest yoga tantra (*anuttarayogatantra*). The most advanced of the four classes of tantra.

hungry ghost (*preta*). A being born in one of the unfortunate classes of beings who suffers from intense hunger and thirst.

I-grasping (*ahaṃkāra*). Conceiving and grasping the I (one's own self) as inherently existent.

ignorance (*avidyā*). A mental factor that is obscured and grasps the opposite of what exists. There are two types: ignorance regarding ultimate truth and ignorance regarding karma and its effects.

immediate motivation (*tatkṣaṇa-samutthāna*). The motivation that occurs at the time of the action.

imperceptible form (*avijñapti-rūpa*). A subtle form that is not perceivable by the sense faculties and arises only when a person has a strong intention.

impermanence (*anitya*). The transient quality of all compositional phenomena and functioning things. Coarse impermanence can be known by our senses; subtle impermanence is something not remaining the same in the very next moment.

inattentive awareness (T. *snang la ma nges*). A consciousness that doesn't ascertain its object, even though that object appears to it.

inferential reliable cognizer (*anumāna-pramāṇa*). An awareness that knows its object—slightly obscure phenomena—nondeceptively, purely in dependence on a reason.

inherent existence (*svabhāva*). Existence without depending on any other factors; independent existence. According to the Prāsaṅgika Mādhyamikas, inherent existence does not exist.

interpretable sūtra (*neyārtha sūtra*). A sūtra that speaks about the variety of phenomena and/or cannot be taken literally.

invariable karma. Second-link formative karma that is the cause for rebirth in a specific meditative absorption and no other.

karma. Intentional action; it includes intention karma (mental action) and intended karma (physical and verbal actions motivated by intention).

karmic seeds. The potency from previously created actions that will bring their results.

latencies (*vāsanā*). Predispositions, imprints, or tendencies.

liberation (*mokṣa,* T. *thar pa*). A true cessation that is the abandonment of afflictive obscurations; nirvāṇa.

liberation (*vimokṣa, vimokkha,* T. *rnam thar*). In both the Pāli and Sanskrit traditions, this refers to the eight liberations, the mind's temporary release from defilements that is brought about by mastering certain meditative skills.

liberation (*vimukti,* T. *rnam grol*). In the Pāli tradition, nirvāṇa is what is realized in the experience of liberation (*vimutti*); liberation is a conditioned event, whereas nirvāṇa is not.

Mādhyamika. A proponent of Buddhist tenets who asserts there are no truly existent phenomena.

Mahāmudrā. A type of meditation that focuses on the conventional and ultimate natures of the mind.

meditative equipoise on emptiness. An ārya's mind focused single-pointedly on the emptiness of inherent existence.

mental direct reliable cognizer. A nondeceptive mental awarenesses that knows its object by depending on another consciousness that induces it.

mental factor (*caitta*). An aspect of mind that accompanies a primary consciousness and fills out the cognition, apprehending particular attributes of the object or performing a specific function.

meritorious karma. Second-link virtuous actions that create the cause for a fortunate rebirth in the desire realm.

mind (*citta*). The part of living beings that cognizes, experiences, thinks, feels, and so on. In some contexts it is equivalent to primary consciousness.

mindstream (*cittasaṃtāna*). The continuity of mind.

mine-grasping (*mamakāra*). Conceiving and grasping mine—what makes something mine—as inherently existent.

monastic. Someone who has received monastic ordination; a monk or nun.

Mount Meru. A huge mountain at the center of our world system, according to ancient Indian cosmology.

natural nirvāṇa (*prakṛti-nirvṛta*). The primordial emptiness of inherent existence of the mind.

naturally abiding buddha nature (*prakṛtisthagotra*, T. *rang bzhin gnas rigs*). The emptiness of the mind that is not yet freed from defilements.

nature truth body (*svabhāvika dharmakāya*). The buddha body that is the emptiness of a buddha's mind and the true cessations of that buddha.

New Translation schools. The Kagyu, Sakya, and Geluk traditions that formed in Tibet beginning in the eleventh century, after the decimation of the Dharma during the reign of King Langdarma (r. 838–41).

nirvāṇa (P. *nibbāna*). The state of liberation of an arhat; the purified aspect of a mind that is free from afflictions.

nirvāṇa with remainder (*sopadhiśeṣanirvāṇa*). (1) An arhat's nirvāṇa with the remainder of the polluted body while an arhat is still alive. (2) Prāsaṅgikas: an arhat's nirvāṇa in postmeditation time when the appearance of inherent existence still remains.

nirvāṇa without remainder (*nirupadhiśeṣanirvāṇa*). (1) An arhat's nirvāṇa without the remainder of the polluted body, attained after an arhat passes away. (2) Prāsaṅgikas: an arhat's nirvāṇa while in meditative equipoise on emptiness where no appearance of inherent existence remains.

nonabiding nirvāṇa (*apratiṣṭha-nirvāṇa*). A buddha's nirvāṇa that does not abide in either cyclic existence or personal liberation.

nonaffirming negative (*prasajyapratiṣedha*, T. *med dgag*). A negative phenomenon in which, upon the explicit elimination of the negated object by an awareness, another phenomenon is not suggested or established.

nonreturner (*anāgāmi*). The third level of a Fundamental Vehicle ārya who will no longer be born in the desire realm.

object of negation (*pratiṣedhya*, T. *dgag bya*). What is to be refuted—for example, a self-sufficient substantially existent I or inherent existence.

observed object (*ālambana*, T. *dmig yul*). The basic object that the mind refers to or focuses on while apprehending certain aspects of that object.

once-returner (*sakṛdāgāmin*). The second level of a Fundamental Vehicle ārya who, in addition to eliminating three of the five lower fetters, has subdued sensual attachment and malice to a certain degree and will only be born in the desire realm one more time before attaining arhatship.

ordinary beings (*pṛthagjana, puthujjana*). Sentient beings who have not realized emptiness directly and are not āryas.

parinirvāṇa. The nirvāṇa after death attained when an arhat or buddha dies.

perceptible form (*vijñapti-rūpa*). Forms that can be perceived by the sense faculties.

permanent (*nitya*). Unchanging, static. It does not mean eternal. Permanent phenomena do not depend on causes and conditions.

permanent, unitary, independent self. A soul or self (*ātman*) asserted by non-Buddhists.

person (*pudgala*). A living being designated in dependence on the four or five aggregates.

polluted (*āsava*). Under the influence of ignorance and its latencies.

Prāsaṅgika. The Buddhist philosophical tenet system whose views are most accurate.

prātimokṣa. The different sets of ethical precepts for monastics and lay followers that assist in attaining liberation.

primary consciousness (*vijñāna*). A consciousness that apprehends the presence or basic entity of an object, which are of six types: visual, auditory, olfactory, gustatory, tactile, and mental.

pure grounds. The eighth, ninth, and tenth bodhisattva grounds. These bodhisattvas have eliminated all afflictive obscurations.

pure land. Places created by the unshakable resolve and merit of buddhas where all external conditions are conducive for Dharma practice.

reliable cognizer (*pramāṇa*). A nondeceptive awareness that is incontrovertible with respect to its apprehended object and that enables us to accomplish our purpose.

reliable cognizer based on authoritative testimony. An inferential cognizer knowing very obscure phenomena that cannot be established through direct perceivers or other inferential reliable cognizers but only by depending on the authoritative testimony of a trustworthy source, such as a credible person or scripture.

rigpa. According to Dzogchen, an undefiled, subtle consciousness that pervades all mental states. It is comparable to the fundamental innate mind of clear light in the New Translation schools.

ripening result of karma. The karmic result that is a rebirth; the five aggregates a being takes.

Sautrāntika. A Buddhist tenet school that espouses Fundamental Vehicle tenets and asserts both external objects and apperception to be truly existent. It is considered higher than the Vaibhāṣika school.

self (*ātman*). Refers to a person or to inherent existence.

self-grasping (*ātmagrāha*). Grasping inherent existence.

self-sufficient substantially existent person (T. *gang zag rang rkya thub pa'i rdzas yod*). A self that is the controller of the body and mind. Such a self does not exist.

sense faculty. The subtle material in the gross sense organ (eye, ear, nose, tongue, and body) that enables perception of sense objects.

sentient being (*sattva*). Any being with a mind, except for a buddha.

serenity (*śamatha*). A concentration arising from meditation and accompanied by the bliss of mental and physical pliancy in which the mind abides effortlessly without fluctuation for as long as we wish on whichever virtuous object it has been placed.

six perfections (*ṣaḍpāramitā*). The practices of generosity, ethical conduct, fortitude, joyous effort, meditative stability, and wisdom that are motivated by bodhicitta.

solitary realizer (*pratyekabuddha*). A person following the Fundamental Vehicle who seeks liberation and who emphasizes understanding the twelve links of dependent arising.

space particle. Subtle particles that bear traces of the other four elements and are the source of all matter. They persist during the dormant stage between one world system and the next and act as the substantial cause for the coarser elements that arise during the evolution of the next world system.

śrāvaka (hearer). Someone practicing the Fundamental Vehicle path leading to arhatship who emphasizes meditation on the four truths of the āryas.

stream-enterer (*srotāpanna*). The first level of a Fundamental Vehicle ārya who has eliminated three of the five lower fetters.

substantial cause. Whatever is the main thing that turns into a result. For example, wood is the substantial cause of a table; the carpenter is a cooperative condition.

subtlest mind-wind. The indivisible subtlest mind and subtlest wind that is its mount.

suchness. Emptiness.

superknowledge (*abhijñā*). Special powers gained through having deep states of concentration.

supreme dharma stage of the path of preparation. The fourth and last stage of the path of preparation. At this time, one is an ordinary being. After this, one becomes an ārya.

syllogism (*prayoga*). A statement consisting of a subject, predicate, and reason, and in many cases an example.

tathāgata. A buddha.

tathāgatagarbha (buddha essence). Its general meaning is buddha nature; sentient beings' potential to become fully awakened.

transforming buddha nature (*samudānītagotra,* T. *rgyas 'gyur gi rigs*). Any mind that is not freed from defilements, whose continuity goes on to awakening, and that serves as the basis for the emptiness that is the naturally abiding buddha nature.

true cessation (*nirodhasatya*). The cessation of a portion of afflictions or a portion of cognitive obscurations.

true existence (*satyasat*). Existence having its own mode of being; existence having its own reality. According to the Mādhyamikas, true existence does not exist.

truth body (*dharmakāya*). The buddha body that includes the nature truth body (the emptiness of a buddha's mind) and the wisdom truth body (omniscient mind).

twelve links of dependent arising. A system of twelve factors that explains how we take rebirth in saṃsāra and how we can be liberated from it.

ultimate analysis. A probing awareness seeking an object's ultimate mode of existence.

ultimate truth (*paramārthasatya*). The ultimate mode of existence of all persons and phenomena; emptiness; objects that are true and appear true to their main cognizer.

unfortunate states (*apāya*). Unfortunate states of rebirth as a hell being, hungry ghost, or animal.

union of serenity and insight on emptiness. A meditative concentration on emptiness in which analytical meditation has induced special pliancy and serenity.

unpolluted (*anāsrava*). Not under the influence of ignorance.

unreliable awareness. An awareness that does not correctly apprehend its object and cannot help us accomplish our purpose. These include correct assumers, inattentive perceivers, doubt, and wrong awarenesses.

Vaibhāṣika. A Buddhist tenet school that espouses Fundamental Vehicle tenets, does not accept apperception, and asserts external objects to be truly established. It is considered the lowest tenet school.

veiled truths (*saṃvṛtisatya*). Objects that appear true to ignorance; objects that appear to exist inherently to their main cognizer, although they do not. Synonymous with *conventional truths*.

view of a personal identity (view of the transitory collection, *satkāya-dṛṣṭi*). Grasping an inherently existent I or mine (according to the Prāsaṅgika system).

white appearance, red increase, and black near attainment. Three subtle minds that manifest after coarser minds have absorbed and before the subtlest clear light mind arises.

wisdom truth body (*jñāna dharmakāya*). The buddha body that is a buddha's omniscient mind.

wrong or erroneous consciousness (*viparyaya-jñāna*). An awareness that is erroneous with respect to its apprehended object and, in the case of conceptual cognizers, with respect to its conceived object; a consciousness that cannot certify its object.

yogic direct reliable cognizers. Nondeceptive mental consciousnesses that know their objects by depending on a union of serenity and insight.

Further Reading

Bodhi, Bhikkhu. *The Noble Eightfold Path: Way to the End of Suffering.* Onalaska, WA: Pariyatti Publishing, 1994.

———. *Transcendental Dependent Arising.* Kandy: Buddhist Publication Society, 1980.

Chodron, Thubten. *Don't Believe Everything You Think.* Ithaca, NY: Snow Lion Publications, 2012.

———. *Open Heart, Clear Mind.* Ithaca, NY: Snow Lion Publications, 1990.

Dunne, John. *Foundations of Dharmakīrti's Philosophy.* Boston: Wisdom Publications, 2004.

Dza Patrul Rinpoche. *Words of My Perfect Teacher.* Boston: Shambhala Publications, 1998.

Gyaltsap Darma Rinchen. *The Sublime Continuum Super-Commentary (Theg pa chen po rgyud bla ma'i tikka) with the Sublime Continuum Treatise Commentary (Mahayanottaratantasastravyakhya; Theg pa chen po rgyud bla ma'i bstan bcos rnam par bshad pa)* by Maitreyanātha and Aryasaṅga. Translation and introduction by Marty Bo Jiang. New York: American Institute of Buddhist Studies, Columbia University Press, 2017.

Gyatso, Lobsang. *The Four Noble Truths.* Ithaca, NY: Snow Lion Publications, 1994.

Gyatso, Tenzin, Bhiksu, His Holiness the Fourteenth Dalai Lama. *Beyond Religion.* New York: Houghton Mifflin Harcourt, 2011.

———. *Buddha Heart, Buddha Mind: Living the Four Noble Truths.* New York: Crossroad, 2013.

———. *The Four Noble Truths.* London: Thorsons, 1997.

———. *How to See Yourself as You Really Are.* New York: Atria Books, 2007.

———. *The Meaning of Life: Buddhist Perspective on Cause and Effect.*

Translated and edited by Jeffrey Hopkins. Boston: Wisdom Publications, 2000.

———. *The Wheel of Life: Buddhist Perspectives on Cause and Effect*. Somerville, MA: Wisdom Publications, 2015.

———. *The World of Tibetan Buddhism*. Boston: Wisdom Publications, 1995.

Gyatso, Tenzin, Bhiksu, His Holiness the Fourteenth Dalai Lama, and Thubten Chodron. *Buddhism: One Teacher, Many Traditions*. Boston: Wisdom Publications, 2014.

Ireland, John. *The Udāna and the Itivuttaka*. Kandy: Buddhist Publication Society, 2007.

Lati Rinpochey, and Elizabeth Napper. *Mind in Tibetan Buddhism*. Ithaca, NY: Snow Lion Publications, 1986.

Maitreya, Arya, and Jamgon Kongtrul. *Buddha Nature: The Mahāyāna Uttaratantra Shastra with Commentary*. Ithaca, NY: Snow Lion Publications, 2000.

Reat, Ross, trans. *The Śālistamba Sūtra*. Delhi: Motilal Banarsidass, 1998.

Rinchen, Geshe Sonam, and Ruth Sonam. *How Karma Works: The Twelve Links of Dependent-Arising*. Ithaca, NY: Snow Lion Publications, 2006.

———. *The Three Principal Aspects of the Path*. Ithaca, NY: Snow Lion Publications, 1999.

Sopa, Geshe Lhundub, with James Blumenthal. *Steps on the Path to Enlightenment: A Commentary on Tsongkhapa's Lamrim Chenmo*, vol. 4, *Samatha*. Boston: Wisdom Publications, 2016.

Sopa, Geshe Lhundup, with Beth Newman. *Steps on the Path to Enlightenment: A Commentary on Tsongkhapa's Lamrim Chenmo*, vol. 3, *The Way of the Bodhisattva*. Boston: Wisdom Publications, 2008.

Sopa, Geshe Lhundup, and David Patt. *Steps on the Path to Enlightenment: A Commentary on Tsongkhapa's Lamrim Chenmo*, vol. 1, *The Foundation Practices*. Boston: Wisdom Publications, 2004.

Sopa, Geshe Lhundup, with Dechen Rochard. *Steps on the Path to Enlightenment: A Commentary on Tsongkhapa's Lamrim Chenmo*, vol. 5, *Insight*. Boston: Wisdom Publications, 2017.

Tegchok, Geshe Jampa. *Practical Ethics and Profound Emptiness: A Commentary on Nagarjuna's Precious Garland of Advice to a King*. Boston: Wisdom Publications, 2017.

———. *Transforming Adversity into Joy and Courage*. Ithaca, NY: Snow Lion Publications, 2005.

Tsering, Geshe Tashi. *The Four Noble Truths*. Boston: Wisdom Publications, 2005.

Wangchuk, Tsering. *The "Uttaratantra" in the Land of Snows: Tibetan Thinkers Debate the Centrality of the Buddha Nature Treatise*. Albany: State University of New York Press, 2017.

Index

A

Abhayākaragupta, 326
Abhidammattha Saṅgaha, 270
Abhidhamma, Pāli
  on anger, feelings accompanying, 109
  on birth, 189
  on form realm, 344n17
  on pollutants, 98–99
  on rebirth-linking consciousness, 170, 347n53
  on underlying tendencies, 88, 89, 90
Abhidharma, 67, 141, 144, 145, 345n31
Abhirati, 44
absolutism. *See* extreme of absolutism
abstract composites (*viprayukta-saṃskāra*), 90, 127, 128, 132, 259
access concentration, 242–43, 349n67
addictions, 58, 60, 240
affirmative phenomena, 132
affirming negative, 262–63
afflictions, xiv, 11, 123
  abandonment of, views on, 125
  as adventitious, 136, 279–80, 281, 283, 324, 351n83
  as antidote to afflictions, 117
  as beginningless, 135–36, 280
  bondage of, 49–50
  choosing most problematic, 113–14
  coarse, 31, 75, 116, 126, 241, 305
  control by, 26, 56
  correct attitude toward, 63–64
  counterforces to, 35, 114–16
  definitions of, 64–65
  duḥkha and, 20, 21, 22–23, 48
  eighty-four thousand, 65–66, 101, 307
  emptiness/wisdom in, clarification of, 299, 330–31, 333, 334, 335
  as enemies, 119–20, 121
  ethical dimensions of, 110–11
  identifying, 112–13
  and ignorance, relationship between, 63, 73, 75, 101, 103, 156, 345n26
  as illusory, 121
  immediate motivation for, 163
  initial practice with, advice for, 115–16
  innate and acquired, 31, 124–25, 128, 306, 308
  lists of, 65–66
  manifest and seed forms of, 127–28
  misconceptions about, 36
  nature of, variant views on, 106
  in Pāli and Sanskrit traditions, comparisons of, 88–89, 94, 96, 345n31
  as primary in true origins, 123
  principal factors causing, 106–8
  in pure land, 258
  releasing, 232
  sequential development of, 104–6
  subtle, 32, 75, 126
  three principle, 64 (*see also* three poisons)
  in twelve links, 193, 194
  two facets of, 283
  See also latencies; root afflictions; seeds, afflictive
afflictive obscurations, 259

of āryas, 161
of bodhisattvas, 257
to buddha nature, 307, 308
karma and, 123, 346n40
manifest afflictions and seeds as, 127–28
purification of, 130
relinquishment of, 9, 15, 293
on śrāvaka path, 255, 262, 264, 265, 349n71
afflictive views, xvi, 66, 77, 86, 88, 98, 109
aggregates
arrogance and, 71, 72
clinging to, 10, 12, 53–54, 182, 343n1
craving for, 255
at death, 190
dependent nature of, 237
disenchantment with, 245
distorted conceptions about, 50
emptiness of, 23–25
four of formless realm, 41
fourth, seeds and latencies in, 132
grasping as inherently existent, 162
ignorance and, 74–75, 345n25
impermanence of, 21–22, 244
knowledge and vision of, 243, 244
as lacking inherent existence, 206–8
name and form in, 170–71
in nirvāṇa with and without remainder, 9, 264, 265, 293, 346n38, 349n71
perishing, view of (*see* view of personal identity)
pliancy and, 241
realms of existence and, 41
rebirth and, 10
as resultant rebirth renewed existence, 187
ripening of (*see* ripening result of karma)
self and, 6, 14, 25, 26, 27, 56, 57, 97, 159, 160
as selfless, 25–26
six cognitive faculties in, 172
specific I of, 332–33
suffering of, 12, 13–14, 53–54, 191
as supreme, erroneous view of, 82
as unsatisfactory by nature (*duḥkhatā*), 22–23, 24, 48, 49
aging, 187, 221
birth as cause of, 188
control of, 103
suffering of, 13, 48, 53, 54, 56, 58
uses of term, 189
aging or death (*jarāmaraṇa*), 190–91
Akaniṣṭha, 42, 44
Ākāśagarbha Sūtra, 131
Akṣobhya Buddha, 44, 258
altruistic motivation, 3, 164, 218. *See also* bodhicitta
Amitābha Buddha, 44, 167, 258
analogies and metaphors
amputation of hands and feet, 249
asbestos cloth and dirt, 280, 321, 351n87
bubbles, 64
climate, 287
clouds in sky, 100
dark room, seeing clearly in, 104
delicious but poisonous drink, 179
Dharma as medicine, 1–3, 39, 40, 121
elephant in thatch house, 155
flames, 9, 206, 270–71
flight of birds, 256
four great elements, 171
homeless shelter, 307
house, designing and moving in, 150
incarceration, 217
leper, 223–24
log burning to ashes, 333–34
master and servant, 103
mirage, 207
mirror, appearance in, 205
moon reflected in water, 205
for nirvāṇa, 272
plantain tree trunk, 64
rope as snake, mistaking, 104, 160
rosary, 327
Santa Claus, 245
seal on wax, 206
seed and sprout, 213, 214
seeds, 7, 29

for self and body, relationship between, 80–81
sky lotus, 212
smell of onions, 259
still lake on cloudless night, 242
sun, 54
thieves masquerading as friends, 63–64
two sticks leaning on each other, 170
two-pointed needle, sewing with, 76
volcano, 54
water drop in ocean, 131–32
weary traveler, 242
woodcutter, 243
See also nine similes for buddha nature
analysis, 58, 102–3, 108, 207, 208, 220, 243, 244
Ānanda, 67–68, 117, 118, 188–89, 270
anger, 64
abandonment of, 125
antidote to, 115
arising of, 107
auxiliary afflictions of, 92, 93–94
depression and, 102
destruction of roots of virtue by, 131–32
feelings accompanying, 109
fetter of, 98
as grasping to inherent existence, 161–62
identifying, 113, 114
innate and acquired, 124
karma and, 48, 54
manifest and seeds of, 127–28
nonvirtue of, 68
objects and forms of, 69–70
as obscuration to buddha nature, 304, 308
physical and mental feelings and, 50–51
physical sensations and, 106, 113
questioning logic of, 65
repressed, 128
righteous, 113
strength of, 100
subtle, 75
twelve links and, 197
underlying tendency of, 89, 91, 345n31
See also animosity
animal realm, 45, 46, 47, 166, 187, 189, 257, 307, 344n20
animal sacrifice, 82, 184
animosity, 27
arising of, 105
hell realm and, 47
immunity to, 247
motivation of, 164
as obstruction to buddha nature, 305, 308
as root affliction, 11, 74, 88, 155–56, 259
See also anger
antidotes, 280, 281
cessation and, 15, 16
forgetting to apply, 197
habitual afflictions and, 107
skillful application of, 116
for specific afflictions, 114–15
in weakening underlying tendencies, 89–90
wisdom realizing selflessness as, 35
anti-gods (*asuras*), 45, 344n19
anxiety, 50, 101–2, 115, 136, 241
apasmāra (forgetful makers), 46
appearances
in bardo, 199
conceptual, 180, 289
dependent arising of, 212
dualistic, 259, 260, 265
as illusions, 206, 207
of inherent existence, 130, 259–60, 265, 278, 346n43
snang ba, translation as, 259, 346n43
vividness of, 250
apprehended object, 78, 349–50n77
Approaching the Buddhist Path, xiii, xiv, 319
arhats, 260, 349n74
consciousness of, 168
craving and clinging, lack of, 182, 185
feelings of, 178
fetters and, 87
ignorance, lack of, 161
karma of, 255–56

mental bodies of, 250, 257, 265, 306, 351n84
nirvāṇa of, 9, 264, 272–73, 349nn71–72
peculiar behaviors of, 130, 260–61
rebirth of, 43, 44
true cessation of, 31
arhatship, 16
afflictions eradicated at, 125, 248–49
attaining, 91, 247
of Buddha, 223
desire for, 68, 69
emotions at, 118
karmic seeds at, 130
preventing, 97
in Vaibhāṣika and Sautrāntika systems, 293
arising, abiding, ceasing, 21–22, 133
arrogance, 61, 66, 341
abandonment of, 125
acquired, 124
as antidote to itself, 117
antidotes to, 115
fetter of, 97, 98
haughtiness and, 96
order of arising of, 104, 105
and self-confidence, distinctions between, 73
types of, 71–72, 95, 346n36
underlying tendency of, 89
as virtuous, 68
ārya bodhisattvas, 17
afflictive obscurations of, 307
mental bodies of, 250, 257, 351n84
rebirth of, 43–44, 199, 257
stages of, 257–58
suffering, lack of, 249
ārya path, 250–51, 254–56, 262, 272, 292, 294, 349n74
Āryadeva, 23, 47–48, 49
Āryaratnakara Sūtra, 207, 211
āryas, 5
four qualities of disposition of, 292
in Fundamental Vehicle, 306
ignorance of, 161
karma of, 249, 351n84
as lacking inherent existence, 207–8
minds of, 274
qualities of, 300
realization of, 236
rebirth of, 43, 199
seed of afflictions of, 303, 307
śrāvaka and bodhisattva, differences between, 17
Asaṅga, 293, 296
on asuras, 45
on causal dependence, 211–12
commentary to *Sublime Continuum*, 302, 315
on first-link ignorance, 159–60
on twelve links, 173, 196–97
See also *Compendium of Knowledge* (*Abhidharmasamuccaya*); *Śrāvaka Grounds* (*Śrāvakabhūmi*)
asceticism, 35, 60, 82, 83, 97, 184
aspiration, 52, 257
and attachment, differences between, 66–67, 68
for awakening, 57–59, 67
for liberation, xvii, 39–40, 52, 57–59, 67, 189, 218, 288
worldly, 166
astronomy, 143, 148
Aśvajit, 233
attachment, 11, 60, 64, 66, 88, 246
abandonment of, 125
acquired, 124
and anger, relationship of, 70
antidotes to, 114–15
arising of, 107
auxiliary afflictions of, 92, 93–94, 101–2
bodily sensations and, 106
to cherished belief, 85–86
clinging and, 183
craving and, 179
to emotions as *mine*, 102–3
fear of relinquishing, 117–19
feelings accompanying, 109
fetter of, 98

floods (*ogha*) and yokes (*yoga*) of, 346n37
identifying, 113
immunity to, 247
karma and, 48
and love, distinctions between, 113
manifest and seeds of, 128
as obstruction to buddha nature, 303–4, 305, 308
order of arising of, 104, 105
pleasurable feelings and, 50–51
pollutant of, 99
releasing, 22
and self-grasping ignorance, distinctions between, 75
strength of, 100
types of, 66–68
underlying tendencies of, 89, 90, 91, 345n31
virtuous and nonvirtuous, 68–69
attention, mental factor of, 171–72
Augustine, 135
Autocommentary to the "Supplement" (Candrakīrti), 261
auxiliary afflictions, 65, 87, 88
feelings accompanying, 109–10
in Pāli tradition, 94–96
primary consciousness and, 111
in Sanskrit tradition, 92–94
aversion, 23, 59, 91, 94
Awa Pangchu, 336
awakening, xvi, 3, 162, 274–75
aspiration for, 57–59, 67
attaining, 207–8, 251, 342
of Buddha, 233, 234, 267
conviction in, xvii
creating causes for, 219
mental consciousness at, 333
motivations that impede, 250
in pure lands, 258
in tantra, 288–89, 321
two obscurations at, 259
variant views on, 292–93, 350n79
wrong views and, 86
See also buddhahood
awakening activities, 250, 258, 278, 301, 310, 311, 312, 315, 316, 323
awareness, 93, 173, 298–99. *See also* inattentive awareness; introspective awareness

B

bardo (intermediate stage)
birth in, 189, 255
body in, 186
clinging in, 182
karmic appearances in, 199
karmic ripening in, 167, 347n52
renewed existence in, 185, 186
twelve links in, 200
basis of designation, 9, 21, 132, 186
behavior
anger and, 70
changing, 112
from craving, 15, 25
examining, 199
habitual, 107
harmful, relinquishing, 67
instinctual, views on, 152–53
nonvirtuous, not abandoning, 88, 94
observing one's own, 113
bhavaṅga, 175–76, 347n53
Bhāvaviveka, 153, 228–29
Big Bang theory, 8, 142–43, 148, 149
Bimbisāra, King, 155
birth
as beginning of resultant rebirth, 187
eleventh-link, 188–89, 191
four types of, 173, 189
suffering of, 13, 53, 56
black near attainment, 128, 328, 332
blame, 29, 40, 199
bliss, 43
attachment to, 89, 183, 204
craving for, 67
of deva realms, 46
in dhyānas, 91, 110
suppression of, 167
in transcendental dependent origination, 239, 242–43

bodhi, 274–75
Bodhi, Bhikkhu, 347n46
bodhicitta, 1, 59, 288
  of arhats, 257
  of āryas, 207–8
  buddha nature and, 313, 327
  causal and immediate motivations for, 164
  clinging to self-interest and, 69
  five factors that hinder developing, 341–42
  generating, 193, 218, 226, 310
  merit of, 131
  on path of accumulation, 254
  in transforming buddha nature, 298
  wrong views regarding, 86
  See also great resolve
bodhisattva grounds, 125, 128, 258, 298, 299, 307
Bodhisattva Grounds (*Bodhisattva Bhūmi*, Asaṅga), 296
Bodhisattva Vehicle, 259, 293, 296. *See also* Mahāyāna
bodhisattvas
  afflictions eradicated by, 125, 128
  aspiration of, 59
  deeds of, 226, 295, 313
  as fields of merit, 251
  nirvāṇa sought by, 266
  path of, 17, 44, 69, 254, 257, 265, 306, 319, 349n68
  rebirth of, 9, 228–29
  See also ārya bodhisattvas; pure-ground bodhisattvas
body
  and afflictions, physical sensations of, 106, 112–13
  attachment to, relinquishing, 60
  as attractive, counteracting notions of, 23–24, 116, 221
  in bardo, 186
  biology and karma of, relationship between, 153–54
  as conditioned by seeds and latencies, 188
  development of, 174–75, 177
  distorted conception of, 22
  ethic neutrality of, 138
  in highest yoga tantra, 286
  impermanence of, 14
  inner elements of, 150
  instinct and, 153
  of light, 154
  mental, 250, 257, 265, 306, 351n84
  mind and, 8, 112–13, 144–48, 174–75
  mindfulness of, 27
  momentariness of, 26
  as object of clinging, 170–71
  possession of, 208–9
  sense of self and, 6
  as unsatisfactory by nature, 48–49, 50, 53–54
Brahmā, 24
Brahmins, 24
brain, 106, 278, 286
breath, counterforce of, 115
Buddha
  on aging or death, 190
  on arhatship, 248
  asceticism of, 35
  awakening of, 233, 234, 267
  as Bhagawan, 278
  on birth, 188–89
  on body, possession of, 208–9
  on causality and conditionality, 6–7, 144, 156, 232
  on condition for craving, 181
  on disenchantment, 245–46
  divine food from fodder, story of, 178
  as doctor, 1
  first teaching of, 10
  on four truths, 39, 40, 52
  on his spiritual journey, 59
  homage to, 270
  on ignorance, beginninglessness of, 159
  on knowledge and vision of liberation, 249
  on knowledge and vision of things as they are, 243
  on nihilism, 81

on nirvāṇa, 247, 268–69, 272
parinirvāṇa of, 118–19
as proof of buddha nature, 317
refusal to answer certain questions, 141, 208
respecting, 2, 342
sensual pleasures of, 222, 223
and sentient beings' buddha nature, 304, 305, 306, 307, 309–10
skillful teaching of, 340
subtle karmic seeds of, 132
on true duḥkha, 53
on two kinds of happiness, 231
using general I, 333
Wheel of Life image of, 156
buddha activities. *See* awakening activities
buddha bodies, four, 9, 234
buddha bodies, three, 314
buddha nature and, 293, 296, 311, 312–13
Dzogchen and Mahāmudrā views of, 335
as innate in sentient beings, misunderstanding, 335–36
seed as basis for actualization, 323–24, 327–28, 329–30
subtlest mind-wind and, 302
three stages of, 330
buddha nature/disposition/essence, 222, 293, 350n78
awakening and developing, 313–14
as both object and subject, Seventh Dalai Lama's presentation on, 322–23
Cittamātrin view of, 293–96
clear light mind and, xvi, 326–27, 328, 341, 351n83
defiled, four types of persons having, 296
denying existence of, 316–17, 342
as dharmakāya, 311–12
difficulties in understanding, 315–16
impeding and stimulating, 295–96
in inanimate phenomena, mistaken notion of, 299
as interpretable teaching, 338–39
in *Laṅkavatāra Sūtra*, 326
Madhyamaka view of, 296–301
purpose in understanding, 338, 340, 341–42
regarding as special, realization required for, 300
textual sources on, 296
three aspects of, 310–14
See also naturally abiding buddha nature; nine similes for buddha nature; transforming buddha nature
Buddhaghoṣa, 143–44. See also *Path of Purification* (*Visuddhimagga*, Buddhaghoṣa)
buddhahood, 335
attachment to, impossibility of, 67
five factors that hinder, 341–42
higher rebirths toward, 166
subtlest clear light mind and, 288–89
two obscurations at, elimination of, 130, 259, 278–79
unpolluted body of, 258
variant views on, 292–93, 296, 350n79
See also awakening
buddhas, 3, 9, 258
acts of, 144
appearance of, 20, 326
"attachment" of, 69
consciousness of, 168
feelings of, 178
as fields of merit, 251
ignorance, lack of, 161
karma, lack of, 250
knowledge of karma of, 150
minds of, 274–75
nonabiding nirvāṇa of, 266
purpose of becoming, 226
sentient beings potential to become, 136, 222, 277, 301
true cessation of, 31
two truths, knowledge of, 260
wheel-turning, 45, 292–93
Buddhism, xv, 63, 240, 254

C

Candrakīrti, 105, 133
  on arhats' latencies, 261
  on having-ceased, 133
  on impermanence, 54–55
  on karmic seeds and latencies, 134
  See also *Clear Words*; *Supplement*
caste system, 24, 261
causal dependence, 211–12, 217
causality/causation, 84, 143–46, 158, 232, 297. *See also* dependent arising
causally concordant results, behavioral and experiential, 130
cause and effect, interrelated systems of, 154, 212
causes and conditions, 142, 244
  as beginningless, 212
  Buddhist view of, 6–8
  as dependent arising, 156
  disintegration in, 133
  of duḥkha, 26, 30
  interconnectedness of, 158, 205–6
  for liberation, creating, 236
  mistaken appearances of, 207
  nirvāṇa's absence of, 268
  for origin of universe, 143–44
  of saṃsāra, 232
  in three times, 210
celestial bodies, 146
central channel, 288–89
change
  causality and, 143
  duḥkha of, 13, 22, 47–48, 50, 51, 56
  impermanence of, 54–55
Changkya Rolpai Dorje, 335–36
Chim Jampelyang, 67
Christianity, 135, 142
Cittamātra school
  on afflictions, 66
  on aggregates at nirvāṇa, 9
  on buddha nature, 293–96
  on clear light mind, 351n83
  on consciousness and objects, 288
  on ignorance, 73, 162
  on mind and form, 146
  on purifying karmic seeds, 132
  Reasoning Proponents subschool, 265, 293–94, 296
  Scriptural Proponents subschool, 169, 293, 294, 349n72, 350n79
  on seeds and latencies, 346n42
  on virtues, 138
clairvoyance, 260–61, 303, 305
clear light mind, xvi, 274, 324
  adventitious defilements and, 279–80
  as basis for excellent qualities, 282
  as buddha nature, xvi, 326–27, 328, 341, 351n83
  causal, 330, 332
  example and actual, 289
  primordial, 283–84
  stability of, 298
  subtlest, 275, 325
  in Sūtra and Tantra, distinctions between, 328–30, 331
  in third turning, 320, 321, 322, 323
  variant views on, 284, 349n77, 351n83
  See also fundamental innate clear light mind
Clear Words (Candrakīrti), 263–64
clinging
  to aggregates, 10, 12, 53–54, 343n1
  antidotes to, 114–15
  four types, 68–69, 183–84
  impermanence and, 26
  in meditation, 241
  to painful feelings, 203
  rebirth and, 15
  releasing, 50
  at time of death, 182, 186
cognitive faculties
  afflictions and, 121
  after death, 171
  arising of, 182
  craving and, 14, 179, 191
  impermanence of, 54
  mindfulness of, 204
  objects of, feeling, 176–77, 183
  obscuration of, 277–78
cognitive obscurations, 259–62

of arhats, 265–66
of ārya bodhisattvas, 258
to buddha nature, 308–9
cessation of, 31
latencies of afflictions as, 130
manifest, 260
collection of merit, xvi, 131, 228, 306, 313–14
collection of wisdom, 131, 298, 313
collective unconscious, 136
Commentary on Bodhicitta (Nāgārjuna), 321
Commentary on Reliable Cognition (*Pramāṇavārttika*, Dharmakīrti), 19
on counterforces, 280–81
on duḥkha, 48, 57
on mind's transformation, 281
on nature of mind, 279
on order of afflictions, 105, 106
Commentary on the Awakening Mind (Nāgārjuna), 206–7
Commentary on the "Pristine Wisdom on the Verge of Transcendence Sūtra" (Kelzang Gyatso), 322–23
compassion
of bodhisattvas, 9
of buddhas, 69
and determination for freedom, relationship between, 228
developing, 193
effort in cultivating, 122
ethical conduct and, 241
freedom from craving and, 180
inability to generate, 342
limitless cultivation of, 282
mental factor of, 64–65
motivation of, in twelve links, 198
for oneself, 222
for ourselves and others, 225, 226–27
primary consciousness and, 138
righteous anger and, 113
of Śāriputra, 118
seeds of, 128
for suffering of others, 103, 219
in transforming buddha nature, 298
in unawakened mind, 316
valid foundation for, 280
as virtuous mental state, 111
without attachment, 60
wrong views regarding, 86
See also great compassion
Compendium of Determinations (*Viniścaya-samgrahaṇi*), 250
Compendium of Instructions (Śāntideva), 131
Compendium of Knowledge (*Abhidharmasamuccaya*, Asaṅga), 11, 18, 31
on afflictions, 64, 65–66, 89
on auxiliary afflictions, 92–94, 96, 345–46n34, 346n35
on bardo, twelve links in, 200
on dependent arising, 157
on fetters, 98
on virtue, five types, 138–39
on wrong views, 86
Compendium of the Mahāyāna (*Mahāyānasaṃgraha*, Asaṅga), 293
competition, afflicted and positive aspects of, 95
concealment, 93, 109, 345–46n34
conceit, 95–96, 115, 118
conceit of I am (*asmimāna*), 71, 72
concentration
alternating, 43
attachment to, 89, 183, 204
craving as inspiration in, 67
in experiencing subtle impermanence, 14
full, 242
limitless cultivation of, 282
relaxed feelings from, 60
seeds of, 128
single-pointed, 41, 116, 137, 148, 253–54, 278, 286
in suppressing defilements, 204
in transcendental dependent origination, 239, 242–44
two principal faults of, 254
concentration, higher training in, 1, 129–30, 226, 241, 253

conception, 15, 168–69, 170, 173, 174, 190, 202
conceptual fabrications, 245
conceptualizations. *See* distorted conceptions
conditionality, 13–14, 156, 209, 210, 232, 244, 267. *See also* twelve links of dependent origination
conditioned phenomena, 210
  analysis of, 243
  buddha nature as, 293, 323–24
  death as, 190
  disenchantment with, 246
  duḥkha and, 29
  having-ceaseds as, 133
  impermanence of, 54–55
  path as, 273
  sentient beings as, 226
  three characteristics of, 244
  three types, 127, 144, 159
  transforming buddha nature as, 298
  true paths as, 37
conditioning action, 165. *See also* formative actions (*saṃskāra karman*)
conditions, three types, 176
confidence, xiv
  in awakening, 279, 334, 340
  false sense of, 92
  lack of, 93
  in mind's ability to transform, 283
  in nirvāṇa, 231, 232
  stable, 240
  in true path, 35
confusion
  ignorance and, 68, 73, 74
  immunity to, 247
  karma and, 48
  as obstruction to buddha nature, 308
  as root affliction, 1, 11, 88, 259
  between virtue and nonvirtue, 115
  from wrong views, 85
Connected Discourses on Causation, 157
conscientiousness, 96, 138, 139, 155, 193
consciousness
  afflictive, 128, 169
  of arhats' realization, 272–73
  arising of, three conditions for, 176
  bases of, 278
  as basis of designation of self, 186
  and brain, Buddhist view of, 106
  Buddhist and Western views of, compared, 136–37
  causal, 165, 168, 169, 177, 182
  as clear and cognizant, 332
  coarse and subtle, 284, 349n77
  at conception, 15, 202
  conceptual, 346–47n43
  continuity of, 6, 206, 265, 349n72
  momentariness of, 55
  name and form as mutual conditions of, 170
  psychological causality and, 143
  resultant, 168–69, 171, 177, 188
  six types, 169, 170, 172, 173, 260
  true paths as, 12
  Vaibhāṣika view of, 90
  variant views on, 169
  See also foundation consciousness; primary consciousness
contact
  mental factor of, 171–72
  in twelve links, 176, 177–78
contemporary society, 101, 107, 112, 221–22
contempt, 94–95, 261, 341, 342
contentment, 55, 291, 292
continuities, of type and substance, 333–34
conventional existence, 81, 157, 211, 214, 260
conventional level of truth, 18, 208, 214, 285, 286, 316
conventional nature (*svabhāva*), 279
conventional reliable cognizers, 25
cooperative conditions, 29, 30, 148, 149
correct mental direct perceivers, 298–99
cosmic substance. *See* primal matter
cosmology, 141–43, 144–48, 154
counterforces, 114–16. *See also* antidotes
covetousness, 66, 94, 130, 187

craving
afflictions related to, 94
as antidote to itself, 117
antidotes to, 114–15
and clinging, relationship between, 182, 183
duḥkha of change and, 56
and feeling, space between, 177–78
forms of, 99
freedom from, 180
as grasping to inherent existence, 161
ignorance and, 202
nirvāṇa and, 271
in origin of duḥkha, 11, 12, 14–15, 28–30, 59
releasing, 50
types of, 179–80, 184
Vaibhāṣika emphasis on, 292
virtuous and nonvirtuous forms of, 67–68
creators, 6, 7, 24, 29, 30, 31, 55, 84, 85, 86, 135–36, 142
innate clear light mind as, 287–88
refutation of, 144, 145, 158, 211, 212
cruelty, 70, 92, 345–46n34
cyclic existence (*saṃsāra*), xiii, xvi, 55–56, 307
as beginningless, 49, 52, 135–36, 159, 218–19
bondage to, 186
clinging to, 69
craving and, 180
cutting root of, 12, 19, 204, 236
dependent arising of, 214–15, 237
determination for freedom from, 39–40, 52, 57–59, 227–29
disadvantages of, 49, 51–52
disenchantment with, 23
eliminating causes for, 218
formative karma and, 164
freedom from, 27, 36
as illness, 1–3
in Indian tradition, 10
innate clear light mind as basis of, 287–88
meditation on defects of, 219–20
mind as basis for, xiii–xiv, 297, 328
releasing attachment to, 22
remedies to, 191, 233, 348n60
renouncing, 54, 167, 190
root and ultimate root, distinctions between, 162
root of, 11, 75, 78, 98, 161
roots of in Pāli tradition, 202
as self-perpetuating, 177
terror of, 200

D

daily life
afflictions in, 126, 232
attachment in, 66
clear light mind in, 349–50n77
craving in, 180
duḥkha in, 63
lack of mindfulness of karma in, 250
reflecting on lack of inherent existence in, 221
six sources in, 174
Darwin, Charles, 154
death, 187
birth as cause of, 188
clinging at, 182, 183–84, 186
consciousness at, 128, 283, 284, 286–87, 349–50n77
craving arising at, 15, 179, 186
disadvantage of, 52
elements at, 147
karmic seeds ripening at, 26
lord of, 155
meditating on, 219
mind-wind at, 146, 301, 328
mini-, 167, 347n52
name and form at, 171
primordial mind at, 335
pristine wisdom at, 322
renewed existence during, 186
seeds of self-grasping at, 128
state of mind at, 167
suffering of, 13, 48, 53, 54, 56, 58
uses of term, 189

view of extremes at, 208
See also aging or death (*jarāmaraṇa*)
deceit, 93, 95, 109, 345–46n34, 346n35
defilements, xiv, xvi
ability to be eliminated, 297
as adventitious, 291, 301, 302, 313, 316
classifications of, 87, 100, 101
emptiness of, 64
eradication at arhatship, 248, 272
as fetters, 129
in fourfold cessation, 15–16
indentifying, purpose of, 87–88
subtle, 278
as underlying tendencies, 89, 129
definite emergence (*niḥsaraṇa*), 33
delight, 240, 241, 242
demons, 46
dependent arising, 6–8, 56, 156, 157–58, 238, 273, 347n48. *See also* twelve links of dependent origination
dependent designation, 157, 273
dependent origination, transcendental, 238–49, 274
depression, 48, 101, 102, 106
Descent into Lanka Sūtra (*Laṅkāvatāra Sūtra*), 326, 337–38, 339–40
desire. *See* sensual desire
desire realm, 41, 44–45
attachment of, 89, 153
clinging in, 183
craving of, 223–24
ethical dimensions of, 111
feelings in, 109
hindrances in, 100
latencies of sense faculties in, 135
lower fetters and, 97
mind in, 286
obscurations to buddha nature in, 303, 304, 305, 308
renewed existence in, 187
ripening of karma in, 167
twelve links in, 173
types of karma in, 166, 249
desire-realm devas, 44–45, 46
devas, 44–45, 46, 166, 173, 187, 189, 305
Dhammadinnā, 79
Dhammapada, 256
Dhammasaṅgani, 88
dhammata, 144, 347n45
Dharamsala, example of karma and environment in, 150–51
dhāraṇī, 232–33
Dharma
actions of, 69
as antidote to afflictions, 114
arrogance due to, 72–73
attachment to, views on, 60–61
gratitude toward, 204
Jewel of, 253
meanings of term, 114
as medicine, 1–3
resilience in practicing, 30
respecting, 2
study and investigation, importance of, 337
See also three turnings of Dharma wheel
Dharma practice, 58, 60, 65, 219–22
dharmadhātu. *See* nature of phenomena (*dharmadhātu*)
dharmakāya. *See* truth body (*dharmakāya*)
Dharmakīrti, 336. See also *Commentary on Reliable Cognition* (*Pramāṇavārttika*)
dharmatā, impermanence of, 55
dhyānas, four, 41, 42–44, 344n10, 344nn12–15
analytical meditation and, 244
attaining first, 243
factors of, 242–43
feelings in, 109
joy in, 241, 349n67
neutral feelings in, 177
overcoming underlying tendencies in, 91
seven preparations for, 186, 348n58
dhyāni buddhas, five, 147
Dignāga, 336
discouragement, 93, 113, 221–22, 316, 341

discrimination, 42, 171–72, 177
disenchantment, 239, 244–46
disintegration, 21–22, 23, 54–55, 133, 245, 262, 271
dispassion, 239, 246–47, 274
disposition
  ārya, 292–93
  five types, 294–95, 311, 312
  See also buddha nature/disposition/essence
dissatisfaction, 14–15, 28, 54, 223–24, 240
distorted attention (*ayoniśo manaskāra*), 66–67, 70, 76, 107–8, 163, 164, 197
distorted conceptions, 25, 101, 107–8, 119–21, 199, 316–17, 341–42. *See also* four distorted conceptions
Distortions of the Mind, 20
distraction, 93, 94, 253, 287
divine eye, 47, 120, 305
Dodrubchen Jigme Tenpai Nyima, Third Dodrup Rinpoche, 331, 335, 336
doubt
  about true path, 34
  antidotes to, 122
  and anxiety, relationship between, 102
  contemplating four truths in eradicating, 19
  and curiosity, differences between, 76
  deluded, 66, 76, 88, 89, 97, 98, 99, 115, 125
  feelings accompanying, 109
  freedom from, 210
  inclined to correct conclusion, 298
  order of arising, 104, 105
  types of, 76
  underlying tendencies and, 129, 345n31
dreams
  appearances as, 206, 207
  latencies of, 135
  mind in, 176, 286
  objects in, 172
  unconscious in, 136
duḥkha (unsatisfactory circumstances), xiii, xvi, 141, 245
  aggregates as basis of, 171
  between aging and death, 190–91
  arising of, analyzing, 58
  Asaṅga's ten points on, 54–57
  cessation of, 32, 237
  contemplating, 49
  creating causes for, 198
  dependent arising of, 214–15
  of desire realm, 45
  determination to be free of, 227–28
  Dharma Jewel and, 253
  eight unsatisfactory conditions of, 53–54
  eliminating causes for, 218
  four attributes of, 20–27
  as illness, 1–3
  impermanence and, 23
  links that are, 193–94
  nature of, 11, 12
  nonvirtue as cause of, 137
  origin of (*see* true origins (*samudaya-satya*))
  of others, meditating on, 122
  as proximate cause for faith, 239, 240
  reflecting on, purpose of, 39–40, 57
  renouncing, 10
  three types, 13, 22, 33, 47–50, 50–51, 55–56, 123, 226
  twelve links and, 235
  wrong views about, 184
Dzogchen tradition, 283–84, 324–25, 327, 331, 334–35

E

educational system, 122
effort. *See* joyous effort
ego-identity, 61, 179
eight worldly concerns, 53, 166
eightfold path, 12, 232, 234, 240, 253, 343n9, 348n60
Eight-Thousand-Line Perfection of Wisdom Sūtra (*Aṣṭasāhasrikā Prajñāpāramitā Sūtra*), 297
elements, 147–48, 150, 171

Elucidation of the Five Stages of Guhyasamāja (Tsongkhapa), 285
emanation body (*nirmāṇakāya*), 9, 288
manifestation of, 309, 310
pure lands of, 44
subtlest wind and, 302
transforming buddha nature as, 313, 314
emotions, xvi
as afflictions, 278, 279
in contemporary society, 101
differences in, 64
disadvantages of, 119–21
general antidote to, 115
habitual, 107
ignorance and, 37
learning to identify, 96
as motivation, 58
multipronged approaches to healing, 102
as obstruction to buddha nature, 305
overwhelming, 22–23
repression of and seeds of, differences between, 128
twelve links and, 197, 203
emptiness, 37, 256, 343n3
of agent, action, object, 207
of aggregates, 23–25
and causal dependence, compatibility of, 217
clear light mind and, 284, 321
of defilements, 64
direct realization of, 125, 251
in examining duḥkha, 54, 56, 57
fallacious reasoning on, 124
fear of, 338
five factors that hinder realization of, 341–42
of four truths, 18
free from elaborations of inherent existence, 264
in highest yoga tantra, 288–89
meditating on, 131
motivation to understand, 168, 193
as nature truth body, 9, 288, 302, 339
nirvāṇa as, 270, 273
obscurations to direct perception of, 162
of persons and phenomena, 232
of phenomena, 207, 213
posited in relation to objects, 300
reflecting on, 116
in second turning, 319
and selflessness, Prāsaṅgika view of, 25
subtle, 27
of true cessations, 12
twelve links and, 157, 158, 211
two types of buddha nature and, xiv
as ultimate virtue, 138–39
See also wisdom realizing emptiness
emptiness of mind, 35
buddha nature and, xiv, 296, 300, 305, 306, 320, 325, 326, 328, 338
and buddhahood, relationship between, 298
of buddhas, 302
of buddhas and ordinary beings, 274–75, 299–301, 312, 315–16, 323, 339
as foundation of dharmakāya, 311
joy of realizing, 304
as nirvāṇa, 262, 263, 264, 285
nothing to be added or removed from, 326
in Sūtrayāna, 322
tantric view of, 275
as ultimate nature, 327
and voidness, differences between, 336
wisdom as, 331
Engaging in the Bodhisattvas' Deeds (Śāntideva), 119–21, 139–40
enjoyment body (*saṃbhogakāya*), 9, 288
actualizing, 308, 309
pure lands of, 44
subtlest wind and, 302
transforming buddha nature as, 313, 314
enlightenment. *See* awakening
environment, 221
afflictions triggered by, 108
elemental particles of, 146–47
as external true duḥkha, 11
impermanence of, 54

karmic causes of, 150–52, 165
in manifold world, variant views on, 145–48
origins of duḥkha and, 141
in realms of existence, 41
environmental result, 130
equanimity, 91, 342
to feelings, 181, 204
in form and formless realms, 167
in freedom from craving, 180
of Śāriputra, 118
virtue of, 138
virtuous mental states and, 109
"Essence of Dependent Arising Dhāraṇī," 233–34
Establishment of Mindfulness Sutta (Skt. *Smṛtyupasthāna Sūtra*), 12, 45
ethical conduct, 1, 253
delight and, 240–41
disregarding, 286
distorted notions of, 184
ignorance of, 68
mindfulness and awareness in, 254
rebirth due to, 45
in restraining defilements, 129
sensual pleasure and, 183
wrong views and, 86
ethical restraints, 12, 82, 109, 172, 288. *See also* precepts
ethics, 83, 84, 143, 167
evolution, 149, 153
excellent qualities, 60–61
at buddhahood, 130, 274, 278
deceit regarding, 95
disposition as source of, 294
as limitless, xiv, 281–82
meditating on, 164
valid foundation of, 139, 280
existence
attachment to, 89, 97
craving, antidote to, 115
craving for, 179, 180–81, 184
floods (*ogha*) and yokes (*yoga*) of, 346n37
pollutant of, 98, 99
See also inherent existence
extreme of absolutism, 81, 83, 88, 181, 184, 208, 217, 345n28
extreme of nihilism, 81, 83, 88, 181, 208
counteracting, 217
craving for nonexistence and, 179, 184
three types of, 84

F

fainting, 170, 176, 286
faith
lack of, 93
limitless cultivation of, 282
seeds of, 128
for subduing hindrances, 242
in Three Jewels, 58, 164
in transcendental dependent origination, 239, 240–41
in transforming buddha nature, 298
virtue of, 138
fear, 70, 101–2, 113, 122, 221, 241, 255
feeling, aggregate of, 172
feeling, mental factor of, 171–72
accompanying afflictions, 109–10
impermanence of, 54
mindfulness of, 27
with three types of craving, 179–80
with three types of duḥkha, 50–51
with three underlying tendencies, 91
in twelve links, 176–78
fetters, 87, 97–98
abandoning, 243, 246–47
five lower, 129, 255, 345n31
final vehicles, variant views on, 264–65, 294–95, 296, 349n72
five hindrances, 15–16, 88, 99–100, 242, 243
five paths, 254, 265, 299, 349n68
accumulation, 254, 257, 265, 349n68
meditation, 16, 125, 160, 258, 307
no more learning, 16, 255, 258
preparation, 250, 254, 257, 349n68
See also path of seeing
five pure abodes, 43, 44, 344n12
floods (*ogha*), 346n37

forgetfulness, 93
form body (rūpakāya), 234, 288
  deity visualization and, 298
  at parinirvāṇa, 9
  subtlest wind and, 302
  transforming buddha nature as, 313, 314
  two collections and, 139
  See also emanation body (*nirmāṇakāya*); enjoyment body (*saṃbhogakāya*)
form realm, 41, 42–44, 344n10, 344nn12–15
  attachment to birth in, 89, 97, 99
  clinging in, 183
  craving for bliss of, 67, 69
  ethical dimensions of, 111
  feelings in, 109
  impediments to attaining, 99–100
  invariable karma of, 166–67, 249
  mind in, 286
  obscurations to buddha nature in, 303, 304
  renewed existence in, 186, 187
  twelve links in, 173
formative actions (*saūskāra karman*), 123, 165
  bondage of, 186
  causal and immediate motivations for, 163–64
  cessation of, 262
  feeling and, 177
  innate self-grasping and, 161
  latencies and having-ceaseds in, 134, 165
  nonvirtuous, 111
  projecting rebirth, 185
  and renewed existence, relationship between, 186, 187
  as root of saṃsāra, 236, 237
  three types, 166–67
formless realm, 41–42, 44, 344n10
  attachment to birth in, 89, 97, 99
  bodies in, variant views on, 171, 348n55
  clinging in, 183
  craving for bliss of, 67, 69
  ethical dimensions of, 111
  feelings in, 109
  impediments to attaining, 99–100
  invariable karma of, 166, 167, 249
  mind in, 286
  obscurations to buddha nature in, 303, 304
  renewed existence in, 186, 187
  sense faculties, lack of in, 135
  twelve links in, 173
form-realm sphere of consciousness (*vacaracitta*), 44
fortitude, 1, 15, 64, 115, 131, 240, 241, 295
foundation consciousness, 146, 169, 288, 293, 294
Foundation of Buddhist Practice, The, xiii, xiv, 63
four distorted conceptions, 343–44n9
  afflictive views and, 82
  emptiness in overcoming, 37
  formative karma and, 163
  ignorance of, 74
  reflection on opposites, 220–21
  true cessation and, 33
  true duḥkha and, 20–22, 26
  true origins and, 30
  true paths and, 36
four extremes of arising, 213–14, 237, 339
four fearlessnesses, 233–34
four formless absorptions, 41–42, 43, 110, 186, 243, 344n10, 348n58
Four Great Kings, 45, 46
four māras, 278
four opponent powers, 132
four truths of the āryas, xvi
  absence of experiencer of, 208
  coarse and subtle, 18–19, 31
  framework of, 5
  ignorance of, 74–75, 159, 243
  naming of, 10
  nature of, 11–12
  practice and results of, 17–18
  realization of, 91, 232, 248, 267
  sixteen attributes of, 19–37, 253
  three turnings of Dharma wheel and, 319–22, 324

in twelve links, 235
worldview of, 240
in "Ye Dharmā" Dhāraṇī, 233–34
See also individual truth
four ways of maturing disciples, 313
Freud, Sigmund, 136
fundamental innate clear light mind, xvi
buddha nature and, 324, 331
in Dzogchen and Mahāmudrā, 327, 331
as ever-present, 332
in highest yoga tantra, 286–87, 321, 325
transformation of, 280
two qualities of, 328
Fundamental Vehicle, 306. *See also* Sautrāntika school; solitary realizers; śrāvakas; Vaibhāṣika school

G

gandharvas, 46, 202, 348n61
garuḍas, 46
Gedun Drupa, First Dalai Lama, 145
Gelukpa tradition, 324–25, 335–36
generation and completion stages, 288
generosity, 1, 138
ethical dimensions of, 111
limitless cultivation of, 282
rebirth due to, 45
sensual pleasure and, 183
virtuous mental states and, 109
wrong views and, 85
genetics, 106, 153, 154, 188
global warming, 152
God, 6, 29, 135–36
grasping
counteracting, 285
of ignorance and view of personal identity, distinctions between, 161
inherent existence, 18–19, 69, 111, 161–62, 264, 334 (*see also under* ignorance)
self-sufficient substantially existent person, 74, 75, 103, 126, 162
subtle and coarse, 78
true existence, 74, 250, 334
gratification, danger, escape, 222–25
great compassion, 265, 294, 304, 306, 349n76
great resolve, 257, 265, 294
Great Treatise on the Stages of the Path (Tsongkhapa), 105, 251
Greater Discourse on the Destruction of Craving, 202
greed, 66, 88, 94, 114–15
Guhyasamāja Tantra, 146, 321
Guṇaprabha, 292
Gungtang Konchog Tenpai Dronme, 336
Gyaltsab Darma Rinchen, 23, 327, 331

H

habits/habitual tendencies, 65, 115, 127, 130, 165, 170, 188, 261
happiness, xiv
afflictions accompanied by, 109
afflictions sabotaging, 112, 120
arising of, analyzing, 58
creating causes for, 30
of current life, 69, 219–20, 250
from Dharma practice, 22
doubt and, 102
as duḥkha, 47–48, 53
illusion of, 48–49
lasting, 246
levels of, 60
money and, 224
renunciation and, 10
saṃsāric, karma ripening as, 249
sources of, 28
types of, 231
virtue as cause of, 137, 292
wishing for others', 226–27
Haribhadra, 285
harm/harmfulness, 109, 112, 120, 125, 183, 218, 247, 345–46n34
hatred, 94
anger and, 70, 88
antidote to, 115
effects of, 122
nonvirtue of, 68
as obscuration to buddha nature, 304
order of arising of, 104, 105

haughtiness, 66, 92, 96, 110, 345–46n34
having-ceaseds (*naṣṭas*), xv, xvii, 127
  formative karma and, 134, 165
  nirvāṇa and, 263
  renewed existence and, 185
  ripening of, 167
  in twelve link cycles, 197, 198–99
  variant views on, 132–34, 347n44
Heart of Dependent Origination (*Pratītya samutpāda hṛdaya kārikā*, Nāgārjuna), 193
Heart of the Middle Way (*Madhyamaka-hṛdaya-kārikā*, Bhāvaviveka), 228–29
heedlessness, 94, 96
hell beings (*nārakas*), 45, 46, 47, 166, 173, 187, 189, 257, 307
Hevajra Tantra, 302
highest yoga tantra, 322
  on buddha nature, 301–2
  on death process, 182
  fundamental innate clear light mind in, 320–22, 324, 328, 331
  mind, two types in, 332
  on mind and body, 146, 286
  practices of, 288–89
hindrances. *See* five hindrances
Hinduism, 142
holy objects, actions involving, 164, 251
human birth, 138, 171, 172, 187, 198. *See also* conception; precious human birth
human potential, 53, 58, 106, 136, 277, 301
human realm, 45, 46, 140
hungry ghosts (*pretas*), 45, 46, 47, 166, 187, 189, 257, 307, 344n20
hypervigilance, 102

I

I, general and specific, 332–33
icchantika disposition, 295, 350n79
ignorance, xvii, 1, 10, 11, 52, 64, 66, 98–99
  abandonment of, 125
  aggregates and, 14, 23–24
  auxiliary afflictions of, 93–94
  as beginningless, 135–36, 159
  bondage of, 186
  as causal motivation, 163
  cessation of, 232, 236–37, 262, 292, 298
  counteracting, 34, 253
  craving and, 28, 181
  death and, 190
  feelings accompanying, 109, 177, 178
  first-link, 161–62, 163, 165, 166, 202
  floods (*ogha*) and yokes (*yoga*) of, 346n37
  grasping inherent existence, 11, 19, 25, 34, 36, 74, 75, 114, 126, 161, 163, 237, 297
  ground of latencies of, 306, 308, 351n84
  impermanence and, 21
  of karma and effects, 68, 73–74, 304
  latencies of, 249–50, 257, 259, 262
  mixed and unmixed, 110–11
  neutral feelings and, 50–51
  non-afflictive, 261–62
  as not present at buddhahood, 320
  as obscuration to buddha nature, 304–5, 306, 308
  as obscuration to seeing duḥkha, 240
  and other afflictions, relationship to, 63, 73, 75, 101, 103, 156, 345n26
  as root of saṃsāra, 75, 98
  severed at root, 191, 280
  strength of, 100
  underlying tendency of, 89, 91, 345n31, 345n33
  variant views and meanings of, 73–76, 159–61, 345n24
  view of personal identity and, 78, 104
  wrong views and, 85–86
  See also confusion; self-grasping ignorance
Illumination of the Thought (Tsongkhapa), 127, 299–300
illusory body, 258
immediately preceding condition, 176, 189
imperceptible forms, 12

impermanence
of afflictions, 90
of aggregates, 21–22, 244
Buddhist understanding of, 26, 343n2
coarse, 21, 54
as counterforce, 114
dependent origination and, 238
duḥkha and, 23, 24, 54–55, 56, 57
of having-ceaseds, 133
meditating on, 219, 220–21
of mind, 8
mistaking as permanent, 20–21, 27
of results, 7
subtle, 14, 21, 54, 56
of twelve links, 206
inattentive awareness, 298
inconsideration, 88, 94, 109, 345n34
India, spiritual traditions of, 10
infancy, 129, 203
inferential cognizers, 54, 240, 298–99
inherent existence, 130, 346n43
afflictions and, 108
of agent, object, action, 111
appearances of, 130, 259–60, 265, 278, 346n43
contemplating absence of, 180
counterforce to grasping at, 114
duḥkha's lack of, 36–37
emptiness of, 134, 214, 263
of four truths, lack of, 18
grasping, 18–19, 69, 111, 161–62, 264, 334 (*see also under* ignorance)
noninherent existence and, 36
reflecting on, 52, 210–11, 221
refutation of, 237, 262
of saṃsāra and nirvāṇa, 285
in twelve links, lack of, 204–6
insecurity, 73, 101–2
insight (*vipaśyanā*), 19, 27, 183, 204, 243, 244–45, 246, 254, 297
insolence, 95
integrity
lack of, 88, 93–94, 109, 345n30, 345n34
limitless cultivation of, 282
virtue of, 138
intention
of arhats, 256
of bodhisattvas, 257
body and, 209
in determining virtue and nonvirtue, 137–38
examining, 250
of formative action, 165
as having-ceased, 133
influence on bodily elements, 146
karma and, 130–31
as karmically active renewed existence, 187
mental factor of, 171–72, 177
to renounce saṃsāra, 54
twelve links and, 197
introspective awareness, 112, 137, 178, 181, 203, 204, 244, 254
Islam, 142
Īśvara, 145, 212

J

Jainism, 6. *See also* Nigrantha tradition
jealousy, 95, 345n34
anger and, 70, 92
antidotes to, 115
of anti-gods, 45
feelings accompanying, 109
fetter of, 98
identifying, 113
Jñānaprasthāna, 345n31
joy
and bliss, distinctions between, 242
in buddha nature, 342
in concentration, Buddha's, 223
from connecting with others, 60
in first dhyāna, 91
five degrees of, 241, 348–49nn66–67
increasing, 109
in saṃsāra, instability of, 11
in transcendental dependent origination, 239, 241–42
joyous effort, xiii, 1, 138, 221, 228
Judaism, 142
Jung, Carl, 136

K

Kālacakra Tantra, 141, 144, 146–47, 149, 288
Kamalaśīla, 46
karma, 10, 50, 193, 194, 297
accumulation of, 250, 349n68
body and, 146, 209
bondage of, 49–50
causality of, 143
causes and conditions of, interrelated, 205
from clinging to sensual pleasure, 183
collective, 148, 149, 152, 153, 154
control by, 56
craving and, 15
demeritorious/nonvirtuous, 166, 187, 249
destructive, 88
diversity of beings and, 55
duḥkha and, 20, 21, 22–23
four branches of, 165, 168
ignorance of, 68, 73–74, 304
importance of understanding, 236
instinct and, 153
invariable, 41, 42, 43, 249
latencies of, 130–32, 133–34, 148, 153, 169
laws of nature and, 148–49
and merit, relationship between, 139
meritorious, 166, 249
and natural law, relationship between, 150–51, 153–54
as present motivations, 152
in pure lands, 258
in realms of existence, 41, 46, 166–67, 249
ripening of, 15, 103, 132, 149, 167, 177, 185, 187 (*see also* ripening result of karma)
root afflictions and, 68
as source of manifold world, 145–46, 148, 150
on śrāvaka ārya path, 255
subtle mind and, 287
in true origins, 346n40
unpolluted, 249–50, 251, 257, 258, 308, 351n84
view of personal identity and, 79
virtuous mental states and, 109
wrong views and, 85, 86
See also formative actions (*saṃskāra karman*); polluted karma
karmic seeds, xv, xvii, 130–32
as adventitious, 136
afflictions needed for ripening of, 123
causal consciousness and, 168
of completing karma, 256
consciousness and, variant views on, 169
continuity of, 170
craving and, 30
formative karma and, 165
from four distorted conceptions, 26
having-ceased and, 132, 133–34
as neutral, 137–38
nourishing, 182–83, 198, 199
preventing ripening of, 132, 193
at rebirth, 15, 167, 182, 188
renewed existence and, 185
in twelve link cycles, 197, 198–99
Kelzang Gyatso, Seventh Dalai Lama, 322–23, 324, 325, 327, 329, 331
killing, 65, 82, 84, 112, 184, 256
kiṃnaras, 46
kindness, 60, 84, 115, 166, 183, 222. *See also* loving-kindness
King of Concentration of Sūtra, 2
knowledge
of all phenomena, 277–79
conceptual, 243
reviewing (P. *paccavekkhaṇa ñāṇa*), 248
true, 75
knowledge and vision of liberation, 248–49
knowledge and vision of things as they are, 239, 243–46

L

latencies, xvii, 260
of afflictions, 114, 130, 134, 188, 257, 260–61, 278, 305–6, 308

in Cittamātra school, 146, 288, 293, 294, 346n42
of cognitive obscurations, 259
continuity of, 170
of ignorance, 249–50, 257, 262
of ignorance, ground of, 306, 308, 351n84
instinct and, 153
of karma, 130–32, 133–34, 148, 153, 169
neutrality of, 137–38, 139
and original sin, comparison of, 135–36
purification of, 274
as seeds or potencies, 127
types other than affliction and karma, 135
unconscious and, 136–37
laxity, 254
laziness, 93, 94, 113, 219–22
lethargy, 88, 93, 99, 109, 345–46n34
Letter to a Friend (*Suhṛi-lekha*, Nāgārjuna), 51, 251
liberation, 10
afflictive obscurations at, 123, 259, 346n40
and arhats' nirvāṇa, distinctions between, 273–74
aspiration for, xvii, 39–40, 52, 57–59, 67, 189, 218, 288
compassion and, 225
craving for, 67–68
creating causes for, 219, 236
distorted notions of, 184
full, two aspects of, 247
higher rebirths toward, 166
ignorance eliminated at, 162
inspiration for, 23
knowledge of destruction of pollutants and, 247–49
as lacking inherent existence, 207–8
mistaken views of, 32–33, 35, 36, 42
motivations that impede, 250
as possible, 106, 239, 279–81
proximate cause of, 238–39, 246
shift in perspective from aspiring, 227–28
terms translated as, 273–74
wrong views and, 86
Library of Wisdom and Compassion, xiii, xiv–xvi, 106
life-continuum, 347n53
Longchenpa, 330–31
Lotus Sūtra (*Saddharma Puṇḍarīka Sūtra*), 296
love, 113, 180, 298, 316, 342
loving-kindness, 88, 115, 116
Luminous, 291
lust, 24, 114, 116, 222
lying, 15, 65, 74, 184. *See also* deceit

M

Madhyamaka school, 68, 331
on aggregates at nirvāṇa, 9
on buddha nature, 296–301
on clear light mind, 351n83
on emptiness, 343n3
four truths, approach to in, 17–18
on ignorance of ultimate truth, 73
on mind and form, 146
on one final vehicle, 296
on purifying karmic seeds, 132
Māgandiya, 222–25
Mahāmati, 337, 338
Mahāmudrā tradition, 324–25, 327, 331, 334–35
Mahāparinibbāna Sutta, 98
Mahāyāna, 313
buddha nature as basis of, 301
disposition for, 294, 295
reverence for, 306
śrāvakas and solitary realizers entering, 257, 265, 293, 348n72, 349n68
Maitreya, 45, 157. See also *Ornament of Clear Realizations* (*Abhisamayālaṃkāra*); *Sublime Continuum* (*Ratnagotravibhāga*)
malice, 94, 97, 99, 130, 345n31
Māra, 20, 44, 343n7
materialism, 68, 92, 181
Materialists (Cārvākas), 28–29, 30
mātṛkas, 46

matter
four great elements and, 171
as obstruction, 277
primal, 29, 85, 143, 212, 213
scientific view of, 8, 143
space particles and, 147
Maudgalyāyana, 132, 233, 256
meal chant, 226–27
media stimuli, 107
meditation
analytic, 220, 244
attainment at extinction of defilements, 272, 349n74
consciousness developed through, 137
to counteract laziness, 219–20
daily practice of, 116
on emptiness, prerequisites for, 157–58
inner object of, 242
joy in, 241
latencies surfacing through, 135
limited goals in, 220
on mind, two methods of, 336
on nature of mind, 334–35
on refutation of inherent existence, 262
restlessness during, 66
transforming buddha disposition and, 294
See also insight (*vipaśyanā*); serenity (*śamatha*)
meditative absorptions
cessation and, 15–16
clinging in, 183
of form and formless realms, 41, 42, 44, 166–67, 243, 344n10
mistaking as nirvāṇa/liberation, 32, 35, 36, 184
seeds of afflictions and, 303
seven preparations for, 186, 348n58
meditative equipoise on emptiness, 134, 260, 265, 266, 294, 300
meditative stability, perfection of, 1, 342
memories, 135, 170, 178
mental consciousness
buddha nature and, 299, 350n80
Cittamātrin view of, 293
continuity of, 332
embryonic, 171
general and specific, 333
having-ceaseds of karma and, 134
ignorance and view of personal identity, accompanied by, 160
objects of, 172
polluted, 168
severing, 293
mental factors, 159, 160
accompanying consciousness, 171–72
afflictions as, 64, 90
bondage of, 63
continuity of, 126–27
in determining ethical value, 163
five omnipresent, 170, 174, 175
psychological causality and, 143
seeds of virtuous, 131
virtuous, 138
mental faculty, 172, 173, 174, 175, 202, 278
mental states
contradictory, inability to experience, 128, 164
obscuration of afflictive, 278
strength of mental factors in, 172
as transient, 180
virtue and nonvirtue of, 137–38
virtuous, 65, 90, 109, 113, 138–39, 298, 299, 345–46n34
mere designation, 6, 64, 162, 186, 205, 206
mere I, 6, 78–79, 81, 134, 159, 169, 205
merit, 139, 222, 251, 254, 288, 313. *See also* collection of merit
mind, 9, 58, 279
ability to transform, 297
afflicted views and, 82
as basis of saṃsāra and nirvāṇa, xiii–xiv, 297, 328
and body, relationship between, 8, 106, 112–13, 144–48, 174–75
and brain, wrong views of, 84
Buddhist and Western notions of, compared, 136–37
clarity and cognizance of, 277, 279, 280
conventional and ultimate, xvii

happy, maintaining, 60, 109
impermanence of, 14
mindfulness of, 27
momentariness of, 8, 26
in Pāli tradition, potential of, 291
at path and fruit, 246–47
refined states of, 44
in saṃsāra and nirvāṇa, differences between, 286, 287
sense of self and, 6
similar to correct view, 250–51
substantial cause of, 8
transformation of, three factors, 281–82
universal, wrong view of, 85
unpolluted (T. *zag med sems kyi nus pa*), 134, 169, 292, 298
See also clear light mind; emptiness of mind; nature of mind; subtlest mind-wind
mindfulness, 137
afflictions and, 108
on aggregates, 244
of craving, 180, 181
developing, 254
in experiencing subtle impermanence, 14
of feelings, 178
four establishments of, 27
lack of, 112, 203
of motivation, 218
of sense objects, 204
of three doors, 193
mind-moments, 189
mind-training teachings, 58
Mipham, Ju, 212
miserliness, 66, 67, 92, 95, 98, 109, 345n34
momentariness, 8, 13–14, 26, 54, 347n49
motivation
attachment and, 68
causal and immediate, 163–64
for Dharma study, 1–2
due to afflictive emotions, 103, 112, 120
due to fetters, 129
in eliminating afflictions, 117
in five dispositions, 294–95
karma and, 152
limited, 250
mindfulness of, 218
nonvirtues due to, 139
polluted virtuous, 162
in three types of karma, 166
virtue due to, 138
See also altruistic motivation

N

Nāgārjuna, 68, 193, 206–7, 321, 339, 351n83. See also *Letter to a Friend* (*Suhṛi-lekha*); *Praise to the Sphere of Reality* (*Dharmadhatū-stava*); *Praise to the Supramundane* (*Lokātītastava*); *Precious Garland* (*Ratnāvalī*); *Treatise on the Middle Way* (*Mūlamadhyamakakārikā*); *Versed Commentary on the Rice Seedling Sūtra* (*Śālistamba Sūtra Kārikā*)
nāgas, 46
Nālandā tradition, 266
name and form, 168, 170–72, 174–76, 177, 273, 348n54
name of result given to cause, 185, 187, 311, 330–31, 349n76
natural laws, 148–49, 150, 151, 152, 153
natural phenomenal causality (P. *dhamma niyāma*), 143–44
naturally abiding buddha nature, xiv, 296–98, 338
as always present, 301
as Buddha's intended meaning, 338
as empty nature of mind, xiv, 300, 306, 328
as nature truth body, 266, 309, 313, 314
in third turning, 322
three characteristics of, 293–94
and transforming buddha nature, relationship between, xiv, 296, 299, 301, 312–13, 328, 329
nature body of buddha (*svabhāvikakāya*), 329
nature of mind
and afflictions, variant views on, 283–84

defilements and, 100
direct perception of, 327
meditation on, 334–35, 336
mental bodies and, 257
natural inclination of, 281
nirvāṇa as, 9, 262, 263–64, 266
in Pāli tradition, 291
purity of, 274, 279, 280, 302
realization of, 35, 36
as stable basis for excellent qualities, 281–82
three characteristics of, 323
ultimate, 31, 287, 297–98, 320, 326, 331
as undefiled, 324
nature of phenomena (*dharmadhātu*), 300, 311
nature truth body
appearance of, 307
as bodhi, 275
emptiness of awakened mind as, 9, 288, 302, 339
naturally abiding buddha nature and, 296, 298, 309, 313, 314
nonabiding nirvāṇa as, 266
twofold purity of, 301, 313
nervous system, 106
Nettippakaraṇa, 68
New Translation schools, 283, 284
Ngok Lotsawa, 296
Nigrantha tradition, 30
nihilism. *See* extreme of nihilism
nine similes for buddha nature, 302–3
buddha image in lotus, 303–4, 311
buddha statue in tattered rag, 307, 313
chart of, 308–9
gold in filth, 301, 305, 312, 316
golden buddha statue in dust, 308–10, 313
honey with bees, 304, 311–12
kernel of grain in husk, 304–5, 312
sprout hidden in peel of fruit, 306, 313
in three aspects of buddha disposition, 314
treasure under earth, 305–6, 313
universal monarch in womb of destitute woman, 307–8, 313
nirvāṇa, xiii, 52, 237, 343n3
afflictions overcome at, 125
analogies and synonyms for, 272
of arhats, 306
as cessation of duḥkha and its origin, 267–68, 271
etymology of, 268
fourfold classification of, 18, 263, 343n4
fundamental innate clear light mind as basis of, 287–88
general description of, 262
glimpsing, 232
as highest health, 224
as lacking inherent existence, 207
mind as basis for, xiii–xiv, 297, 328
mistaken notions on, 32–33, 271
mundane happiness and, 231–32
natural, 18, 263–64, 274, 285, 298, 331
as nonaffirming or affirming negative, views on, 262–63
as object of mediation, 268–71
Pāli views, reconciliation of, 272
with remainder, 247, 256–57, 293, 349n71
and saṃsāra, equality of, 284–86
in Sanskrit and Pāli traditions, comparison of, 273
three aspects of, 270
without remainder, 9, 257, 346n38
with and without remainder, variant views on, 264–66, 293
See also nonabiding nirvāṇa; true cessation (*nirodha-satya*)
Nirvāṇa Sūtra, 296
nominal existence, 205–6, 207, 208
nonabiding nirvāṇa, 18, 228–29, 259, 262, 266, 298, 306, 309
nonaffirming negative, 262–63
nonattachment, 138, 272, 292
noncomposite phenomena, 331
nonexistence, craving for, 179, 181, 184
non-knowingness, four causes of, 261–62

nonreturners, 16, 43, 87, 91, 97, 98, 125, 185, 247, 255
non-seed latencies, 127
nonvirtue, 140, 157
afflictive views and, 82, 83, 86
dispositions and, 294, 295, 296
five types, 139
intention and, 137–38, 218
purifying, 132, 225
and virtue, discerning between, 115
nonvirtuous actions
attachment and, 68
formative karma of, 163, 187
ignorance and, 111
seeds and latencies of, 130
ten nonvirtues, 66, 85, 96, 130–31, 163, 204
Numerical Discourses, 238

O

object condition, 176
objects
apprehended, 78
causing afflictions, 107, 108
conceived, 78
and consciousness, relationship between, 349–50n77
craving for, 180
desirable, clinging to, 183
mental, latencies of, 135
mind's cognizance of, 277–79
observed, 78, 81
polluted, 66, 67
six, 203
See also sense objects
objects of negation, 19, 25, 126
obstinacy, 95
obstructions, types of, 277–79
Ocean of Reasoning (Tsongkhapa), 214
offerings, 251
ogress and monkey, union of, 154
omniscient mind, 9, 275, 335
clear light mind's transformation to, 324, 329
obstructions to, 278
realizations of, 279
subtle mind-wind and, 288, 302
once-returners, 16, 87, 185, 247, 249, 255
one taste, 284–85
oral teachings, xv–xvi
ordinary beings
afflictions due to bodies of, 106
and āryas, differences between, 236, 255, 300
attachment to views by, 82
and bodhisattvas, differences between, 257
buddha nature obscurations of, 303, 304, 306, 307, 309, 315–16
coarse selflessness realized by, 19
dualistic appearances of, 260
first-link ignorance of, 161
in form and formless realms, 41, 42–43
general and specific I of, 332–33
innate craving and clinging of, 183
karma of, 249, 250, 251
minds of, 274, 297
on paths of learning, 304, 306
in pure lands, 258–59
purification of nonvirtue by, 132
rebirth of, 190, 199
subtlest mind-wind/clear light mind of, 146, 280, 301–2, 349–50n77
underlying tendencies in, 129
original sin, 135–36, 221–22
Ornament of Clear Realizations (*Abhisamayālaṃkāra*, Maitreya), 296, 327
on abandonment of afflictions, 125
buddha nature in, 320
nothing to be added or removed verse in, 325, 326
on twelve links, 157
Ornament of Clear Realizations commentary (Haribhadra), 285
outflows, 99

P

pain, 48, 54
afflictions and, 110
of bodhisattvas, 228, 257

duḥkha of, 13, 22, 47, 50, 55, 191
in duḥkha of change, 51, 56
equanimity toward, 118, 256
of hell beings, 45
karma and, 132, 151, 153, 209
proper attitude toward, 40
in twelve links, 172, 177, 179, 191, 203, 226
Pāli tradition, xiv–xv
on absence of substantial experiencer, 208–10
on afflictions, 88, 125
on antidotes, 117
on arrogance, types of, 71, 95, 346n36
on asuras, 344n19
on auxiliary afflictions, 94–96
on birth, 189
on cessation, 15–16, 343n3
on clinging, 184–85
on craving, 180–81
on dependent origination, 157, 159, 238–49
on eightfold path, 12, 34
on fetters, 97
on five pure abodes, 44
on form realm, 344n14, 344n17
on ignorance, 74–75, 98
liberation, use of term in, 274
on Maitreya, 45
on mind's potential, 291
on name and form, 171–72
on nirvāṇa, 266–73
on pollutants, 98–99
on rebirth-linking consciousness, 169–70, 347n53
on remedy to saṃsāra, 348n60
on renewed existence, 187–88
on seeing and meditation, 346n41
on six realms, beings of, 46
on six sources, 173–76
on three trainings, 343n9
on twelve links, 200–202
on twenty false views of real self, 79–81
on underlying tendencies, 88–91, 129–30
parinirvāṇa, 9, 44, 119, 144
Parting from the Four Clingings (Sachen Kunga), 69
partless particles, 147
path
as lacking inherent existence, 207
of learning, 306, 307
method aspect of, 312, 314
three principal aspects of, 251, 288
transforming external difficulties into, 58
wrong views and, 86
Path of Purification (*Visuddhimagga*, Buddhaghoṣa), 157, 200
on absence of experiencer, 208, 209
on afflictions, 88
on duḥkha, 40
on nirvāṇa, 271
on renewed existence, 187
on six sources, 175
path of seeing, 16, 90, 161
actualization of, 306
afflictions abandoned on, 125, 160, 307, 308
on bodhisattva path, 257, 258
on śrāvaka path, 254–55
wisdom of, 132
path wisdom, 246
peace
of arhats, 247, 257, 265, 349n72
compassion and, 122
of concentration, 16, 177, 183, 223, 244
in daily life, 58, 59, 60, 63, 180, 221
of nirvāṇa as, xiii, 31–32, 33, 34, 37, 39, 40, 228, 231–32, 253, 271–72
of relinquishing afflictions, 15, 51, 86, 279
wishing for others', 226
peak of saṃsāra, 41, 42, 167, 286
peer pressure, 107
perception, 130, 259, 346n43
Perfection of Wisdom sūtras, 274, 296, 320, 322, 325, 326, 329, 338
permanence
Buddhist understanding of, 343n2

causality and, 142
of emptiness, 298, 300
of having-ceaseds, views on, 132–33
mistaking impermanence as, 20–21, 27, 101
of naturally abiding buddha nature, 299
of nature body of buddha, 329
view of, 81, 181 (*see also* extreme of absolutism)
person, xiv, xvii, 24, 81. *See also* self; self-sufficient substantially existent person
pervasive duḥkha of conditioning, 13–14, 26, 48–49, 50, 56–57, 191, 257
phenomena
affirmative, 132
clear light mind as source of, 287–88
contemplating divisions of, 115
emptiness of, 207, 213
as knowable, 137
manifold, 285
mindfulness of, 27
noncomposite, 331
Prāsaṅgika view of, 25, 26
same taste of, 312
self-grasping, 162
unborn nature of, 319, 321
See also conditioned phenomena
Pilindavaccha, 261
piśācas, 46
pleasure
craving and, 14–15
levels of, 60
mistaking duḥkha as, 20–21, 22, 27
saṃsāric, attachment to, 59–60, 219, 227–28
of three worlds, 58–59
worldly, futility of, 218
See also sensual/sensory pleasure
pliancy, 138, 239, 241–42
pollutants, 87, 98–99, 256
abandoning, 243
knowledge of destruction of, 238–39, 243, 247–49, 274
mind's freedom from, 264
polluted karma, xiii
causal motivation for, 163
at cessation, 9, 34
control by, 26
ethical value of, 249
as origin of suffering, 11, 18, 123
possessions, 59–60
power of the basis/field, 164, 251
practitioners, 40, 225–26, 291
Praise to the Sphere of Reality (*Dharmadhatū-stava*, Nāgārjuna), 274–75, 280, 284, 321, 330
Praise to the Supramundane (*Lokātītastava*, Nāgārjuna), 214–15, 326
Prāsaṅgika Madhyamaka, 20
on afflicted views, 86
on afflictions, 66, 111, 125, 126
on buddha nature, 338–39
on cessation, 12, 31
on clear light mind, 351n83
on emptiness, 25
on four truths, 18–19
on having-ceased, 132, 133, 165
on ignorance, 73, 74, 75, 98, 159, 232, 347n49
on karmic seeds in mere I, 169
on nirvāṇa with and without remainder, 265–66
on non-afflictive ignorance, 262
on root of saṃsāra as subtle ignorance, 162
self, view of in, 6
on true path, 34–36
on view of personal identity, 77, 78, 81, 161
on virtues, 138
prayers, 3, 257, 258
precepts
bodhisattva, 131, 295
prātimokṣa, 138, 294, 295
Precious Garland (*Ratnāvalī*, Nāgārjuna)
on arrogance, 71–72

on first-link ignorance, 162
on four extremes of arising, 237
on nirvāṇa, 263
on wheel of existence, 194
precious human birth, 250
appreciating, 203–4, 219
body as support of, 60
clinging to, 182–83
potential of, 281
as result of merit, 222
wasting, 21
pretension, 93, 95, 109, 345–46n34, 346n35
primal matter, 29, 85, 143, 212, 213
primary consciousness
as buddha nature, 327–28
of ignorance and afflictions, 111
intention and karma in, 130–31
mental factors and, 75–76, 283, 345n26
as virtuous and nonvirtuous, 138, 139
prostrations, 133–34, 251
Proximate Cause Sutta (*Upanisā Sutta*), 238
Puchungwa, 225, 226
pure lands, 44, 167, 258
pure-ground bodhisattvas, 130, 260
cognitive obscurations of, 258, 308–9
consciousness of, 168
feelings of, 178
ignorance, lack of, 161
motivation of, 164
purification, 193, 254
false views about, 83
forgetting, 197
of mind, 262
of nonvirtue, 132
of twelve links, forward and reverse, 234–35, 238
purity, twofold, 266, 301, 313, 339

Q

Questions of Upāli Sūtra (*Upālipariprcchā Sūtra*), 131

R

radiance, five-colored, 147
realms of existence
craving for existence in, 180–81
duḥkha of, 29–30
forms of attachment in, 89
innate afflictions in, 124
karma in, 41, 46, 166–67, 249
naturally abiding buddha nature in, 301
psychological states, viewing as, 47
rebirth in, 46
reflecting on dependent origination and, 218
renewed existence in, 185, 187
twelve links in, 173
types of, 41
on Wheel of Life, 156
reasoning, 124, 262, 280, 282, 336–37. *See also* four extremes of arising
rebirth, xvii
of bodhisattvas, 9
Buddhist view of, 7–8
cessation of, 37, 237, 247
choice in, 199
clinging to, 182
continuity in, 134
craving and, 15
cycles of, in twelve links, 158
direct perception of, 137
formative karma and, 165
fortunate, aspiration for, 40, 67
infinite numbers of, 52, 195, 219
innate and acquired afflictions and, 124, 125
innate clear light mind during, 287
karma and, 153, 166–67
karmic seeds ripening at, 26
of nominally existent I, 205–6
realms of, actuality of, 46
of self, views of, 5–6
on śrāvaka ārya path, 255
subtle afflictions at, 75
third-link consciousness and, 168
time between, debates about, 189

unfortunate, 120
on Wheel of Life, 156
wrong views regarding, 84
rebirth-linking consciousness, 169–70, 347n53
red increase, 128, 328, 332
reflections
on afflictions, 121–22
on afflictive emotions, 103–4
on antidotes to strongest afflictions, 116
on Asaṅga's ten points, 57
on auxiliary afflictions, 96
on buddha nature, four puzzling points of, 317
on buddha nature in sentient beings, 340
on causality, 8
on clinging, four types, 185
on compassion for others, 227
on craving, 31, 181
for death and dying, 188
on dependent arising, three characteristics of, 215
on disadvantages of cyclic existence, 52–53
on excellent qualities, 282–83
on feelings, 110
on feelings and craving, 178–79
on fetters, 98
on five afflictive views, 87
on formative karma, 168
on four attributes of duḥkha, 27–28
on four truths, 36–37
on ignorance and formative karma, 164–65
on innate and acquired afflictions, 126
on lack of inherent existence, 210–11
on leper seeking happiness, 225
on media's influences, 108
on nature of mind, 281, 325
on nine similes for buddha nature, 310
on nirvāṇa, 34
on obscurations and defilement, 16, 279
on pleasant feelings as unsatisfactory, 51
on root afflictions, 76
on seeds and latencies, 134
on stages of path, 258–59
on twelve links, 191, 199, 238
on virtue and nonvirtue, 140
refuge, 59, 204, 240
regret, 99, 109, 345–46n34
reliable cognizers, 240, 298–99, 300
renewed existence (*bhava*), 182, 185–88, 189
renunciation, 10, 69, 231
reputation, attachment to, 66, 68
resentment, 70, 92, 94, 107, 298
antidote to, 115
feelings accompanying, 109
as obscuration to buddha nature, 304
three levels of, 129
restlessness, 66, 88, 92, 97–98, 99, 109, 241, 254, 345–46n34
results, types of, 130
Rice Seedling Sūtra, 157, 158, 194, 201, 204, 205, 211–12
rigpa, 283–84, 324, 327
ripening result of karma, 14, 130, 138, 153, 171, 172, 185, 188, 256, 304
rituals, 82–83, 97, 184
root afflictions, xvi, 64, 65–67, 88, 89, 109, 110–11. *See also* afflictive views
roots of virtue, 83, 85, 88, 131–32, 139–40, 292

S

Sachen Kunga Nyingpo, 69
Śakra, 45
Sakya Paṇḍita, 296–97
Sāṃkhya tradition, 6, 143, 339
saṃsāra. *See* cyclic existence (*saṃsāra*)
Saṃsāra, Nirvāṇa, and Buddha Nature, overview of, xvi–xvii
Sanskrit tradition
on afflictions, 88, 89
on auxiliary afflictions, 92–94
on dependent origination, 157, 159
on emptiness, 343n3

on eradicating underlying tendencies, 90
on fourth dhyāna, 344n14
liberation, uses of term in, 273–74
Maitreya in, 45
on ten root afflictions, 88, 345n31
on three trainings, 343n9
on twenty false views of real self, 79–81
Śāntideva, 131. See also *Engaging in the Bodhisattvas' Deeds*
Śāriputra, 118–19, 233, 270–71
Sarvāstivādin Abhidharma, 345n31
Sautrāntika school
on aggregates at nirvāṇa, 346n38
on ārya disposition, 292
on attachment, latent and manifest, 90
on buddhahood, 292–93
on continuity of mental consciousness, 169
on first-link ignorance, 162
on nirvāṇa, 264–65
on purifying karmic seeds, 132
on virtues, 138
science
instinctual behavior in, 152–53
origin of universe in, 142–43, 148
treatment of disturbing emotions through, 106
as unable to remedy true duḥkha, 48–49
sectarianism, xv
seeds
of bodhicitta, 164
factors of, 260
from holy objects, 251
and latencies, distinctions between, 127
of virtue, 137
See also karmic seeds
seeds, afflictive, xvi–xvii
as cause of afflictions, 106–8
function of, 127–28
obscuring buddha nature, 303–4, 308
reflection on, 128–29
underlying tendencies and, 129–30
uprooting, 262
views on, 90
self, xvi, 115, 255
as beginningless, 6–8
cessation of, views on, 9
clinging to, 183, 184
as designation, 7–8, 134
distorted conception of, 20, 21, 27
as general I, 333
as permanent, unitary, independent, 6, 23–25, 26, 27, 77–78, 181
production from, refutation of, 339
refutations of, 332, 333
two contextual meanings of, 343n6
in understanding underlying tendencies, 90
unobservability of, 56
views of, 5–6, 337
See also mere I; person
self-confidence, xiii
and arrogance, distinctions between, 73
four types, 233–34
increasing, 122, 241
lack of, 219
self-grasping, 61, 75–76
arrogance and, 71
manifest and seeds of, 128
in pure lands, 258
two types, 77, 79, 162
self-grasping ignorance, 259, 298, 304
definition of, 74
innate and acquired, 124, 161
latencies of, 130
Prāsaṅgika view of, 75, 351n83
as root of saṃsāra, 37, 68
and self-grasping, distinctions between, 75–76
in twelve links example, 197
variant views of, 162
wisdom in dispelling, 26, 35
selflessness, 321, 337
in examining duḥkha, 54, 56, 57
fear of, 338
in first turning, 319
ignorance of, 73
meditating on, 19, 131

and nirvāṇa, distinctions between, 273
of persons and phenomena, 26, 233
Prāsaṅgika view of, 25, 126
reflection on, 98
subtle, 27
variant views on, 159–60
view of personal identity and, 78
wisdom analyzing, 250
self-mortification, 184
self-recrimination, 102, 214
self-sufficient substantially existent person
aggregates and, 25, 26, 27, 104
clinging to, 184
four truths and, 18–19, 31
grasping at, 74, 75, 103, 126, 162
variant views on, 159, 160–61
view of personal identity and, 78, 103
sense consciousness, 168, 286, 294, 320, 350n80
sense faculties, 135, 286
sense objects, 108, 112, 204, 222–23, 240
sense organs, karmic influence on, 154
senses, 44, 68, 91, 344n17
sensual desire, 89, 91, 97, 98, 99, 345n31
sensual/sensory pleasure
clinging to, 183, 184, 185
craving and, 179, 180, 184, 231–32
distinctions in, 60
duḥkha of change and, 47–48
origin, disappearance, gratification, danger, escape, 222–25
unsatisfactory nature of, 204
sentient beings, 121
afflictions of, 31, 32
altruistic motivation toward, 3
basic nature of, 136
buddha nature of, xiv, 299, 310–14
buddhahood of, variant views on, 265, 283
buddhas' compassion for, 69
as conditioned phenomena, 226
diversity of, 55
and environment, Abhidharma view of, 145–46
and environment, tantric view of, 147, 148, 149, 150
first-link ignorance of, 161
innate buddha body of, refutation of, 335, 337–40
in manifold world, 145–46, 148
potential of, 262, 277, 292
receptivity to buddha activity by, 278, 301, 323
six classes of, 41, 44–45, 46, 50, 52
subtlest mind-wind in, 301
thirty-three classes of, 41–45
See also ordinary beings
serenity (*śamatha*), 27, 204, 241, 242, 253–54. *See also* access concentration
Seventh Dalai Lama. *See* Kelzang Gyatso, Seventh Dalai Lama
sexual relationships, 66, 114, 221
shamelessness, 345n30
Shorter Series of Questions and Answers, The (*Cūḷavedalla Sutta*), 79–80
sickness, suffering of, 13, 53, 54, 56, 58
signlessness, 270, 272
six perfections, 1, 295, 313, 342
six realms, 41, 44–45, 46, 50, 52, 156
six sources (*Saḍāyatana*), 172–76, 177
six stains, 345–46n34
Sixty Stanzas of Reasoning, commentary (Candrakīrti), 133
sleep, 93, 109–10, 175–76, 286, 345–46n34
sleepiness, 99
Smṛtyupasthāna Sūtra. See *Establishment of Mindfulness Sutta*
socialization, 136
solitary realizers, 43, 294, 305–6, 349n68, 351n84
Song of the Experience of the View (Rolpai Dorje), 335–36
soul, 24, 78, 85, 181, 184, 206, 332, 333, 337
space particles, 146–47, 148, 149
speech
of buddhas, 139, 312
harsh words, 92, 197, 198, 345–46n34
sphere of reality, 323

spiritual masters/mentors, 71, 95, 167, 219, 295
spite, 70, 92, 109, 345–46n34
Śrāvaka Grounds (*Śrāvakabhūmi*, Asaṅga), 19, 54
śrāvakas
entering Mahāyāna, 349n68
karma of, 249
mental bodies of, 351n84
obstructions to buddha nature of, 305–6
realization of, 17
rebirth of, 43–44, 199
vehicle of, 294
stages of the path (*lamrim*), xiv
stealing, 65, 66
stinginess, 46, 95
storehouse consciousness. *See* foundation consciousness
stream-enterers, 16, 17, 349n74
entering path of, 246–47
fetters and, 87, 125, 184–85
karma of, 249
realization of, 233
twelve links of, 255
underlying tendencies of, 90, 129
strong determination, 16, 31, 52, 96, 122, 210, 217, 225, 227–28, 294
study, guidelines for, 1–3
Sublime Continuum (*Ratnagotravibhāga*, Maitreya)
on buddha activity, 331
on buddha nature of sentient beings, three reasons for, 310–13
on clear and luminous mind, 324
on defiled buddha nature, 296
on difficulty of understanding buddha nature, 315, 317–18
Dzogchen/Mahāmudrā perspective on, 335
on nine similes for buddha nature, 302–10
nothing to be added or removed verse in, 325, 326–27
on purpose of teaching buddha nature, 341
on true duḥkha, 17
subsequent attainment, 260
substantial causes, 8, 147, 149
subtlest mind-wind, 9, 146, 147, 148, 150, 288, 301–2, 348n55
suchness, 236, 312, 314, 322, 326, 338
suicide, 58, 179
Sukhāvatī, 44, 258, 265
Sumaṅgala-vilāsinī (Buddhaghoṣa), 143–44
superknowledges, 137
supernormal powers, 256
Supplement (Candrakīrti), 127, 131, 139–40, 146
supramundane path, 90, 246, 268, 270, 271, 272
supreme dharma stage of path of preparation, 250
Supreme Net Sutta (*Brahmajāla Sutta*), 83–84
Sūtra of the Enumeration of Phenomena That Is Called "Discerning the Divisions of Existence, and So Forth," 211
Sūtra of the Tathāgata's Inconceivable Secret (*Tathāgatācintya-guhya-nirdeśa Sūtra*), 228
Sūtra on the Code of Ethical Conduct (Guṇaprabha), 292
Sūtra on the Ten Grounds (*Daśabhūmika Sūtra*), 190
Sūtra Unraveling the Thought (*Saṃdhinirmocana Sūtra*), 294
sūtras, definitive and provisional, 311, 312, 314
Sūtrayāna
on afflictions, 334
on buddha nature, 296, 322, 324–25, 328, 329
on cause for all saṃsāra, 275
on clear light, 287
on clear light mind, 327, 328, 329, 332
on mind, levels of, 286
on mind and form, 146

on nature of mind, 283
on wisdom, 331
Svātantrika school, 138, 162, 169, 264, 265
Sword of Wisdom for Thoroughly Ascertaining Reality (Mipham), 212
syllogism, 25

T

Tantrayāna, 251
causal clear light mind in, 332
cause for all saṃsāra in, 275
cessation, view of in, 9
fundamental innate clear light mind in, 328
illusory body in, 257–58
on mind, levels of, 286
mind and form in, 146
nature of mind in, 283–84
subtlest mind-wind in, importance of, 288, 349–50n77
taking attachment on the path in, 68
See also highest yoga tantra
tathāgatagarbha. *See* buddha nature/disposition/essence
Tathāgatagarbha Sūtra, 296, 302, 325, 337
Teachings of Akṣayamati Sūtra (*Akṣayamatinirdeśa Sūtra*), 131
Tears Sutta, 49–50
ten full entanglements, 345n34
Tenzin Gyatso, Bhikṣu, His Holiness the Fourteenth Dalai Lama, xv–xvi, xvii–xviii
theism, 135–36, 142, 339
Thirty-Seven Practices of Bodhisattvas, The (Togme Zangpo), 58–59, 218
Thirty-Three Devas, 45, 344nn18–19
thirty-two signs and eight marks, 139
thoughts
discursive, 242
habitual, 107
identifying afflictive, 112–13
verbal stimuli, impact of on, 107
three doors, formative actions of, 165
three higher trainings, 1, 12, 129–30, 226, 240–41, 251, 253–54, 343n9
Three Jewels, 58, 60, 67, 97, 164. *See also* refuge
three poisons, 11, 64, 74
iconography of, 155–56
latencies of, 259, 304
nirvāṇa as eradication of, 267–68, 272, 274
three types of feelings and, 50–51
See also anger; attachment; ignorance
Three Principal Aspect of the Path (Tsongkhapa), 227
three times, 29, 210, 238, 297, 333
three turnings of Dharma wheel, xvii, 304, 325
buddha nature in, 319–22, 341
first turning, 10–11
relationship between, 322
sequence of, 324
three vehicles
āryas of, 161, 210, 236
as final, 294–95, 349n72
five paths of, 250, 254
nirvāṇa in, 343n4
true paths of, 34
Tibetan people, origin legend of, 154
Togme Zangpo, 58–59, 218
Tongme Sangpo, 116
transforming buddha nature, xiv, 293, 294, 298–99
development of, 302, 306, 311
as form bodies, 313, 314
and naturally abiding buddha nature, relationship between, xiv, 296, 299, 301, 312–13, 328, 329
purification of, 334
and seed serving as basis for actualization of buddha bodies, 327–28
sense consciousness and, 350n80
in third turning, 322
as wisdom truth body, 298, 304, 309
transitory collection, view of. *See* view of personal identity

Treasury of Dharmadhātu (Longchenpa), 330–31
Treasury of Knowledge (*Abhidharmakośa*, Vasubandhu), 18, 19, 31
on abandonment of afflictive views, 125
on afflictions, 65, 66, 67, 104–5
on arrogance, types of, 71
on bardo, twelve links in, 200
cosmology in, 154
on defilements, additional categories of, 345n34
on fetters, 97
First Dalai Lama's commentary on, 145
on floods (*ogha*) and yokes (*yoga*), 346n37
on form realm, 44
on ignorance, 75, 160
on ignorance, mixed and unmixed, 110–11
on manifold world, arising of, 145–46
on motivation, two forms, 163
on pollutants, 99
on Realm of Thirty-Three Devas, 344n18
on six realms, 46, 47
on twelve links, 157, 173
on underlying tendencies, 89
on wrong views, 86
Treatise on the Middle Way (*Mūlamadhyamakakārikā*, Nāgārjuna), 157, 213, 236–37, 269–70, 285, 297
true cessation (*nirodha-satya*), xvii, 17
on ārya path, 292
of buddhas' mind, 302
and *cessation*, distinctions in meaning, 262
final, 275
four attributes of, 31–34, 37, 253
four types in Pāli tradition, 15–16, 343n3
nature of, 12
nature truth body as, 9
Prāsaṅgika view of, 265
in Sanskrit tradition, 273–74
in second turning, 319
in third turning, 320
twelve links and, 235, 236–37
true existence
emptiness of, 158, 213–14, 236, 285, 313, 347n48
grasping, 74, 162, 250, 327, 334
in nirvāṇa with and without remainder, 343n4
superimposition of, 341–42
true origins (*samudaya-satya*), xvi–xvii, 63, 123, 250, 334
and afflictive obscurations, difference between, 346n40
four attributes of, 28–30
karmic seeds as, 130
nature of, 11, 12, 14
in twelve links, 194, 203, 235
See also afflictions; karma
true path (*mārgasatya*), xvii, 17, 233–34
in common tradition, 253
emptiness of, reflection on, 37
four attributes of, 34–37
in highest yoga tantra, 321
nature of, 12
realization of, 300
in third turning, 320
twelve links and, 235
wisdom realizing emptiness as, 236, 237
true sufferings. *See* duḥkha (unsatisfactory circumstances)
truth body (*dharmakāya*), xvi, 234, 275, 309, 311, 314, 339. *See also* nature truth body; wisdom truth body
Tsongkhapa, 103, 214, 227, 285, 335, 337. See also *Great Treatise on the Stages of the Path*; *Illumination of the Thought*
Tsultrim Zangpo, 335
Tuṣita, two places named, 45
twelve links of dependent origination, xvii, 6–7, 232, 347n48
as afflictions, karma, duḥkha, 193–94
break in between feeling and craving, 177–78, 181, 204, 226
cessation of, 237, 262
creating new set, 167, 347n53

examples of, 197–98, 202–3
explicit presentation of, 194–96, 201
forward and reverse order of, 157, 158, 234–37
four groups in Pāli tradition, 200–202
ignorance in, 73, 74, 111
implicit presentations of, two, 196–97
interconnection of, 186, 204–5
as lacking inherent existence, 206–8
meditation of, benefits of, 217–19
natural phenomenal causality of, 144
overlapping sets of, 198, 200, 201
in pure lands, absence of, 258
purpose of understanding, 210
sequence of, 191
solitary realizers and, 294
specificity of terminology of, 158–59
on śrāvaka ārya path, 255
textual sources on, 156–57
three levels of contemplating, 225–26
ultimate nature of, 211–15
in "Ye Dharmā" Dhāraṇī, 233
two collections, 139, 296, 306
two obscurations, 259–62, 278–79, 283, 302, 342
two truths
defilement of apprehending as different, 259, 260, 278
definitive and provisional sūtras and, 311
four ārya truths and, 18
obscuration of, 130
simultaneous realization of, 279, 309, 329
See also conventional level of truth; ultimate truth/nature

U

Udāna, 268, 269
Udāna commentary, 261
Udāyana, King, 155
ultimate analysis, 18, 134, 169, 207–8
ultimate truth/nature
as buddha essence, 304, 309
of buddhas and sentient beings, 307
ignorance of, 73
nirvāṇa as, 263
pristine wisdom realizing, 322
saṃsāra and nirvāṇa in, 284–86
as self-revealed, 327
true duḥkha and, 18
unconscious mind, Western psychological view of, 136–37
underlying tendencies
continuity of, 129–30
three most dangerous, 90–91
variant views on, 88–90, 345n31
union of serenity and insight, 27, 204, 254
universe. *See* world systems
unmadas (crazy makers), 46

V

Vaibhāṣika school
on afflictions, 66, 106
on ārya disposition, 292
on buddhahood, 292
on cessation, 9, 346n38
on continuity of mental consciousness, 169
on first-link ignorance, 162
on having-ceased, 347n44
on nirvāṇa, 264–65
on non-afflictive ignorance, 261–62
on purifying karmic seeds, 132
on underlying tendencies, 90
on virtues, 138
Vaiśesika tradition, 30
vajra-like concentration, 309
Vajrayāna. *See* Tantrayāna
Vasubandhu, 159–60. See also *Treasury of Knowledge* (*Abhidharmakośa*)
Vātsīputrīya school, 90
veiled truths, 260, 311, 314
verbal stimuli, 107, 108
Versed Commentary on the Rice Seedling Sūtra (*Śālistamba Sūtra Kārikā*, Nāgārjuna), 205, 212
Vibhaṅga, 88, 189
victim mentality, 29

view holding erroneous views as supreme, 82, 98, 104–5, 125, 183
view of extremes, 81, 86, 141, 217–18
  abandonment of, 125
  aggregates in, 346n38
  clinging to, 183
  as ethically neutral, 110, 111
  order of arising, 104, 105
view of personal identity, 82, 345n31
  abandonment of, 125
  analysis of, 244
  as antidote to itself, 116–17
  arrogance and, 71
  clinging to, 183–84
  control and, 103
  discouragement and, 221
  as ethically neutral, 86, 110, 111, 163
  as fetter, 97, 99
  ignorance and, 104
  twenty false views stemming from, 79–81
  two facets of, 78–79
  underlying tendencies to, 129
  variant views on, 77–78, 159, 160–61, 162
view of rules and practices, 82–83, 98, 345n27
  abandonment of, 125
  clinging to, 184
  as fetter, 97, 99
  order of arising, 104, 105
  as underlying tendency, 345n31
views
  clinging to, 183, 184–85
  distorted, 58
  false, 162
  floods (*ogha*) and yokes (*yoga*) of, 346n37
  grasping and, 69
  pollutant of, 99
  underlying tendency of, 89
  See also afflictive views; wrong views
violence, 46, 70
virtue
  concordant with liberation, 164
  destruction of, three levels, 131
  five types, 138–39
  and nonvirtue, discerning differences between, 137–39
  rejoicing at, 73
  See also roots of virtue
virtuous actions
  clinging as motivation for, 184
  formative karma of, 163
  karmic potency from, 182–83
  mundane, renewed existence due to, 187
  polluted, seeds and latencies in, 130
  ten, 187, 204
virtuous mental states, 65, 90, 109, 113, 128, 138–39, 298, 299, 345–46n34
visualization practice, 298
volitional actions. *See* formative actions (*saṃskāra karman*)
vows. *See* ethical restraints

W

Wayman, Alex, 343–44n9
Wheel of Life, iconography of, 155–56
white appearance, 128, 182, 328, 332
winds, subtle, 287, 288–89, 328, 349–50n77. *See also* subtlest mind-wind
wisdom, 262
  afflictions and, 108
  analytical, 342
  aptitude for, levels of, 204
  as cause for future arising of wisdom, 284, 349n76
  concentration as precursor to, 243
  determination to cultivate, 103
  developing, 19, 180
  in enhancing excellent qualities, 282
  five types, 147
  gradual process of, 232
  objectless/nonobjectifying, 319–20
  penetrative, 16
  perfection of, 1, 342
  pristine, 292, 293, 313, 314, 321, 322, 330
  as root of virtue, 88
  seeds of, 128

subtle levels of mind and, 288
in transforming buddha nature, 298, 306
turning inward to, 245
See also collection of wisdom
wisdom, higher training of, 1, 130, 226, 241, 253
wisdom realizing emptiness, 136, 326, 330
as all-encompassing counterforce, 114
clear light mind and, 280
cultivation by advanced-level practitioners, 226
ignorance eradicated with, 26, 191, 237, 297–98, 334
as natural nirvāṇa, 264
nirvāṇa and, 262
purification by, 132
reflecting on, 52
as true path, 34–36, 253
wisdom realizing selflessness, 9, 12, 17, 35–36
wisdom truth body, 9, 275, 288, 329, 339
attaining, 312
collection of wisdom and, 298
subtlest mind-wind and, 302
transforming buddha nature as, 298, 304, 306, 309
wise and unwise, distinction between, 236
wishlessness, 270
world systems, 144
general Buddhist view of, 145
tantric view of, 146–47
two points of sentient influence on arising of, 149, 150–51
worldly paths, 35, 36
wrath, 92, 94, 345–46n34
wrong views, 20–21
abandonment of, 125
acquired, 124
as afflictions, 278, 279
clinging to, 124, 183, 184
cutting root of virtue, 140
effects of, 85–86
feelings accompanying, 109
habits and, 107
and ignorance, distinctions between, 86
logic and, 85, 86
manifest and seeds of, 128, 130
as obstruction to buddha nature, 305
order of arising, 104, 105
rebirth due to, 46
reflecting on dependent origination and, 218
types of, 83–84, 345n29

Y

yakṣas, 46
Yaśomitra, 90
"Ye Dharmā" Dhāraṇī, 232–34
yogic direct reliable cognizers, 27
yokes (*yoga*), 346n37

About the Authors

THE DALAI LAMA is the spiritual leader of the Tibetan people, a Nobel Peace Prize recipient, and an advocate for compassion and peace throughout the world. He promotes harmony among the world's religions and engages in dialogue with leading scientists. Ordained as a Buddhist monk when he was a child, he completed the traditional monastic studies and earned his geshe degree (equivalent to a PhD). Renowned for his erudite and open-minded scholarship, his meditative attainments, and his humility, Bhikṣu Tenzin Gyatso says, "I am a simple Buddhist monk."

Peter Aronson

BHIKṢUṆĪ THUBTEN CHODRON has been a Buddhist nun since 1977. Growing up in Los Angeles, she graduated with honors in history from the University of California at Los Angeles and did graduate work in education at the University of Southern California. After years studying and teaching Buddhism in Asia, Europe, and the United States, she became the founder and abbess of Sravasti Abbey in Washington State. A popular speaker for her practical explanations of how to apply Buddhist teachings in daily life, she is the author of several books on Buddhism, including *Buddhism for Beginners*. She is the editor of Khensur Jampa Tegchok's *Insight into Emptiness*. For more information, visit sravastiabbey.org and thubtenchodronbooks.org.

Also Available from the Dalai Lama and Wisdom Publications

Buddhism
One Teacher, Many Traditions

The Compassionate Life

Ecology, Ethics, and Interdependence
The Dalai Lama in Conversation with Leading Thinkers on Climate Change

Essence of the Heart Sutra
The Dalai Lama's Heart of Wisdom Teachings

The Good Heart
A Buddhist Perspective on the Teachings of Jesus

Imagine All the People
A Conversation with the Dalai Lama on Money, Politics, and Life as It Could Be

Kalachakra Tantra
Rite of Initiation

The Life of My Teacher
A Biography of Kyabjé Ling Rinpoche

Meditation on the Nature of Mind

The Middle Way
Faith Grounded in Reason

Mind in Comfort and Ease
The Vision of Enlightenment in the Great Perfection

MindScience
An East-West Dialogue

Opening the Eye of New Awareness

Practicing Wisdom
The Perfection of Shantideva's Bodhisattva Way

Science and Philosophy in the Indian Buddhist Classics, vol. 1
The Physical World

Sleeping, Dreaming, and Dying
An Exploration of Consciousness

The Wheel of Life
Buddhist Perspectives on Cause and Effect

The World of Tibetan Buddhism
An Overview of Its Philosophy and Practice

Also Available from Thubten Chodron

Insight into Emptiness
Khensur Jampa Tegchok
Edited and introduced by Thubten Chodron

"One of the best introductions to the philosophy of emptiness I have ever read."—José Ignacio Cabezón

Practical Ethics and Profound Emptines
A Commentary on Nagarjuna's Precious Garland
Khensur Jampa Tegchok
Edited by Thubten Chodron

"A beautifully clear translation and systematic explanation of Nagarjuna's most accessible and wide-ranging work. Dharma students everywhere will benefit from careful attention to its pages."
—Guy Newland, author of *Introduction to Emptiness*

Buddhism for Beginners

Cultivating a Compassionate Heart
The Yoga Method of Chenrezig

Don't Believe Everything You Think
Living with Wisdom and Compassion

Guided Meditations on the Stages of the Path

How to Free Your Mind
Tara the Liberator

Living with an Open Heart
How to Cultivate Compassion in Daily Life

Open Heart, Clear Mind

Taming the Mind

Working with Anger